FROM SIBERIA TO AMERICA

Boruch B. Frusztajer

DATE DUE

Individual Histories

FROM
SIBERIA
TO
AMERICA

FROM
SIBERIA
TO
AMERICA

A Story of Survival and Success

A Memoir by
BILL FRUSZTAJER

UNIVERSITY OF SCRANTON PRESS
Scranton and London

Library of Congress Cataloging-in-Publication Data
(Has been applied for but is not available at time of publication.)

Distribution:
UNIVERSITY OF SCRANTON PRESS
Chicago Distribution Center
11030 S. Langley
Chicago, IL 60628

PRINTED IN THE UNITED STATES OF AMERICA

CONTENTS

FOREWORD

*As if a man did flee from a lion, and a bear met him; or went into
the house, and leaned his hand on the wall, and a serpent bit him.*
– Amos 5:19

THIS MEMOIR is a remarkable story of endurance and heroism. The
Soviets occupied considerable areas of eastern Poland under the Nazi-
Soviet non-aggression agreement of August 1939 and their goal was
to sovietize these areas, described as "western Belarus" and "western
Ukraine," as rapidly as possible. One way of doing this was by mass deportations of "anti-Soviet elements." Hundreds of thousands of Christian and Jewish citizens of the second Polish Republic were deported
in four mass-scale tides into the depths of the Soviet Union. These
people were sent to the famine-ridden steppes of Kazakhstan or to
taiga of the Komi Republic and many parts of Siberia where they were
surrounded by totally alien and hostile natural conditions. The death
rate in the convoys and at the place of stay exceeded ten percent. In
addition there were smaller-range deportations to closer destinations,
but always among total strangers affecting at least another 50,000 persons. Tens of thousands of young men were forcibly enlisted into the
Red Army, in which they served as compulsory workers in construction battalions, while several score thousands of prisoners of war were

employed as laborers in, as it was put in the highly euphemistic manner of the period, "the distant regions of the Soviet Union."

The Frusztajer family was one of those who suffered in this way. Indeed this memoir provides one of the best accounts available of what deportation and work in Siberia entailed. The Frusztajer family had led a comfortable life in Warsaw, where Bill's father was an accountant and property developer. His paternal grandfather had owned a large estate near Lublin and had been murdered before the war by his estate manager. The memoir provides a fascinating picture of the life of an acculturated Jewish family in the Warsaw of the 1930s.

Having fled eastward to Rovno (Równe) in September 1939 they soon found themselves under Soviet rule. They sought safety by moving to a smaller town, Mos´ciska, but like many others among the refugees they decided not to take Soviet citizenship, an act regarded by the Soviets as disloyal, which led to their arrest and deportation eastward in June 1940. Bill's mother, who had already once been transplanted when she moved from Russia to Poland to marry his father, lost her sanity in the face of the appalling conditions in which she had to live. She had to be institutionalized and died in June 1942. Bill was barely ten when he was deported and owed his survival partly to his native resilience and resourcefulness, which he put to good effect when he had to work in Siberian mines. Even more important in his survival was his father who became "a calm beacon of wisdom and decency" and was able to organize the fifty families of the deportees so that they could survive in the small and isolated settlement in Siberia where they found themselves. The fact that Bill's father was fluent in Russian also gave him an advantage in dealing with the Soviet bureaucracy, as did the fact that he had been a political prisoner in Siberia before World War I.

Like the other Jewish deportees to the Soviet Union who returned to Poland after the war, Bill and his father found themselves in a difficult and often hostile environment when they resettled in Kłodzko (formerly Glatz), near Wrocław, in May 1946. A combination of bitter memories and a dislike of the increasingly repressive Communist system which was fastening its hold on the country led him to escape to

England in 1947. His departure from Poland was another case in which his father sacrificed himself for the benefit of his son. Fortunately Bill's father was able two years later to leave Poland for Israel.

Bill had an uncle in London who was a prosperous doctor with consulting rooms on Devonshire Place—Bill's early British years are described with great humour—who made it possible for him to obtain an engineering degree and become involved in the early development of the computer industry. After his move to the United States in 1956, where he met his wife, Olga, and established a family, he has had a highly successful career in this area which he describes in an engrossing way in the second part of the memoir.

Bill himself has argued that "the years I spent in Russia strongly influenced my ability to function in the West. Practical skills of fending for food, keeping warm in the Siberian climate, and outwitting Communist security services were of little direct use in a capitalist country, but persistence, self-confidence and the ability to cooperate with others—all qualities developed under conditions of life-threatening adversity—proved to be helpful in establishing and managing commercial enterprises in a market economy." Certainly his ability to triumph over adversity is an inspiring lesson for us all, demonstrating how an indomitable human spirit can navigate seemingly impossible circumstances and build a life of meaning and accomplishment. I feel privileged to provide a short introduction to this moving work and very much hope it obtains the wide readership it deserves.

ANTONY POLONSKY
Brandeis University

AUTHOR'S PREFACE

In 1939 Poland was attacked by Germany and Russia, becoming the first casualty of the Second World War. The two powers ruled the country as allies for almost two years before turning on each other in 1941. The invaders were controlled by the most vicious dictators of the twentieth century, Adolf Hitler and Joseph Stalin. Driven by different philosophies, they used similar methods to achieve their ends: Hitler built extermination camps to eliminate people who did not conform to his vision for a new world, while Stalin sent his victims to Siberia. My parents and I were caught in Stalin's web. In June 1940 we were arrested by the Russian Secret Service in the small town of Mos´ciska, in Eastern Poland, and deported to Siberia. Our torturous journey in cattle cars, slave ships, and crowded trucks lasted eight weeks; our detention in the Soviet Union lasted six years.

Over the centuries, Russian regimes had used Siberia as a giant penal colony. Millions of exiles perished there; others, including my mother, were driven to insanity, while still others were left with deep emotional scars. I was among the more fortunate victims. Despite terrible deprivations of hunger, work in permafrost-bound mines at the age of eleven, and the early loss of my mother, I emerged seemingly unscathed and even physically, emotionally, and morally fortified by my

Siberian ordeal. In 1947 I escaped to England, where, with the help of a strong-willed uncle, I obtained an engineering degree and became an early participant in the budding semiconductor industry. Since moving to the United States in 1956, I established a series of silicon-based high technology companies, which afforded me a level of professional and financial success unimaginable in Siberia.

This book tells my story beginning in Warsaw with my birth in 1930, and describing my happy childhood until the outbreak of World War II, my formative teenage years under the guidance of an extraordinary father in the Soviet Union, and finally my life in the West.

Most of the book is devoted to two seemingly disconnected—if not diametrically opposed—topics: Survival in the Soviet Union and entrepreneurship in the United States. Self-analysis is a perilous exercise, but in retrospect it seems that the years I spent in Russia strongly influenced my ability to function in the West. Czesław Miłosz wrote, "Banishment is destructive—but if it does not destroy you it will make you stronger." I choose to believe that my years in Siberia have made me stronger. Practical skills of fending for food, keeping warm in the harsh Siberian climate, and outwitting Communist Party security services were of little direct use in a capitalist country, but persistence, self-confidence, and the ability to cooperate with others—all qualities developed under conditions of life-threatening adversity—proved to be helpful in establishing and managing commercial enterprises in a market economy.

Lenin's own words provide a good summary of the nature of Soviet oppression. Historian Richard Pipes, in his book *Communism: A Short History*, quotes Lenin's reference to the "dictatorship of the proletariat"—a term used by the Bolsheviks to confer legitimacy on their rule—as "power that is limited by nothing, by no laws, that is restrained by absolutely no rules, that rests directly on coercion."[1] Lenin's was not merely a prescription to be followed sporadically; it formed the basis of control over the population in everyday life. The tentacles

---

1. V. I. Lenin, Polnoe Sobranie Sochinienii, fifth ed. (Moscow, 1958-1965), vol. 41, p. 383.

of the Communist Party and Secret Police penetrated every facet of the Soviet Union to ensure strict conformance with the official dogma. All towns, villages, schools, commercial enterprises, and, of course, the Soviet Army had to function under the watchful eyes of Communist Party cells and detachments of the KGB and its predecessors.

Lenin's rejection of limits for the Communist Party did not apply to the common people, who had to follow strict rules. The slightest hint of criticism of the prevailing order, even in jest, was strictly forbidden and carried the threat of severe punishment. People, of course, concealed their disapproval in public, but the muzzling of free speech penetrated deep into families as well. Parents were afraid to discuss matters in front of their children for fear that their offspring might repeat a forbidden phrase in public. At work and school there was prescribed language for compulsory praise of the Communist system and its "great" leader, Stalin, and the authorities were vigilant, unforgiving, and cruel. Indeed, their presence was so pervasive and powerful that, decades later—even after the collapse of the Soviet Union—it took me a long time to believe that the Communists were no longer in power. Only after Leningrad had been officially renamed St. Petersburg did I become convinced.

How did many of us survive and keep our sanity in the face of such monolithic, overwhelming, and malevolent authority? In addition to an inborn healthy mind, a healthy body, and a strong survival instinct, I ascribe my deliverance primarily to two factors: my young age and my father's wise and loving guidance. If one had to pick an age for Siberian exile, ten would be a good choice. Youth, of course, does not diminish the effects of physical deprivation, but as a child I did not fully appreciate the consequences of our fate. I grew from a ten-year-old child to a sixteen-year-old teenager, absorbing the restrictions imposed on us. Although not without grief, I accepted the hunger, the cold climate and political deprivations as people who live near an active volcano accept frequent earthquakes—the realities are inevitable and you just have to get used to them and proceed with the rest of your life. We quickly learned what to say, what topics to avoid, and how to act to conform to the established order.

There were positive aspects of our situation. We realized that we would benefit greatly from mutual support among members of our small exile community. Some among the fifty families dumped in an abandoned isolated Siberian settlement were better equipped for survival than others, so by pooling our resources, we made all our lives more bearable. Our plight taught us the art of cooperation, even as we learned the art of individual survival.

After escaping to England in 1947, I settled in the United States in 1956. I founded my first silicon-based high technology company in Cambridge, Massachusetts, in 1959. There was little in my background to prepare me for the role of an American manager. As our enterprise prospered, I realized that in contrast to other organizations I had seen—especially those in Russia—a commercial company in this country enjoyed an amazing autonomy and freedom of action: It could set its own internal rules, determine a working environment, and institute compensation privileges unencumbered by external traditions and dogmas. Eventually my goal became to run my companies for the benefit of our employees. To achieve this end, I became the sole owner of my operations, eliminating the need to satisfy external stockholders. Although we did not fully achieve my ideal of creating an oasis of sanity in this crazy world, we came close enough to demonstrate that our main concern was the dignity and personal growth of our employees and that we would not sacrifice those qualities at the altar of greater business "success."

I have noticed that many young survivors of the Holocaust or Siberian exile owe their lives to a caring and resourceful parent. I was blessed with just such a father, who guided me through the perils of Soviet exile and later arranged my escape to England. In many ways this book is a tribute to him from his grateful son.

Boston
January 2006

BOOK ONE
SURVIVAL

Midway upon the journey of our life
I found myself within a forest dark,
For the straightforward pathway had been lost.
—*Inferno*, DANTE ALIGHIERI (1265–1321)

EXILE

AT ABOUT ELEVEN O'CLOCK ONE MORNING IN JUNE 1940, an army truck pulled up in front of our house. Russian soldiers wielding rifles with fixed bayonets burst into our room and barked an order: *"Sobiraities!"* they shouted: Pick up your things and get going.

Most people accustomed to Western ways would find it difficult to appreciate the horror of such a situation. It would be terrifying anywhere for armed men to burst in and order the unsuspecting occupants to board a waiting truck, but if this happened in the United States or Western Europe, the victims could at least hope that the police would apprehend the kidnappers and rescue them. In our case, the police were the kidnappers, and we knew there was neither appeal nor hope of deliverance.

Despite the shock of the incursion, my mother showed a great deal of courage. Refusing to budge without her husband, she told me to run and fetch my father from his office in the nearby small town of Mościska. I started for the door, but found it blocked by a giant of a man whose enormous hand completely covered the doorknob. With the full strength of a furious ten-year-old, I grabbed his fingers and tried to dislodge his hand from the knob. Why he did not send me flying across the room, I will never know. Perhaps he was amused by my puny efforts, because I could not move even a single finger. After a short conference among the intruders, the Russian commander sent several of his men to fetch my father, leaving three soldiers to guard us. I expected a quick resolution of our problem after my father's return, for he had always seemed to be in control of every situation. But there was little he could do. He merely asked to be allowed to collect the meager possessions we had rescued from our home in Warsaw a year earlier, shortly after the German invasion of Poland.

Now, surprisingly, the Russians became polite and accommodating. This sudden change in the soldiers' demeanor was not, of course, a change of heart. They were merely applying one of the many methods oppressors use to control their victims. A cousin who survived the Auschwitz concentration camp told me after the war about the impeccable manners of a German officer who greeted them on arrival at the camp. With a single gesture he either condemned weak inmates to death by directing them to a crematorium or prolonged the lives of healthy-looking potential workers by steering them toward the barracks. After the harsh treatment the prisoners had received from the train guards, they found the officer's politeness disarming and meekly followed his directions without realizing the consequences of his choice.

We loaded our belongings onto the open army truck with the help of the soldiers and rode to the railroad station to join the deportation train. On arrival, we were packed into one of the freight cars already filled with other unfortunates. It was a cloudy, murky day, and when the big sliding door closed behind us we were plunged into near-darkness, except for the meager illumination of four small windows. I became aware of slow movements of human arms and legs on tiered wooden platforms on either side of me, the rest of the bodies obscured by the close spacing of the berths, but not until my eyes adjusted to the twilight could I see the owners of those limbs. Gradually people began to crawl out from their large shelves and greeted us in subdued voices. They had arrived in the cars only the previous night, but their slow speech and hesitant movements made them seem like ancient veterans of this dark underworld.

It is strange how in an instant fate can change your status, your way of life, your priorities and your outlook. In the morning we had been relatively free people with the usual concerns about earning a living, achieving good marks in school, and attending to the endless details of everyday life. By afternoon we had become a part of a huge Russian subculture of political prisoners, whose personal goals and freedoms had been left behind. This world had an entirely different set of ambitions, hopes, and behavior, along with its own jargon invented to describe the unique situations and events occurring behind bars; it had its own form of humor, code of integrity, and modesty. It was surprising how quickly—in a matter of hours—we slipped into our new roles and adapted to these new realities.

The interior of the freight car, which would be our home for the next four long weeks, was a dismal affair. The joke was that the cars were designed to house six horses or thirty people, and there were, in fact, thirty-two men, women and children in our container. The boxcar had a sliding door on each side and, high above the floor, four small, rectangular openings that served as windows. Two huge wooden platforms were built into each end of the car. These bunks spanned the full width of our container and extended seven feet from end walls to the sliding doors. The bottom shelf was two feet above the floor, and we used that gap to store our possessions, the top shelf was fixed about three feet above the bottom platform. We spent most of our time lying or crouching on these shelves or standing in the space between the two sliding doors, one of which was nailed to within a foot of its closed position. The gap was covered by a board except for an opening about one foot square near the floor, where a short, sloping trough projected up from the hole to provide a toilet facility. Someone suspended an old sheet from the ceiling to shield the trough from general view, but it was a poor privacy screen and did nothing to contain the smell or provide protection against the flies and other invading insects that flew all over the car when we were stationary.

But the flies were not our biggest problem. The crowded conditions, confinement in the car, stale air, and lack of water or washing facilities soon resulted in our being completely infested with lice. We spent most of our time killing one kind that covered our bodies and another that nested in our hair. They multiplied at a prodigious rate that nullified our efforts to reduce their numbers. We not only fed them with our blood but also unwittingly scratched open wounds into our skins. Those lice were with us until we reached our final destination two months later. Even more oppressive than the infestation of lice, however, was our terrifying ignorance. We knew nothing about our final destination, how long our journey would take, and what would happen to us upon arrival.

Our train consisted of about seventy cars: sixty transporting two thousand prisoners, the rest reserved for the armed guards. Sometimes the train would roll along all day without stopping; at other times it would pause at a small station for a few minutes or pull to a dead-end line for hours or even days. As soon as we stopped, the guards jumped out of their cars and placed themselves strategically along both sides of the train. Most days, two men from each car were recruited to fetch buckets of hot water, boiled cereal, and bread. Two couples had brought tea leaves; while the supply lasted, they shared the tea they brewed with other occupants of our car.

Refugees quickly learn the essentials of vagabond life, discovering that the items most critical to survival are warm clothing, sturdy shoes, rudimentary dishes, and simple cutlery. My parents had brought metal cups and three sets of cutlery when we left Warsaw in September 1939, fortunately affording each of us a spoon, fork, and knife. Most of our companions had their own kits as well, sparing us the indignity of lapping like dogs straight from the bowl or stuffing cereal into our mouths with our fingers. We never knew when the train would stop and new provisions would become available. Most of us saved part of the rations for the inevitable long hours, or even days, of scarcity. Although we did not starve, the amount of food was too miserly to satisfy normal needs, and our journey introduced us to a state of hunger which persisted, almost without a break, during our subsequent long years in Siberia.

Twice during our trip we were marched a few hundred at a time to a steam bath. Those occasions seemed like an incredible luxury: we could leave our cages, walk in open space, remove our clothes and expose our bodies to air, water and steam, and wash off the accumulated filth. The cleanliness was momentary, however, for we could not launder our clothes and had to don the same lice-infested garments after emerging from the steam bath.

Even though the atmosphere in the cars was somber, the human spirit is hard to break, and morale was not as bad as might be imagined. Still a child of ten, I was not sure how the adults felt, but I don't remember any fights or major quarrels despite the congestion and terrible conditions. In retrospect I marvel at my own initially calm state of mind. Clearly, being locked up with thirty strangers for four weeks in a small railroad freight box, having my blood drained by lice, and being hungry most of the time was a deplorable experience, but I remember taking it largely in stride. As a child, I did not appreciate the dangers facing us, and, bad as it was, I was distracted from the horror of our situation by the novelty and adventure of our trip.

The guards, while committed to preventing escape, were not crude or cruel. I don't recall any insults or beatings, except when a few men and women jumped out of the stationary cars to relieve themselves in full view of the others to avoid using the hated troughs. In many cases, the guards ignored those excursions as long as fewer than about a dozen individuals left the train and stayed within a couple of feet of the cars. Occasionally such fugitives were pushed and ordered to return immediately, and in a couple of cases shots were fired to frighten them.

We defied our jailers as much as we could. For instance, we were successful in opening the sliding door that wasn't nailed down, a feat accomplished only when the train was in motion, because the guards almost always closed the doors as soon as the train stopped. It seems trivial now, but at that time this continuing battle over the door was one of our main preoccupations. The guards tried to defeat us by securing the door with a large latch. We found that by extending a long stick or umbrella through a window we could unlatch the door and slide it open. The guards' response was to secure the closed latch with nuts and bolts. But we found that the windows were large enough for a slim person to slip through, and several of our young men, their legs firmly held by others inside the car, leaned out to loosen the bolts and open the latch. The guards soon ran out of bolts, and with padlocks not readily unavailable in Russia, we were able to keep the door open for daytime travel, closing it at night to prevent small children from tumbling out.

The open doors did not encourage escape, since jumping from a fast-moving train is a dangerous proposition. We also realized that a foreign escapee caught without documents in the heartland of Russia would almost certainly face summary execution. Nonetheless, the open door gave us the illusion of freedom. No less important were the satisfaction of outwitting our captors—even in such a small conquest—and the feel of the fresh, cool air clearing the atmosphere of our crowded, otherwise airless jail.

My fellow sufferers on that journey are beyond my recall. Naturally I remember my parents, but the others have dissolved into one amorphous group of indistinguishable bodies and faces, like a distant band of inmates dressed in identical prison garb. I know that it was the young men who leaned out to unlock the sliding doors. I remember that men fetched the food, but I cannot recall their faces. One person I clearly remember was the boisterous middle-aged woman who leaped from the car to relieve herself on the ground nearly every time our train stopped. She was not an exhibitionist—indeed, by that time most of us had lost our sense of modesty. She simply wanted to avoid the humiliating trough in our car. The guards tolerated her behavior, seemingly amused by the sight of this crouching woman with her lifted skirt. The floor of our boxcar usually towered over her head, and she always had to be pulled back inside by her arms when she had finished—not an easy task—especially when the train had begun to move.

Over the years I have wondered why I don't recall the faces or personalities of our companions. The passage of time is probably one reason, along with my young age and our appalling circumstances. Normally, differences among people are enhanced by the details of their past, their current situation, and their ambitions for the future. For us, most such details were simply irrelevant as distinguishing features. The past did not matter, the present was the same for all, and we all aspired to the same, simple goal: survival. We had no control over our fate, and there was, therefore, little room for expressing our personalities. Some inmates were innately more outgoing than others, but our sudden transition into the world of herded confinement cast an identical spell of doom over everyone.

Our numbed lives did benefit from occasional acts of kindness. At a few stops, in a small town or village, a middle-aged woman would run to the train, choosing a car not immediately attended by a guard, and quickly hand the occupants food, usually a small melon or a loaf of bread impaled on a long stick extended toward the little windows. As soon as the transaction was finished, she would run away. Surprisingly, the guards tolerated those incursions, but it was obvious from the women's frightened faces that they knew they were taking a considerable risk. Food was scarce everywhere in Russia, and people could be arrested as counterrevolutionaries for lesser transgressions than feeding political prisoners. The women's actions were amazing feats of compassion and kindness. Admiring their courage, we wondered whether they had lost sons or husbands to the Communists and perhaps were hoping that their generosity would be rewarded by similar actions toward their imprisoned relatives. Years later I learned that compassion for political prisoners among the ordinary population, terrorized as they were by the oppressive Russian governments, had a long tradition in that long-suffering country. Despite their best efforts, the Communists were not able to eradicate the kindness of the Russian people.

Bad as the situation was for all detainees on that train, my parents had more reason to worry than the other prisoners, in view of the fact that this was my father's second exile to Siberia. The first time in 1913, at the age of twenty, he had been banished to that forbidding land by the Tsarist authorities. Such horrible things happened in Poland because of the country's proximity to the Russian "bear." The Tsarist government may have felt threatened by him because of a trip he took to Belgium before the First World War, and on his return to the Russian-occupied part of Poland he was accused of being a Western spy. Whatever the reason, my father found himself in a small Siberian town near Petropavlovsk at the beginning of World War I, where he witnessed the Communist Revolution and the subsequent Civil War. He wrote to his brother in Poland in 1922, asking him to send documents—presumably including a birth certificate—that would prove his Polish nationality and pave the way for him to return home. The Soviet authorities were not swayed by his documents or his pleas for freedom, however, and they kept him in Siberia. When he was finally able to leave his exile settlement, he moved to Petropavlovsk, where he met my mother, a descendant of several generations of Jewish settlers transplanted to Siberia from Russia's western lands. In a later chapter, I describe how my father ran afoul of the Soviet authorities there and how my parents eventually escaped, illegally crossing the nearest border to China. Escapees and their families recaptured by the Communists almost invariably faced immediate execution; accordingly, my parents were terrified that if our jailers learned of my father's past, such would be our fate.

Our train kept rolling eastward through towns unknown to most of us. Having been expelled along the same route twenty-seven years earlier, however, my father knew Russian geography well, and the long Trans-Siberian Railroad stretching from the Urals to the Pacific Ocean was eerily familiar to him. Without acknowledging his previous unfortunate adventure in Russia to the others, he informed my mother and me about our changing geographical location.

At first, my father was surprisingly optimistic about our chances of survival. He equated our banishment with the much more benign Tsarist displacements of entire families to Siberia, when families were usually expelled for a limited time and then allowed to return home. Such a fate was not a pleasant prospect, but it was at least one that promised survival. We found out later that he was right about our survival for the wrong reasons, for this time our captors were planning a one-way trip.

Our journey continued slowly but steadily. We knew we were in Siberia when we reached the town of Chelabinsk and crossed the Ural mountains. We then passed Petropavlovsk, my mother's birthplace, then Omsk, Novosibirsk, Krasnoyarsk, and finally Irkutsk. In Irkutsk we were taken off the train and herded directly into a transit camp, which consisted of a number of low, dilapidated barracks surrounded by a high barbed-wire fence. A wide strip of neatly groomed sand was spread outside the fence to display the footsteps of potential escapees, and armed guards monitored the facility from strategically located watchtowers.

It was a forbidding and sinister place, but after our four-week train journey the camp seemed almost luxurious. The weather was glorious, and we could observe the clear sky and the bright sun without the confining walls and roof of the cattle car. There was plenty of room to walk around, and the bunks in the barracks were more spacious than our sleeping shelves on the train. We had access to water, both for personal hygiene and for laundering our clothes, and food, although still limited basically to soup and hot cereal, was plentiful, even though we had to stand in long lines to reach the field kitchen. It was almost with a feeling of regret that we left the camp on densely packed trucks a week after our arrival. The trucks took us to barges on the Angara River, where we endured the worst conditions of the entire trip. The dark, oppressive holds of the vessels resembled the interiors of eighteenth-century slave ships that ferried human cargo across the Atlantic, being lined with tiers of closely spaced bunks where we lay most of the time. Thankfully, unlike the victims of the slave trade, we were not in chains, but were allowed to climb the narrow ladders leading to the deck to wait our turn in the latrines (although the guards forced us below if the lines grew too long). The latrines were simple, long wooden booths constructed to overhang the upper deck. Inside, we were close enough to touch each other while sitting over holes cut in long boards, but unlike the situation on the train, men and women were not crowded into the same stalls—a minor but welcome concession to privacy. There were no washing facilities, and the drinking water must have been contaminated, because diarrhea spread rapidly and resulted in longer lines to the latrines.

After a five-day trip on the Angara River, we left the barge in Za-yarsk and traveled by truck for a day and a half to Ust-Kut on the

Lena River. We were tightly packed into those open trucks with the inevitable soldiers, one per truck, to guard us. The ride on an unpaved Siberian road would have been bumpy and uncomfortable in any vehicle, but it was especially rough on a Russian truck. The Russians had a knack for producing goods of such low quality that even when brand new they appeared to be old and unreliable. True to form, our trucks were shoddy, dirty, and seemed likely to disintegrate with each bump on the road. A few years later, when we saw American trucks delivered to Russia as part of wartime aid, the contrast revealed the Soviet vehicles in an even less favorable light.

From Ust-Kut a ship took us along the Lena and Vitim Rivers to Bodaybo. This final leg of the trip lasted eight days, with conditions somewhat better than those on the Angara barge. In Bodaybo we were separated into several groups, with each party assigned to a different final destination. My family was guided to a train on a narrow-gauge railroad that took us to a gold mining settlement named Vasilevskii

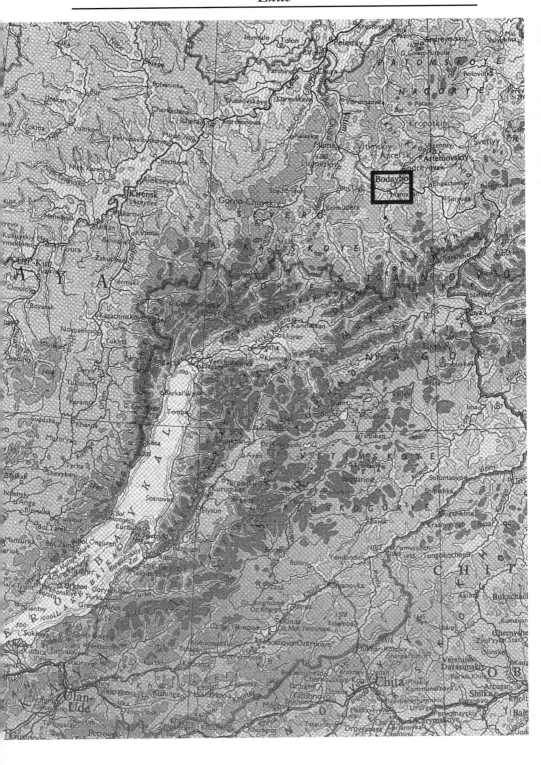

Priisk about thirty-five miles away. From there it was a relatively short one-hour truck ride along a narrow winding dirt road cut through a dense forest to Priisk Konstantinovskii, "Konstantinovskii Mining Village."

My father was generally familiar with that remote part of Siberia, and correctly estimated our approximate location. We had covered more than a thousand miles on our circuitous river route, and were now about 600 miles northeast of Irkutsk, the closest city along the Trans-Siberian Railroad. We were separated from it by Lake Baykal and hundreds of miles of taiga—the wild, uncharted, northern forest. Moscow lay nearly 3,000 miles west, the Sea of Okhotsk and the Pacific coast nearly 1,000 miles east. With the possible exceptions of Antarctica or the North Pole, it would be difficult to find a place anywhere on earth more remote from centers of civilization.

When we left Irkutsk, I sensed a steadily rising anxiety among the members of our group, including my father. Even the vast Siberian landmass has its limits, and it was clear that our long weeks of travel would soon bring us to our final destination. The presence of the train, even in the midst of the thinly populated landscape, had given us the temporary illusion of civilization. But now the rivers, with their hundreds of miles of uninhabited shores, told a different story. We were being isolated from the rest of the world. There was nothing but water, forest, and sky—no people, and not even wildlife, for even wild beasts shunned this forsaken part of the globe. Terms like "extinction," "exile," and "vanishing without a trace" were uttered with increasing frequency. Were we being taken to some remote dump to be disposed of like so much human garbage?

I now realize how fortunate I was to be a child of ten in that golden moment between childhood and adolescence. Younger children had greater nutritional and physical requirements to nourish their immature bodies, while teenagers had greater emotional needs. The adults faced backbreaking work, and they also understood the gravity of our situation, reaching a level of anxiety that I was spared. Our fearsome plight gradually pushed most of them into a state of helplessness and despair. Big and strong for my age, I was more optimistic than they. Yet I still wanted to believe in the infallibility and strength of my parents. The deeper into Siberia we went, the more I realized that they were losing control over our destiny. In the case of my father, the cumulative effects of the ruthless German and Soviet invasions of Poland, the fear of being discovered as a previous escapee from the Communists, our long tortuous journey east, and the desolation of our surroundings gradually increased his fears about our impending fate. I sensed his growing nervousness and tried to clear away those thoughts as quickly as they formed, but by this time even I was feeling at some deep level that we were being cast adrift into a cruel wilderness without a map, without means of support, and without a chance of escape. In short, my initial buoyancy was beginning to fade.

Approximately fifty families rode the open trucks that brought us from Vasilevskii to our final destination, an abandoned penal mining settlement, Priisk Konstantinovskii. On arrival we were ordered to assemble in front of a small log cabin. There, waiting for us, was our new *Komendant*, an NKVD officer named Mironov. A slim young man of medium build, wearing a military uniform and armed with a large pistol hanging at his side, he surveyed us indifferently. In a voice reminiscent of a bored travel guide, he informed us that we had been brought there to work in the gold mines.

"Here you will spend the rest of your life," he announced. "You can forget your Poland. The conditions will be hard, but you will get used to them. And if you don't, you will die."

CHILDHOOD

THE YEARS BEFORE EXILE were mostly peaceful, except for one event that might be taken as an omen of the times to come. I was probably three years old at the time, which would have made the year 1933. We lived on Miła Street in Warsaw. In Polish the word Miła embodies several concepts. It can mean "dear," referring to a loved one, or it can stand for "pleasant," "agreeable," or even "charming." The street, as I realized when I was old enough to understand such things, did not live up to any of the qualities suggested by its name, but was merely a perfectly ordinary street somewhere in the middle of Warsaw. During World War II, it became part of the Warsaw Ghetto, and it played a role during the 1943 Ghetto uprising. One of the first armed skirmishes between the Germans and the Jewish insurgents occurred at Miła 61. A command base was established at Miła 63 and a bunker at Miła 18, which became the title of Leon Uris's novel based on the desperate last stand of the Warsaw Jews in 1943.

On that night in 1933, I was awakened to the sound of loud screams in our apartment. The bedroom lights were out, but in the adjacent living room my parents were moving around frantically, shouting, "Thieves, robbers! Look what they tried to do to our door!" I crawled out of bed more out of curiosity than fear and walked to the front entrance. Our maid stood there, speechless, staring at the cause of this commotion.

Left: Poland, 1932.
Below left: My mother and I.
    Poland, 1932.
Below right: My father at a
    Polish resort, 1937.

The heavy wooden door had sprouted several holes, drilled from outside, that formed a neat circle near the inside locks. Whoever drilled those holes planned to complete the circle with a small saw to produce an opening large enough for a hand to reach inside and open the locks. Fortunately our terrified maid heard the noise and scared off the burglars with her screams. Later the police told us that others had not been so lucky; the criminals had honed their approach and managed to burglarize other apartments in our building.

In 1933 the Nazis became the only legal political party in Germany. Dachau concentration camp opened in June. Adolf Hitler became German Chancellor in July. After President Hindenburg's death in August 1934, Hitler assumed the self-created post of "Führer," absolute leader of Germany and its people.

When I was five years old, we moved a few blocks to another apartment at 27 Karmelicka Street. There we acquired our first telephone number, which I was instructed to memorize in case I lost my way in the city. (I remember it still: 11-70-56.) The new apartment was larger, and its location on the second floor made it easier to reach than our previous sixth-story address. Similar to other structures in that part of Warsaw, our building presented a continuous wall to the street, with windows, balconies, and a tall opening guarded by a heavy gate that led to a public inner courtyard. The building completely surrounded the courtyard, which served as a sheltered space for use by the tenants as well as by street performers and pushcart vendors peddling fruits, vegetables, fabrics, buttons, soap, and other household products. The most vocal of these vendors were artisans who sharpened cutting implements. They promised to fix broken scissors, restore old knives, and bring new temper to knife blades. "New for old, new for old," they cried in Polish and Yiddish. Their machines looked big, heavy, and awkward to carry, but the vendors set them up quickly and invariably attracted all of us children, who were fascinated by the bright stream of sparks generated by the grinding process. Tailors carried sewing machines on their backs and were able to produce whole new garments, such as shirts, trousers, suits, and dresses, either in the courtyard or in the buyer's apartment.

Above: My mother. Petropavlovsk, Siberia, 1920.
Right: My father (seated) and uncle Leon. Poland, 1913.
Below: My mother (standing) with her parents in the foreground, and other family members. Petropavlovsk, Siberia, 1920.

My two favorites were the fire-eaters and knife-throwers. The latter would place a young woman against a vertical backdrop and throw knives perilously close to her body. In the grand finale the knife thrower, wearing a black blindfold, hurled a knife a distance of fifteen feet and knocked a cigarette from the girl's mouth. It was a scary sight, and I wondered how long the girl could survive those dangerous performances. Not until fifty years later did I discover that the performance relied on an optical illusion: Knives hidden behind the backdrop would spring forward one at a time through covered holes arranged in an outline around the girl's body. The performer was merely pretending to throw the knife. Instead of launching it toward the girl, he concealed it in his sleeve as his hand moved forward, then placed it again in his hand as he reached into the prop box for the "next" one. The mind betrays us, bends us to the conjurer's will, constructing a trajectory where none exists—literally in thin air.

Our new apartment on Karmelicka Street had a living room, one bedroom, a bathroom, a kitchen, and a foyer. In typical East European fashion, the living room served also as the dining room, although it was not divided into two separate sections. It was dominated by a large, round table that we used for all social activities, and it was where I ate, did my homework, and played chess and where my parents hosted their guests. On a few occasions when my parents left me alone with our maid, I circumnavigated that table on my little bicycle. Those rides required considerable skill, for the room was not large and the space between the table and the furniture along the walls was limited to three or four feet. But by pushing the chairs under the table and steering carefully, I managed to complete a few circles without running into any stationary objects. I landed in trouble when I was asked to explain the origin of tire marks on the polished floor. The punishment for leaving the objectionable trail could not have been too severe, because the thrill of riding in defiance of parental authority continued to outweigh the fear of unpleasant consequences. It also helped that I had a close relationship with our maid, who offered to help me restore the shine to the soiled floor after my rides. Polishing the floor was hard work and she insisted that I help her do it. Whether this was by our maid's design or by accident, our conspiracy eventually discouraged my illicit excursions.

There were just the three of us in the family—my father Mieczysław (Moshe in Hebrew), my mother Miriam, and I—and we led a quiet home life. An accountant and real estate developer, Father was always busy. He left home early in the morning, came back for supper, and went out to another job in the evening. He worked six days a week, including Sundays, staying late in bed only on Saturdays when he read the paper. Father was of medium height, his thick black hair neatly arranged close to his head with the help of a net, which he wore at night. He had a thin face, straight nose, full lips, and penetrating dark eyes which, along with his impeccable dress, gave him an air of vitality and decisiveness. The eldest of six children, he became the unofficial head of his family after his parents' death, and it was not unusual for my aunts and uncles to come to our apartment for professional and personal advice.

My father was not a strict disciplinarian and we were quite close, a relationship which later helped us survive the war together. He was not a believer in physical punishment, but I do remember one occasion when I received a severe spanking for stealing a coin from my mother's purse. For a while my mother gave me money once a week to buy a comic sheet. Eventually she decided that I should not waste my time on comics and denied me funds for their purchase. I was heartbroken. I enjoyed the comics, especially the weekly adventures of "Pat and Patachon," characters similar to Mutt and Jeff, and I devised a scheme that I thought would circumvent the restriction. I took a ten grosz coin, equivalent to a few pennies, from my mother's purse and bought the comic sheet. After reading it I tried to return it to the seller for, I hoped, a full or partial refund. He refused to cooperate and I brought the comics home. That led to an inquiry about the source of my funds and to the aforementioned punishment. I never held the spanking against my father, but after his death I learned from a close friend of his that he deeply regretted the physical punishment he had inflicted upon me, evidently feeling guilty about it for the rest of his life. I am sure my father thought that I would forget the incident, and that is why he never brought up the subject. He was always my hero, but knowledge of his remorse elevated him even higher in my estimation.

My mother was a slim, attractive woman about five feet, five inches tall. She had light brown curly hair and brown eyes, and her large forehead emphasized the fair complexion of her well-proportioned oval face. She nursed me tenderly when I was ill during winter months and otherwise catered to my every need. She closely followed my progress in school and was immensely proud of my scholastic achievements. But despite her devotion to my father and me, I believe she was a lonely woman. Born in Siberia in 1900, she came to Poland in her mid-twenties after marrying my father. She thus had no prior knowledge of the Polish language and never felt completely at ease in her new country. By the time I was born, she had learned to speak Polish well, but not without a slight Russian accent and occasional grammatical errors.

The new language was not the only cause of her discomfort in Poland. The contrast between her early years in Tsarist Siberia—often considered Russia's wild frontier—and pre-Second World War European urban Warsaw was enormous. Apart from my father she knew no one in Poland, and she probably felt like an outsider among my father's numerous relatives. Her extended family lived in China after their escape from Communist Russia, and she missed her parents, her brothers, and her sister. She was a reserved woman and had a good, but not close, relationship with my father's siblings.

My parents spoke Russian at home, but never attempted to teach me the language; they spoke Polish to me and seemed to relish their ability to discuss in Russian issues they wanted to keep confidential. Four of my father's married brothers and sisters lived in Warsaw, and we frequently saw my aunts and uncles as well as my cousins. The most festive of those visits occurred during Hanukkah, when all my relatives gave me Hanukkah geld (coins) for chocolates and ice cream.

Two of my cousins lived immediately above our apartment. They were almost my parents' age and had a son one year my junior. His name, like mine, was Bronek, and we often played together after school. Every one of my father's siblings had a son named Bronek. We were all named after my paternal grandfather, the patriarch of the family. His name was Boruch, "the blessed one" in Hebrew. It was the habit of even assimilated Jews in Poland to give their children Hebrew names, even though in everyday life they were called by Polish names that were similar and easier to pronounce, such as Bronek. At the time of this writing only two Broneks out of the original six of our family are still alive. Two died of natural causes, two perished during the Holocaust, and one, who now lives in Sweden, is an Auschwitz survivor. I, the sixth Bronek, now live in Boston, Massachusetts.

My paternal grandfather was murdered just before World War I on his own farm, although the circumstances remained a mystery to me while I was growing up. I learned more details through a chance acquaintance with Ed Cohler, a former neighbor in Lexington, Massachusetts, long after my arrival in the United States. Ed was actively investigating his own Eastern European origins and had collected many references on his lineage, including Polish and Russian texts, which I translated into English.

Ed became interested in my origins. I had done little study of my own lineage, but I related the stories I had heard in childhood about my grandfather's large estate near Lublin, in southeastern Poland. My father's town had been described both as Rachów and Annopol, and I wasn't sure which name was correct, or even if the names referred to two separate towns. Ed asked a lot of questions, and it was almost midnight when he left our house. Early next morning he called, barely able to contain his excitement.

"I have wonderful news for you," he said. "Late last night I found a reference to your grandfather's estate in my files. I almost woke you up in the middle of the night. Both names, Rachów and Annopol, are right."

Ed opened up a wonderful source of information for me. I had not been aware that after the Second World War, the survivors of many Jewish communities in Poland wrote commemorative books (Yizkor books) describing their *shtetls*. These books were joint efforts of the survivors in Poland and the towns' emigrants abroad. Ed found a reference to one of those books in his home library: *Rachov/Annopol, Testimony and Remembrance*, published in Israel in 1978. Ed's reference included a table of contents, and the name of the second chapter was "The 'Rachov' Farm—a Jewish Estate." Ed suggested that the book would be available at the YIVO Institute for Jewish Research in Manhattan.[2]

I was able to find the book in the library of the YIVO Institute during my next trip to New York. Most of the text was in Hebrew and Yiddish, but there was also an eighty-page summary in English containing a wealth of information not only about my grandfather but also about previous generations of ancestors. It also unraveled the mystery of the town's two names. During the reign of Poland's King Bolesław Śmiały (the Brave) in the eleventh century, a woman named Anna Rachowa left her land to two sons. The settlement on her land was named "Rachów" ("Rachov" is the anglicized spelling). After she built a church on her land in honor of her patron saint, St. Anna, the community was given the name "Annopol," but the old name stuck, and "Annopol" was not fully accepted until the end of World War II.

My grandfather owned a large estate in that town. Contrary to popular belief, not all Jews in Poland were artisans, craftsmen, or small businessmen. There were a number of Jewish landowners, especially in southern Poland. In Warsaw, I was often entertained by stories of my father's childhood on the family estate. My grandfather owned 500 horses to work the 7,500 acres of land and the phosphate mines. The phosphates, used as Sztuczny nawóz (chemical fertilizer) were mined for sale both in Poland and abroad.

My grandfather's murder is described in the book in Hebrew by a local resident, W. S. Flishinski. Here is a translation of his description:

The Murder of Boruch Frusztajer

On that fateful night, I was staying with my friend [presumably my father], the son of Boruch Frusztajer, the owner of the Rachov farm, at the manor on the road leading to the estate. Very early in the morning, people rushed in screaming, woke us up and told us that Boruch had been murdered at night on his way home.

---

2. YIVO was founded as the Yidish Scientific Institute (*Yidisher visnshaftlekher institut*) in 1925 by scholars in Berlin and Vilna, Poland. In 1940, it transferred its mission to New York City.

Half awake, we rushed from our beds to see what had happened. When we arrived at the murder scene, we saw the following: Boruch Frusztajer was lying on the ground with his legs pointing toward the town. The bullet had struck the back of his head. He did not die immediately and his head movements produced a wide depression in the ground. And here is the story behind the murder. At two o'clock after midnight when Boruch Frusztajer was returning to his estate from a card game at uncle A. Berfman's house, a gentile to whom Boruch promised the position of estate manager ambushed him. Since Boruch did not come through with his promise, the man hated him. At that time there was a great deal of strife among all social classes in Russia [Poland was then under Russian rule] and that was the way the assassin carried out his grudge against the Jewish owner of the estate.

After some time the man was accused of the murder. The trial took place in Janów, but the accused was exonerated due to insufficient evidence. It may well have been that the matter was hushed up because of the anti-Semitism that existed at that time in all layers of Polish society, Russian rulers, and the justice system.

My father and his siblings were still young at the time of their father's murder. They knew little about business and lost the property to a Mr. Rosenberg. After the war my father introduced me to Mr. Rosenberg's son in Israel. The son did not even bother to deny his father's shady handling of the transaction. In fact, lending truth to the saying, "The apple does not fall far from the tree," Mr. Rosenberg the younger, an Israeli pharmacist, also managed to swindle my father out of some money. He did this by raising funds from several investors, including my father, to import medical drugs that were in short supply in Israel during those early years. The drugs turned out to be sugar. Mr. Rosenberg, Jr., was convicted of a criminal offense and punished accordingly. Unfortunately, my father never recovered his investment.

Back in Warsaw, the cousins who lived in our building had an apartment identical to ours except for the extra room that belonged to their son, Bronek. Both parents worked: The father was a partner in a wire factory, the mother a pharmacist. They had a car, which was considered a luxury. Bronek was one year my junior, and I acted almost as his older brother. I taught him to play chess and tried to engage him in boyish horseplay. Although we enjoyed each other's company and spent a lot of time together both at home and in the parks, we never became close friends, perhaps because of our age difference.

My formal education started in kindergarten, essentially a room in a private apartment. I have only a vague recollection of the place and the children who were my playmates, but I remember my first disastrous day in school very well. I was taken there by my mother and left in the first-grade classroom. Our first task was to draw a cat based on a tall, slim black silhouette cut out against a white background. For some reason, I refused to do it. The teacher, unable to persuade me, tried to steer me to another table to draw a different object. I rebelled against this project, too, balking at the physical coercion, and hit the teacher with a clenched fist. My first day in that school was also my last. I don't know whether I was expelled or whether my parents decided that I needed new surroundings, but the following day I was taken to another school. There—probably surprising my parents—I soon became not only a good student but also one with exemplary behavior.

My new school was a small, private Jewish academy that enrolled a hundred boys in six grades. Housed on the top floor of a large residential building, it occupied what must have been several converted and connected apartments. There were six classrooms, a few teachers' offices, and one large room with a stage for school performances and meetings. There was also a room for sports activities, which generally consisted of jumping on a pogo stick and playing "basketball." That game had all the rules of real basketball except that there were no baskets. We scored by shooting the ball past defending goalies through two doorways at opposite corners of the room. The ceiling was about eight or nine feet high, preventing all but low passes to the other players. The floors creaked and nails had the nasty habit of popping up, despite the teachers' valiant efforts to keep them hammered down. I once managed to fall on one of those nails, and its head tore a large hole in my left knee. Fortunately it missed the critical parts of the joint and caused little lasting damage, but it left a big scar in the shape of a cross, serving even today as a reminder of my early athletic enthusiasm.

I was not very good at this game of basketball and developed an adversarial relationship with the supervising teacher, who was not above dispensing mild physical punishment. One of his nasty habits was to sit down next to us while we were resting and slap our thighs while saying, "This is where I would build a house if I had a million złotys." If the saying was supposed to be funny, none of us understood the joke. I was subjected to that painful, slapping treatment on several occasions when the teacher was particularly displeased with my handling of the ball. But while basketball was not my game, I did take to the pogo stick and soon became the school's acknowledged pogo stick champion. I earned that exalted title by staying on the stick longer than other boys, spanning greater distances with a single jump, and vaulting over such high obstacles as benches and chairs. Not a particularly useful skill, but it impressed my children many years later when I was able to give them lessons.

The school was a strict but supportive place. The headmaster, Mr. Kaplan, walked around with a long wooden ruler he used to dispense punishment by hitting the backs of the boys' hands. Fortunately only Mr. Kaplan and our "basketball" coach believed in corporal punishment. Other teachers employed more humane penalties, such as additional homework and detention after school.

I remember the time I was subjected to Mr. Kaplan's ruler for misconduct outside the classroom. I lived less than five minutes' walk from the school. Half way home was a stand for *doroszki,* horse-drawn hackney carriages similar to those that carry tourists around New York's Central Park. These were the principal means of transportation for hire in Warsaw. While walking home with a couple of my classmates, I decided to play a joke on one of the drivers by asking him how much he would charge to take me home. He anticipated earning a good fare until he heard my destination, just a few steps away, and his initial hopeful expression changed quickly to anger. I didn't realize that this farce was being played out within earshot of my own classroom teacher, and the next day at the beginning of class my teacher announced that he was going to punish one of his better students. For the duration of the forty-five minute session, I had to stand in the corner facing the wall. For good measure I later received a slap on my wrist from Mr. Kaplan's wooden ruler; evidently my teacher had shared his information.

In general, a friendly atmosphere prevailed in the classrooms, but there were occasional conflicts. My first introduction to the evils of this world (a mild version, indeed) occurred in the second grade during the celebration of some religious holiday. The school organized a feast in our gym, serving delicious desserts. Unlike most other boys who immediately devoured the tastiest pieces, I saved my favorite item for last, planning to crown the occasion with that delectable treat. Just as I was about to savor my final reward, one of my classmates grabbed it from my plate and stuffed the whole thing into his mouth. There was nothing I could do to get it back, and little profit in attacking the guilty boy; a fight in full view of the teachers during our celebration would have been unthinkable. I just had to suffer in silence and reflect on the ugly side of human nature, something I would learn much more about in the years to come.

The school curriculum was quite demanding. We covered the subjects taught in standard Polish elementary schools as well as topics related to Judaism. We studied scriptures, Hebrew language, Jewish history, Israel, and Zionism, spending probably one-third of our school day on those subjects. Sad to say, I retained little of what we learned. My Jewish elementary education ended with the outbreak of the war when I was nine years old, and all I remember are most of the letters of the Hebrew alphabet and a few Hebrew poems and songs. Subjects learned at such an early age and then abandoned are easily forgotten.

At one point my teachers decided I showed an inclination for music and prevailed upon my parents to take me to a music school. The admission test was quite simple. The teacher drummed several rhythms on the lid of a closed piano and asked me to repeat them. The result, as the teacher immediately informed my mother, was not very impressive but good enough to be admitted to the school. My mother enrolled me as a violin student, and I was to begin my musical education in September 1939. World War II, of course, put an end to those plans.

Close friendships developed at school. One of my friends was Abram Wołoszko, who lived near our building. I could walk to his place without crossing a street, and I was allowed to make frequent visits without parental supervision. He came to see me quite often, too, but his apartment was more fun. His family was large, and his father had a business at home. Home workshops were not unusual in Warsaw, producing such commonly made products as wooden implements, neckties, clothing, toys, and other hand-made objects. My friend's father produced wooden rulers, and two people were needed to operate his machine: One turned a large engraving wheel with an attached handle, while the other fed wooden blanks and removed the marked rulers. Abram's entire family participated in the process, and I was always eager to help. The place was cluttered with packages. The whole apartment smelled of the ink used to smear the periphery of the engraving wheel. The ink found its way all over our hands and faces. The noise forced everyone to speak loudly, adding to the tumult so delightful to a young boy.

I don't recall many birthday parties, but I always received birthday presents, usually books and toys. On one occasion I got a toy car with a battery and working headlights. I also remember a running battle with my mother about excessive reading in bed. She insisted on switching off the lights after a certain hour, but one night I decided to outwit her by covering my head with a blanket and using the lights of my new car to read in the dark. The blanket must have been translucent, however, because my mother soon returned to the room and confiscated my new source of illumination. I pleaded with her to let me read my new books, but she would not listen. My only consolation was deciding that if I ever had children, I would let them read books in bed as long as they liked—and I kept my promise.

During the school year, my daily routine varied little. I walked to school in the morning and returned home around two in the afternoon. I had lunch with my mother and then did my homework. Later my mother and I would spend several hours in the nearby park with my upstairs cousin Bronek and his governess. Our favorite activities were feeding the abundant red squirrels and, in the right season, playing games with chestnuts, where the chestnuts themselves were the prize.

I often took my bicycle to the park. On one occasion a stranger, a boy my age, pleaded with me to let him ride my bicycle. Foolishly, I agreed. He promptly steered into a woman and almost knocked her down. The boy ran away, and the woman, rather than trying to catch him, grabbed my bicycle and refused to return it to me. I ran to fetch my mother, who was horrified to see me without the bicycle. Returning to the scene of the accident, we saw a small crowd gathered around the injured woman, and there was a lot of shouting and arguing. At first the woman, to whom one boy must have looked very much like another, accused me of running into her, but she finally released the bicycle. Needless to say, the incident taught me to be much more careful about lending my bicycle to strangers.

During the cold winter months, I often went to a neighborhood skating rink, and sometimes on Saturdays I went to the movies. Shirley Temple was a great favorite of mine, but I also enjoyed Polish films. At first I did not understand that films told a story; I thought they were just a collection of moving scenes. The first film I actually understood was called Chłopcy z Placu Broni (Boys from the Arms Square). Based on a novel, The Paul Street Boys (the title was changed in the Polish version), by Hungarian author and playwright Ferenc Molnár,[3] it told the story of a group of boys who used a building lot as a playground, which they were forced to defend against a gang of bigger boys. Their defense was successful, but the victory was hollow, for one of the defenders—a small, sick boy—died of an illness caused by the fight. And almost immediately, construction began on the lot, ending its use as a playground for anyone.

I remember the miraculous feeling of discovery that came with understanding my first film—something akin, I imagine, to solving a great mystery or seeing the world in a new light. The last film I saw

---

3. Ferenc Molnár (1878-1952) was celebrated all over the world at the height of his fame in the 1920s and 1930s. Today he is best remembered in the West for the play *Liliom*, on which Rodgers and Hammerstein based their musical *Carousel*, and for adaptations of his farce *The Play's the Thing* by P.D. Wodenhouse and Tom Stoppard (the latter as *Rough Crossing*).

before the war was "Snow White and the Seven Dwarfs," which my mother promised weeks in advance. It was screened at an elegant new theater, a building with a majestic lobby, thick carpets, and plush seats. It seemed like a palace to me, intimidating but surely an appropriate backdrop for my newly discovered art form.

Every year my mother and I spent my summer vacations in various resorts in the Polish countryside, while my father remained in Warsaw attending to his work. The two most memorable places were the Tatra mountains in southern Poland and a resort on the Baltic sea. The mountains were magnificent, and we explored them in long walks and gentle climbs. Although I enjoyed these outings, I was bewildered by the frequent stops the adults made to admire the scenery, which I didn't appreciate nearly as much as they did. On the other hand, I loved everything about the mountain people, admiring their dress, their dialect, their singing, and their crafts. The mountaineers' walking sticks were famous throughout Poland, and the toy boats—which closely resembled the real craft used to navigate the swift, shallow rivers of the region—gave me hours of pleasure in my bathtub at home. I admired the skill of the carvers, and even learned to make primitive shepherd flutes on my own. The flutes actually were easy to make: One started by cutting a branch about one-inch in diameter from a bush, trimming it to the right length, and then tapping it for a few minutes with a heavy wooden stick to loosen the bark. When removed from the branch, the bark retained the form of a tube to serve as the main sound chamber of the flute. Both ends of the tube were then sealed with short plugs cut from the original branch, the plug at the far end forming a tight seal, and the one close to the player's mouth trimmed to form a narrow slot for air to pass through. The final step was to cut half a dozen small, evenly spaced holes in the side of the tube. I must have made a dozen of those flutes.

The summer we spent in Copoty on the Baltic Sea was equally memorable. We stayed at a small pension, a kind of country inn with room and board. The place was near a large, expensive hotel which we admired from a distance. The hotel's opulently dressed, fashionable clientele

Uncle Ilya (left), my parents, and
I at the beach in Copoty, Poland,
1932.

seemed to be of a different breed; it didn't even occur to us to visit that august establishment. (By a strange coincidence, I spent a night at that hotel after the war, on my way to England.) The Baltic fishermen in Copoty were not nearly as colorful as the Tatra mountaineers, but I enjoyed watching them return with their catch early in the morning, their sailboats (I don't think their craft had engines) presenting a picturesque sight as they approached the harbor. I frequently joined the group of townspeople who waited on shore to bargain for the fresh fish.

That summer we traveled to nearby Danzig (now Gdańsk), then a nominally independent city-state that was actually under German control. Among other sights, we visited an old castle, well equipped with torture chambers. One of its halls was full of niches carved into the walls a few feet above the floor. The niches were just large enough to hold prisoners who, in the Middle Ages, were wedged inside with their faces toward the wall and locked in position by iron bars fastened across their backs. I thought of that castle in 1980 when, under the leadership of Lech Wałęsa, the Gdańsk shipyard workers mounted the first serious challenge to Soviet rule—a challenge that was an important stage in the collapse of the Soviet Union. And so the city where I first saw instruments of repression later became a beacon of freedom.

In 1939 my parents must have judged me mature enough to spend a summer without them, and they sent me off to Śródborów, a small resort town near Warsaw. There I stayed in a pension that catered to adults and also provided a camp-like environment for children. I was part of a small group of perhaps twenty youngsters supervised by adult counselors, and I remember the summer as an enjoyable one, although I don't recall exactly how we spent our time. There was no nearby river or lake for swimming, but we played basketball, volleyball, and other games.

It was there that I first fell in love. The girl was probably one year my junior, and unfortunately I don't recall her name. We knew nothing about sex—at least I didn't—and we did not even hold hands during our long walks in the countryside. I didn't think of our relationship as a romantic one, although it must have been. To me she was an exquisite creature—well dressed, gentle, and delicate—and she always greeted me with a beaming smile. We spent a lot of time together walking and discussing our future. We spoke of getting married and moving to London, where we would both become doctors. We even decided we would have independent practices, with adjacent offices but separate outside doors, and each would have a car. We kept our involvement and our plans secret. Although she lived in Warsaw, our paths never crossed again. I hope she escaped the horrible fate of Warsaw's Jewish inhabitants and survived the Holocaust.

OUR CHILDHOOD musings about the future—moving to London and entering the medical profession—show that my parents' plans for me were already firmly in place. One figure who was always discussed with a great deal of awe in our household was my Uncle Ilya, my mother's brother, who was a distinguished British surgeon. Living in London, he loomed large in my mind: My father made me memorize his address and promise that if I ever were destitute, I would contact him immediately. Later, during the war, when everything seemed lost, the knowledge that I had Uncle Ilya in London helped me sustain hope for survival. In my boyish daydreams I even fantasized that my uncle and I piloted a bomber in a raid on Berlin and delivered a devastating blow to the German war machine. My parents intended to place me in a boarding school in England after I finished the sixth grade in Poland so that I could complete my education under my uncle's tutelage, then work with him as a doctor and eventually take over his practice. My uncle strongly supported those plans. He and my aunt had no children of their own, and besides, as I later learned, he had been a great supporter of his extended family, helping several relatives who found themselves in trouble during World War I and the Russian Revolution.

After annexing Czechoslovakia in March 1939, Hitler demanded the right of passage between mainland Germany and East Prussia through the so-called Polish "corridor." He also complained about the "mistreatment" of ethnic Germans in Poland, a charge he had leveled against the Czechs before invading their country. In May the Nazis signed a "Pact of Steel" with Italy; in August they concluded the infamous Ribbentrop-Molotov Non-Aggression Agreement with the Soviets.

I was supposed to stay at the camp in Śródborów until the end of August, but my mother took me home a few days early. By then the rumors about impending war were growing louder, and my parents wanted me to be home with them. They had good reason to worry: The war broke out just a few days after my return.

WAR

By the beginning of 1939, war had become the main topic of conversation among our relatives and friends. Radio programs extolled the readiness of the Polish army. Posters with military themes appeared on the streets of Warsaw. A widely disseminated slogan boldly proclaimed "JESTEŚMY SILNI, ZWARCI, GOTOWI" ("We are strong, united, prepared"). Some people were reassured by the patriotic fervor, others were extremely worried. I was nine years old, too young to appreciate the gravity of the situation, but I was confident that Poland could take care of itself.

An early hint of the coming upheaval in Europe was the addition to our household of a middle-aged Jewish refugee whom Hitler had expelled from Germany in late 1938. Elegantly dressed and distinguished looking, this gentleman stayed with us for almost a year before emigrating to the United States. He did not speak Polish, and only my father was able to communicate with him, in German and Yiddish. He was not related to us, nor was he a friend or even an acquaintance, but it was quite common for Jews to shelter their co-religionists in times of trouble. His living with us seemed at the time to be a very natural event. In the years to come, I saw many examples of mutual help among Jewish refugees.

Anti-Semitism had always existed in Poland, but it seemed to gather momentum as the country inched toward war. I began to hear stories of Jews beaten by hooligans, with the police intervening half-heartedly or looking the other way. The atmosphere grew tense for Jews in the streets, and parks became more dangerous. Orthodox Jews were especially vulnerable because of their distinctive attire. I never witnessed physical violence, but I often heard insults being hurled. About a third of Warsaw's population was Jewish, and there were many predominantly Jewish neighborhoods. The Catholic churches dispersed throughout the city occasionally posed a particular problem for religious Jews. Christian Poles usually took their hats off when passing a church, while the Jewish custom called for heads to be covered. That difference was exploited by hooligans, who waited outside a church and challenged Jews to uncover their heads. Some Jews did so out of fear, while others ignored the hooligans, despite their threats.

On one occasion I became terrified and angry during a demonstration by a group of young men who were marching through the park and shouting in unison a catchy rhyme that loses some of its color in translation:

Warszawa i Kraków	Warszawa and Kraków
to miasta Polaków	are Polish towns
a wy żydy świnie	and you Jew Swine
siedźcie w Palestynie.	stay in Palestine.

Such anti-Semitic slogans and insults in the streets and parks of Warsaw made the atmosphere increasingly tense, as did the signs appearing in some shop windows proclaiming *Firma Chrześcijańska* (A Christian Establishment), to differentiate those stores from Jewish-owned businesses, presumably to attract Christian shoppers and possibly as protection from hooligans intent on breaking the shop windows in imitation of the German *Kristallnacht* (Night of Broken Glass), an event marking the beginning of the Holocaust.[4]

---

4. Louis I. Snyder, *Encyclopedia of the Third Reich* (New York: Paragon House, 1989), p. 201. On the nights of November 9 and 10 in 1938, gangs of Nazi youth roamed through Jewish neighborhoods in Germany, breaking windows of Jewish businesses and homes, burning synagogues, and looting. In all, 101 synagogues were destroyed as were almost 7,500 Jewish businesses. Some 26,000 Jews were arrested and sent to concentration camps, and others were physically attacked and beaten, of whom 91 died.

Poland has been accused of being the most anti-Semitic nation after Germany. It is not difficult to understand why. Like many Jews, I never felt quite at home in prewar Poland. All my friends were Jewish, and my parents did not socialize with Christian Poles. No one told me that I did not belong there, yet I "knew" that I was different from our Christian neighbors, and not just in the religious sense. That is to say, I felt to some extent an impostor and a trespasser in someone else's land. I was sure that the Christian Poles were physically stronger than the Jews and that we had to avoid fighting with them at all costs because of the certainty that we would be beaten up. Besides, our adversaries would be justified in hurting us because we were second-class citizens who should be satisfied just to be allowed to live in their country. I suspect my parents harbored similar sentiments. We never discussed this subject, but they must have conveyed their own fears to me in many subtle ways.

It was in Poland that the Germans built most of their concentration camps and exterminated the majority of the six million Jews who died during the Holocaust. Many Poles knew about those camps, yet did nothing to stop the slaughter. Indeed, there were many instances of Christian Poles refusing to hide Jews, and even going out of their way to betray them to the Germans. Discovery of the massacre of Jews by their Christian Polish neighbors in Jedwabne during the German occupation only added force to this argument. Nor does comparison with other countries show Poland in a favorable light. Danish citizens, at tremendous personal risk, saved practically their entire Jewish population by smuggling them into Sweden. Even the Italians, Germany's staunchest allies, made valiant efforts to protect Italian Jews. To add the final insult to what was probably humanity's greatest injury, many Christian Poles greeted the few Holocaust survivors after the war with renewed anti-Semitism and pogroms, causing the loss of even more Jewish lives. The Catholic Church did little to change the attitude of its people, and in many instances contributed to fostering bigotry and hatred against the Jews.

And yet closer examination reveals many of these charges to be less than fair. Harboring a Jew was punishable by death. German posters[5] such as the one below made that fact abundantly clear, and terriúfying:

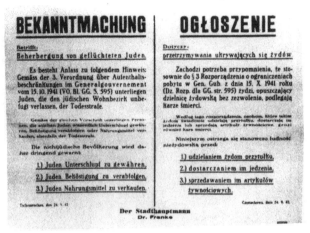

NOTICE

About the harboring of escaping Jews

This is a reminder that pursuant to the third Decree of General Government dated 10/15/41 (G.G. Decree, page 595) concerning residence restrictions, Jews who leave [the] Jewish quarter without permission are subject to the death penalty.

The Decree also states that persons who knowingly help those Jews with shelter, give them food, or sell them food are also subject to the death penalty.

The non-Jewish population is hereby firmly warned against:
1. Giving Jews shelter
2. Giving them food   Chęstochown 9/24/42
3. Selling them food   Der Stadthauptmann
                            Dr. Franks

It took extraordinary courage, devotion, and idealism for Poles–and there were a fair number of them—to shelter their Jewish neighbors. It is true that the Danes faced the same risks, but there were only ten

5. *Żegota: The council for Aid to Jews in Occupied Poland 1942-1945,* Irene Tomaszewski and Tecia Werbowski (Montreal, Quebec, Canada: Price Patterson Ltd.), p. 28.

thousand Jews in Denmark, compared with over three million in Poland. Placing the extermination camps in Poland certainly held strong appeal to the systematic Nazi mind: After all, Poland had by far the largest Jewish population in Europe, and locating concentration camps there saved transportation and other logistical costs.

It is also instructive to compare the betrayal rate of Jews in Warsaw and in the Netherlands. Gunnar Paulson estimates that in Warsaw 13,000 to 17,500 Jews survived out of 23,500 who remained in hiding on the "Aryan side." In contrast, in Holland, primarily in Amsterdam, there were only 10,000 to 15,000 Jewish survivors out of the 20,000 to 25,000 who had gone into hiding.[6]

> The overall survival rate in Holland was thus 40–60 percent, and in Warsaw . . . 55–75 percent. Thus, the attrition rate among Jews in hiding in Warsaw was relatively low, contrary to expectations and contemporary perceptions.
>
> Despite frequent house searches and the prevailing Nazi terror in Warsaw (conditions absent in the Netherlands), and despite extortionists, blackmailers, and anti-Semitic traditions (much less widespread in the Netherlands), the chance that a Jew in hiding would be betrayed seems to have been lower in Warsaw than in the Netherlands.

The Israeli Holocaust Museum, Yad Vashem, has honored the so-called "righteous gentiles," who at great personal risk sheltered Jews during the war, saving them from certain death. More than six thousand Christian Poles were among those righteous gentiles, the largest single ethnic group to be so honored. This is not altogether surprising, of course, in view of the large Jewish population in prewar Poland.

A small rescue group known as Żegota illustrates the polarized relationship between Christian and Jewish Poles during World War II. Żegota operated by providing Christian identities, food, and shelter to escaping Jews. Organized by the Polish Government in exile in London, it included people of both faiths. One of Żegota's main concerns was the

---

6. Gunnar S. Paulsson, "The Demography of Jews in Hiding in Warsaw, 1943-1945," *"Polin* vol. 13 (London and Portland, Oregon: The Littman Library of Jewish Civilization, 2000).

fate of the few Jews who managed to escape from the Warsaw Ghetto. In many instances, the fugitives were stalked outside the Ghetto walls by thieves who demanded their victims' possessions, including their clothing. The Jews were totally defenseless. Cries for help would attract German guards and result in immediate execution. Żegota members, most of whom were Christian Poles, tried to defend the escaping Jews, and even killed their attackers.

The war started on the first of September 1939. I certainly did not appreciate its significance or the danger it posed for my family. By then, most of the windows in Warsaw were crisscrossed with sticky tape to minimize the danger of shattering glass, and there was a total blackout each night. The blackout was strictly enforced, and the names and addresses of people who left their lights on at night were announced on the radio. The radio broadcasts were also full of troop movements and the progress of the war. Initially the Poles fought valiantly and the German progress was slow. During the first few days of the war, Warsaw was spared any serious aerial attacks, and I don't remember much shooting or bombing. I have a recollection of airplanes flying over, but I saw no damage in our part of town. So at first, my life went on more or less as usual.

Then, on the sixth of September, around midnight, radio broadcasts informed us that the Germans had broken through the Polish defenses and that Panzer columns were advancing toward Warsaw. Colonel Roman Umiastowski, acting under orders from the supreme military commander, issued a radio appeal for able-bodied men to leave Warsaw and move toward Poland's eastern borders, where new fighting units would be organized. The Army's appeal and the German advance posed a major challenge, and a decision had to be made quickly about whether or not to leave Warsaw. Clearly it was a wrenching choice. If you left, you would immediately become homeless. Where would you go? What would you take with you? Would you be able to buy food? There were few banks in the countryside where one could get cash, and even if currency was available, the chances were good that it would be useless. I remember watching anxiously as my father paced up and down in our apartment, his palm occasionally touching his forehead. Suddenly he announced his decision: We were going to leave.

Left: A map showing the 1939 partition of Poland by the Nazis and Soviets along "Ribbentrop-Molotov line."

Below: Polish refugees leaving Warsaw, Poland, ahead of German occupiers. September, 1939

There is little doubt that his choice saved my life. Most of my extended family stayed behind, and almost all of them, including several aunts, uncles, and cousins, were later murdered by the Nazis. And we left just in time, for it took the Germans only two days to reach Warsaw and put it under siege on the tenth of September.

My parents informed the building manager of our decision to leave. Our maid promised to stay behind to guard the apartment, or so we understood. The manager, Pan Franciszek (Mr. Franciszek), was stunned. He was a short but well-built, broad-shouldered, muscular man. He stood in our doorway with his hands at shoulder level, pressed rmly against the door frame to form a well-meaning but determined barrier as he tried his best to persuade us to remain. "Panie Mieczysławie," he pleaded, "where are you going? Why are you leaving us? England and France have now entered the war. Germany cannot hold out against them. The whole thing will be over in a few short weeks, or even days. Please stay." Fortunately, my father ignored those pleas, explaining that he was heeding the Army's appeal to join Polish forces in the East. He accurately foresaw the great dangers to come, including the expected deadly German aerial bombardment of Warsaw. He wanted to move our family eastward, away from the front, hoping to avoid the scene of the most ferocious fighting.

We left the following day in two big wagons drawn by draft horses similar to the enormous Clydesdales shown in traditional Budweiser advertisements. Three families traveled in our group. Our wagon, which we shared with another family (my parents' friends), was pulled by one horse; the other wagon, with two horses, belonged to the owners of the moving business that supplied our means of transport. Our immediate "fellow travelers" were a married couple with a boy two years my junior and the husband's brother.

It was dark when we finished loading our possessions—primarily valuables and clothing. The wagon was crowded with people and hastily thrown bundles. The adults rearranged the luggage to create a "bed" for the other boy and me. Placed side by side, and covered with small blankets, we were told to go to sleep. I realized soon that my neighbor's mother was pulling off my blanket to cover her son, but I was afraid to say anything even when I began to feel cold. My mother, seeing me uncovered, re-spread the blankets to cover both of us, but then I felt the blanket moving once again. This charade was repeated several times until my mother caught the other woman stealing my blanket. After a short, sharp exchange, the woman agreed not to uncover me again.

I was wide awake when we came to the outskirts of Warsaw. The road was filled with refugees, army vehicles, horses, and crowds of people. Deep, wide trenches had been dug in the road to delay the movement of German tanks and motorized units, and we had to snake our way past these obstacles, making our progress slow and difficult. Surprisingly, everything was orderly and calm, as the refugees all cooperated and helped each other.

During the next few days we inched our way eastward. The roads, horizon to horizon, were choked full of refugees like us, and we saw every conceivable type of vehicle. Most were horse-drawn carts, but there were also cars, trucks, bicycles, motorcycles, and, perhaps most incongruous, out-of-gas cars pulled by horses. As might be expected in wartime, our progress was not peaceful. Several times a day, low-flying German planes strafed the road. As soon as we saw or heard German planes approaching, we ran for cover among trees, bushes, or fields on the side of the road. I was scared but not terrified; never having seen death, I did not appreciate the danger, even though on several occasions my father lay on top of me to shield me with his body. Typically the planes flew in groups of three, in triangular formations. They flew very low, perhaps twenty feet above the ground, and often we could see the pilots' faces shielded with goggles in what seemed like open cockpits.

One day we found ourselves pulling out of a village with a Polish Army unit whose soldiers were riding on a few dozen horse-drawn carts. Appearing as if from nowhere, a swarm of German planes attacked the convoy. This episode brought home the full, horrible reality of war. The planes flew low over us, firing at everything in sight, then soared into the sky and circled back, for what seemed like hours. The troops were defenseless. They had no antiaircraft artillery, and their rifles were pitifully ineffective against the German planes. The roar of the engines, the deafening loudness of machine gun fire became numbing and disorienting, and we were completely helpless as bullets rained onto the ground and the wagons around us. Incredibly, no one in my immediate vicinity was killed or even wounded—or so I thought at the time, as I was quietly led away by my parents immediately at the end of our ordeal.

After that incident we traveled at night, hiding in the woods during daylight hours. Every day my father went out in search of food, usually procuring it from local peasants in exchange for Polish currency or articles of clothing. During those days there was little for me to do, and at night, while we traveled, I fell sound asleep. Our huge horses were gentle and friendly creatures, and I spent most of my time with them, hugging their enormous legs, climbing on their backs and chasing away flies. The horses grazed all day in an open field. I wasn't allowed to sit on them for very long, because my parents were afraid that if the German planes came, I would not have enough time to climb down and run into the woods.

Two weeks after leaving Warsaw, we came to the town of Rovno (Równe in Polish), which we thought to be far enough east to be safe from the war. It was, indeed, far enough, because the next day the Soviet Red Army entered the town. The Russians were welcomed with open arms. Crowds of jubilant people lined the main street, greeting the Soviet troops with flowers, food, singing, and slogans. "Russia is with us," the people shouted. "together we'll march on Berlin," and "Long live Russia!" Tanks led the troops, with soldiers sitting atop open turrets. I thought those soldiers would be vulnerable in combat, and I couldn't understand who was driving the tanks. My father explained that the soldiers normally sat inside the closed turrets and the drivers were hidden inside the tanks. He was unusually grim and so, I noticed, were a number of people around us.

That day, despite my young age, I somehow knew that a major upheaval was taking place in the world. True, during the last three weeks I had seen German planes and witnessed their deadly fire power. But they seemed distant and transient, like big, black flying hornets on a temporary visit from another world. Russian troops were right next to us, their huge tanks appearing even bigger by contrast with the narrow streets they gouged with their caterpillar tracks. The long guns extending from the turrets heralded aggression and conquest. The troops, packed into trucks that followed the tanks were dressed in shoddy, unfamiliar foreign uniforms and clearly did not belong in our country. Poland had been invaded and divided among its three neighbors 150 years prior to this incursion, but this time, I sensed, the conquerors were more vicious, more intent on wiping out the Poland we had known forever. Perhaps it was the naïve who were greeting the Russians—those who had forgotten the last Soviet invasion a mere twenty years earlier. Others, my father among them, had a clear understanding of the Communists' plans. I desperately wanted to know what was happening, and I remember trying to frame a question in words that would be appropriate for this solemn occasion. Drawing on the most sophisticated resources in my young vocabulary, I asked my father if the eastern lands of Poland would now belong to Russia. Unusually grim, he evaded the question.

The Soviets were not, of course, there to help Poland, but to fulfill the terms of a secret Soviet-Nazi nonaggression pact signed before the outbreak of the war. The pact contained provisions for joint occupation of Poland, and the Russians wasted little time in establishing control over their portion. They mounted a massive invasion of the country, with NKVD personnel following closely behind frontline troops. The man in charge of establishing the Soviet order in this newly conquered land was Nikita Khrushchev, a loyal henchman from Stalin's inner circle and a future ruler of the Soviet Union. His task was "to conquer and Sovietize, to expropriate and collectivize, to organize new party and state institutions, and to make sure (the population) opted 'voluntarily' to join the Soviet Union of Socialist Republics."[7]

---

7. William Taubman, *Khrushchev, The Man and his Era*, p. 137. (New York: W.W. Norton & Co. 2003). On page 136 Taubman further states: "All told, one and a quarter million people (including Jews, Ukrainians, and Byelorussians, as well as Poles), or nearly 10 percent of the total population, were deported from western Ukraine and Byelorussia to the Soviet interior. Approximately half a million were imprisoned during the twenty-one months of Soviet rule between 1939 and 1941, including about 10 percent of all adult males. Some fifty thousand were executed or tortured in prison, while three hundred thousand more perished during deportation or in exile."

1940: A year of triumph for the Nazis and the Soviets. Holland and Belgium surrendered to the Germans in May; In June the Nazis occupied Norway and entered Paris. Soviet troops occupied Lithuania, Latvia, and Estonia in July. With their eastern boundaries secured, the Nazis started their blitz against England on September 7, and the Italians invaded Egypt on September 13.

The atmosphere in the town changed overnight. Every day Russian troops marched menacingly through the streets, wielding their bayonet-tipped rifles and singing military songs. Within days, small groups of armed young men wearing conspicuous red armbands descended on the town. They surrounded buildings, checked papers, searched dwellings, and sometimes arrested people. There were a number of fights, often accompanied by warning shots, as those being arrested tried to escape. The young men with red armbands were Polish or perhaps Ukrainian, but no one—at least none in my sight—questioned their authority. The tension infected our own household, in a room we had rented in an apartment building. When one day I dropped a heavy object on the floor during my father's afternoon nap, he jumped up from his couch with a loud scream.

At first we did not understand exactly what was going on, but soon the situation became clear. Starting with Lenin, the Communist Party in the Soviet Union had established a ruthless totalitarian state and demonstrated how a minority—admittedly an armed minority—could control a country much larger than the United States. One successful tactic they employed immediately after seizing eastern Poland was what might be termed "preventive maintenance." Like all autocratic parties, the Russians relied on terror to enforce their power. But the Bolsheviks (Russia's Communist Party) elevated the art of terror to new heights. Most dictators eliminate their opponents. Russian Communists arrested and deported those who *might conceivably become their opponents in the future*.[8] Among the first victims of this strategy were members of

---

8. Russia has had a long history of suppressing dissent. Under a 1878 law, special police answerable directly to the Tsar could take "preventative measures"—i.e., administer severe penalties on mere suspicion of political crimes. According to historian Richard Pipes, this was one of the features that made "… the police institutions of the late imperial Russia the forerunner, and, through the intermediacy of corresponding

all Polish political parties, including even Polish communists. It may seem surprising that the Russians feared their Polish counterparts, but Stalin believed that only his party should wield unlimited power. The same line of reasoning led much later to animosity between the Soviet Union and Communist China.

The deportations did not stop with people involved in political activities but soon engulfed those in business, government, the army, teachers, and clergy—anyone who might have a reason to be dissatisfied with the Russian occupation. These mass arrests were carried out with total disregard for human rights or any legal process. If the members of the Communist security apparatus did not like or trust someone, they simply eliminated him. Nor was this practice confined to individuals. Shortly after the invasion, a Russian soldier was attacked by local Polish peasants. A few nights later, their village was surrounded by Russian troops, who dragged all the inhabitants—men, women, and children—from their houses and shipped them to an unknown destination. We did not know it at the time, but the Communists had begun massive population displacements as a means of establishing their authority almost as soon as they seized power in Russia. In several instances, the populations of entire regions where disloyalty was suspected were relocated. Three of the biggest cases involved the forced and brutal exile of 450,000 ethnic Germans who had lived on the river Volga since 1762, half a million native Chechens, and 180,000 Tartars (descendants of Ghengis Khan warriors) who had settled in the Crimean peninsula in the fifteenth century.[9] Nor did the Communists confine their resettlement schemes to Asian minorities: Millions of Slavs—Russians, Ukrainians, and Byelorussians—suffered a similar fate, but the emptying of entire regions was restricted to non-Slavic nationalities.

communist institutions, the prototype of all political organs of the twentieth century." (Richard Pipes, *Russia under the Old Regime* [New York: Penguin Books, 1977] p. 302.) The Soviet laws and enforcement practices were, of course, much harsher than those of their Tsarist predecessors. There is credible evidence that, despite growing opposition to the imperial rule in the last decades of its existence, the total number of political prisoners jailed, exiled, and executed in Tsarist Russia was in the thousands, or possibly in the tens of thousands. In Soviet Russia, under a much broader definition of the term "political prisoner," similar numbers reached millions, if not tens of millions.

9. For a fuller discussion of this topic, see Robert Conquest, *The Nation Killers (Soviet Deportation of Nationalities)* (New York: The Macmillan Co., 1970).

The large-scale expulsions eliminated nearly the entire population in those regions. Stalin was determined to wipe out all traces of displaced minorities from their ancestral lands and gradually settled the vacant areas with ethnic Russians and a sprinkling of other nationalities. The emptied towns and villages were given new Russian names, and the regions were no longer shown on maps as separate entities. By strange coincidence, our family was transplanted in 1944 to the formerly Volga German region.

In his 1899 novel "The Resurrection," Leo Tolstoy described the indiscriminate arrests made by the Tsarist Police. His words can easily be applied to the plight of the innocent people rounded up by the NKVD:[10]

> Those people were treated the way fishermen treat the catch snared in dragnets: they haul everything on shore and then select the big fish they need, paying no attention to the small fry which perishes, drying out on shore. [In] the same way, the authorities rounded up hundreds of people who were not only not guilty but clearly not capable of harming the government, and sometimes kept them for years in prisons where they contracted tuberculosis, were driven to insanity, or committed suicide; and they were kept there only because there was no reason to release them and, as an aside, being handy they could be used to clarify some points in an ongoing investigation.

Of course, the Soviets had good reason to doubt the loyalty of their southern and eastern populations. Moscow ruled a colonial empire created by the tsars in a manner reminiscent of western European conquests. One technical difference was that western European countries were bounded by the Atlantic Ocean and had to build navies to subjugate distant lands. Russia, ruling a much vaster continent, had been able to conquer its future colonies by land. Yet the conquered people were as different from the Russians as the Asians and Africans were from their French or British masters, and they yearned just as fervently for the freedom they had once known. In the view of the Bolsheviks,

---

10. Leo N. Tolstoy, *Voskresenie (Resurrection)* (Moscow: Terra, 1993), p. 459. Translated by the author.

this desire for freedom by their colonial subjects justified the suspicion and brutal treatment their new masters were now free to exercise.

During the Cold War, the colonial origins of Tsarist Russia and the Soviet Union were not widely recognized in Europe and America. Apologists for the Communists claimed that the Soviets' subversive international behavior was merely a reaction against a threat of invasion by foreign powers. Soviet propaganda made the case that over the centuries, Russians had been surrounded and continually attacked by hostile neighbors, and they were simply responding to that danger. The historian Richard Pipes convincingly demolishes that argument by pointing out that Russia became the largest country in the world not by being invaded but by invading others:[11]

> One can dismiss the explanation most often offered by amateur Russian "experts" (although hardly ever by Russians themselves) that Russia expands because of anxieties aroused by relentless foreign invasions of its national territory by neighboring countries. . . . Common sense, of course, might suggest . . . that a country can no more become more spacious as a result of suffering constant invasions than an individual can gain wealth from being repeatedly robbed. But common sense aside, there is the record of history. It shows that far from being the victim of recurrent acts of aggression, Russia has been engaged for the past three hundred years with single-minded determination in aggressive wars, and that if anyone has reason for paranoia it would have to be its neighbors.

The British once were fond of saying that the sun never set on the British Empire. The Soviet Empire rivaled the British one, spanning eleven time zones—almost half the globe. The very size of the Soviet Union made internal deportations an effective means of political control. After gaining power, the Communists dispersed millions of real and imaginary opponents across Siberia, which stretched for thousands of miles from the Ural Mountains to the Pacific Ocean and from China to the Arctic Sea. Communication and transport among the regions of

---

11. Richard Pipes, *Survival Is Not Enough* (New York: Simon and Schuster, 1984), p. 38.

that huge area were under strict government control, making organized opposition virtually impossible. Soviet authorities were not concerned that their hunt for potential dissenters caught millions of innocent people in their far-flung nets. On the contrary, large-scale deportations became an added deterrent to resistance and yet another tool of the mass terror originally established and publicly legitimized by Lenin.

Decades later, when I gave a talk in the Boston area about my Siberian experience, a listener asked me if the large-scale deportations were a waste of Russia's meager economic resources: "How could Russia devote so much effort to such large relocations?" she wanted to know. I replied that the deportations probably brought a net economic benefit to the government by providing abundant slave labor for Russia's massive building projects. The labor was cheap, not only because these so-called "enemies of the people" were not paid for their work, but also because no provisions had to be made for normal living facilities, warm clothing, or sufficient food. All those items would indeed have constituted a substantial expense in the remote areas of Russia, but they were simply not provided. When the workers died under the harsh conditions of life in Siberia, they were simply replaced by a continuing stream of additional prisoners. Recruitment of detainees was centrally planned, and each region of the country was required to fill quotas. Under that system, it was not surprising that after the 1917 October Revolution, the Bolsheviks "found" literally millions of spies and *vrediteli* (wreckers or evil-doers, from *vred*, meaning "harm") among the population of the Soviet Union.

My questioner in Boston did not understand that in Stalinist Russia, political reliability took precedence over economic considerations. Wholesale resettlements of ethnic minorities served a primarily political, not an economic, strategy. All other considerations ranked a distant second.

The arrests and deportations that eventually imprisoned our family were not improvised actions. They were, as I later discovered, part of a broad strategy formalized in the Soviet Penal Code. Loosely translated, Article Seven[12] of that code referred to "defensive measures" to be taken

12. Ugolovnyi Kodeks RSFSR (1934), Gosudarstvennoye Izdatelstvo, Sovietskoye Zakonodatelstvo.

not only against people who committed "socially dangerous" acts but also against those who were potentially dangerous due to past "criminal associations" and those associated with undesirable past activities. Those undesirable past associations and activities could include owning a small business, receiving a letter from abroad, listening to a foreign radio broadcast, expressing discontent with life, or being a close or even distant relative of someone in a Soviet jail. Such a broad interpretation allowed the authorities to label virtually anyone a socially dangerous person, whether or not he had even thought about committing an anti-Soviet action. One's only hope in cases of past "transgressions" was that the commentary attached to Article Seven of the Code limited the penalty to exile. But that restriction applied only to courts. The NKVD did not have to respect that limitation, or any other.

It was easy for the authorities to obtain information on the local population in occupied eastern Poland, for records were easily available. It was more difficult for them to check the backgrounds and determine the loyalties of people like us, who were refugees from the German-occupied part of Poland. But the NKVD was nothing if not creative. Shortly after the Soviet invasion, the authorities ordered the entire population to register with the police. Documents were checked frequently, and if you lacked proof of registration, you were arrested and questioned. No one wanted to be subjected to this treatment because the outcome of any NKVD interrogation was seldom favorable. A bitter joke circulating at that time proclaimed that it would be just as hard to prove you were not a goat as it would be to convince the authorities that you were not guilty of a crime. During the registration process my father was asked a seemingly innocuous question: "Do you want to stay here or do you want to go home to Warsaw?" At the time Warsaw was occupied by the Germans, and the question seemed harmless enough, since the Russians and Germans were allies. My father chose to go home, which was the wrong answer. All those who wanted to leave the Russian-occupied part of Poland were labeled "socially dangerous elements" and exiled to Russia. Presumably, this policy was based on the unassailable logic of NKVD-think: "You want to leave us, therefore you don't like us. Well, we have a place for people who don't like us."[13]

But at this point, for us, registration and exile were still in the future, and my family decided to leave Równe for a smaller town farther south. By then the war in Poland was over and the country neatly divided between Germany and Russia. Our plan was to use one of the horse-drawn wagons that had brought us from Warsaw. The two wagons were parked in the courtyard of our apartment building; the horses had been taken to a farm where they worked in the fields to earn their keep. The original owner of the wagon objected, arguing that the wagon was still his on the grounds that the money we had paid for it was now worthless. We did not know how the argument would end, but as it turned out, the outcome was straightforward and final. During the night before our departure, someone slashed the pneumatic tires of our vehicle. We suspected the previous owner, but had no proof. Since replacements could not be obtained, we left by train.

Our destination was Mościska, a small provincial town which, like the rest of eastern Poland, was under Russian occupation. We rented a room with kitchen privileges in a farmhouse in a Ukrainian village just outside town. My father found work as an accountant in a printing shop that produced various leaflets as well as the local newspaper. My mother looked after us at home. At first the shop had only a primitive foot-operated press, which could hold nothing larger than a single, small, newspaper sheet. I occasionally helped run the press, which was pretty hard work for a nine-year old child. But evidently my coordination and dexterity were adequate for the task, and soon I was running the machine at a smooth, fast pace. I stood on one foot and operated the pedal with the other. Every few seconds, when the press opened, I removed the newly printed leaf with my left hand and simultaneously inserted a new sheet with my right. I had to perform this maneuver quickly enough to keep my hand from being crushed between the two moving plates.

---

13. Our designation as "socially dangerous elements" suggests that the "legal" authority for our exile was contained in Article 7 of the Soviet Criminal Code (see footnote 12). Presumably our past "criminal associations" were our lives in Poland, which according to the Soviets was a fascist country, and the proof of our "potential danger" to the State was our wish to return there despite its occupation by another fascist government.

After a time the shop installed a large Russian printing press that accepted paper the size of two newspaper sheets, which were automatically fed by the machine. This press was driven by a big flywheel that required two people to turn it. Frequently, I was a member of the turning team. I was never paid for the work; I just joined in to help when I visited my father after school.

Going to school at Mościska was not a simple proposition. The three distinct schools were taught in Polish, Ukrainian, and Yiddish. Initially I attended the Jewish school, but since I did not understand the language, I was transferred to the Polish school. That did not last very long either. I don't remember the details, which probably had to do with my being the only Jewish student there, but I was soon transferred to the Ukrainian school. There were other Jewish students in my new surroundings, and I had no trouble picking up the Ukrainian language, which is related to Polish. Needless to say, I don't recall learning very much that academic year. My lack of progress was not the fault of the educational system. The schools were well organized, the teachers competent, educational standards high, and classes limited to approximately thirty students. But the frequent transfers and generally unsettled political situation were not conducive to education.

One lecture, however, stands out in my memory. During the first week of school we were treated to a long talk about the evils of religion. The teacher explained how religion was used to exploit the workers by asking them to ignore their suffering in this life in return for rewards after their death. In fact, there was no God; the capitalists had concocted the entire idea of deity and church to transform workers into docile employees who would meekly accept the appropriation of the fruits of their labor by the ruling classes. Priests and rabbis should not to be trusted, since they were the primary implementers of the capitalists' appropriation schemes, both in Europe and in European colonies. It was no accident that imperialists dispatched missionaries to undeveloped countries, we were told. Capitalists were not content to exploit their own workers and peasants; their greed drove them to rob the entire world. And what better way to subjugate native populations of Asia,

Africa, and the Americas than by implanting a religion that advocates nonviolence, obedience to authority, and acceptance of poverty as a ticket to glory in the life to come? "The meek," after all, "will inherit the earth," or so preached the clergy.

At that time I paid hardly any attention to this indoctrination, probably because religion had not played a large role in our household. In Warsaw we celebrated religious holidays at home, and I studied scripture in school, but I was not aware of the moral dimensions of religion. At the age of nine it seemed strange to learn that God had ceased to exist, but I accepted our teacher's words at face value. At the end of the session she asked the class whether God existed, and we responded in unison with a loud "NO!"

During the few months between October 1939 and the summer of 1940, we witnessed many arrests as the NKVD continued to discover undesirables and "enemies of the people." Our family attempted to lead a quiet existence, applying the age-old tactic of remaining inconspicuous during troubled times. We occupied modest quarters, did not join any organizations, and avoided associations with people who might be controversial in the eyes of the new authorities. We did not think that we would become targets for deportation.

We were wrong. We discovered that the Russians had considered my father's wish to return to Warsaw to be a major crime. In view of what we now know, it may seem strange that my father expressed the desire to go to the German-occupied part of Poland, but at the time it was not an illogical decision. The Germans and Russians were allies, and the question posed to my father seemed candid enough. In fact, we occasionally saw German military staff cars with what appeared to be high-ranking officers passing through Mościska, presumably on the way to friendly transactions with Russian authorities. Also, in 1940 few people could imagine the extent of Hitler's true plans. And, finally, my father had had firsthand experience with the Russian Communists and understood the evil nature of their regime.

A small diversion should further clarify my father's choice. As I have pointed out, he had been exiled to Siberia by the Tsarist Government in 1913 and was still there during the Communist Revolution,

ets. Years later, he told me that the
ich better than those we were to ex-
. In fact, other than being restricted
did quite well during his first exile,
the World War I, the International
iary for forwarding correspondence
war in Germany and their families
father's Siberian town tried to corre-
d, since most of them were illiterate,
people who professed an ability to
ny, of the letters reached their desti-
ither for help. The outcome, he told
uickly reached its intended recipient
received. Other mothers asked him
ly gratifying results. My father as-
write well and legibly, with beautiful
sors were almost illiterate and prob-
ably incapable of addressing the envelopes properly. The Russians in his
town refused to believe so straightforward an explanation; they were
convinced that my father had a "lucky hand" and was a saintly man.
His fame spread rapidly and soon people were coming from a hundred
miles away to ask him to send letters. They usually brought gifts in the
form of eggs, milk, bread, and live farm animals. There were even instances of his visitors falling on their knees and kissing his hands. The
Russians in that area were simple, honest, religious, and sincere people,
who showed their gratitude in a most demonstrative way.

After the fall of the Tsarist regime my father moved to Petropavlovsk,
a small town on the Trans-Siberian Railroad that lay three hundred
miles east of the Ural Mountains. The town had been founded in 1752,
and the railroad arrived in 1896. By 1917 its population had grown to
50,000 inhabitants. In Petropavlovsk, my father met his future father-
in-law, Nicolai Vitenson. The two formed a trading company when
Lenin declared the "New Economic Policy" (NEP), which restored a
certain amount of private enterprise. Under the new law, which eased
food shortages in Russia almost overnight, entrepreneurs were allowed

to open small companies. My father called the new operation Paitorg, a name sufficiently similar to state-run enterprises not to arouse too much resentment among the local officials. Their shop was essentially a department store that sold food and clothes. Most of their business was derived not from retail sales but from trade in food, supplies, and furs with trappers and hunters living along the great rivers of northern Siberia. I owe my existence to that enterprise, because it provided the opportunity for my father to meet my mother, Miriam Vitenson, the daughter of his partner. My parents were married on June 7, 1922.

After Lenin's death in January 1924, Stalin started dismantling the NEP. Most of the participants in that program were gradually eliminated by the GPU, an early predecessor of the KGB. Fortunately my father knew someone who worked in an informed position, and he was warned the day before his planned arrest. The only course of action was to make for the nearest border, which he did, escaping to China that same day and leaving everything behind. At that point he was married, but my mother crossed the border at a later date and eventually joined him in China. My maternal grandfather also escaped to China, where he lived until the late forties, later moving to Australia after the Chinese Communist Revolution. After a couple of years in China, my parents managed to return to Poland, where I was born.

As a result of my father's firsthand experience with the Communist system, he knew what to expect when Russia invaded Poland in 1939. Not only were the Russians ruthless with their own people, they were also quick to settle old scores when they occupied new territory. There was no doubt in my father's mind that he would be arrested and either shot or sent to a concentration camp if they realized he had escaped from Russian authorities during NEP. My father still knew relatively little about the Germans in 1939, but he had no doubts about Russian intentions, and it therefore was logical for him to decide to return to the German-occupied part of Poland. In retrospect, through sheer luck, that was the right decision for the wrong reason. Those who chose eastern Poland were allowed to remain there, but the region was later occupied by Germans, who wiped out practically the entire Jewish population.

My father's fear of discovery was based on the assumption that the Russians kept complete records of those who escaped from their clutches. Until recently I thought that his fear had been groundless, but a few years ago, during a conversation with a friend who now lives in Schenectady, New York, I learned otherwise. In fact, the Soviets kept records of all sorts of people, on the chance that they might find them useful for their twisted purposes at some future date. The family of this friend was deported from Poland to the Kazakhstan region of the Soviet Union in 1940. His father was a Polish communist who had worked for Red Army intelligence during the 1917 October Revolution. After the deportation, the Soviet authorities learned of his past and arrested him.

The reason for his arrest was simple. At the time of his dedicated service to the revolutionary cause, the Red Army was under the control of Leon Trotsky. When Stalin later came to power, he found it convenient to accuse Trotsky of treason in order to eliminate him. The Soviet propaganda machine then made the name Trotsky synonymous with evil, and anyone even remotely connected to Trotsky, even a foreign spy who had worked selflessly for the Communists, became guilty by association and a candidate for execution. Like countless other Russian prisoners, he simply vanished. Perhaps his remains were buried in a mass grave, with a bullet in the back of his head—a favorite method of Soviet executioners. Or perhaps his tired bones, covered with malnourished flesh, had been put to rest in a shallow hole dug above the permafrost in the frozen north.

SIBERIA

WE WERE ALL SOBERED by the cold greeting from Mironov, the young Komendant with the large pistol who had told us we were doomed to die in the place of our exile. In Russian, the phrase "you will die" has two forms: *Umriosh* applies to a human, *sdohniesh* refers to an animal. Mironov used the latter, leaving no doubt about our status. When someone asked about food rations, Mironov had a ready answer: *"Chelovyek nie svinya, vsyo syest"* (Man is not a pig, man will eat anything), implying that our food would be worse than what was fed to pigs—animals that eat almost anything. Then he added, "The harder you work, the more you'll eat. He who doesn't work, doesn't eat." He paused to let his words sink in, then added, "Those of you, men and women, who are fit to work *(trudosposobnyie)*, be ready tomorrow morning at six o'clock. Trucks will transport you to a mine in a neighboring Russian village. You will return here at night." He waved his arms dismissively and instructed us to occupy any of the log cabins in that desolate, abandoned settlement. As an afterthought he added, "You'd better fix those huts well or you will perish *(sdohnietie)* like dogs from the cold when winter comes."

Bewildered and exhausted from the long journey, we surveyed our new "home," standing in the middle of a heap of our belongings—a collection of tattered suitcases, burlap bags, and amorphous bundles of clothes held together by knotted bed sheets. These were now the entirety of our worldly possessions, hurriedly collected in Poland only two months before—in another era, another world. We examined our immediate surroundings closely, believing that we might spend the rest of our lives there, for generations of Poles before us had been deported to Siberia, never to return home, and there was no reason to doubt the *Komendant's* words. There were no roads between us and the nearest railroad station. Rivers provided a means of travel, but they were navigable only during the short summer. During the long winter they were frozen to ice and could be used as roads for trucks and sleds, but such transport was a hazardous undertaking.

We were isolated not only from the distant land of our birth, but even from the nearest Russian settlements. Our small, abandoned village of Priisk Konstantinovskii was completely surrounded by tall, steep mountains without visible breaks. Indeed, had we not just been delivered by trucks, we might have assumed that the mountains formed an impenetrable barrier around us. The village consisted of thirty or forty log cabins scattered in irregular fashion between a swift, shallow mountain stream on one side and a now-abandoned gold mine on the other. Footpaths wound randomly to each of the cabins, none of which were on the same horizontal plane. At night, when a dim light shone through the windows, the village probably resembled a Christmas card depicting an old Alpine settlement, a fairy tale scene where Gepetto might have lived. But any such resemblance was strictly wishful; the primitive, run-down cabins were anything but cheerful.

This was no fairy tale, and our plight was desperate indeed. True, we were not surrounded by a barbed-wire fence studded with watch towers, waiting to be fed into Auschwitz-like furnaces and converted into dark smoke. But unaware of the fate that would meet our brethren in the Holocaust, it was difficult to imagine a worse situation. We had just traveled for two weeks through a thousand miles of virtually impassable taiga northeast of Irkutsk, itself a remote town three thousand miles east of Moscow. We would surely remain trapped here until a slow death from hardship ended our suffering. Having been officially notified of our subhuman status, we faced hard labor, hunger, and complete lack of medical attention. Worst of all was our feeling of utter helplessness. Not only were we plunged into the vast, lonely, and inhumanly frigid expanse of Siberia, but we had also been enslaved by the cruel, seemingly invincible, and implacable NKVD apparatus well designed to crush resistance and eliminate the faintest hope of survival.

Over the years I have occasionally wondered how we coped with our utter powerlessness in a situation that was apparently hopeless and, for many, ultimately fatal. A ten-year-old observer tends to have a selective memory and to be an unreliable witness; nevertheless I have tried to resurrect my own feelings and to recall the reactions of the adults, especially my own parents. The picture remaining in my mind is quite different from what might be expected in our circumstances. Clearly we were tired, intimidated, and depressed when, after our long journey, we received such a hostile and pitiless greeting from our *Komendant*. But we were not desperate. When Mironov walked away from us I don't remember any wailing or cries of despondency. Few of us knew how to refurbish damaged log cabins, yet we all plunged into the task with nervous vigor. Poles are energetic and buoyant people, and we responded to this challenge with hard work. There must have been disagreements and perhaps even quarrels among us, but I don't remember any. Instead, I recall the adults treating each other with respect and politeness, in that formal Polish way, addressing each other as Mr. or Mrs., as if we were still living in refined circles in Poland.

I don't know why there were few manifestations of helplessness and despair, but I recall that the seventeenth-century poet Richard Lovelace wrote from prison:[14]

> Stone Walls do not a Prison Make,
> Nor iron bars a cage:
> Minds innocent and quiet take
> That for a hermitage.

---

14. *To Althea, from Prison*, Richard Lovelace (1618-1657).

Like Richard Lovelace, we did not feel guilty of any crime. This and our blissful ignorance of Stalin's heinous crimes preserved what surely had to be an irrational hope, or perhaps rationalization, that somehow our innocence would eventually be recognized and we would be freed.

Or there could be a simpler explanation. Analogies are seldom perfect, but perhaps our situation had something in common with the tragedy befalling a person who loses a close member of his family. It is said that during the first few days following the death of the loved one, the grieving relative is too busy with receiving visitors and funeral arrangements to brood over his loss. It is only when life resumes its former rhythm and returns to "normal" that the full impact of the tragedy becomes apparent and depression sets in. In our case the "tragedy" continued without respite and, perhaps for this reason, eventually lost its shock effect. Our life never got "back to normal," and we just did what had to be done without complaining—after all, there was no one to listen to our complaints. The business of survival was a full-time occupation and brought what for us was the only gratification that mattered—survival itself. That task kept us busy and left little time for speculation about the future.

Nothing, of course, could compensate for the frequent deaths in our small community. During the four years of internment, about one third of our people died not at the hands of NKVD but from "natural" causes—disease, cold, hunger, hard labor, and the inability to cope with the primitive conditions of life in Siberia. No matter how busy we were and how well we eventually adapted to our circumstances, those losses continually reminded us of the horror of our situation. My own mother was to become one of those casualties.

The village had been abandoned twenty years before our arrival, and the log cabins showed the effects of the harsh Siberian climate, including broken windows, missing doors, and leaky roofs. Most of the dwellings had three small rooms and a kitchen, and each hut was shared by three families. We spread out, trying to divide ourselves into smaller groups of people who had become friends during the long journey. We chose cabins that showed the least amount of damage, and over a period of just a few days, refurbished them using materials salvaged from the irreparable dwellings. Our methods, we later learned, followed the typical pattern of Soviet scavenging. New materials for construction, such as spare mechanical parts, were always in short supply, and the Russians were accustomed to cannibalizing one structure or machine in order to repair another. We also used materials from other huts to make primitive beds, tables and chairs. As in Colonial America, nails were one of the most valuable commodities, and we pulled every surplus rusty nail we could find from walls or floors, usually damaging and bending them during the extraction process. We quickly learned to straighten these recycled nails with an axe; the trick was to hit the bent nail without smashing the fingers that held the nail in place. Most of us had never used an axe, and at first the task was fraught with accidents. Out of necessity we learned quickly, but not before inflicting considerable damage to our hands.

I don't remember how we acquired our primitive tools, but the community shared several handsaws, and every family soon had its own axe. We learned that an axe was essential to survival in Siberia; it was a universal tool for most types of repair, as well as for cutting down trees and splitting logs for fuel. Initially, we had little contact with the local Russian population, but eventually we realized that the axe was so vital to their survival that it was virtually an object of reverence among them. We, too, came to respect this tool, maintaining it properly and sharpening it with abandoned grindstones we found in the village. In our room the axe occupied a place of honor, hanging prominently on two nails driven into the wall.

Surprisingly, the village had electricity. We later discovered that the power came from a settlement ten miles away where our people were taken to work in the mine. It had been brought to our village long before our arrival to operate the now-exhausted gold mine. Most cabins had bare wires running along the ceiling, and in others we installed new wiring by stripping it from empty huts. We had a limited supply of electric bulbs, and someone managed to construct a bulb receptacle from two pieces of bare, rigid wire and a few layers of newspaper. Later another inventor developed an improved version by using a piece of wood. Those innovations were widely copied because there was not a single bulb receptacle in the place. As the bulbs burned out, a few of us even became skilled at repairing them. We learned to shake the bulb in such a way that the end of the burned-out filament slipped out of its supporting structure and came to rest on the lead that brought power into the bulb. Most of the time, the current welded the loose wires together and the connection would remain in place when the bulb was turned on. The repairmen were in great demand. We could usually repair the same lamps several times, although each restoration shortened the filament and reduced the useful life of the bulb.

One hut housed the food store run by a Russian woman who issued our daily ration of 800 grams of bread to mineworkers and 400 grams to dependants judged to be too weak for reasons of health or age to be employed in the mines. Each month we also received a small ration of flour, cereal, potatoes, salt, and sugar, and occasionally there was a piece of smoked fish. The taiga around us provided additional staples: we gathered mushrooms, berries, and *krapiva* (nettles). The latter were boiled in water and provided the base for rudimentary soup. Two items could be preserved for the winter: *brusnika* (mountain cranberries) and *gruzdi* (agaric mushrooms). The *brusnika* resembled cranberries, except for their smaller size and greater hardness than the cultivated American variety. Easily frozen outside during the long winter, they retained their taste and texture once thawed. The *gruzdi* mushrooms could be preserved in salt water in the few containers we had brought from Poland, and also provided sustenance during the cold winter months. Despite all these provisions, however, the daily pangs of hunger stayed with us throughout the long years of our Siberian exile. Fortunately, by the time we were deported to Russia, the Soviets had realized that keeping their captives on a starvation diet was detrimental to the country's economic interests; starving exiles did not make sturdy laborers, and the rations were adjusted to provide enough sustenance to enable people to work. In her book *Gulag, a History*, Anne Applebaum states:[15]

---

15. Anne Applebaum, *Gulag, a History* (New York: Doubleday, 2003), p. 184.

From 1939, it seems that Beria [Lavrenti Beria, head of NKVD]—with presumably Stalin behind him—no longer explicitly intended the Gulag camps to be death camps, as some of them had been, in effect, in 1937 and 1938. Which is not to say, however, that their administrators were any more concerned with preserving human life, let alone respecting human dignity. From 1939 on, Moscow's central concerns were economic: prisoners were to be slotted into the camp's plans like cogs in a machine."

Applebaum's comments refer to improved conditions in the Gulag concentration camps, but Moscow's new economic concerns could also be applied to people in our category—captives interned in special, isolated exile settlements. The new policy kept the workers among us from starving, but those of us unable to work or not enterprising enough to harvest food from the forest suffered from severe malnutrition.

The only permanent Russian presence in the settlement, other than the woman who ran the store, was *Komendant* Mironov, who lived with his wife in a big log cabin. He always carried a pistol and was the supreme authority over our fifty families. We seemed to be unlikely candidates for the designation of "socially dangerous elements," yet there we were, exiled in Siberia for this so-called crime. I can say with confidence that none of us harbored any plans for the overthrow of the Soviet government. None of us were previously wealthy "exploiters of the workers" or even former members of Polish political parties.

The majority of our group came from lower-middle-class backgrounds. Three families were Christians, the rest Jews. Some had owned small businesses, such as shops, inns, or taverns; others had been self-employed tailors, cobblers, bakers, or peddlers. One old man who shared our cabin was a basket weaver. He found certain Siberian bushes ideal for basketry and practiced his skill in our new surroundings. His baskets ranged in size from a few inches across to large trunk-like containers. I volunteered to help him, and in the process acquired rudimentary skills of the craft. Our community also had musicians, accountants, a dentist, and a few intellectuals, including teachers and a college professor. One couple's specialty was the breeding of bees.

Many of the Jews came from a strong Orthodox religious background. They held clandestine religious services—an illegal activity—and studied the sacred books they had managed to bring with them from Poland. Most of them did not speak Polish, at least not well, and Yiddish was the preferred language. I did not speak Yiddish before the war, and it was in eastern Siberia, of all places, that I picked up a basic knowledge of that tongue.

Gradually my father became the unofficial, unelected leader of our small, banished community. He had always commanded respect from those around him, and he continued to do so in Siberia. It was not what he did but who he was—a modest, unassuming and compassionate man, always ready to help. Father had many talents. Above all, he was endowed with common sense and intellectual curiosity, and he felt at ease with every member of our little Polish community. The Christian Poles and assimilated Jews found him to be an excellent conversationalist. He spoke and wrote Polish well and, as mentioned previously, had beautiful handwriting. Aside from my mother, he was the only one among us who had been in Russia before and witnessed the Bolshevik Revolution. The ways of the Communists was our main topic of conversation and his previous experience helped him contribute valuable insights. And even though part of our community consisted of religious Jews who seemed unaware of secular matters, my father found common ground with them. His mother had wanted him to be a rabbi, and in his youth he had attended religious schools. He was fluent in spoken and written Yiddish, and as a result of his rabbinical studies was well versed in Jewish liturgy. He understood the religious Jews' point of view.

He was also, along with my mother, the only member of our community who spoke and wrote flawless Russian, a skill that immediately made him our unofficial spokesman and writer of petitions to Russian authorities who, in turn, turned to him to communicate with our members. In Warsaw his counsel had been solicited by members of our extended family; in Siberia he advised our companions on work-related problems, family matters, and Siberian survival skills, or simply listened sympathetically to their woes. In a few cases, he even wrote letters to

Stalin for those members of our group naïve enough to think that their protestations of innocence would bring them a reprieve from Siberian exile. My father's activities brought emotional relief to a few neighbors, though it did little to alleviate our own family's physical discomforts.

In summer, all men and women judged to be fit for labor were transported by truck six days a week to work in the gold mine in the neighboring Russian village, ten miles from our *priisk*. We mined in the winter as well, but then the mineworkers stayed in barracks near the mine and came home only on Sundays, our day of rest. Mothers with young children were excused from work, and because I was ten, my mother qualified for this exemption.

As winter approached, our main concern was staying warm. Each cabin had a large brick stove, with a cooking surface. We had to keep the fire going nearly all day with wood from trees we chopped down. Although we were surrounded by forest, harvesting logs was not an easy task. It meant venturing into the woods on steep mountainsides in punishingly cold weather—often with temperatures below −40 degrees Fahrenheit—to cut down live trees which we then dragged back to the village in snow that was often more than six feet deep. Few of our people were qualified for this task, as it took great effort to trample the snow around the trees we intended to fell. After producing what was essentially a well around our target, we had to wield an axe—initially a foreign implement to us—and strike accurate blows below the level of the surrounding snow to harvest as much of the trunk as possible. Each tree, once felled, had to be dragged home in deep, dense snow, an exercise so laborious it was not unlike hauling a burden with heavy weights tied to each foot. With the passage of time, many of us became quite adept at this task. In later years we cut trees during the summer, making the job easier and allowing the wood to dry before we burned it. But during that first winter we were completely unprepared.

The clothes we had brought with us were of little use in the Siberian climate. Most of us managed to barter with Russian mine workers, exchanging various personal belongings for warm clothing. Each one of us had been given only one set of Siberian clothing, consisting of trousers and a jacket both padded with cotton wool. Those garments had to last us for many years, and we all became experts at patching tears and supplementing them with mittens assembled from old scraps of cloth and cotton. Adequate boots, however, were impossible to improvise. Leather boots or shoes were completely useless there, and the only way to keep warm was to wear *valenki*, big shapeless felt boots. Somehow my father managed to get *valenki* for himself, my mother and me. Others were not so lucky. Another boy my age developed frostbite on all his toes early that first winter during one of his tree-harvesting trips. He was unable to walk and spent the rest of the winter in bed while his toes rotted away. There was no doctor in the village and no access to any medication, and he just had to hope that his wounds would heal naturally. By the spring he started walking slowly on his stubby feet, but two years later he died from another undiagnosed illness. We had carved a chess set together, improvised a chessboard, and played chess and checkers almost every day. He seemed quite cheerful during his illness and grateful that he regained the ability to walk, even though the effort was painful and his progress unsteady. I cannot vouch for his state of mind, but perhaps he felt that his predicament was preferable to total disability and death.

Soon after our arrival we found that the village was infested with field mice and occasional rats. It was quite normal for mice to run around the rooms in broad daylight, and there was little we could do to scare them away. We eventually got used to them and would probably have tolerated their company had they not developed into such fierce competitors for our precious food. They defeated all our efforts to safeguard our supplies—gnawing into potatoes, biting their way through the bags holding our grains. But one method of storage circumvented the mice's best effort: suspending the food from a hook fastened to the ceiling. Storing food that way was very inconvenient, to say nothing of conspicuous; our supplies were visible to everyone else, especially to Mironov who became suspicious whenever he thought we had more food than our meager rations allowed and inquired about them immediately. To avoid this public display, we built mousetraps of many varieties. The only materials we had were bits of string, lumber, and nails, and there were lots of mice to catch, but our people showed great creativity in their efforts. By pooling our resources, we devised a simple, effective design. In its final version the trap consisted of two wooden planks about ten inches long, four inches wide, and half an inch thick. At one end the planks were hinged together with a piece of string, and at the other kept open at about a thirty degree angle with two small, strategically placed notched rods. The lower plank rested on the floor, the upper was weighted by a heavy rock. Bait, usually a piece of bread, was tied to one of the small rods. A gentle tug on the baited rod disturbed the delicate balance and brought the weighted plank crashing down on the unsuspecting rodent.

The traps were surprisingly effective, and each cabin was soon equipped with several of them. But the task of removing and killing the animals was distasteful, and sometimes dangerous. Occasionally, several mice were ensnared at one time and were frequently still alive in the trap; the rats were often caught by their tails and moved menacingly toward anyone who approached them. We had to smash the hapless animals' heads with a heavy object and then remove the squashed bodies, making sure, especially in the case of rats, that there was not enough life in them to bite us.

One day my father largely solved the rodent problem by importing a cat from a Russian village. It was a small, cuddly specimen, yet extremely efficient in exterminating mice and rats. The rodents soon avoided our cabin entirely. We loaned the cat to our neighbors, with similar results. Although people still occasionally saw mice in their cabins, that single valiant cat largely controlled the plague, or at least reduced it to the point where it could be managed by mousetraps.

I cannot but wonder at our people's inventiveness and adaptability. The resources at our disposal seemed pitifully inadequate for our purpose, yet we quickly learned how to fix dwellings, repair electric bulbs, and build mousetraps. We harvested food and fuel in a totally unfamiliar forest and climate. We fashioned and learned to maintain clothing that guarded us against the bitter cold, and we managed to accomplish

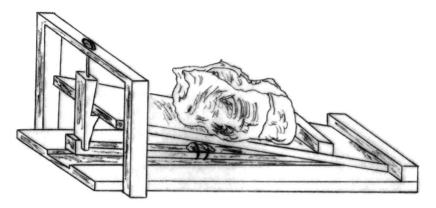

Improvised mousetrap that helped contain the plague of mice and rats in Siberia, 1940.

all this in a matter of just a few weeks before the onset of the Siberian winter. Perhaps the best way to describe this process is "improvisation with limited skills and practically nonexistent resources in the face of severe need." Yet, at the time, no one considered our achievements extraordinary. It is possible that those survival techniques boosted my self-confidence and made a lasting impression on my young mind, for I think that the ability to improvise stayed with me for the rest of my life.

There was one other unique factor that boosted my confidence while we were in Siberia: my father's abilities and personality. We tend to judge our well-being not in absolute terms but in comparison with our surroundings. He was, no doubt, the most respected man in the village and the best provider—qualities that made me feel much luckier than our neighbors. The pride I felt in being the son of such a man helped me maintain my optimism.

No one was blessed with sufficient quantities of food, but some people felt the shortages more acutely than others. Several families with many children relied on only one breadwinner, while others had members who were ill and unable to work. It took only a couple of weeks after our arrival in the village to organize what can be described as a mutual self-help organization, in which two trusted individuals were designated to collect food for those with the greatest need. An observer from the West might easily have judged those collections to be futile, for the donations usually amounted to no more than small pieces of bread perhaps one cubic inch in volume, along with a few spoonfuls of flour and sugar. But in reality, offering these small items constituted acts of great compassion because those making the donations often went hungry as well. Although the identity of the recipients was never revealed, it was generally known which families depended heavily on community aid. We also had no assurances that the food collectors would not appropriate the offerings, but the unspoken code of honor was sufficiently strong that we had no doubt the food was reaching its intended recipients.

Such mutual help was by no means unique to our village. It was quite widespread in Soviet and German camps during the Second World War, although it took place mainly among individuals rather than an entire community. The cooperation was mutually beneficial. Elie Wiesel eloquently describes his experience in Auschwitz:[16]

> (The Germans) . . . tried to get the inmates to think only of themselves, to forget relatives and friends, to tend only to their own needs, unless they wanted to become "Mussulmen." But what happened was just the reverse. Those who retreated to a universe limited to their own bodies had less chance of getting out alive, while to live for a brother, a friend, an ideal, helped you hold out longer. As for me, I could cope thanks to my father. Without him I could not have resisted. I could see him coming with his heavy gait, seeking a smile, and I would give it to him. He was my support and my oxygen, as I was his.

I, too, would like to think that by being objects of my father's love, my mother and I contributed to his survival by giving him another reason to live.

During that first winter, a young couple fell in love and were married, though the celebration was tempered with disappointment on the part of the young man's family because they had lost a breadwinner. We had music. Two musicians had brought their violins, while others had saved

---

16. Elie Wiesel, Memoirs. *All Rivers Run to the Sea* (New York: Alfred A. Knopf, 1995), p. 81.

strings for a cello and a bass. By using ordinary wooden planks, they fashioned instruments that resembled a cello and a bass to a remarkable extent, except that their contours were straight rather than curved. Someone made a drum as well, and soon we had a village orchestra which, at least to my young ears, sounded as good as any other I had heard.

Another source of amusement was the small reindeer herd that appeared with its three shepherds as if from nowhere at the beginning of the winter. I visited the shepherds often in their hut at the edge of the village. The herders had Asian features and clearly sprang from one of the many native Siberian ethnic groups. They spoke Russian with a heavy accent. I spoke Russian well enough to communicate with them, and our long conversations helped develop my knowledge of the language. I don't know if the men were nomads or if they worked for the state, like nearly everyone else. They told me the reindeer grazed in the taiga during the summer, and the men just followed them, finding winter shelter in different villages. They must have lived off the reindeer, drinking their milk and slaughtering them for food, but despite our friendship I never saw any meat in their hut. Meat, of course, was too precious a commodity to share with relative strangers. Milking reindeer was a laborious task; they had to milk several animals to fill a single glass. But it tasted much sweeter than cow's milk and was more viscous, and the shepherds often shared it with me. The reindeer were gentle creatures that looked like small cows with antlers, ambling about while foraging for food under the snow. Village children hugged and wrestled with them, and occasionally tried to ride them. The docile creatures usually accepted and even enjoyed these advances, never resisting, but when pestered beyond a certain point they simply trotted away. In the spring the shepherds and their herd disappeared as mysteriously as they had materialized during the winter.

With the passage of time, we began to accept the reality of Mironov's original statement about our living and dying in Konstantinovskii. Hitler and Stalin were still friends and the war was going well for the Germans. We received no information about the rest of the world except for an occasional copy of Pravda or other Russian newspapers that proclaimed the great 1940 German victories over the Allies and lavishly praised the heroic German people for their valiant struggle against the British and French imperialists. I know my parents worried because I was not attending school, and they saw the absence of schooling as further evidence of the Russians' intentions to keep us there for the rest of our lives. There was no school in the village, and we were not allowed to leave our settlement. We had no books, no paper, and no writing implements that would have allowed my parents to tutor me at home. But even if those supplies had been available, I doubt they would have tried to provide me with home education. They were both too busy ensuring our survival,

The June 1941 German advance into Russia was swift and decisive. Within six months Nazi troops reached Minsk, Leningrad, Kiev, Kharkov, Sevastopol, Rostov, and Moscow. On December 6 the Russians launched a major counter-offensive around Moscow. On December 7 the Japanese bombed Pearl Harbor. The following day the United States and Great Britain declared war on Japan. On December 11 Germany declared war on the United States.

and the uncertainty of our future did not elevate tutoring to the level of urgent priority.

Even so, many people never gave up hope. While they may have been afraid to complain too loudly about their miserable living conditions, they talked surreptitiously about their plans for the future and what they would do on their return to Poland. I am sure those faint hopes helped keep them alive. And although it seemed improbable at the time, our situation was about to take a dramatic change for the better for a reason none of us could have foreseen. The Germans invaded Russia in June 1941 (ten months after our arrival), shifting our entire universe overnight. Once they learned about the attack, the adults immediately sensed it would have a profound effect on our future. Indeed, in only a few days, Mironov's attitude toward us changed. Instead of calling us enemies of the people, he now addressed us as normal human beings—even allies. He even told us that plans were being made to move us to a Russian village and give us equal rights with Russians! We could imagine no greater turnaround.

The German attack had forced the Russians to change sides in the war and join the Allies. On July 30, 1941, General Władysław Sikorski, the head of the Polish government in exile in London, signed an agreement with Ivan Mayski, the Soviet ambassador to Britain, granting amnesty to "'all Polish citizens who are at present deprived of their freedom on the territory of the USSR.' . . . Both Gulag prisoners and deported exiles were officially freed. . . ."[17] The NKVD officially confirmed in writing the change in our status on September 7, 1941. I still have the battered certificate they issued on shoddy paper proclaiming that, based on the Ukaz of the Supreme Soviet, my father had been granted amnesty and had the right to reside in the territory of the USSR except in areas adjoining national borders, forbidden zones, and other restricted places of "first and second categories." The certificate was valid for three

17. Anne Applebaum, *Gulag, a History* (New York: Doubleday, 2003), p. 451.

months until December 7, at which time it was slated to be replaced by a passport.

I remember no greater jubilation than when those announcements swept through our community. I think our joy was even greater that day than at the conclusion of the war. We rejoiced in the poetic justice of the two unholy allies, Hitler and Stalin, now fighting each other; more importantly, we could now dare to believe that our nightmare might someday come to an end and we might eventually return to Poland and resume our former lives.

We were transferred to a Russian village during one of the coldest winter days I can remember. The ten-mile trip took about three hours. There were no thermometers, but the local Russians estimated the temperature at −60 degrees Centigrade (−75 degrees Fahrenheit). We traveled on sleds pulled by reindeer and covered ourselves with coats, blankets, and anything else we could find. My job was to hold our faithful cat on my lap. He seemed satisfied with his confinement and under all those blankets he radiated enough heat to keep my hands and chest warm for the entire trip.

Our new neighbors were descendants of early settlers, previous exiles, or people who, for a variety of reasons had simply been assigned to Siberia by Soviet authorities. On the whole they were kind, simple people, and welcomed us into their midst. The majority of the villagers were women and children, since most of the able-bodied men had been drafted into the army. The men left behind were members of the "militia" or NKVD, or officials of the Communist Party. Young men were also needed to perform critical tasks in the mines, such as heavy drilling and blasting. Women were expected to perform most of the other manual tasks below ground.

Our new village, Priisk Krasnoarmieiskii, with its hundred or so buildings which resembled American log cabins, was larger than our previous settlement. The procedure for building these dwellings, which ranged from single family huts to barracks that housed up to twelve families, was a source of great curiosity for me, and later I made it a point to watch the construction process. My interest was motivated partly by natural curiosity and partly by the insecurity caused by the Russian authorities' total control over our lives. I thought that, should the need ever arise, I would know how to build an elementary shelter to house our family and save us from certain death in the unforgiving Siberian climate.

The only tools required to build these simple cabins were an axe and a wood drill. The cabins had no foundation; the builder started by laying logs horizontally in a square to define the size of the house. He cut a notch close to the end of each log to dovetail it with the next one, which was laid at right angles to the first. He then carved a wide shallow groove in each successive log, which was laid on top so that the curvature of the groove fit snugly over the log below. The logs were also joined by vertical dowels made at the site and inserted into holes drilled into each successive trunk. These dowels were especially important in places where openings were left for doors and windows. Moss was used to caulk the joints. The ceiling and the floor were formed by boards cut with an axe from timber at the site. The roof was constructed of a simple truss overlaid with boards, and the floor of the small attic was covered with a thick layer of soil. The final step was to seal the layers of moss with wet clay both on the inside and outside of the house. I marveled at the speed of these rough builders. Once the wood was at the site, two men could put together a cabin in a couple of weeks.

The layout of our village seemed completely arbitrary and chaotic. Most villages in Europe and the western part of Russia consisted of houses that lined both sides of a central road. Our *priisk* had no road leading into or through it; rather, the cabins were connected by narrow meandering paths. The key point of the village was the termination of a branch of the narrow-gauge railroad, which was the only means of transportation connecting us with the outside world. Within a few feet of the end of the rail line stood the village store.

I remember that site well because it was there at the tender age of twelve that I became somewhat of a celebrity. People gathered there daily to wait for the train to take them to work and, in my case, to school. My arrival was always eagerly awaited by other exiles because

I was invariably up to date on all the latest war news. My information came from the "radio" of a Russian family with whom we shared our dwelling in one of the barracks. They did not actually have a radio, but a loudspeaker attached to a network of wires connecting some of the houses to a central receiver in a different village.

I listened eagerly to the news and tried to memorize all the details. The format of the information was always the same. Newspapers and radio discussed the rapid Nazi advances into Russia. The media identified cities captured by Germans, but the elaborate descriptions of major battles and smaller skirmishes told a different story. The reports quoted daily losses of the German and Soviet Armies, including the number of planes, tanks, artillery pieces, and soldiers lost on both sides. The German figures always exceeded the Russian casualties by a wide margin. The arithmetical account was followed by descriptions of several battles, most of them won by the Red Army. Despite heavy Russian defeats in the early stages of the war, the broadcasts implied that it was the Germans who were losing the contest.

No one else in our group had access to a radio, and on my arrival at the "station" I was always asked to recite the latest news. Most people were skeptical of the reports, though they never showed it, because having such doubts about Russian victories was tantamount to treason. Some just enjoyed hearing the fact that the war was proceeding. Those who spoke no Russian and barely understood my report in Polish asked every day in Yiddish at the end of my talk, *"S'git fur Yidn?"* ("Is it good for the Jews?") I invariably answered affirmatively. Very few of our people spoke Russian, so my command of the language and my access to the world outside Siberia gave me a position of prominence. Soon I felt responsible for disseminating the news and began to prepare for my daily delivery. I discussed the war with my teachers and the few intellectuals among our people to gain better perspective on the situation, and I incorporated editorial comments into my "briefings."

The normal work week, like the school week, was six days long, with Sunday designated a day of rest. The mines, however, operated seven days a week, twenty-four hours a day, and those who had enough energy to work on Sundays were rewarded with coupons that could be exchanged in a special store for food and scarce goods, primarily fabrics that could be fashioned into primitive garments, buttons, threads, and vodka. Occasionally tools such as needles, scissors, and eating utensils were also available. Vodka was especially prized as "liquid currency" that could be exchanged for almost anything.

Not everyone, of course, drank vodka. There were major cultural differences between our group and the local Russian population, and one of the biggest was in the rate of alcohol consumption. Our people did not drink, while most of the Russian men drank ceaselessly when vodka or beer was available. Whenever a shipment of beer came to the village cafeteria (or *stolovka*, literally a place with tables), the Russians drank to excess. The *stolovka* did indeed have tables, but despite its designation as an eating establishment, it was open at unpredictable times and offered no food. The only occasions on which it could fulfill its intended purpose were when it served beer, which was brought to the village at irregular intervals. At those times customers would team up in groups of three or four and go to the *stolovka* with a bucket and their own metal cups, since glasses were not provided. The buckets would be filled from kegs and then brought to the tables, where the customers would dip their cups and drink. When they emptied the pail, it would be refilled until their money ran out or until the revelers' legs became too unsteady to support the weight of their bodies. I remember on several occasions seeing men lying in the snow unconscious and foaming at the mouth. Fortunately those instances were rare, because few people could afford the "luxury" of frequent excessive drinking, and alcohol—like everything else in Russia—was in short supply.

Attendance at work was strictly enforced. A person absent from duty without a valid excuse was punished according to the feared "6–25" formula: a 25 percent loss of pay for the following six months. If another unexcused absence occurred during those six months, the punishment was six months' confinement in a gulag under severe conditions that could easily result in death. The gulag concentration camps have been eloquently described by Alexander Solzhenitsyn in *Gulag Archipelago* and by other writers. The camps subjected prisoners to forced labor, unheated, cramped sleeping quarters, and meager rations.

The only valid justification for missing a day of work was a medical certificate of illness, and only one person in the village could issue such a document. This "doctor" was a midwife of dubious medical qualifications. Her primary diagnostic technique was to take the patient's temperature. If it was not elevated, the person was judged to be healthy. Few people had their own thermometers, and those who felt sick took an enormous risk by not catching the six a.m. train to the mines without being sure that their sickness would manifest itself in a fever at the examination. If the temperature proved to be normal, it would be too late to go to work. The only recourse then to secure a certificate was to offer a bribe. It is easy to imagine the potential for corruption under the existing conditions. The midwife was not unaware of the value of her services, and she sold them for an appropriate price. It was hard not to resent this woman: She was a parasite who preyed on sick people and extorted money from individuals whose financial needs were greater than hers. Adept at taking bribes, she was less proficient at dispensing medical help. Beyond that, she was not well trained and had no medical equipment other than the thermometer and a stethoscope. Her only medicines were powders, probably modified forms of aspirin. Dental care was not available, and the only cure for a toothache was to soak a piece of cloth with vodka and hold it against the offending tooth with a clenched jaw.

Life among the Russians, while an improvement over our previous conditions, was still tough. We remained stranded under the oppressive Stalinist regime where even a casual criticism of the Communist system brought heavy penalties; indeed, a less-than-admiring remark about Stalin could bring a death sentence. Living conditions in the primitive Siberian villages—cramped quarters, no running water, not even elementary sanitation, and the isolation thousands of miles from civilization—exacted a heavy toll. Poor clothing, scarcity of food, and lack of control over one's destiny were constant reminders of our miserable existence.

And yet, in comparison with our previous confinement to the isolated village of Konstantinovskii, our new status seemed like a new lease on life. Instead of being treated like subhuman animals, we led a normal[18] Russian existence, such as it was, and were no longer taunted with expressions like "Forget your Poland!" or told that we were to die in the miserable, abandoned, deteriorating *priisk*. Equally important was the resumption of my education. Our *priisk* had had only an elementary school, but higher grades were available in Priisk Vasilevskii, ten miles away along the narrow-gauge railroad. The school had two shifts, and while we lived in Krasnoarmieiskii Priisk, I was assigned to the second shift, catching the noon train to attend classes and returning home at eight in the evening.

Shortly after signing the Sikorski-Mayski pact, the Russians allowed the Polish Government in exile to open an embassy in Moscow and a consulate in Krasnoyarsk, Siberia. A Polish consular representative, Jan Mucc, visited our area in 1942. To my amazement, I found his comprehensive report in Hoover Institution Archives at Stanford University in 2004. The report provides a painfully accurate description of our conditions in Siberia. Here is my translation from the original Polish of extracts from that report:[19]

> I left Irkutsk for Bodaybo by plane on 7.11.1942. I arrived in Bodaybo on 7.14. 1942 after a 2333 km. journey. I was met at the Bodaybo airport by miserable looking people. I left for our meeting place followed by a column of these pitiful, tattered, penurious, wasted and destroyed people. I spent the entire day and night listening to the grievances and grief of our citizens.
>
> On 7.15 I visited the Head of NKVD and the Chairman of *Obispolkom* (Civilian Government). The same day we held a solemn meeting for 2000 Polish citizens. I delivered a short report on the political situation and described the views of the Polish

---

18. The Russians had, of course, adapted to the local conditions much better than we did. I assume that those among them who could not adapt had long been dead. The survivors were able to work, learned how to procure food from the forest, knew how to keep warm, and had small families—at most two to three children to support. Many of our people were completely helpless. They were physically weak, suffered from various ailments, and were not prepared for primitive conditions and manual labor. I was the only child in our family, whereas others had several children to feed. The "normal" Russian experience in Siberia was considerably more brutal to us than to the local population.

19. Hoover Institution Archives, *Poland. Ambasada* (Soviet Union) Records, box 44, folder 13.

Government (in London) and the Embassy in Russia about our responsibility to our citizens. I reported that "Poland has not perished" (Polska nie zgineła), that Poland is fighting, that her armed forces are growing on land, in the air, and on the sea. Rabbi Dym followed with a beautiful speech. He blessed Poland and the Polish Army in Hebrew. He announced that there are 2,000 Jewish Polish citizens (in addition to 300 Christian Poles) in Bodaybo. He said, "No one other than the Polish Government has any claim to us and we are loyal to the death to our Government." He further stated that the Polish Jews categorically reject foreign "care." "We want and demand 'care' from the Polish Government. We want to fight against the German gangs under Polish banners. We want to die for Poland. God help us in that." He stopped and the hall loudly sang the Polish national anthem and echoed the rabbi's speech with cries in honor of Poland and General Sikorski.

From 7.14 to 7.20 I visited gold mining settlements and mica mines whose workers included 280 of our citizens. The gold fields are situated in several directions up to 400 km. from Bodaybo. They are reached by rivers or narrow gauge railroad. I saw beautiful countryside: mountains that reach the sky, beautiful forests crisscrossed by enchanting streams. It is a wonderful sight for a Government official to admire, but visiting our people and seeing them deprived, clothed in rags, their hungry bodies with protruding bones, looking as if they emerged from graves and pushing wheel barrows with gold-yielding soil is true hell. Food—800 grams of bread and light soup and that is all. The workers are children, the elderly, and women who still retained some remnants of health.

From 7.20 to 7.22 I visited barracks housing some of our citizens. The barracks are horrifying, filthy, so called *obshchezytie* (communal quarters) intended for 50 people but housing 100 to 200 under unhygienic conditions. Sixty-five percent of the people were suffering from tuberculosis, rheumatism and heart diseases caused by the climate and inadequate nutrition. From 7.22 to 7.24 I visited houses for 700 invalids and children unable to work—sick and wasted people. Wherever I looked I saw miserable people, resigned to their fate, as if the world did not belong to them.

During my visit I was invariably asked, "When are we going to be helped? We are naked and hungry." I answered the best I could.

I tried to console them. Often I clenched my teeth to hide my tears. . . . For several days I talked to groups of our citizens and they all begged to be rescued because they feared they would not survive the third winter. I was visited by mothers, old people, and young orphans. Those who have not seen these starving people beseeching help will not believe my report. . . .

On 7.31, followed to the airport by a crowd of our citizens, I left for Irkutsk. . . . I reached Irkutsk on 8.5. and immediately went to *Obispolkom*. Chairman Komisarov listened to me and issued instructions that will help our citizens in Bodaybo. The same day I saw the Head of NKVD, who immediately greeted me with, "Finish your business and go back to Krasnoyarsk. We have nothing to talk about.

When I visited the archive, it had not yet been fully indexed, and it was by pure chance that I came across the word "Bodaybo" in a thick binder that must have listed thousands if not tens of thousands of documents. At first I thought I must have made a mistake: I did not think that our remote, isolated region would come to the attention of the Polish Consulate, nor did I think that the Russians would allow a Polish official to visit this place of banishment. Nervously, as if afraid to bring back the ghosts of my Siberian childhood, I approached Irena Czernichowska, the Polish librarian at the Hoover Institution. She was most helpful, and within a quarter of an hour she brought me the box containing the report. I hardly believed my eyes. There in front of me at Stanford University, a place as different from my Siberian exile as I could possibly imagine, was a document written in Polish by a visitor who had not only evaluated our situation, but because of his diplomatic status, dared to challenge the all-powerful NKVD and was able to leave the area alive. The report transported me back to Siberia, and it took several days before I could sleep well at night. I now looked on our predicament as an adult, with a hopefully more mature mind, and perhaps for the first time in my life I could appreciate the full horror of our Siberian existence.

The reader may well ask, "How did you survive those terrible conditions?" I have already spoken about my physical strength, the resourcefulness of my father, and, perhaps equally important, my young age as factors that allowed me to adjust to our new life. Some of us adapted to our new conditions, others did not. Numerous members of our community could not stand the psychological shock, perform the heavy mine work, or engage in other, occasionally illegal activities to procure extra rations. Gradually the hunger and despair sapped their strength and often left them vulnerable to disease. Lack of medical attention, the harsh climate, and the promised life sentence in Siberia completed their destruction, driving the poor sufferers to an early demise.

One of my activities that brought extra rations was my Sunday work in the gold mines. We exchanged the special coupons I received for sugar, butter, and even vodka, which we invariably sold on the black market at a handsome profit. The work was not compulsory—in fact, I had to lie about my age, which was barely 12—because it was illegal to employ children under 16, but evidently I was tall and mature looking enough to go underground. The work, of course, was grueling and dangerous, and from time to time the constant pressure to perform, coupled with generally lax Soviet safety standards, resulted in accidents—fortunately none of them fatal in our mine.

Ironically, in comparison with work on the surface, mining was considered desirable because of the relatively moderate constant temperature of the underground working environment. We were in the region of permafrost, where soil deeper than just a few feet is permanently frozen and almost rock solid; only the surface layer melts during the brief summer. While it was difficult to extract this hard soil, the sheltered surroundings in the mines were vastly preferable to the extreme winter cold and sweltering, mosquito-infested summer air above the surface.

The mining process started with drill operators boring deep holes at the ends of shafts to accommodate sticks of dynamite. The explosions ripped out huge openings and produced large clumps of frozen soil, which were then broken into smaller pieces by pneumatic hammers. We were assigned separate piles of frozen earth, and the amount transported by each worker was carefully measured. My job usually consisted of loading the smaller fragments into a wheelbarrow and delivering the load along a lengthy corridor to a long conveyor belt that carried the soil to the surface. The quota of soil we were expected to transfer was hard to meet without nonstop labor. Since our reward was proportional

Photograph of Soviet gulag mining operations, 1940's.

to the results achieved, we worked hard to fulfill the quota and to be allowed to work in the future.

In the final stage, the conveyor belts delivered the frozen soil into one of several huge chambers on the surface to be steam-heated for several hours. When melted, it was expelled into long troughs and propelled by a stream of water past horizontal wooden bars fixed along the bottom at right angles to the flow. Since gold is heavier than other soil ingredients, it was the first substance to be trapped behind those bars, where it could be collected at the end of the shift. This extraction method was inefficient, but it worked to our benefit, because in the summer we were encouraged to pan for the gold that still remained in the processed tailings, which were dumped around the mines. We then used the gold as currency in the special store that accepted the coupons for Sunday work. Gold could also be sold surreptitiously on the black market.

I was the only boy my age working in the mines to earn extra food for my family, and I was proud of my achievement. Initially, however, I felt completely out of place in that dark world. The thin tree trunks that held up the ceilings of the previously excavated passages looked fragile and inadequate for their intended purpose. I worried about the weight of the soil above us; if the supports gave way, it could break through the barrier and bury us in an instant. I consoled myself with the thought that no mine disasters had been reported in our area. Fortunately for my peace of mind, I did not know that such accidents were never announced in the Soviet press; indeed, talking about them was tantamount to treason—even simple fires were kept secret. Everything belonged to the state, and disruptions, however small, suggested incompetence in the *Sovietskoi Vlasti* (the Soviet Rule). Criticism of the Soviet Government was an unforgivable sin with the result that Russia was officially presented as an utterly efficient, fair, and error-free country.[20]

I worried about my ability to carry out my assignments in the mines. Still a young boy and on my first job, I was for the first time in my life working alongside adults and being expected to perform at their levels. Initially I felt like an intruder, an underage impostor who would soon be found out and ejected for his presumptuous behavior. But I recovered my composure later that first day. Several women were performing similar tasks, and I was able to maintain their pace. The traditional miners' solidarity also worked in my favor; far from scrutinizing my performance, my coworkers welcomed me into their midst. Supervisors were less congenial, but they were fair and gave me full credit for my work.

Occasionally I felt sorry for myself, knowing that, had I been lucky enough to be born in a country untouched by war, I would have been engaged in more pleasant activities, like other young boys. But in retrospect I feel that laboring in the mines did me no harm. The underground

---

20. Perhaps nothing illustrates the devastating effect of the virtual prohibition of criticism of the Soviet Rule as well as the initial steps Mikhail Gorbachev, the last leader of the Soviet Union, took to try to reform Russia's failing economy. One of his first innovations was to introduce *"Glasnost."* The root of the word is *glas,* an old form of *golos,* meaning voice. *Glasnost* stands for public discourse of issues at hand. Gorbachev hoped that in the absence of market forces, which automatically eliminate inefficient enterprises, the previously forbidden voicing of discontent would naturally revive Soviet commercial practices and lead to restructuring or overhaul *(perestroika)* of the Communist economy. We know now, of course, that this did not happen. Central planning, absence of competitive markets, and the muzzling of the Russian people did irreversible harm. Eventually the Soviet economy collapsed under the weight of its own restrictions and, in the process, inevitably took down with it the Communist regime.

work was exhausting, and I was always dead tired at the end of the eight-hour shift, but the exercise probably helped to transform me from an illness-prone child into a reasonably healthy and strong teenager. That strength came in handy in later work in Russia and in holding my own in various situations involving other young adults. Many years later my mining experience made me feel quite "at home" when one of our companies became a supplier to the mining industry and I visited coal mines in Pennsylvania to see our equipment in action.

My weekdays were busy and followed a well-defined routine. The first chore of the day was to fetch two pails of water from a stream a half mile away. Carrying the water became a ritual significant beyond the mere act of transporting two pails, and many of us honed our skills to achieve maximum efficiency and make the task more pleasant. We hung the buckets on a yoke which some carried on their shoulders and others laid across their backs. During the winter the stream was covered with one to two feet of ice, and the buckets had to be lowered through a round hole cut in that frozen barrier. On especially cold days we carried an axe to remove the ice that had formed at the bottom of the hole during the night. The challenge was to fill the pails to the rim and to carry them without spilling any of the precious water. On very cold days this was not much of a problem, because the top of the water froze on the way, sealing in the liquid. On most days, however, the air temperature was not low enough to freeze the water on the way home, and we had to walk smoothly to keep the buckets from swinging. We soon learned that we could accomplish this by keeping the upper body stiff and walking in short rapid steps. The ultimate achievement was to carry three buckets. I was one of the few to master this feat by placing the yoke with two buckets on my left shoulder and holding the third in my right hand.

To supplement the rations provided by the state and items we harvested from the forest we grew our own potatoes and cabbage, but the results were uneven in that unfavorable climate. The region had two seasons: a short summer and a long winter. Snow began falling at the beginning of September and by the middle of the month the ground was usually covered with a solid layer that did not fully melt until the following June. During one difficult season, early snowfalls made the harvest barely sufficient to provide seed potatoes for the following year. Cabbage fared better than potatoes; either the variety we planted ripened without forming a solid head, or the short growing season simply left it in the form of open leaves, but there was always some harvest. We pickled the vegetable to preserve it during the winter, making a form of sauerkraut. In the initial step we cut the leaves into shreds and placed them in a small barrel. We then compacted the cabbage into a layer about eight inches thick by jumping up and down inside the barrel. We sprinkled salt on top of the flattened layer and continued the process with more cabbage until the barrel was almost full. The top was then covered with a wooden disc and weighted with a heavy stone. After a few days, when the cabbage juices overflowed the wooden barrier, we took the barrel outside where the freezing temperatures preserved the pickled cabbage for the winter. After the liquid froze, we removed the rock and the wooden disc and used an axe to hack away pieces of frozen sauerkraut for our meals.

One of my other duties was providing fuel for the stove. We lived in a long barracks comprised of eight units, constructed of horizontal logs. Each unit of three rooms and a shared kitchen housed three families, one to each room. The rooms were defined by partitions that rose short of the ceiling, providing little privacy both within the family or among the group. Every three days, each family took its turn building and maintaining the fire in the stove. The fire burned from morning until early evening, and the heat retained by the bricks kept us warm throughout the night.

Our primary fuel was silver birch logs, and procuring an adequate supply was a major undertaking. Although our village was surrounded by trees, previous logging left birches that were too thin for firewood in the immediate vicinity, and we had to go high into the mountains to do our cutting. This was much easier in the summer than in the heavy winter snows. Many of us found a favorite spot, cut trees, cleared them of branches, and stacked them in a secret place. We hoped this location would be difficult for others to find but possible for us to remember in the fall when the early snows would make it much easier to transport the logs to the village on a primitive sled.

Initially I accompanied my father to harvest the trees, but within a year or so I was going by myself. Axes remained our only implements for cutting, and we became adept at using them. The thickness of the birches we harvested was about six to eight inches, and chopping them down was not very difficult. When I went with my father, we took turns with the axe, while contending with a common summertime hazard in the Siberian woods: mosquitoes. The human body responds slowly to mosquito attacks. By the time we feel the bite, a lot of blood has already been sucked out, and the discomfort lasts for hours. I could never understand why the body does not give a quicker signal of the mosquito's assault, to enable us to swat it before it has a chance to consume such a substantial amount of blood. Nor could I understand where all those mosquitoes were coming from; there did not seem to be enough wildlife to sustain such great numbers of them, and they could not have lain dormant waiting for us to appear in the woods.

We did our best to collaborate in combating the mosquito menace. While my father chopped down trees, I stood guard and tried to prevent these flying pests from landing on his back or tried to kill them if they penetrated my defenses. My father perspired more heavily than I did, probably because he worked harder, and invariably became their preferred target. He did not react well, or at least not silently. I felt uneasy at his lamentations and also somewhat guilty that I suffered less than he did and could more easily deal with my discomfort.

When I was still only twelve years old, I convinced my father that I was handy enough with an axe to become the sole procurer of logs. The school was closed in the summer, and at my age I did not have to work, so I had ample time to visit the forest. He, of course, had to work all year, and welcomed my commitment to prepare our winter fuel. I cut the trees into ten-foot lengths and stored them in an inconspicuous place. On the way back to the village, I dragged one or two trees down with me and cut them into logs of a suitable size for the oven. When fall came, I transported the hidden logs by stacking them on a small sled produced by a local Russian craftsman, tying them down, and maneuvering the assembly down the mountain—not an easy task. I tried to stay in tracks made by others, but it was not unusual to develop too much momentum and end up deep in virgin snow.

Procuring the logs was hard work, but at my age it was also fun. It gave me the satisfaction of doing something useful and, in fact, essential to our survival. Few pre-teenage boys can boast such an accomplishment. Also, the process of cutting trees, chopping them into logs, and splitting the logs, all with a single axe, required a lot of skill and produced immediate, tangible results. As with carrying water, we tried to make the log production process quick and elegant. The best way to divide the long trunks into logs was to cut the timbers at a forty-five degree angle. The challenge was to administer successive axe blows close to the mark made by the first impact. That way little lumber was wasted, and the logs flew apart with minimal effort. The same applied to splitting logs. Only two blows were required if the second swing guided the axe into the first split. Finally, there was the satisfaction of stacking the logs in neat piles, reminiscent of the joy a boy gets constructing pyramids from toy building blocks.

Our logs were stored unprotected outside the cabins, but there was surprisingly little pilferage of wood in the village. In the cold Siberian winter, wood was essential for survival, and stealing it would be considered a heinous and unconscionable act. I did hear of cases where felled trees were stolen in the mountains; I also heard stories of people drilling holes in their logs and filling them with gunpowder to produce an explosion in a thief's oven. In retrospect, I think these gunpowder stories were circulated to prevent theft, because I never saw or heard firsthand any such explosions.

In addition to a Polish family, we shared our quarters with a Russian woman and her son, Sasha, who was two years my senior. He was the one who received the radio broadcasts that would become such a good source of information for me. He also showed me how to trap rabbits, which were completely white in the winter and gray in the summer. I never saw any rabbits running free in the wild, but it was easy to find their tracks in the snow. Sasha was good at catching them. He managed to procure a supply of steel wire from a secret source and learned to soften the metal by bringing it to a red heat in our oven. He then formed sliding snares, placed the loops in vertical positions above the rabbit tracks and secured the free end to a tree. It was important not to touch the wire with bare hands after the heat treatment because doing so would leave an odor the rabbit could detect. Rabbits had the habit of retracing their steps, and as they hopped along they would literally jump into the loops, which then tightened like a noose around their necks and suffocated them. Sasha knew how to skin them without damaging the fur, which he sold to the State. The meat was an important source of protein for his family.

One day he found a freshly trapped snow-white fox in one of the snares. Sasha and another boy brought the snarling predator home and barricaded the animal under a table in their small room. Sasha quickly found ways to feed the fox. He caught white birds called *snegurochki* (snowbirds) about the size of a sparrow that flew in small flocks around the village. The trapping methods were somewhat similar to catching rabbits, except the snares were made of different material. Sasha pulled a few hairs from the tail of one of the village horses, cut the strands into three-inch sections, knotted the pieces into sliding loops, and attached the snares to a wooden board. He sprinkled breadcrumbs or grain on the board, placed it in a prominent open space, and chased the birds until they saw the food and landed on the board to eat it. It took Sasha only seconds to trap two or three birds in the snares. He then grabbed them, brought them home, and threw them alive to the fox, which ate them whole. I felt uneasy about having the fox locked up in our barracks, for the animal was restless and looked extremely vicious. I also felt sorry for the poor birds that served as its food. After a few days Sasha took it away, after maneuvering it into a flour sack and sold it to a government office in charge of procuring pelts.

On another occasion, Sasha's creativity went a little too far when he played a trick on me that I feared would leave me permanently blind.

He had a bottle of vinegar and a small box of baking soda. Considering the food shortages, I have no idea where he found these things. He sprinkled soda powder into a dish of vinegar, which started bubbling, and suggested I light a match. While I was doing it, he threw the liquid into my face. My attention was on the match and it all happened so fast that I didn't have time to close my eyes. The liquid flooded my eyes, produced excruciating pain, and completely obscured my vision. After a few minutes I managed to open one eye. It took about half an hour before I realized I could also see with the other eye. Fortunately Sasha and his mother moved out shortly afterwards and were replaced by a Polish family.

IN 1941 MY MOTHER fell seriously ill, and we took her to a hospital about ten miles from our village where she was diagnosed with a severe heart condition. It was a small hospital, and I was surprised at the cleanliness of its rooms, the apparent efficiency, and the friendly attitude of its staff. The hospital was, after all, a government institution, and we were not used to kind treatment by any Russian official. My father and I took my mother there on the narrow-gauge railroad and left with the feeling that she was in good hands.

Just a few days later, however, mother staggered back into our barracks at about four o'clock in the morning. She was in a terrible state, completely exhausted, and so cold she could hardly move. She was almost incoherent as she tried to tell us what had happened. On the previous day the hospital's heating system had broken down and the authorities moved all the non-ambulatory patients into one room. Those who could still walk were simply discharged and told to go home. There was no transportation available at night, no telephones, and no other shelter, so my mother was forced to walk ten miles in the cold Siberian night carrying her small bag of possessions, primarily a few precious articles of clothing. The thought of leaving her personal effects behind to make the trip easier never entered her mind, since those things could not be replaced. Whereas the long walk would have been challenging even for a healthy person, it was devastating for my mother. But then, life was cheap in Siberia, and although we were shocked, we were not altogether surprised at the hospital's action. She, of course, had had no voice in the matter. We gave her something hot to drink and put her to bed.

That was the last time I saw her sane. When she woke up, her rational mind was gone. It was not easy to accept the fact that my mother had suddenly—overnight in fact—become a different person. She never became violent, abusive, or loud; on the contrary, she was submissive and quiet. She recognized only my father and me, but was otherwise completely unaware of her surroundings. And although her speech was clear, her conversations were unintelligible. She lost all sense of time, often getting out of bed to wander about the room and the kitchen in the middle of the night, sometimes waking our neighbors. One of the most striking changes was her abrupt switch from speaking Polish to Russian, the language of her childhood. My parents had spoken Russian at home before the war, but they switched to Polish for fear that the NKVD would want to know why my mother spoke Russian and would discover that my parents had escaped from the Communists after the Revolution. But we no longer worried about her speaking that language. The tragedy of her insanity overshadowed any fear of discovery; after all, it was expected that an insane person might do unusual things.

My mother's condition completely changed my life. Because my father worked six days a week, I had to look after her, and for the next few months I could not attend school. She required constant attention. Her heart condition and physical strength were no better than before she went to the hospital, and by this time she didn't even know how to function properly. I fed her, washed her, and dressed her. She could not control her bodily functions, and we had no such things as geriatric diapers or disposable paper towels. Bedpans were not available, and one of my hardest tasks was the daily hand-washing of soiled sheets and blankets. People feel sorry for the washerwomen who have to wash clothes by hand in the river. My task was much harder because the local river was frozen during most of the year, and the water had to be fetched and heated before the washing could be done. Soap was not always available, so I often did the washing in plain water and finished by placing the clothes in a cauldron of boiling water.

We tried again to place my mother in the hospital, but the authorities did not accept her, citing overcrowding. Finally after about three months, a hospital in Bodaybo offered her a bed. Bodaybo was 45 miles from our village. We left my mother at the new place with serious misgivings. The new hospital was bigger and more impersonal than the first, and the greater distance made it much more difficult for us to visit her. She was unaware of what was happening, and we worried about the possibility of abuse by the hospital personnel. I visited her once a week for about three weeks. I think she recognized me, but she was a pitiful sight. Her face was swollen, her eyes dull, and her words, while clear, did not produce a logical sequence. She was one of many patients in a big room

The last photograph of my mother, 1942.

that was dingy, dark, and inhospitable. All the patients looked dejected, thin, and miserable, but except for my mother, they appeared to suffer only from physical disabilities. Her combination of physical and mental problems made her an outsider even in that marginal world. We considered bringing her home, but the doctors advised against it.

About three weeks later we were notified of her death. I don't remember how we found out. The local police probably received a phone call and came to our barracks. When my father and I went to Bodaybo to arrange for the burial, we were told she had regained mental clarity on her last day and had talked about her family. Seemingly at peace with herself, she was calm and knew she would die soon. She also seemed to realize that she would not see us again and asked the nurses to give us her love. The end came within twenty-four hours of regaining her senses.

My last memory of my mother is very disturbing. Wrapped in a white sheet, she lay on a big wooden box in the mortuary of the hospital. Jewish burial practice calls for the body to be washed before placement in the coffin, and two women were there to perform the ritual. When they turned her body over, we saw a large bed sore on her back, with several fat worms already attached to it. The worms had come from the box below, which contained several other bodies.

The funeral took place on the same day, with my father and me the only mourners. We were in a strange town, and while we knew a few people there, funerals were too frequent to merit attendance by anyone but immediate family. She was buried in an unmarked grave, but several months later we erected a gravestone prepared by one of our fellow exiles who was a stone mason. A flat stone placed in a vertical position, it bore a simple chiseled Hebrew and Polish inscription giving her name, date of birth, and date of death: June 9, 1942. My father promised to return after the war to exhume the body for a decent burial in a Jewish cemetery in Poland, but I am sure he knew even then that he was unlikely to be able to fulfill that promise.

There were few cases of insanity among our exiles, but then my mother had a harder burden to bear than most. At eleven I did not appreciate the tragedy of our situation, but later, after piecing together my parents' casual remarks, I think I understood her agony. She felt tremendous guilt and lived in constant fear that her Russian accent, an incorrect phrase, or an unguarded remark might expose her origin and bring calamity upon our family, for the NKVD delighted in destroying fugitives fortunate enough to escape their clutches. She and my father constantly admonished me not to speak of their flight from the Bolsheviks less than two decades earlier, but could a child be trusted to hold his tongue? On more than one occasion

My father in 1942.

she apologized to my father for being such a burden, saying that he would not have been in constant danger of exposure and possible execution had his wife been like the other women in the village.

If my father's love for my mother and me helped him survive Siberia by giving him someone other than himself to fight for, the opposite may have been true of my mother. Now that I have my own children, I cannot imagine a greater calamity befalling a mother than to see her child victimized, hungry, and left languishing in Siberia without hope for the future. All the mothers there must have suffered agonies at that prospect, but perhaps she had more reason to lament my fate. I had been one of the most promising students in our school in Warsaw, and just a few months before the outbreak of the war my mother had traveled to London to enroll me in one of England's most prestigious boarding schools, where I was to continue my studies when I turned twelve. The contrast between that bright prospect and the dismal reality of Siberia must have deepened her despair immeasurably. Her mind could no longer cope, and when her body failed her as well, she found escape in insanity.

SIBERIAN SCHOOL

IT WAS HARD FOR ME to cope with the emotional roller coaster that followed my mother's death. My first reaction was utter amazement that the world around me did not seem to change in the slightest. People still went about their business as if nothing had happened. The other feeling, which I was ashamed to admit to myself but eventually shared with my father, was a feeling of relief that the inevitable had happened. Along with my tremendous sense of loss came a sense of release from the responsibility of caring for an invalid. I felt guilty at harboring such thoughts, but my father reassured me that they were perfectly normal and in no way showed callousness or lack of love for my mother.

Our pain was eased by the moral support of friends and neighbors in our village. On one occasion I shall never forget, a Russian woman asked me, as I stepped off the train from Bodaybo, if my mother was dead. When I confirmed it, she just stood there on a high spot of the village and started wailing, "Oh, you poor orphan. What will you do, poor orphan?" She had a strong voice and her cries penetrated the entire village for about five minutes until I reached our barracks. People gave free vent to their feelings there and most of them, having lived through major tragedies themselves, sympathized with others in their misfortunes.

Despite my grief, I began to recover quickly from my mother's death. Just a few days afterward, I went back to school to see if I could still take the final examinations. I don't remember how I accomplished that feat, but I know I did not lose that year's school credit. I had always been a good student, although I seldom studied. At that time the Russian school system followed a predictable routine: Each class started with an oral presentation of the previous lesson's homework by students picked at random, then the teacher explained a new topic. Newspapers were the only paper available in reasonable quantities, and we used them to prepare written homework by writing large, heavy letters over the print. Between my domestic duties of housekeeping and procuring fuel and my long commute, I did not have much time left after school. Although I don't think I did it consciously, now that I look back at my activities analytically I think I must have subconsciously designed an approach to beat the Soviet school system. My strategy was to praise Soviet Communism and Stalin during my presentations, an approach that helped me receive consistently high grades with little work.

I had missed a whole academic year when we first arrived in Siberia because we had been isolated from the Russians and our village had no school. But when we were moved to Krasnoarmieisk, I made up the lost year by skipping one grade in a ten-grade school in Vasilevskii Priisk. By that time I spoke Russian fluently. Twelve years old, I picked up languages easily, like most children of that age. The Russian children were friendly and did not overtly discriminate against me as a foreigner, although over the next few years I was exposed to several difficult incidents, including tough fights in which I was singled out for special treatment.

I have very favorable recollections of Russian schools. The school building I attended was a one-story L-shaped log barracks with a long corridor on one side and classrooms on the other. Offices for teachers and a small gymnasium were located at the far end of the corridor. There were approximately thirty students in each grade, and we always occupied the same classrooms, with teachers rotating to teach their various subjects.

I enjoyed all subjects, but science and mathematics were my favorites. At the time, I explained my leanings toward them by the fact that once you understood science and mathematics, you had to do very little work, whereas the other disciplines required extensive study and memorization. Russian schools awarded grades from one to five, with five being the highest. Grade one was reserved for a particularly bad performance and was seldom used. Those students who received all fives were known as *otlichniki* (literally, "those who are distinguished"). Those with fives and up to two fours were called *udarniki* ("hitters"). The names of the *otlichniki and udarniki* were posted in a prominent place in the corridor, and I was generally among them, though not always as an *otlichnik*.

A number of incidents, most of them pleasant, come to mind when I think of those days. The school had a small library devoted primarily to works by Marx, Lenin, and Stalin, but there were about half a dozen books on popular science topics. I particularly enjoyed a series written by Yakov Perelman, which included titles that could be roughly translated as "Engaging Arithmetic," "Engaging Algebra," and "Engaging Physics." Other books described ways to make model water turbines, steam engines, electrical motors, transformers, simple radios, and radio-controlled ships. The models used rudimentary construction materials such as tin cans and wood, and, in the case of radios, relied on electrical sparks as transmission elements. I made a few models with varying degrees of success. The water turbines worked beautifully, but the steam engines hardly moved.

The books and classroom matter provided topics for lively conversation with my physics teacher. After a while he brought me to one of the storage rooms and showed me a number of electrical instruments, such as voltmeters, ammeters, and galvanometers. Even now I remember how attracted I was to them. The galvanometer was probably eighteen inches high, with a horizontal scale at the top and a central vertical needle which pivoted at the bottom and reached the center of the scale. The needle was designed to deflect right or left, depending on the polarity of the voltage applied.

My teacher said he could not demonstrate any of these instruments because he needed a battery to drive them and there were no batteries available.[21] Having seen large, wet batteries in one of the small, narrow-gauge railroad stations, I asked the stationmaster why they were there. He told me they were used for signaling. Knowing the batteries would be useful in school, I embarked on a campaign to procure at least one of them to power the electrical instruments. I remembered that we had brought an electric flashlight with us from Poland. The flashlight's batteries were long gone, but it had a small bulb that I hoped would still be in working order. After a few visits to the station and several conversations with the stationmaster, I was able to interest him in trying the bulb. He connected it to one of the big batteries and it lit up. Evidently he had never seen a small, three-volt bulb, and he was so intrigued that he gave me one of the wet cells in exchange for the flashlight.

I was twelve years old and immensely proud of that early achievement in procurement. The physics teacher was thrilled to get the battery, and he gave me the task of preparing a demonstration of electrical instruments in several classes. I enjoyed these sessions immensely. Never having seen electrical instruments before, I was very impressed with the movement of needles, the actions of electromagnets, the ringing of bells, and other phenomena that seemed almost miraculous. Perhaps those early experiences influenced my eventual decision to study electrical engineering.

The school had no playing fields, and sport was never part of the curriculum. People were too busy surviving, and in any case playing fields would have been covered by deep snow during the school year. Seldom used, the gym was too small for basketball, and the only equipment was a horizontal bar and two rings suspended from the ceiling on heavy ropes. During the breaks between classes, we played chess on tables set up in the school's corridor, and although we had no chess clocks to

---

21. I still find it impressive that this primitive school in our remote region of Siberia had a wide range of electrical instruments. I suppose their presence demonstrated the high levels of technical education the Russians strived for. It was also emblematic of the Soviet system that, having supplied necessary instruments, it failed to provide the means to use them.

pace us, we usually managed to finish two or three games during the ten-minute breaks. To this day I tend to be a fast player, and have little patience for deep analysis.

My relationships with my classmates and teachers were generally good. Most of the teachers came from the European part of Russia and had been educated in large Russian cities, including Moscow and Leningrad. At that time, teachers graduating from college had no choice about where they worked, and simply went where the authorities sent them. Most of them were women, many of whom were refined, sensitive, fragile individuals not prepared for the rigors and crude simplicity of Siberian life. Their origins outside Siberia and my Polish nationality gave us something in common, but it was an unspoken link; we simply understood that unlike most others there, we had seen another part of the world. I remember once passing the cabin of a teacher of Russian literature. Probably in her mid-twenties, this small, frail, dark-haired woman was trying to split logs that had been delivered to her door and lay scattered in the snow. She was wielding an axe that seemed larger than she was, producing only a tiny scratch in the log, and then raising the axe again to deliver another ineffective blow. It was dark, and from the sight of the trampled snow, it was clear that she had worked hard for some time without any success. I took the axe from her and within minutes, sent the split logs flying, eliciting a look of infinite gratitude from her. As I was leaving, she broke into tears—a display she made a valiant effort to conceal. Although she was an attractive young woman, no romantic thoughts or fantasies entered my mind. Teachers were held in high esteem in that supposedly egalitarian Russian society; indeed, we showed our respect by standing whenever the teacher entered the classroom. Any action that might have disturbed our teacher-student relationship was unthinkable.

I participated in several school plays, and one year I became the editor of the "Wall Newspaper." As the name implies, the "Wall Newspaper" was a collection of hand-written articles (we did not have a typewriter) posted on a school bulletin board. It announced school events, arrivals of new teachers, and politically correct topics, including the conduct of the war and the advantages of the Soviet Communist order. Most, if not all, editions also contained praise for the infinite wisdom of Comrade Stalin. Like all writing in the Soviet Union, the production of the newspaper was strictly supervised to assure conformance to accepted political standards.

Occasionally the school held dances, with someone playing a bayan, a kind of large accordion, but on the whole, extracurricular activities did not play a big part in school life. Nor did we tend to meet after school, everyone being busy doing chores at home and having little time for social life, at least in the early grades. That situation changed for me somewhat later, in another school in the European part of Russia.

An unpleasant incident occurred when I was fourteen years old. Brewing for some time, it was partially caused by the peculiar differences in the attitudes of students in Polish and Russian schools. In Poland, at least in the schools that I attended, children seldom avoided fights when they were provoked. Even if challenged by a bigger and stronger student, we stood our ground and resisted. It may not have been a wise course of action, but we fought back, not out of fear of being branded a coward, but to preserve our dignity. Perhaps it was that mindset that sent Polish cavalry against German tanks in 1939 with such disastrous consequences. At the same time, this attitude may also have contributed to Polish Solidarity's almost quixotic defiance of the Russians in the shipyards of Gdańsk in 1980—a challenge that contributed significantly to the fall of the Communist regime.

Students in Russian schools reacted differently to intimidation. If one was challenged by a stronger rival, the custom was to step aside or run away. My imported attitude of defiance was therefore a source of annoyance to the school bullies. Because I was tall in comparison with Russian students and too strong to be attacked successfully by anyone in my class, it took students in higher grades to give me a good fight. Those upper classmen were taken aback by my unwillingness to submit to their bullying tactics. A few one-on-one skirmishes proved inconclusive, but on one occasion, three older students decided to teach me a lesson. They waited for me on a narrow snow path on my way home from school.

Before I describe the battle, perhaps I should describe the battlefield, because the topography that produced those narrow snow paths may be peculiarly Russian. In the summer the villages were crisscrossed with paths connecting the randomly placed houses. In the fall the snow began to accumulate and was never cleared, but people continued walking along the same paths, creating narrow troughs. Loose snow filled the depressions and was compacted by people's feet until the hard paths had risen to the level of the adjacent surface. This process continued throughout the winter until the paths and the surrounding snow cover had gradually risen several feet above the ground. The paths were normally very narrow, and two people coming from opposite directions had to move sideways at the last moment to pass each other, almost in an embrace as if they were on a balance beam high above the ground. Stepping off the path meant sinking into the deep snow to the sides, and it was difficult to climb back onto the hard surface. There was no danger of suffocating in the snow—it was not powder and would not collapse and cover you—but one could easily drop three or four feet below the surface.

My challengers chose the site of the ambush well, waiting for me at a spot where the path was just wide enough for two or perhaps three people. I saw them and guessed their intentions, but they knew I would not turn back. The initial stage of the fight did not last long. It was an unequal struggle, and I soon found myself lying on my back three feet below the surface, looking at the sky through an opening the width of my body. I was in a helpless position. My only course of action, other than lying there ignominiously, was to get up and drag them into the snow with me. I did just that, one at a time. Since I was about three feet lower, I had the advantage of being able to grab their feet. A sharp pull on the boots, which were resting on a slippery surface, and the assailants went flying into the deep snow. Unfortunately, their higher elevation enabled them to kick me in the face. Luckily, the felt boots softened the blow, but I was soon on my back again in deep snow and bleeding. The damage was not as bad as it looked, though I ended up with a split lip, which to this day bothers me in cold weather.

The fight did not result in permanent animosity between my three assailants and me. I think they received a minor punishment from the school, but they never bothered me again. The incident did nothing to lessen my resolve to resist intimidation.

During my teenage years I began to discover the joys of literature and history. The Russian ways of teaching these subjects were different from those in the United States. We studied a broad outline of European literature without concentrating on any single work in great detail. We studied Russian translations of English, French, and German works by listening to the teacher describe their contents and occasionally read excerpts from them. We memorized passages from some better-known works—for example, I still remember parts of Hamlet's "To be or not to be" soliloquy in Russian. The main point of studying Western literature in Russian schools was hardly literary, but rather to show us the principal theme the authors supposedly wanted to convey: oppression of the masses by slave masters, feudal lords, and capitalists. Dickens was emphasized as a particularly effective advocate of the oppressed classes. From there it was a short step to explaining that all those wrongs were redressed in Russia after the Communist Revolution, that the West had not changed a great deal since the days of Dickens, and that the working masses all over the world admired the Soviet system and longed to be liberated from their oppressors.

The study of Russian literature was much more thorough, and we actually read several books. Sometimes our teachers read aloud in class. I found Russian poetry beautiful and always looked forward to reciting poems in the classroom and on the school stage. On one occasion I was asked to read a poem on the local "radio." Like many Russians, I was particularly captivated by Pushkin. In addition to his novels in poetry and prose, he composed numerous short poems. I was fascinated by the beauty of his language, the suspense he created in his novels, his vivid descriptions of places, actions, and events, and his ability to condense his thoughts into just a few lines. Of the favorite poems I remember from my school days, most are by Pushkin and Lermontov. Pushkin was, of course, famous for his many amorous conquests, and I eagerly read his love poems and envied what I thought was his bold and romantic approach to women.

We studied many other wonderful fiction writers and playwrights, including Derzhavin, Griboiedov, Ostrovsky, Gogol, Tolstoy, and Chekhov, usually discussing only the content and "social significance" of their work. Conspicuously absent from our reading list were extensive works by Dostoevsky, whom I had discussed with my father; only passages of his works were included in a volume of short extracts from the writings by Russian authors. The teachers produced vague explanations for this omission. In later years I wondered whether the authorities felt that Dostoevsky's religious views presented too serious a challenge to their beliefs, and whether his descriptions of Tsarist prisons were too close to the Soviet reality for comfort. Recently I found no lesser authority than Stalin himself confirming that the omission had not been accidental. Referring to Dostoevsky, he told Milovan Djilas, a leading Yugoslav Communist: "A great writer and a great reactionary. We are not publishing him because he is a bad influence on the youth."[22]

In the higher grades we switched to more contemporary Soviet literature, including works by Sholohov, Gorky, and Mayakovsky. I almost landed in serious trouble in the tenth grade when we studied Sholohov's novel, *Podniataia Tselina,* or Virgin Soil. One of the characters was a hard-working farmer who was eventually persuaded by a counterrevolutionary not to support the collective farm. The teacher's interpretation of the author's message was that the farmer should be severely punished. I felt that in recognition of past services, he should be forgiven his opposition and convinced through discussions to come back into the fold of the collective farm. I don't know what the other students felt about the situation; most just watched passively as I argued my points with the teacher. Two students strongly argued that anyone who was even temporarily swayed by counterrevolution was not a reliable member of society. "If it happened once, it will happen again," they said, "and one cannot trust a potential enemy of the people." As

22. Milovan Djilas, *Conversations with Stalin* (New York: Harcourt Brace Jovanovich, 1962), p. 157.

the classroom discussion proceeded, I noticed the frightened expression on most students' faces. It did not take me long to realize that I was on dangerous ground, and I brought the debate to an end. Free thought and free speech were not tolerated in Russia, and the slightest deviation from the Communist Party line brought severe punishment. Defending even a fictional enemy of the people in a seemingly innocent classroom discussion could have resulted in imprisonment for my father and me, and I think I realized this barely in time.

Our study of the Soviet Constitution in the seventh grade provided a beautiful illustration of Soviet propaganda. In our weekly classes we analyzed that document's articles and compared them with related practices in the Western countries. It must be difficult for a Westerner brought up in the democratic tradition to understand the hypocrisy of those studies and the fact that all students accepted the teacher's words without question. I don't know how many of my classmates believed the subject matter. I certainly did not, but I kept quiet.

The Soviet Constitution boldly proclaimed Soviet citizens' right to free speech, and the teacher stated that this was not the case in the West, where capitalists controlled the press and workers could not voice their grievances. We were told that the capitalist countries exercised censorship of mail, but that that was not the case in the Soviet Union. Although few of us knew what the Western practices were, we all realized that what was taught about the Soviet Union did not correspond to reality. Yet somehow the two incompatible positions reconciled themselves in the students' minds in much the same way that people accepted Communist slogans describing our happy lives in a workers' paradise in the face of daily repression, suffering, and hunger.

One paragraph of the Constitution stands out in my mind. It described the emblem of the Soviet Union, the hammer and sickle inside a circle of wheat bound by a ribbon displaying the names of all Soviet republics. The emblem, the teacher said, symbolized the nature of the Soviet Union: the hammer and sickle proclaiming the brotherhood of the workers and peasants, the sheaf of wheat showing the peaceful pursuits and brotherhood of all republics. "Much as the imperialists try to hide it, the capitalist national emblems also represented the nature of their countries," the teacher continued. Those emblems were bloodthirsty animals and birds. The British lion and the American eagle illustrate the true predatory character of their imperialist masters, we were told, and the emblem of the Tsarist regime, blissfully replaced by the Communist system, was a double-headed eagle, inadvertently revealing the ultimate villainy of pre-Revolutionary Russia. It was hard to argue with that impeccable logic. Although such explanations may seem comical today, those crude indoctrination methods were persuasive to many Russians, who were denied access to alternate points of view. Here is how Richard Pipes describes Soviet propaganda:[23]

> Propaganda was not a Bolshevik invention, of course. . . . The novelty of what the Bolsheviks did lay in the centrality of propaganda in Soviet life: previously used to touch up or to distort reality, in Communist Russia it became a surrogate reality. Communist propaganda strove, and to a surprising extent succeeded, in creating a fictitious world, side by side with that of ordinary experience and in stark contradiction to it, which Soviet citizens were required to pretend to believe. This was made possible by the monopoly the Communist Party secured over sources of information and opinion. The effort was undertaken on so vast a scale, with such ingenuity and determination, that in time the imaginary world it projected eclipsed for many Soviet citizens the living reality.

I liked history and geography, and both subjects were taught thoroughly. My only problem was that we had to memorize many facts, and that meant a lot of studying, which I did not like to do. We covered history from the dawn of humanity to current events. The facts were important, but their interpretation carried equal weight. As was to be expected, we were taught that the entire human history was a prelude to the Communist Revolution, which was to fulfill all aspirations and potentials of mankind. Just as we studied the alleged differences between the Soviet Constitution and constitutions of the West,

23. Richard Pipes, *Russia Under the Bolshevik Regime* (New York: Harcourt Brace Jovanovich, 1962), p. 157.

so were historical facts compared with the existing situation in the Soviet Union. For example, we discussed the treatment of slaves in ancient times in conjunction with the safeguards embodied in the Soviet Constitution but not in comparison with modern working conditions in other countries, leaving the impression that only the Communist Revolution had ended the abuse of the underprivileged masses.

Geography was relatively immune from heavy-handed propaganda, but it brought us a measure of frustration. We had good wall maps of the world, which created an illusion of accessibility to other parts of the planet. In reality, we were not allowed to travel more than about fifty miles within our region of Siberia. I had to content myself with merely finding Paris, London, and other great cities of Western Europe on the map. The study of foreign countries reaffirmed for me the existence of places where people led normal lives without NKVD control. I envied them and harbored hopes of one day joining that world. I also felt that the inhabitants of those faraway places were endowed with almost superhuman qualities: They seemed more dignified, more capable, more cultured, and, because they had built a better world, more deserving of good fortune than we were.

Despite my interest in geography, I was bored by the need to memorize populations of foreign cities, lengths of rivers, and heights of mountains. Somehow, however, I always found ways of getting good marks without studying all those statistics. In one geography test, for example, I used the Russian passion for propaganda against the system. Coming to the examination room completely unprepared, I worried that I might have to repeat the course the following year yet—quite unexpectedly—I was awarded the highest grade. Year-end examinations were oral rather than written. The teachers wrote three questions on slips of paper and put the slips on a table, blank side up; each student then selected a slip at random. Fifteen to twenty minutes were allowed to examine the questions, study the wall maps, and prepare answers. The three questions that I drew were:

    1. What is the commercial output of Byelorus?

    2. Describe Pamir and Pamiro-Alai.

    3. What is the climate of the Amur *(Priamurie)* region?

I did not remember studying these topics, so I improvised, reasoning that the most likely product of Byelorus would be agriculture. I expounded on the great agricultural achievements under Stalin, the happiness of the peasants on collective farms, and the efficient machinery that the Soviet government provided under Stalin's guidance. The examiners were sufficiently impressed with my knowledge and attitude to interrupt my answer and ask me to proceed to the next question.

Knowing nothing about Pamir and Pamiro-Alai except that they are mountains in the southern part of the Soviet Union, I quickly found them on the map. The heights of the mountains were clearly marked, and I discovered that the highest peaks were named after Lenin and Stalin. Anything to do with those two Soviet leaders, of course, provided ready-made material, and while I don't remember exactly what I said, no doubt I compared the tall mountains to the lofty heights to which the Communist Party, under Lenin's and Stalin's leadership, was taking the Soviet people and setting an example for the rest of the world.

It is amusing to follow the changes in the political climate of the Soviet Union and today's Russia by examining the various names given what was then Peak Stalin. A 1932–1933 survey confirmed the mountain height at 7,495 meters, USSR's highest point and surpassing even Peak Lenin, which reached a mere 7,134 meters. Then known as Garmo Peak, it naturally was renamed Stalin Peak. In 1962, with Stalin discredited after his death, the mountain was renamed Peak Communism. In 1998, after the breakup of the Soviet Union, which left the Pamir range located in independent Tajikistan, the mountain acquired the designation Ismail Somoni Peak, after the founder of the first Samanide State over a thousand years ago.

Returning to the examination, I had to answer my third question without Stalin's help, for even a man endowed with his extraordinary abilities could not control climate. *Priamurie* refers to the area around the Amur River (the largest in Asia), located in the southeastern corner of the former Soviet Union. Fortunately I remembered that Siberian tigers live in the Amur region of Russia. Although years later I learned that these tigers thrive in snow, at the time of the examination I assumed they, like their Bengali cousins, needed a much more temperate climate—an

1942: A tumultuous year on many fronts. German offensives in Russia and Africa were successful initially, but towards the end of the year Allied troops recaptured part of the territory occupied by the Nazis. The first thousand-bomber British air raid (targeting Cologne) took place on May 30. Stalin and Churchill met in Moscow on August 12. The battle for Stalingrad began on September 19, and on November 13, U.S. troops invaded North Africa. In January SS Leader Heydrich held the Wannsee Conference to coordinate a "Final solution of the Jewish question." In June mass murder of Jews by gassing began at Auschwitz. Professor Enrico Fermi set up an atomic reactor in Chicago on December 2.

anomaly in otherwise cold Siberia—and that is what I described. The region does indeed have a moderate climate because of its location in southern Siberia and its proximity to the Pacific Ocean, and apparently my description was persuasive enough to win over my examiners.

The other subject through which I occasionally bluffed my way was German. All Russian children had to study a foreign language; German was the most common, and the only alternative offered in our region. Many students objected to studying the language of the sworn enemies of Russia, especially when the country was engaged in a bitter war against the Nazis. Our teachers countered this resistance with a quotation from Lenin (always a persuasive argument): "You cannot defeat your enemy without knowing his language." The teachers did not know German well, however, and occasionally when I could not remember a particular word in German, I would say it in Polish, making sure that I confined my deception to words without similar-sounding expressions in Russian. Most of the time I got away with it.

In 1943, when I turned thirteen, we moved to Vasilevskii Priisk. My school was located there, and I no longer had to commute by train. For the first few months we lived in a small "house," called *zemlanka* (from the word *zemla*, meaning soil). The hut was built into the side of a large hill, with only the front wall and part of the roof exposed to outside air—a heat-efficient way of constructing a dwelling. We shared our small shelter, which had a tiny central kitchen, completely dominated by a brick oven, and two side rooms, with a Russian family. I remember that dwelling vividly, because while we lived there, the authorities suddenly demanded that we accept Soviet passports and become Soviet citizens. This development provoked many days and nights of soul searching. Although I have traveled widely since those days, I have never heard of a country forcing its nationality upon foreign citizens. On the contrary, it is usually difficult, and often impossible, for immigrants to become citizens of their new land. I suppose this policy might be considered yet another illustration of how different and unattractive the values of the Soviet state were.

The consequences of becoming Soviet nationals would be catastrophic, we feared, but rejecting the NKVD's latest demands was perhaps an even greater danger. We had already been told that individuals caught without approved documents were subject to punishment under a law prescribing a two-year prison sentence. This perverse logic qualified us as violators, since our prewar Polish papers apparently were not valid in the Soviet Union. The Soviets, of course, had banished us to Siberia without bothering to document our existence with official certificates, and now they were about to use that omission as an excuse—as if they needed one—to thrust their perverse nationality upon us in violation of the 1941 Sikorski-Mayski London[24] agreement, originally designed to free us from their bondage. At the same time, we shivered at the possibility that accepting a Soviet passport, and thus relinquishing our Polish roots, would permanently seal our future in Russia. That fate was too horrible to contemplate, especially since the "amnesty" we had been granted following the German invasion of Russia had rekindled our hopes for eventual deliverance. There was also the terrifying possibility that the question had been posed to test our loyalty and that a wrong answer—like our choice to return home in 1940, which the Communists interpreted as our hostility toward them—would land us in a situation even more lethal than acceptance of the Soviet nationality or two years in a Soviet jail.

---

24. Anne Applebaum, *Gulag, a History* (New York: Doubleday, 2003), p. 49.

The dilemma weighed heavily on both our minds, but I am afraid I was not much help to my father. I trusted his judgment, and left the choice of accepting or rejecting Soviet nationality entirely in his hands. Finally, on the eve of the deadline, we could no longer just debate the issue; that crucial judgment had to be made. That evening lives in memory, for we knew our choice could affect the rest of our lives—perhaps even ending them. I cooked our usual dinner. Apart from our supply of cabbage, we had the means to prepare only three dishes during most of our life in Siberia: porridge, primitive macaroni, and boiled potatoes. Porridge was the simplest to cook: merely throw the cereal into a saucepan and boil the water, adding salt when available. Pasta required more effort: mix flour with water, knead the mixture, and roll it with a bottle, then shred it with a knife before boiling. Cooking potatoes, of course, was simply a matter of peeling, boiling, and mashing with a fork. That fateful evening I prepared porridge.

For a long time we sat in silence. I was now a teenager and better able to sense impending danger. On my father's tortured face, I saw an expression of abject fear, utter helplessness, and resigned surrender. His glazed eyes seemed to contemplate some distant object, as if he wished to be transported away from our miserable surroundings into another, more forgiving reality. He was a man of action, but not immune from despondency and despair. For my part, I examined our room as if to take stock of our situation: It was tiny, with bare walls and living space barely twice the size of the one narrow bed we had to share. Except for a small table and two primitive chairs, it had no other furniture. In one corner rested a neat pile of our worldly possessions, all of which, including our clothing, utensils, cutlery, and a few mementos from Warsaw, would not be too heavy for us to carry on a long march. The porridge that I had just prepared and two spoons rested on our table. We had no plates and always retrieved our food directly from the pot, drawing an imaginary line through the center of the container to gauge the size of our individual portions. The skimpy, squalid surroundings emphasized our helplessness and isolation. We had been left with so little and yet, in addition to coping with our daily hardships, we now had to face this new crisis that loomed like a tidal wave over our heads. Until now our captors had determined our fate. Now, imposing an even greater indignity, they were forcing us to choose between two horrible alternatives—almost like telling us to dig our own graves.

My father lifted his spoon and dug into the saucepan. "Whom do we bother, sitting here and quietly eating our porridge?" he inquired painfully. "Why don't they leave us alone? We have never harmed anyone; is it too much to ask just to be allowed to lead our wretched lives, such as they are, in this cruel, miserable Siberia? Why are we being tested again? Will there be no end to our trials?" Once again he looked into a distance, obviously not expecting me to answer his questions. I think we both knew what our decision would be. We had come to it during many sleepless nights but were too frightened to confirm it openly, perhaps hoping against hope that not resolving the problem prematurely would drive it away.

Like most members of our exile community, my father decided to accept the Soviet passport. If our loyalties were being tested again, that would be the "right" answer. Despite the risk of being stuck in Siberia for the rest of our lives, the alternative of facing a two-year prison term, with its inherently high mortality rate, could be even worse—possibly bringing destruction upon us immediately. And, indeed, the people who refused the passports were promptly arrested. All of them—at least those who survived—applied for Soviet passports within weeks of their confinement. The NKVD took their time before eventually issuing the requested documents to those late applicants, and by the time they were finally released from prison, they were in a pitiful mental and physical state.

Uncharacteristically, the documents proclaiming our Soviet nationality were not long in coming. We regarded them with disdain and fear, as though they would rob us of our personalities and wipe out our past. We did not know how they would affect our future, but the current reality still demanded our full attention. Ignoring distant consequences, we gradually resumed our daily Siberian struggles.

Two other incidents come to mind from our stay in the small *zem-lanka*. The first—not nearly as perilous as the pressure to acquire Soviet nationality, though still unpleasant—was our continuous fight with bedbugs. These horrible insects actually live inside walls; their German name, *wanzen,* from the word *wand,* for wall, is more appropriate than its English equivalent. It was almost impossible to get rid of them. Every night they crawled out of the walls, climbed the legs of the bed, and drank our blood. No amount of whitewashing of the walls made any difference. We moved the bed away from the wall, to no avail. We placed containers filled with water under each leg of the bed, which merely diverted the insects to the ceiling from which they dropped onto us. We killed dozens of them in the middle of the night, but they were back in force hours later.

The second, somewhat humorous incident, involved a severe tongue-lashing I received from a good friend of my father's, Mr. Muszel. When the two of them played chess, almost invariably the game degenerated into loud arguments. My father, the better player, often accused his opponent of cheating by changing the position of his pieces on the board. The provocation for this complaint was Mr. Muszel's habit of lifting one of his chessmen, holding it in the air for a long time, and then placing it on a convenient square—apparently not always a legal one. The arguments always revolved around the starting position of his pieces. One day Mr. Muszel came over when my father was out and, expecting an easy win, challenged me to a game. As things started going badly for him, he became progressively more agitated. Then I discovered that both his bishops were on white squares, a position that could only have been achieved by illegal moves while I was looking away. I burst out laughing and impolitely used one of my father's favorite Polish expressions, "Only a goat moves this way," with the implied but silent conclusion, "but not a chess piece." Mr. Muszel jumped out of his chair, accused me of bad manners, and stormed out of the house. Curiously, few of these heated chess quarrels, like similar arguments over cards, had any effect on friendships. We led our lives on two levels: one, the daily struggle for survival, the other, clinging to vestiges of our previous life by daydreaming, playing chess, debating serious issues, or even organizing musical evenings. Most of us managed to retain a sense of proportion, and disappointments and disagreements encountered in the second, almost imaginary, life seldom rose to the level of destructive feuds.

We left our *zemlanka* after a few months and moved into a big barracks with about twenty rooms on either side of a central corridor. Initially, the entire building was occupied by members of our Polish community. The rooms were separated from one another by flimsy partitions, but each room had its own cooking stove, which also served as a source of heat. It was a relatively pleasant place, with more privacy than in our previous dwellings. Although the living conditions were still primitive and the partitions, though they reached the ceiling, were poor sound barriers, living together with forty Polish families gave us a sense that our community—our "little Poland"—was separated from the ugly reality of the outside world. The teenagers among us formed a closely knit group—so much so, that I still correspond with one of them, who now lives in Sweden.

The mascot of the barracks was a medium-sized dog with reddish fur. No one knew where the dog came from, but we all adopted him, and he adopted us. Despite the scarcity of food, someone always fed him, and he chose different families at random for his sleeping quarters. Sometimes he slept in the hallway, occasionally he was absent at night. He knew every inhabitant of the barracks and growled at strangers. We all believed he could distinguish among Polish, Yiddish, and Russian speakers, and would tolerate only the first two languages. A happy animal, he contributed to our feeling of community. The makeup of our group in the barracks changed radically over the next two years. A few people died from exhaustion or illness, while others were moved to different parts of our region. Gradually, Russians replaced most of the Polish families, until eventually there were only two Polish families left: my father and I, and the five-member family of my father's chess opponent, the Muszels. The atmosphere, too, changed drastically.

The Russian families were headed by either women or old men not fit enough to be drafted into the army. The heads of families did not get along with each other nearly as well as the Poles had, and friendships became less common than feuds.

An awful woman with two small children about three and four years old lived in one of the rooms adjacent to ours. One day I caught her trying to steal a small bag of flour from us. We had built a shelf on one of the walls, high against the ceiling, and stored bags of flour and cereal there, which were practically our only source of food besides bread, which we bought at the store. She was trying to hook one of the bags with a stick she had maneuvered through a space between the wall and our oven. She was making good progress at pulling the bag along the shelf when, fortunately, I returned home and caught her red-handed. She quickly withdrew the stick, but did not seem the least embarrassed.

This woman showed no love for her own children, screaming at them and complaining almost daily as they clung stubbornly to life. Presumably addressing the neighbors or maybe just shouting to herself, she would cry out loudly, *"Chevo ne podyhayut?"* ("Why won't they just die?"). She used the verb "die" as it applies to animals, not people, and it wasn't just a figure of speech: She really wanted them dead. Although constantly mistreated, they—remarkably—proved too resilient for her, at least while we still lived there.

In contrast, our neighbor on the other side was a woman who adored her three small children. Quiet and pleasant, she kept her room clean and the children neat. One day I heard her screaming, "Help, help, my child is dying!" Rushing into her room, I saw her two-year-old baby shaking in wild, rapid convulsions in her arms. The spasms lasted for about a minute before the child went limp and died. Years later in America, when my wife Olga called to tell me that Lisa, our one-year old daughter, had a high fever and was seized with convulsions, I tore home from the office with that scene in mind, fearful that Lisa too was dying. Fortunately, by the time I arrived the convulsions were over, and Lisa was lying peacefully in her crib, exhausted but actually smiling.

The Russian presence in the barracks had a profound effect on the dog's behavior. He seemed completely bewildered, disappearing for several days and then returning to visit the two remaining Polish families. We tried to feed him, but we did not have enough food between us to satisfy him. I knew that dogs were used for pulling sleds, and I thought of making a harness so the dog could help me haul firewood from the mountains, but I never went through with my plan, realizing that one animal would not be of much help. He grew visibly thinner and his visits became less frequent, then one day he left for the last time. Shortly afterward I heard that someone had killed him for meat. I had heard of such cases before, and I believe that the report was most likely true.

The other Polish family in our barracks engaged in gold trading, which attracted the attention of one of the village policemen, or "militiamen," as they were called in Russia. (The term "police" evidently had capitalist or Tsarist connotations, whereas a "militia" was considered to be an organization of the people.) The Polish family was singled out for frequent visits by the militiaman, who demanded petty bribes and hot food. If he detected any resistance, he produced what he claimed was a search warrant. That was enough to grant him whatever he wanted. He occasionally came to our room, but since he could not accuse us of illegal activities and my cooking would not have been to his liking, he eventually left us alone.

There were no bedbugs in our new quarters, and one of our few pleasures was going to bed at night. We were usually weary at the end of the day, and sliding under warm blankets to sleep was one of the few gifts of our Siberian existence. We had brought from Warsaw a pair of down-filled covers made of beautiful Chinese silk. I still remember when they were made before the war: Two seamstresses took over our apartment for a few days to quilt them. One side was pink, the other blue, and both colors were bright and rich. They looked so vivid in contrast to the drab Siberian reality that my parents encased them in plain covers to hide them from the Russian officials, who would surely have considered them opulent objects clearly belonging to someone wealthy and therefore predisposed to counterrevolutionary activities. The down covers were well made and kept us warm even in the coldest weather. Equally important, they provided moral support by reminding us of our cherished past.

Sleep afforded not just physical rest but privacy, and—even more important—a blessed escape from reality. The pleasure of going to bed was so great that both my father and I often emitted spontaneous loud cries of delight on retiring at night. I never had trouble falling asleep, especially after days filled with physical labor. I slept so deeply that on one occasion a friend who was staying with us arrived after I fell asleep and could not wake me by banging on the door with all his might. He woke several of our neighbors who tried to help by striking the walls, but even that was to no avail, and he spent the night sleeping on the floor with other people.

Yet, I did wake up one night when I heard my father groaning as if overcome with pain. He was clearly distraught and I asked him what was wrong. At the time he was working as an accountant for the food distribution organization. The previous day he had been sent to audit the month-end inventory in the village food store and had discovered shortages. The woman who ran the store pleaded with him not to report the shortfall, fearing arrest and a long prison sentence under appalling conditions, with a very low probability of survival. He felt sorry for the woman, whom we all knew, and agreed to sign the papers stating that everything was in order. The hope was that new transactions the following day would make it hard to prove what the inventory had been at the end of the month. Unfortunately, there were occasions when a second inventory was taken by another auditor during the night to check on the first one. If shortages and falsified papers were discovered, both the shopkeeper and the first auditor would be imprisoned. My father was going through agony, fearing that a second audit might be taking place at that very moment.

It must have been two or three in the morning when I suggested that we go to the store to take a look. He readily agreed, because we only had to approach the shop to see if the lights were on. Taking inventory required several hours, and a darkened store would signal that no second check was taking place. We worried that someone might see us close to the shop, which could arouse suspicion, but we decided that the risk was worth taking for the sake of our peace of mind. If questioned, we could always claim sleeplessness.

Leaving the barracks, we closed the door behind us, but then my father stopped, his face distorted with fear. He believed in premonition and by then he was a confirmed pessimist, and he convinced himself that another audit was taking place. He stood still for a while, preferring uncertainty to the awful certainty of bad news that would seal his fate and mine. His visage resembled that of someone who had been unjustly accused and convicted of a heinous crime and was now awaiting a stiff sentence.

Luckily he recovered his composure and we proceeded to survey the village for any signs of activity. Siberian days can be indescribably cold, but the nights are even colder, and this was one of those unbearable nights. A few silver birches scattered through the village, almost as white as the surrounding snow and inexplicably not yet cut down for firewood, stood perfectly still, even their bare branches and the thinnest twigs frozen stiff. Motionless and clear, the air was so heavy it gave the impression of a bitterly cold, dense fluid which, when inhaled in more than the lightest breaths, cut painfully into our nostrils.

The cloudless sky was studded with stars, and a brilliant moon illuminated the village both with direct light and by reflection from the shimmering, pristine layer of snow. We had seen the village hundreds of times, but now it looked foreign and dangerous, a disarray of dilapidated log cabins worn by decades of Siberian winters and neglect by transitory tenants. All was quiet, and no light shone in any house, no smoke rose from any chimney. We took a few cautious steps then stopped, frightened by the sound of the snow crunching underfoot, which seemed to grow louder as we moved forward. We dared not even speak, afraid of adding to the noise.

Suddenly my father uttered a loud, painful cry. "The lights are burning," he exclaimed, "the lights are on!" He seemed about to faint. I didn't see any light in the window, but then I realized what had given him such a fright. A telegraph pole stood in front of the store, and its smooth surface was reflecting the bright moonlight. At first, still in shock, he was too disoriented to understand my explanation. When he finally realized we were safe, he thanked me profusely for suggesting our night trek and for recognizing the reflection. His gratitude almost suggested that I was the one to be thanked for the absence of the second inspection.

My father's leniency towards the shopkeeper did not go unrewarded. The grateful woman, who had probably been selling food on the black market, occasionally gave me a hundred grams more bread than I was entitled to. But her freedom did not last long. A few months later she and a baker were arrested and paraded before a crowd of people waiting for a train. An NKVD operative mounted an improvised soapbox and delivered a scathing speech denouncing the woman and the baker. He kept repeating a favorite phrase: "They stole, and cheated the workers. They stole, and cheated the workers." The harangue lasted for at least ten minutes while the hapless prisoners stood handcuffed under guard in the most conspicuous spot at the station. This public display and humiliation was, of course, a well-honed, widely used tactic designed to blame individuals for all the ills of the Communist economy and to deflect criticism of the state. Although sorry for the arrested couple, we worried for days that the shopkeeper would denounce my father, but she never did. Indeed, she had no reason to add to her record another incident of collusion with an outside inspector.

Her behavior was, of course, by no means unusual. In order to survive, most of us had to turn to activities that were illegal and carried a high degree of risk. I occasionally engaged in illicit transactions involving gold, food, and transportation. Panning for gold was widespread and actively encouraged by the authorities, as long as the proceeds were submitted to a special State store in exchange for precious food. Keeping the gold or selling it elsewhere was illegal, but a small underground network of prospectors and buyers sprang up despite the threat of heavy penalties. My transactions started with a cash purchase of gold from a prospector. I then exchanged the nuggets for butter, sugar, flour, and salt in the special store and took the products to Bodaybo, where I sold them to Polish acquaintances; they, in turn, disposed of them for a profit on the black market. The markup on these transactions was usually two to one—not bad if you ignored the risk and the small size of each deal. In order not to arouse suspicion, the packages I transported had to be small, and the weight of each shipment seldom exceeded three or four kilograms. But even those quantities enabled us to exceed our monthly rations, the profits allowing us to buy more gold which provided food for our own consumption.

I looked forward to those ventures because each trading transaction presented me with a challenge and a new adventure. Obviously I did not fully appreciate the dangers involved, and every time I embarked on the journey I had to convince my father that I had a good plan. He, of course, provided the initial cash. Buying gold was relatively safe because I bought it from people with whom I had established a trusting relationship. Since I also panned for gold, I could pass off the purchased metal as my own at the State store. Transporting the goods was the most dangerous part of the whole procedure. Either my transgressions went undiscovered or the authorities decided not to bother with such petty matters. They may even have considered the activities of youngsters like me to be helpful, since they improved the efficiency of food distribution. Nevertheless, I always took elaborate precautions, such as concealing the goods on my body or carrying very small packages to be as inconspicuous as possible.

Purchasing tickets for our little train was time-consuming and increased the chance that my smuggling would be detected. No lines ever formed at the ticket window, and unless you elbowed your way through the crowd, you were left behind. Realizing that the flow of people at the ticket window followed a predictable pattern, however, I soon developed an efficient technique for buying rail tickets. Those who had already bought a ticket moved backwards away from the window, pushing back individuals located behind them and creating a void which was filled by people at the sides. All I had to do was take a position next to the wall where the ticket window was located, and I would be pushed toward the ticket seller without any effort on my part. Since then, I have observed that similar "hydraulic laws" rule crowd behavior in many parts of the world, and the technique has come in handy for obtaining tickets in other unruly situations.

Later I found an even better method for boarding the train: I developed friendships with the conductors and simply bribed them, eliminating the need to buy tickets for my trips. The act of bribing, however, required considerable skill, since it involved passing money on a crowded train without arousing the suspicion of other passengers.

In short, people become accustomed to living with fear and accept it as a fact of life. My illicit trips added to our ever-present danger, but I learned to tolerate the situation. The extreme optimists among us—and I was in their ranks—just assumed nothing bad would happen, despite our very presence in Siberia, which itself proved that something bad had *already* happened. I devoted little time to logical analysis of this condition, although I am sure my father suffered enormous psychological pain over our predicament.

I was not, however, immune from depression, and during one of my "business" trips I finally came close to despair, feeling I could no longer cope with the tension and the everpresent danger. After selling my contraband goods in Bodaybo to a fellow exile, I stayed with him overnight and shared his bed. He was a big man and a restless sleeper. He snored and woke me every few minutes with his incessant movement, sometimes almost rolling on top of me, sometimes pushing me against the edge of the bed, and I had to hold on hard to resist being pushed to the floor. Sleep was the only refuge from our harsh reality and that day I was deprived of even that modest luxury. In my misery, I came to the conclusion that I just wanted to escape—escape the hardships, escape the illegal trading, escape the hard work, escape the need to fight for survival, escape the hopeless future. But escape how? I knew I could not change our condition, but then I had an idea: If I could get sick, that would provide an escape of sorts, or at least a departure from the daily routine and responsibilities. After an especially strong push from my companion, I decided to go to the outhouse. I put on my felt boots but no clothing over my underwear, then spent as much time in the bitter Siberian night as my body could stand—actually only a few minutes—and that, I thought, would be enough to make me sick. But I did not get sick at all. Perhaps it was just as well, for when I woke up the next morning, my dark mood was gone. I remained healthy—in fact, I don't remember ever being ill during our stay in Russia.

I did have one close call. During one of the trips, I stayed in Bodaybo for a couple of days after disposing of my products. Anxious to keep my father informed, I sent him a note in a sealed envelope, reporting on my successful trip. I wrote my note in a code, which I later realized was easy to decipher, and gave it to a fellow Pole who planned to return to our village before me. A few days after returning home, I asked my father whether he had understood the note. He told me he had received an opened envelope without any contents. He had not been surprised, assuming that either I had been unable to find writing paper or I was sending him a sign that everything went well, thinking it safer not to write anything. There was no doubt in my mind that I had enclosed a note. The man who carried the letter had been rumored to be an informer, and the note's disappearance convinced me that he had given the letter to the local NKVD man, who probably intended to save it for use against my father and me at a later date. After that incident, I watched my courier carefully and decided that the rumors about him were true. I never found proof that he was an informer, but several years after the war a woman in Israel, whom I had known well in Russia and trusted implicitly, confessed that she had occasionally provided the authorities with "innocuous" information on "who said what to whom during some of our discussions." It was, she rationalized, a way for her to get an occasional loaf of bread.

Her confession and the missing note, which thankfully the *Komendant* had not used against us, sadly confirmed that the Russian authorities had managed to recruit informers among our Polish community. I would like to believe that the traitors were few in number, though we suffered from the presence of other unscrupulous characters—even outright thieves. I knew of only two such individuals—one of them, unfortunately, from personal experience.

We seldom knew when bread was going to be delivered to our village store and frequently long lines formed in anticipation of its arrival. Latecomers often handed their ration cards to fellow Poles who had secured a better place in line so that they could buy bread for them. The Russians in line did not object to this practice, even though it delayed their transactions; perhaps they admired our sense of solidarity. I was both a recipient of such favors and also a purchaser on behalf of others. In general the system operated smoothly, but at the beginning of one month a fellow exile bought my bread but blatantly kept my card, claiming he had already returned it to me. I was still a child, while he was a large, strong man, so physical action was out of the question. It was his word against mine and there was nothing I could do but suffer the painful deprivation and share my father's rations for the rest of the month.

The loss of my main source of nourishment was bad enough, but the outrage had other implications. We were in a foreign land under terrible circumstances, and mutual support in our exile community was vital to our survival. Being part of the group reminded us of our previous life in Poland and fed the hope of eventual deliverance. Destroying that trust had a devastating effect on me and caused emotional anguish. Was there no one we could trust, even in our own group?

In addition to sponsoring my trading treks to Bodaybo, my father was involved in a couple of other significant illegal transactions. A Russian watchmaker had developed a method for melting gold and making gold rings. I had panned fifteen grams of gold from the ground around the mine, and my father commissioned him to use this gold to make a ring. This would give us something of value that, we hoped, could be hidden from the Russian authorities and used in case of need. It was illegal to possess the metal in its raw form, but if the ring was discovered, we could claim that we had brought it from Poland. Melting gold was also illegal and carried a long prison term. The watchmaker agreed to make the ring and carved my father's initials in it ("S" was my father's middle initial). I still have it today, weighing 15 grams, it is now worth only around $200.

It is sobering to think that my father literally risked his life for such a small sum, but in Russia in 1943 that ring would have yielded enough for us to live for several months. The poor watchmaker, however, was eventually caught. He pleaded with my father to confirm to the authorities that the only gold he melted was from jewelry he had purchased from our friends, but my father was reluctant to get involved in any defense, since his statements would have been false and therefore dangerous to us. Fortunately my father was never asked to provide any information. The watchmaker was eventually released, and shortly afterwards left the area, a shaken and broken man.

Trading in U.S. dollars also earned income for members of our exiled community in Siberia. A few enterprising individuals had illegally brought dollars from Poland, and they were highly valued in Russia. It is amusing to consider the relative valuation of bills with different denominations. While I don't recall their actual worth in rubles, I remember that a five dollar bill was worth more than five times the value of a one dollar bill, but that a ten dollar bill was worth less than ten one dollar notes. The reason for that anomaly was that a five dollar bill was easier to hide than five one dollar bills, while the value of a ten dollar bill was so great that it lacked liquidity, because it would be extremely difficult to

find a buyer with such enormous purchasing power. A currency market, it seems, can be efficient even in the most unlikely places.

One of the most impressive money transfers I have ever seen was my father's transmittal of $300 from Siberia to New York in 1942. He gave one of our fellow Poles a small sum of money in Russia; in return, that man's relatives in New York paid $300—presumably a negotiated equivalent—to our distant cousin in the United States. Such a "transfer" was illegal and had to be arranged through highly censored mail. No prearranged code existed to communicate the transaction, but somehow the messages, undetected by Russian censors but comprehensible to our

1943 marked a major turning point of the war. In February Germans surrendered at Stalingrad in the first big defeat of Hitler's armies. In May Germans and Italians surrendered in North Africa. The Nazis staged a summer offensive in Russia but were beaten back by Soviet troops. In December the Soviets launched an offensive on the Ukrainian front. Allies captured Sicily in August and entered Naples in October. Italy surrendered on September 8 and declared war on Germany on October 13. In November Churchill, Roosevelt, and Stalin met at Teheran. The Jewish uprising in the Warsaw Ghetto (April-May) was defeated by Waffen SS troops. In June Himmler ordered the liquidation. of all Jewish ghettos in Poland.

respective relatives in New York, were conveyed in the letters sent. The result was that I had the grand sum of $300 available to me on my eventual arrival in England in 1947.

My father and I were better off than most people. Because he worked as an accountant in the State organization that supplied the stores and the cafeteria, he occasionally could acquire additional food. My work in the mines on Sundays and panning for gold in the summer gave us access to the special store, and my illegal trading expeditions to Bodaybo resulted in better provisioning of our little household. Despite all these projects, however, we often went to bed hungry. In fact, in addition to the standard exclamation, "When are we going to be able to reminisce about these times?" it was quite common for us, on going to bed, to ask ourselves, "Shall we ever see the time when we go to bed without being hungry?" Similarly, one of my father's favorite expressions on waking up was *Katorga się zaczyna,* which means *"Katorga* is starting." The word *katorga,* derived from the Greek word *katergon,* meaning "galley," is difficult to translate into English. It implies penal servitude and hard labor in a place of exile, without any hope of deliverance. He was half joking, of course, but it was a bitter joke with only slight exaggeration.

If we try hard enough, most of us can recall a particularly memorable feast in our lives. Mine came around 1943 in a special cafeteria in our village. Years later I would read a great deal about the so-called Soviet *"Nomenclatura"* and their status as the privileged class. The *Nomenclatura* counted among its ranks Communist Party functionaries, KGB officers, and other members of the ruling elite. They enjoyed a considerably higher standard of living than the average Soviet citizen, shopped in special stores, ate in special restaurants, and lived in better quarters. Even a few of our local officials were members of the *Nomenclatura,* but their status was so well hidden I was unaware that one of the small buildings in our village was devoted exclusively to serving this privileged class until one day my father gave me a pass to their exclusive cafeteria. He knew one of the women who worked there and had received the promise of a meal for me.

Having passed that small log building many times, I assumed it was an office, and of course no one asked questions about government offices. Entering the place was quite a revelation. I presented my pass and was shown into a room furnished with six small tables with chairs. The place seemed quiet, orderly and immaculately clean. The woman who knew my father worked in the kitchen, and she gave me a huge meal, adding several pieces of bread. Later in life I have been lucky enough to sample a number of excellent restaurants, but no dining experience can compare to the memory of that surprise meal, which probably consisted of cabbage borscht and undercooked meat and potatoes. The occasion was marred slightly by a diner at the adjacent table. He had several pieces of bread on a plate and, like any good Russian, ate bread with his meal. But when he got up he actually left a few pieces on the table. This was totally incomprehensible, for I could not understand how anyone could have enough bread to leave some behind. If today I saw a diner leaving a million-dollar tip for a server in an ordinary American restaurant, I would be less amazed than I was then by that incredible waste. I was sitting close enough to reach the precious food, but in that exclusive place devoted to serving *Nomenclatura* I was too frightened to move promptly. Before I had time to act, the waitress cleared the table and removed the abandoned, precious bread.

LEAVING SIBERIA

THE SUMMER of 1944 marked our fourth year in exile. We still hoped to return to Poland, but did not expect any changes in our situation until the end of the war. Then came wonderful news: We were told we could leave Siberia and travel westward to the European part of Russia. We could move closer to our homeland! Four years earlier the NKVD had informed us we had come to Siberia to die. If the Communists were wrong about that, they might be wrong about other things. The war was going well for the Allies, and we now dared to believe that it was only a matter of time before we would return to Poland.

There were, of course, many skeptics among us who worried that the Soviets would never allow us to go home, but we had grounds for optimism. Shortly after the 1941 German invasion, Stalin agreed to organize a Polish army in Russia under the command of General Anders. The soldiers were recruited from among Polish exiles in Siberia and other parts of the Soviet Union. After its formation, the army was allowed to move to Iran, which seemed a most encouraging precedent. If other Poles were allowed to wear Polish uniforms and leave Russia, we felt that we, too, had a chance to return to our homeland.

In January 1944 the Soviet Army reached Poland. In June Allied forces entered Rome and staged the D-Day landings on the Normandy coast. In July, Soviet troops liberated the Majdanek concentration camp, and the last use of gas chambers in Auschwitz occurred on October 30. Allies liberated Paris in August and reached the Siegfried Line in September. The Battle of the Bulge in the Ardennes took place between December 16 and 27. The Polish Home Army uprising against the Nazis started on August 1. With his troops across the river from Warsaw, Stalin halted the Soviet advance. The Nazis massacred the insurgent Poles, leaving the country defenseless against Soviet domination.

We did not know at the time that the departure of Anders' army followed disagreements between the Poles and the Russians. Stalin ordered the Poles to the German front before they had recovered from their ordeal in Soviet camps and before they were fully trained for combat. Despite the Poles' eagerness to fight the Germans, General Anders did not want Stalin to use Polish soldiers as cannon fodder, and he refused to rush his troops into battle. Shortly after, the Soviets cut the Polish Army's food rations. Eventually the Polish troops were allowed to leave the Soviet Union. Later, Anders' army fought against the Germans under British command and distinguished itself in a number of engagements, most notably in the battle of Montecasino in Italy.[25]

Stalin did not leave matters there, but organized another Polish Army in Russia by recruiting Poles who remained in his domain after the departure of Anders' troops. This time, however, he liberally sprinkled the army with Russian officers and put it under the command of a Russian general of Polish descent, one conveniently endowed with a Polish name: Marshal Rokosowski. This army fought alongside the Russians, forming part of the force that liberated Poland.

All of this activity bode well for us. We were now allies with the Russians and had reason to feel optimistic—though never quite sure—

___
25. A good reference book on the subject of Anders' Army is Harvey Sarnet, *General Anders and the Soldiers of the Second Polish Corps* (Cathedral City, Calif.: Brunswick Press, 1977).

about our prospects for repatriation to Poland after the war. To say that we were happy about our move west would be a gross understatement.

On the day of the move we gathered all our belongings, put most of them into burlap bags, and loaded them onto the narrow-gauge railroad cars that took us to Bodaybo, where we were housed temporarily in hastily improvised public quarters. A few days later we continued our journey on a large riverboat. The boat trip lasted perhaps a week. The weather was warm, the food plentiful, and the river and its surroundings beautiful. Most importantly, every day of progress downriver took us a day farther from a horrible part of our lives. We occasionally talked about the relatives we lost in Siberia and promised ourselves that some day we would return to exhume their bodies for burial in Poland. I doubt that anyone actually went back.

I joined a group of other young people in singing, telling stories, and dreaming about the future. The river wound its way through thick taiga forest, its straight, tall silver birches *(beryozy)* hugging the shore and receding reluctantly to make room for scant human habitation at intervals hundreds of miles apart. Occasionally, the boat stopped in seemingly uninhabited locations to take on logs as fuel for its steam engines. The logs, mysteriously stacked on riverbanks by unseen woodsmen living in hidden outposts, were heavy and took a long time to carry on board. Several of us in search of physical activity to relieve the monotony of our cramped floating quarters were eager to help the ship's crew. We loaded the fuel in pairs, carrying the three-foot logs on two horizontal poles. It was challenging to carry those huge piles along the wobbly inclined gangplanks that connected ship to shore. On reaching the deck, we would scream, *Poboisia Yama*! ("Watch out below!") before raising one of the carrying poles, lowering the other, and dumping the logs into an open hold. I was a frequent visitor to the boiler room, where I struck up a friendship with the stokers. It was thrilling for me to be allowed to hurl wooden logs into the ship's furnace.

Our group on the barge included many chess players, and we had several homemade chess sets. Someone soon organized a tournament that lasted for most of the trip. I was happy to finish among the top half-dozen players, but I was even more proud that my father won first place.

I don't remember the drive from the Lena River to Angara River; it must have been quick and uneventful. The trip down the Angara was fast, too. Our boat was bigger and faster than the vessel on the Lena, and the distance was appreciably shorter.

When we reached Irkutsk, we spent a few days in a transit camp. We all remembered the prison camp where we were held just four years earlier on our way to a Siberian exile. How different this camp was from the previous one! This time we were not surrounded by barbed wire, and there were no guard towers manned by armed soldiers. The barracks were clean, sanitation facilities adequate, water plentiful, a steam bath was readily accessible, and there was no shortage of food. For some reason the camp was awash in cans of eggplant in tomato sauce. I don't remember how the food tasted. I simply remember that it was plentiful, which was more important than its culinary merits.

Our train journey away from Irkutsk lasted several weeks. We didn't know where we were going, but no one seemed to care as long as we were rolling westward. We loaded our belongings into cattle cars similar to those that had transported us to Siberia, but this time we were less crowded and could keep the doors open or closed as we wished. Most important, we did not have to live under an armed escort. The train made frequent stops where we could use toilet facilities, replenish food and *kipiatok* (boiling water for tea), and take steam baths. The German invasion and Stalin's new dependence on Western support had made a dramatic difference.

Our first stop was sixty miles northwest of Irkutsk in Cheremhovo, where the train crew warned us that the town was infested with thieves. We visited the farmers' market and saw stands offering strawberries, raspberries, cucumbers, tomatoes, and other fruits and vegetables we had not seen since leaving Poland. There had been no stands in Bodaybo, where the summers were barely warm enough to grow potatoes and cabbage. We soon realized why Cheremhovo had earned a reputation for thievery. Teenagers lurked near the stands, waited until sellers were engaged with customers, and then grabbed handfuls of food. No one stopped them as they ran away. The thieves probably carried knives, and it would have been dangerous to interfere. In one incident in the marketplace, knives were drawn and waved threateningly, but fortunately they were not used before bystanders broke up the fight. The thievery and violence did not, however, keep me from my mission. Coming upon a basket of strawberries, I stared at them for long moments in a trance-like state before I could bring myself to put down money. They seemed like food for royalty, and I created quite a sensation when I brought them to the train.

There was little to do on this long journey away from Irkutsk, but I don't remember being bored or even wishing that the trip would end. Perhaps the enforced idleness would have been welcome to any teenage boy; perhaps, despite our welcome westward journey, we still feared the future, because until then we had always expected and usually received the worst. We were not, however, totally idle. There was a boy my age named Gienek in our railroad car, and as time passed we became close friends and partners in a commercial trading venture.

Looking back, I realize that Gienek and I were the only people on the train engaged in this trade. The financial rewards were insignificant, but we were caught up in the thrill of trading. Perhaps this and my illegal and dangerous commercial ventures in Bodaybo were early manifestations of my business interests. At that time I would never have admitted even to myself that such activity was anything but a passing fancy; to think of such trading as an occupation would have been tantamount to a crime in Russia. Trade was frowned upon by the Soviet authorities as "speculation," and the Russian meaning of the word *speculatsia* implies an illegal source of profits. Speculators *(speculanty)* were often jailed in Russia, primarily because the Communists did not understand the value of an efficient distribution system. To them, the creation of goods was the only useful economic activity. Everything else was deemed parasitic. This attitude contributed to the chronic food shortages in the Soviet Union. Collective farms were not efficient producers of grain to begin with, but, to make matters worse, often as much as 30 percent of their output was lost to decay due to the inability of the Russians to bring produce to market.

Gienek and I benefited on a tiny scale from the inefficiency of the Communist commercial distribution system. At every station people sold goods that were not available anywhere else. We started with a small sum of money—probably equivalent to a quarter or two—and bought articles at various stops. Most of the items we traded were hand-crafted wooden toys and articles of basic clothing. Our most profitable deal was a trade in knitted baby booties; we bought three or four home-made pairs and sold them at the next station—probably less than a hundred miles away—for four times our purchase price. Similar transactions kept us occupied throughout the trip. Of course we suffered some losses, but by and large the thrill of being in business and anticipating the trading opportunities at the next stop kept us amused.

The other diversion on our journey was learning geography from my father. He had been to most of the towns we were passing and had stories about them. I remembered that he had discussed this surreptitiously on the way to Siberia because then he had not wanted anyone to know of his former visits to those places. I had not been nearly as interested in his tales then as I was now on our return journey. He was still careful not to advertise his previous stay in Siberia, but this time I listened more closely, now being more mature and better able to understand them. I questioned him about Petropavlovsk, my mother's birthplace. We thought that some of her brothers might still live there, and my father asked several people at the railroad station about my mother's family, taking care not to betray our relationship with them. The Communists harbored deep suspicions about Soviet citizens who were related to foreigners, and a slip revealing my mother's origins could have brought danger to her Petropavlovsk relatives as well as to us. My father must have used a cover story that was sufficiently effective for him to learn that two of my uncles were still practicing medicine in Petropavlovsk. Years later, when they learned we had passed through their city, they told us we should have contacted them; they believed they had enough influence not to be accused of subversive sympathies.

Of course we had no way of knowing that in 1944, and we took the more cautious approach.

The other two highlights of the trip were Novosibirsk and Chelabinsk. We spent a full day in Novosibirsk, which was a huge city in comparison with anything we had seen for years. Even the sight of streetcars amazed us. I had seen streetcars in Warsaw, but for four years in Siberia, horses and reindeer had been the primary means of transportation. The sight of the busy streets of Novosibirsk assured us that we were approaching civilization. After about nine hundred miles additional westward travel we came to Chelabinsk, a town in the Ural Mountains, which form the symbolic border between Asia and Europe. Passing Chelabinsk gave us a great deal of comfort and the feeling that we were really about to rejoin the human race.

The train's final destination was Saratov, a town on the Volga River, four hundred and fifty miles southeast of Moscow. I don't remember if the train was split into sections there or whether it traveled south, dropping off people at different stations. We were taken to a small town, which by coincidence was called Krasnoarmieisk (Red Army Town), the same name as the gold-mining settlement where we had lived not long ago in Siberia. From there we were transferred by truck to Splavnuha—a small agricultural village in the vast Russian steppes. We did not know how long we would be kept there, or even if we would be allowed to leave, but the prospects were encouraging. All in all, our exit from Siberia provided a powerful emotional boost. We found that Rokosowski's Polish army, which included members of our small Siberian community, was now serving along with Russian troops in their offensive to liberate Poland. Wanda Wasilewska, a Polish writer, was allowed to organize a so-called "Union of Polish Patriots" *(Związek Polskich Patriotów)*, in which we became nominal members. The "Union" was clearly sponsored by Stalin and his authorities in the hope that the Poles repatriated from Russia would support the Soviet domination of Poland as a counterweight to the majority of Poles, who had survived the German occupation and were bitterly opposed to the forthcoming Communist rule. We harbored no illusions about this organization, and none of us wanted to see Russian domination of Poland, but its existence suggested a strong possibility that the Soviets would allow us to return home. Still, we could never be sure about our fate, and we assumed we would have to endure Russia for a long time before our hopes were realized.

A SOVIET FARM

BY THE TIME we reached Splavnuha, we had seen many Russian villages, mainly from the train but sometimes more closely during various stops on our journey west. We were familiar with the layouts and dwellings of our Siberian villages, but Splavnuha seemed different, aside from its warmer climate and fertile soil. While still primitive, with no paved roads, electricity, or plumbing, this hamlet was more orderly and better laid out, and had larger, more attractive dwellings than most other Russian settlements we had seen. The houses showed signs of a different architecture, and the people who looked out at us from their yards had happier faces.

We were not mistaken. Our new region had a distinctive past. In 1762 the Russian Tsarina Catherine II, who had been born in Germany, invited German colonists to settle in Russia. Her goal was to bring advanced western agricultural methods to her new homeland. These colonists settled in what is today Saratov province, on the Volga River, and Splavnuha (then called Huk) became one of their remote villages. This new farming population, flourishing in a region of fertile *chernoziom* (black soil) had grown to approximately half a million German inhabitants who, despite the lengthy separation from their homeland, retained much of their cultural heritage. They still spoke German, and even the rubber stamps used in schools and affixed to documents by the ever-present bureaucrats were bilingual. The German influence had survived many generations of settlers and left an unmistakable imprint, making our new village more attractive than the average Russian settlement.

This interesting past, however, did not serve the settlers well. When war came, the Soviet authorities doubted the loyalty of the Volga Germans. As the Nazi forces advanced into Russia in 1941, the Soviets tackled what they feared would become a potential problem with the usual efficiency that they applied to threats, both real and imagined, scattering all of the descendants of the original German settlers throughout Kazakhstan and Siberia. Once the area had been emptied, they installed other people, such as our Polish group, in these now-deserted towns and villages. By the time we reached Splavnuha in 1944, all of the Volga Germans had been displaced.

As one would expect, the change in population did not enhance the area's prosperity. The problem was not just the transition from German to Russian—or, in our case, to Polish—stock. It was the ruthless, hasty abduction of native inhabitants and their gradual replacement by new settlers. During the transition, empty houses deteriorated, machinery rusted, and livestock drifted away. When we arrived on the scene, the village was almost fully occupied and had two functioning agricultural organizations, a Kolhoz and a Sovhoz. The former was an acronym for a collective enterprise, the latter for a Soviet enterprise. A Sovhoz was organized along lines that made it differ somewhat from the better known Kolhoz, but in both cases the State owned "the means of production"—a sacred Soviet canon.

The dirt road that brought us to the village formed the main artery of Splavnuha. Most of the houses were clustered along the main street, with narrow side streets leading toward other dwellings. About two hundred structures housed one thousand inhabitants. A few buildings were brick, others wood; several presented a stucco face to the outside world. There was a bakery, a food store, an elementary school, and even a barbershop, which occupied part of a building used for official purposes. There were stables and warehouses for storing grain and animal fodder. As usual, several small buildings were off limits to ordinary inhabitants, serving as offices and dwellings for the few *Nomenklatura* dignitaries—managers, officials of the Communist Party, and representatives of the NKVD.

Initially we were settled in vacant huts, with several families to a single room. Later we were moved to other dwellings where each family lived in a separate room, often sharing a hut—and a kitchen—with Russian peasants. In addition to working for the State farms, the peasants were allowed to cultivate small plots of land and own one or two farm animals and a few chickens. In most cases those animals were kept in barns, although occasionally, as we later discovered, they lived in the peasants' houses. The peasants' cultivation of small plots was encouraged by the authorities to make up for the notorious inefficiency of Soviet agriculture. These plots occupied a miniscule part of the total land under cultivation in Russia, yet it was estimated that they produced 40 percent of the country's vegetables. During the summer the villagers spread animal dung and other refuse accumulated during the winter into a layer about five inches thick. The material was rolled out to dry and was then cut into brick-sized blocks to be used as fuel for the stoves. *Kiziak,* as it was called, was not pretty and had an unpleasant odor, but it constituted the main fuel for the long winters.

On the day of our arrival, the local Party and NKVD officials held a meeting for us in the village hall. They explained that the villagers worked for either the collective farm or the Soviet farm. We would all work for the latter. They gave the usual pep talk, explaining the need for hard work to produce food for the war effort and for the glory of Soviet agriculture. Diligent work would be rewarded and idleness punished, although neither the nature of the reward nor of the punishment was specified. When the floor was opened for questions, one of our people pointed out that some of us were trained in various trades and professions that might be more useful to the war effort than performing routine farm tasks. This provoked an angry outburst by the party official, who told us that nothing was more important than growing grain and that talk of professional activities was a transparent attempt to exempt the idlers among us from hard work. Such people, he said, were unpatriotic, and such an attitude would not be tolerated among the Russians, much less among the Poles who were guests in the Soviet Union and had to abide by the country's rules.

The situation became tense, but my father resolved it with a conciliatory speech, pointing out that we had as much at stake in the war as the Russians because our entire country had been overrun by the Fascists. We were all eager to work hard, and indeed had already proved our mettle in the gold mines of Siberia. The subject of professions and trades was brought up, he said, to indicate our willingness to tackle any task we were asked to perform. The party officials welcomed this little speech, and we found within a few weeks that the Russian authorities were not totally oblivious to the advantages of professional experience. Two people from our group, a man who had been a baker in Poland and a female trainee, ended up running the village bakery. My father started as an accountant but was soon put in charge of the local consumer service "industry," which consisted of the bakery, grocery store, and barbershop.

We shared a room with two other families. Each of the three families occupied one corner, with the fourth corner left free for a door that connected the room to a corridor leading to a common kitchen and the main entrance. There were, of course, no bathrooms; our sanitary facilities were outhouses. In the absence of any furniture, all activities had to be conducted on the floor. This arrangement posed few problems for us; it was a great improvement over the weeks of close confinement in the cattle cars of the train. After a few weeks, we were relocated to other houses, where each family had its own room, usually with rudimentary furniture. Again, however, there was no running water, and we had to share the kitchen and the outhouse.

Having arrived in Splavnuha in time for the harvest, we were assigned various field jobs. All of the farm workers assembled near the stables early every morning and, tightly packed in horse-drawn carts, were driven into the fields. The lands belonging to the sovhoz were huge, and it took us as long as an hour or more to reach our places of work. Those early morning trips let us shed the remains of slumber, watch the rising sun, and enjoy the camaraderie of the farm hands. Most were women, because the majority of able-bodied men were in military service, but they were strong, able workers and, even more important for those early morning trips, good singers. On most of the morning trips, the women would lead us in melodious, expressive Russian and Ukrainian folksongs. Sometimes, if the carts were far apart, different songs rose from each cart. On other occasions, when the carts moved in close formation, the same powerful song rose from each cart, creating a moving effect of power, joy, and often sadness, but always bringing us closer together and emphasizing our common fate.

Our return trips through the steppes were even more enjoyable. We were all tired after a hard day's work, satisfied with our effort, and looking forward to a well-deserved rest. The mood of the songs in the evenings tended to be heightened: The loud and quick songs were more boisterous, the sad songs more reflective than in the morning. The return trips began in daylight and sometimes ended well after dark. On several of those trips we saw the full moon—which nowhere, I would venture a guess, looks more enormous than on the Russian steppe. Each evening it appeared to rise above a small, nearby mound, almost within our reach, then hover just a few feet above the ground like a balloon tied to a stake by an invisible thread. After a slight hesitation, it would resume its upward journey.

One of the benefits of speaking Russian is the ability to understand, appreciate, and sing Russian folk songs. Those songs can be powerfully uplifting, reflecting, for example, love of the country and the countryside—the latter perhaps a surprising sentiment in view of the harshness of the Russian winter. Many are, of course, love songs with a twist, telling stories of a poor man's love for a woman who has been ordered to marry a much older and richer suitor. This cruel practice occurs in other cultures, but it had a special meaning in old Russia, where the serf often had to secure his landowner's permission for marriage and where parents had to bend to the arbitrary will of their landlords to retain their means of livelihood.

Many ballads feature the river Volga. In a famous song about the folk hero Stenka Razin, a character reminiscent of Robin Hood, Volga is referred to as *Mat Rodnaya,* an expression meaning roughly "my own beloved mother." Another song exalts native fields and woods, but the original Russian *(rodnyie pola i lesa)* is much more intimate and suggests almost a blood relationship between the singer and those rural places. The vast Russian distances and long journeys through snow-covered steppe also gave rise to a genre of songs about coachmen and travelers lost in snowstorms. I can vouch for the accuracy of those songs, because I was once stranded in a particularly severe snowstorm and almost lost my life on the steppe.

Then there are the Russian drinking songs. From their vivid lyrics we can conclude that the reputation of Russians for imbibing large quantities of alcohol is well deserved. Unlike the corresponding German songs, whose steady rhythm invites the drinkers to sway their bodies and wave their beer steins, the Russian songs are quick and boisterous, making you want to jump from your seat and perform one of the aggressive Cossack dances with their vigorous kicks, dizzying pirouettes, and high leaps.

We invariably sang the old ballads that reflected many of the harsh realities of Tsarist Russia, rather than the newer songs commissioned by the Communist Party to praise Stalin and the "glorious" socialist fatherland. The Soviet songs, usually set to a march tempo, were like plastic fruits and vegetables: they had the right shape and luster, but lacked the substance and taste of the real thing. In spirit, many old Russian songs resemble Irish ballads. Both Russia and Ireland have had troubled histories, and their songs reflect the sad heritage of both countries. I have felt for many years that the Russians resembled the Irish more closely than any other group, and I was gratified to hear the writer Frank McCourt[26] confirm my impression during one of his lectures. In Russia, as in Ireland, the songs tend to be sad, melodious, and poetic, and they tell stories that are vivid and credible. Their most

---

26. McCourt is the author of the memoir *Angela's Ashes* (New York: Scribner, 1996).

popular themes are the helplessness of ordinary people in the face of unjust rulers, punishing poverty, and, in the case of Russia, corrupt bureaucracy that had its origins in Tsarist Russia.

Referring to Tsarist bureaucracy, Richard Pipes explains how that entrenched and corrupted caste made life miserable for ordinary Russians:[27]

> The notorious venality of Russian officials, especially those working in the provinces, and most of all in the provinces far removed from the capital cities, was not due to some peculiar characteristic of the Russian national character or even to the low caliber of the people who chose a bureaucratic career. It was inherent in a government which, lacking funds to pay for the administration, not only had for centuries paid its civil servants no salary, but had insisted that they "feed themselves from official business" (kormiatsa ot del).

Early in the eighteenth century the practice was modified, and Russian officials began receiving government salaries. "But the basic problem remained," continued Pipes:

> During Catherine's (II) reign and after it, civil service salaries were so low that most officials could not depend on them to meet their basic living expenses, and had to look around for additional income. . . .
>
> In old-regime Russia, therefore, corruption of public servants was not an aberration, a departure from prevailing norm, such as is common in most countries; it was part and parcel of the regular system of administration. Russian officials had been accustomed since the founding of the Kievan state to live off the land. The central government, hard as it tried, lacked the wherewithal to change this custom. . . . For the overwhelming majority of officials, self-seeking and bribery were a way of life to which they could conceive of no alternative.

The practices of extortion and, to a lesser degree, corruption, persisted until the end of the Imperial period and have been handed along, albeit in modified form, to the Soviet Union, extending even into Putin's Russia. On several visits to Russia since the fall of the Soviet Union, I have witnessed firsthand instances of such malfeasance in Moscow. The

---

27. Richard Pipes, *Russia Under the Old Regime* (New York: Penguin Books, 1977), pp. 282, 283, 284, 287.

script was taken almost directly from Tsarist Russia, where false indictments would be trumped up against merchants, who were then invited to "settle" for "fines" (bribes) that were smaller than the penalties they would have to pay should the case go to court. In post-Soviet Russia, I saw policemen stop traffic "violators," who were encouraged to pay a light fine on the spot instead of having to spend a lot of time at a police station, where they might face a much larger penalty. The transaction was conducted in a calm, professional fashion, with the policeman pretending to do the driver a favor by saving him time and money. The driver, in turn, pretended to be grateful to the officer for his kindness.

The work in the fields that summer was hard, but I enjoyed it, especially in comparison with extracting gold from the cold, dark Siberian mines. The sun was usually bright, the air pure and free from bugs, and the surroundings—a vast expanse of land resembling a boundless, undulating ocean—uplifting. I no longer had to worry about not being able to keep up with my coworkers. At fourteen, I was as tall and strong as most of the women around me, and I could perform my tasks at their pace. Men were scarce, and on the trips to the fields, and even during working hours, some of the younger women were not beyond engaging in mild flirtation with me, providing a measure of distraction from routine work.

My duties consisted mainly of piling straw onto specially adapted wagons and loading big bags of grain into carts for transport to the village. Straw, being light, could be heaped onto carts to a height dwarfing not only people, but also horses. As in carrying water in Siberia, we devised ways to be efficient—for example, in the way we used our pitchforks to hurl straw onto ever growing stacks of straw in the carts. In another instance, we carried the heavy grain bags on our shoulders not, as is usually done, on stooped backs, allowing us to walk upright and making the task much more pleasant and not nearly as punishing to the body. My skill in carrying bags came in handy when I helped my father in his capacity as manager of the organization overseeing the local general store and the bakery. One of his duties was to transport the grain to a mill about ten miles from our village where it was ground into flour. We loaded a horse-drawn cart with sacks of grain and rode slowly through the steppe to the neighboring village, waited for our cargo to be ground into flour, and returned home after dark. A small man, my father could not carry any of the bags, so he relied on me to tackle the loading and unloading at both our village and at the mills.

Most of the trips were uneventful, but they were not without risk. On a few occasions, packs of wolves followed us at a distance. The wolves seldom attacked people, we had been told, but they preyed on foals too young to stay in the stable without access to their mothers' milk. These young animals had to follow our carts when the mares were pressed into service, and we had to make sure they did not lag too far behind. It was not just compassion for the little horses that made us vigilant; we had heard stories about people who received long prison terms when they were found negligent in the loss of their charges to the wolves. Fortunately wolves never approached our cart near enough to pose a danger, but I did get to see them at close quarters, and they were not afraid of us at all. We were on the back of a truck when the driver saw a wolf pack. He stopped and the wolves came almost to within an arm's length of the truck. Their demeanor was that of superior beings who belonged in the steppe, treating us as temporary interlopers. After staring at us for a few seconds, their leader turned and leisurely trotted away, the rest of the pack following.

Our most difficult incident in traveling to the mill was caused not by wolves but by weather. One day it started raining as soon as we left the mill. The rain increased steadily to a fierce downpour, until the dirt roads became muddy and slowed our progress. Soon darkness fell, and the heavy rain made the steppe eerie and threatening. Our horses—we called them "grays"– had difficulty pulling the cart through the thick mud, and our efforts to push the wagon were of little help. We approached a small bridge on a narrow uphill path just wide enough for the cart. As we tried to pull the cart up this incline, one of the wheels slipped off the road. Unable to budge the cart, we were stuck, miles from the nearest village, in total darkness, and under a deluge of rain. Our grays were thoroughly exhausted.

We tried to unload the cart to help free it from the mud, but found that this was impossible in the rain and total darkness. There was a real danger that the cart would slip into the ravine with its heavy load, but our biggest worry was the flour; even if we managed to get it unloaded, it would be ruined by the rain and mud. If that happened, we would probably be accused of sabotage—a fashionable charge in those days. As long as it remained in place, our cargo was protected by a reasonably impermeable cloth. Helpless, we loosened the harness, crawled under the cart, and waited, shivering, until dawn.

Our prospects were bleak. The rain might last for days, and we knew that no one would come to our rescue. There were no telephones in the village, and our coworkers would probably assume we were still at the mill, waiting for the weather to clear. The cart could not be moved in the mud, and we didn't dare abandon it in the fields because we would have been held responsible if the unattended flour was spoiled by the weather or consumed by wolves, vultures, or other animals. We considered the possibility of one of us going by horse to get help, but that, too, would be a hazardous undertaking, for the rains would hide landmarks along the route and it would be easy to become lost on those sparsely populated steppes.

Fortunately, by daybreak the rain had stopped. Hungry, soaked to the skin, and covered with mud, we crawled out from under the cart and unhitched the horses and tied their front legs together with a short rope, allowing them to graze and rest but preventing escape. We unloaded the cart, waited a few hours for the horses to refresh themselves and for the soil to firm up. Then we pulled the empty cart to the top of the ridge, replaced the bags, and slowly returned home. It had been a long and exhausting night, but at least we had not lost our precious cargo.

Most of my father's duties were less physically hazardous, but some were politically sensitive. In addition to raising the efficiency of his subordinates, every manager was expected to engage in periodic political indoctrination to raise "socialist consciousness" among the workers. The usual way of doing this was to hold periodic meetings for the purpose of exhorting employees toward greater effort for the glory of the "socialist motherland" and making plans for better future performance. Even though only six people reported to my father, such meetings had to be formally sanctioned or they were considered illegal. Monitoring meetings involving more than two or three persons was, of course, yet another way the Communist Party controlled the already suppressed population. The standard procedure was to notify the Secretary of the local Communist Party cell well in advance, and to hold the meeting at his convenience. He always attended, presumably to make sure the proceedings were ideologically correct and that no subversive subjects were on the agenda. At my father's invitation, I was present at several of those meetings.

After my father's death I was fortunate to find among his papers the minutes of one of these gatherings. The English translation of these documents is shown below. The original Russian-language documents were prepared by my father and followed the prescribed pompous style of Soviet records. They confirm the selflessness of participants in their work for the common good and, above all, extol the virtues of the "Great Stalin." Despite the high-sounding language, however, the minutes inadvertently reveal the inefficiency of Soviet enterprises. They describe, for example, a shortage of logs to keep the fires burning at the bakery, so that the bakers themselves had to procure fuel. The collective—that is, the group working for my father—had no assured access to a horse and cart, of course, needed to deliver bread. The storage shed was in urgent need of repair, and the Sovhoz could not supply the village with vegetables. It was up to the seven members of the Gortorg Collective—the bakers, the barber, the shopkeepers, and my father—to overcome these impediments. The fact that such simple problems and routine requirements rose to the attention of the official meeting and that the assembly had to delegate its members to "petition" authorities to find a solution provides ample illustration of the deplorable state of Soviet management.

The meeting ended with the decision to challenge the *Gortorg* at a neighboring village to a "socialist competition"—a procedure designed to imitate real market competition. Typically, the criteria for evaluating winners in those socialist competitions were the total output of the enterprise, with no attention paid to the quality of the goods, efficiency of production as measured by profitability (a little-known term in the Soviet Union), or consumer demand for the goods produced. Significantly, the minutes of the meeting record no discussion of previously set targets or the results of other socialist competitions. Such matters were less important than the reiteration of lofty goals and expressions of loyalty to Stalin. Although the minutes do not actually record a decision to praise Stalin, a telegram glorifying the Great Leader was dispatched through an intermediary after the meeting. The telegram read:

Telegram to the Union of Polish Patriots
Chapayev St. 68, Saratov

The Workers' Collective of Polish Citizens at the Splavnuha Sovhoz in Krasnoarmieisk Region, inspired by the joyous news of the liberation of our capital Warsaw and other large cities of our dear Fatherland, which were under the oppression of bloodthirsty German Fascists for more than five years, is sending genuine greetings and deep gratitude to the gallant and invincible Red and, carrying glory for us, Polish Armies. Stop. We ask you to forward in our name genuine thanks to the freedom-loving Soviet Marshall Great Stalin and to assure him that we shall work here selflessly to supply troops at the front. Stop.

***

MINUTES

of the general meeting of the members of the Krasnoarmieisk Gortorg Collective at Splavnuha Sovhoz called on April 2, 1945 by Comrade Director S.B. Frusztajer.

Those present were:

(1) U. I. Pindeyeva, (2) L. Fraind, (3) M. P. Linker, (4) M. Rozner, (5) N. Senkevich, (6) S. B. Frusztajer, (7) Frenkel, and (8) Chairman of Splavnuha Village Soviet, Comrade Dubinin.

Meeting Chairman M. Linker
Secretary M. Rozner

AGENDA

1. How to better organize our work during the sowing campaign.
2. On-time servicing of workers according to Gortorg's standards.
3. Establishing a vegetable garden by Gortorg's workers.
4. Other matters.

After hearing Comrade Frusztajer's report about the extremely important economic and political significance—on the eve of final victory over the German Fascist aggressors—of obtaining a superior harvest, which totally depends on selfless work during the sowing campaign, the attendees unanimously decided:

1. To assure on-time delivery of high-quality baked bread to the Sovhoz workers at the place of their employment. To avoid interruption of baking due to lack of logs for fuel, the Gortorg Collective decided to use its own initiatives to procure wood for the bakery during the sowing campaign.

2. To use all means under the control of our Collective to assure on-time transport of goods from the central base of the Krasnoarmieisk Gortorg in order to issue goods against people's ration cards in accordance with established norms.

3. Regarding the third point it was unanimously decided to organize a vegetable garden by our Collective, taking into account the workdays expended by our members. In order to realize this project, the group delegated to Comrade Frusztajer the task of petitioning the appropriate organizations for appropriating to us a plot of land, horses, agricultural implements, and the essential seeds.

4a. Based on the proposal of Comrade Pindeyeva, it was decided to ask the Sovhoz director to repair a shed at the Sovhoz workshop before 4.10 of this year for temporary storage of bread.

4b.   To deliver bread to the store before 6 A.M. To petition the Director of Sovhoz to assign permanently a cart for delivery of bread.

5.   Based on Comrade Frusztajer's suggestion, it was decided to challenge the member of the Red Army Gortorg Collective at the Nekrasovo Gortorg to a Socialist competition.

Signed:

Pindeyeva	*Linker*
Fraind	*Rozner*
Frusztajer	*Senkevich*
Frenkel	

Stealing was a common and socially acceptable practice that was recognized by everyone except the officials as essential to survival, despite the strict penalties imposed on the perpetrators. Not surprisingly, grain was the chief object of theft, and my father and I often transported stolen grain for many of our friends to be ground into flour at the mill. We all had different methods of stealing. My favorite, which was quite popular, was to wear two pairs of trousers, securely tying the bottoms of the inner pair around my ankles. The second pair, resembling the expansive, loose trousers worn by Russian Cossacks, was worn on top. We poured grain or flour into the inner trousers and relied on the outer pair to conceal our bulging booty. The danger lay not just in being caught stealing or carrying the grain but also in having illegal grain in the house. Unlike flour, which was sold in the store, there was no legal way to acquire grain.

One day as I walked home, a person in plain clothes, who looked suspiciously like an out-of-town policeman, asked me the way to Gienek's house. I was obliged to give him directions, but I remembered that Gienek had a small bag of grain at home. I took a shortcut and ran to warn him. We managed to move the bag to a neighboring house just before the visitor, whose identity I had guessed correctly, arrived and started poking around. My friend escaped disaster on that occasion. Two years later his father was caught stealing a small amount of grain, but fortunately he received a relatively light prison sentence.

My father and I also engaged in "farming" on the side. We borrowed a pair of oxen from the farm, plowed the small field allotted to us, and planted potatoes. The crop was quite respectable and helped us through the winter. One day, my father received a small pig as a reward for fulfilling some kind of a plan. We were unable to raise it ourselves, but my father prevailed upon the State Farm pig attendant to take care of the animal. I visited our pig frequently during the summer. It grew so rapidly that just three months later we were able to sell it for a considerable profit. We also acquired two chickens, which we kept in a small open shed under the outside stairs to our house. These hens appeared to lay more than one egg a day, but we eventually discovered that they were merely hospitable, attracting neighboring birds that also laid their eggs in our little shed. We did not know to whom those extra birds belonged—we just enjoyed their largess.

At the beginning of 1945 the outcome of the war was no longer in doubt. On January 17, Soviet troops captured Warsaw, and liberated Auschwitz on January 26. In February, Churchill, Roosevelt, and Stalin met in Yalta and drew the borders of postwar Europe. The last German offensive of the war, to safeguard Hungarian oil fields, began on March 6. Soviet troops reached Berlin on April 2, leading to Hitler's suicide on April 30. The war in Europe ended on May 8. Atomic bombs were dropped on Japan on August 6 ad 9. The Soviet Union declared war on Japan on August 8. Japan surrendered on August 14.

In the fall I went away to school. Since our village school included only the first eight grades, I had to enroll in the ninth grade at a school in Nekrasovo, an agricultural village eight miles away. As in Siberia, we attended school six days a week. Gienek and I walked to Nekrasovo every Sunday night and returned home late every Saturday. Those walks were somewhat reminiscent of the mill trips with my father. We never missed a Sunday at home, which often meant crossing the steppes in heavy rain, heat, frost, or snow. On many occasions we were thoroughly drenched by a downpour but dried out completely by the time we reached home. Heat and cold did not present a major problem, but we worried about snow, as did our parents.

Snowstorms, and the people lost in them, have often found their way into Russian literature and popular songs, providing the backdrop for any number of romantic and tragic tales. Hiking with no landmarks, little visibility, and no marked roads in seemingly endless steppes can be a harrowing experience. In heavy storms, the snow seemed to fall in one continuous, amorphous mass. Driven by wind, it could cover our footsteps almost instantly and strand a sled in a matter of minutes. To a traveler, the flat, treeless landscape and the swirling white medium created the impression of being at the bottom of a churning ocean. We heard harrowing stories about local people losing their way in the steppes, freezing to death, then being found with their eyes pecked out by birds.

One Saturday night we barely avoided that fate ourselves. As darkness fell, we started home from Nekrasovo under clear skies. We were able to walk briskly until we had reached the midpoint between the two villages, when a sudden, dense snowfall began. We felt reassured by the presence of a small cluster of lonely trees, which we knew were only four miles from our destination. That little grove had been our traditional landmark and showed us we were on the right path. Soon, however, our feet began to sink into the fluffy snow and it became increasingly difficult to maintain our quick pace. The snow and the darkness became disorienting, but we decided to press on toward our village. Since we were four miles from our starting point and four miles from home, retreat would not have been a safer course. I was then fifteen years old and Gienek a year older, and we had confidence in our navigational abilities because we had taken that walk so many times in all kinds of weather. We felt we should be able to cover the four remaining miles without much difficulty.

A compass would have made the journey safer, but such instruments were not available in our part of Russia. The small tree grove provided our only reference point. We set our course and hoped that by following a straight line we would reach the village in about an hour. The temperature dropped, making the snowflakes dryer and producing a firmer walking surface. We exchanged a few remarks, but conversation was not easy in the dense falling snow. At one point we estimated that an hour had passed, then possibly another, and there was still no sign of the village—nothing but steadily falling snow. The realization that we were lost crept up on us.

Initially, we kept our fears to ourselves, as if our uttering them might be overheard by some higher power and bring disaster upon us. I was not yet cold because the struggle to keep moving in fresh snow kept my body warm. But I began to tire. Icicles formed around my eyes, nose, and mouth, and the sharp chill pierced my face. Our pace began to slow and for the first time in my life I questioned the chances of my survival. Would we make it, or would we collapse on the way?

Danger supposedly concentrates one's mind, but my mind wandered in many directions, letting in a flood of images. I remembered a children's play, in Poland, about a plane crashing onto the ice on its way to the North Pole. I recalled the realistic broken fuselage and a protruding damaged wing of the stranded craft. The pilot and two boys survived the accident. Another scene showed them walking across the ice to a field station. They were tired and wanted to rest, but the pilot kept them moving. "If you stop you'll fall asleep and freeze to death in a matter of minutes," he warned. They struggled forward and eventually reached a safe destination.

I also replayed our recent encounter with wolves, imagined stranded travelers with pecked-out eyes, and remembered the short story about a frozen wayfarer who spent millennia haunting others in the snow.

We still had enough energy for a rational discussion. We thought that for the last four miles we had walked in a straight line and that the village was large enough for us to find even if we strayed somewhat from our path, but obviously something had gone terribly wrong. We considered our options. One possibility was to turn left, walk for half an hour and then, if the village was not there, to repeat the procedure to our right. That would work if we had indeed covered four miles from the midway trees and strayed sideways. But we had no way of knowing how far we had walked or whether we could retrace our steps. The snow had slowed our progress, and what seemed like four miles might have been half that distance. If that was the case, we reasoned, our side excursions would simply drain all our energies. We decided to continue to move forward, but half hour later we were still alone in the cold. Not knowing what to do at this point, we just kept moving to take our minds off our predicament. The snowfall grew even heavier. We began to rationalize that rest was essential to survival, and then rest became a more attractive option than survival. We moved like robots, without thought and in total silence—and were close to giving up. Gienek followed me for a while, then I followed him. We lost all sense of time.

Suddenly he uttered an incoherent cry. Stopping, he turned toward me, and exclaimed that he had seen a light. All I saw was the same monotonous, swirling white wall. We dragged our feet awhile longer then, suddenly, we almost bumped into a looming black mass: It was a house. We were back in the village. The next day we learned that it had been nearly dawn when we knocked on the door. Our ordeal had lasted almost all night.

In Nekrasovo we rented space from a Russian family, all of us living in one room just big enough for three beds and a big stove. Our landlady, a fifty-year old peasant woman, and her son Vova had their own beds; Gienek and I slept in another. Vova's grandmother slept on a shelf above the stove, close to the ceiling. Many Russian stoves were designed that way, and the old woman spent most of her time perched there, keeping warm. The house had two rooms separated by a solid wall. The other room served as a small, unheated barn for the cow and the goat. Our landlady, whose job was to tend cows on the farm, supplemented her wages by selling milk. When the goat gave birth, the kids were housed in our room, and in addition to five people sharing cramped quarters, we had three lively little kids jumping wherever their fancy took them. They hardly contributed to the purity of the air or the cleanliness of the floor. Gienek and I had a sack of flour, our main source of nourishment, which the kids seemed to find appealing as a place for performing their bodily functions. After finding the top layer of our bag fouled and removing the rest of the repulsive mess from our flour, we managed to safeguard it from future violations, although I don't remember how we outwitted the little animals.

Gienek and I cooked our own meals, which basically meant fashioning our flour into different forms of dough, which we boiled in water. Each of us also brought a loaf of bread from home each week. Gienek always had the bigger loaf, while I brought more flour, because that was the one commodity my father could buy fairly easily, given his connections to the bakery and the store. We also bought milk from our landlady, although most of the time we could afford only buttermilk that had been centrifuged at the local butter factory to remove most of the fat. We felt deprived at having to drink milk that had already been stripped of what we thought of as its most valuable asset. Ironically, years later in the West I learned that such low-fat milk may actually be more healthful than the whole-fat product.

I enjoyed school and the friendship of Russian students, especially Vova (our landlady's son), who was also in the ninth grade. We had many get-togethers, and the students were supportive of one another. We did not date, but met in groups for conversation, board games, and occasional dances. Our school had no facilities for sports, and in any case that would have been considered a frivolous pastime, especially during the war. The only leisurely physical activity I can remember was my mock fighting with Vova and Gienek. I was much stronger than either of them, probably as a result of my build and my extensive work in the mines and fields. Our fights consisted of their trying to pin me down on the hay that covered the floor of the little barn. I was not an easy target. Surprisingly, since they were approximately my height, our score was even: I managed to immobilize them as often as they could clamp me to the floor.

That academic year passed quickly, and the following summer I worked on the farm for the so-called "Tractor Brigade," where my duties were much better defined than the previous year. My job was to measure and record the fuel levels in the tractor tanks with a dipstick at the beginning and end of each day, and to measure the area that was plowed or harvested. I conducted the second task with a simple instrument consisting of two sticks fixed together at one end and spread two meters apart at the other. The measuring process—probably invented at the dawn of civilization—was accomplished by walking along the edge of the field and flipping the instrument to see how many two-meter intervals fit along the border of the plowed or harvested area.

In the fall I attended school in our region's main town, Krasnoarmieisk, where two high schools went all the way to the tenth grade, the highest grade in the Russian school system. Unfortunately, Gienek did not join me; his Russian education ended with the ninth grade, although later he was able to earn his college degree in Israel. School attendance was compulsory in Russia, but the authorities did not enforce this rule in our community of exiles. It was my father who insisted I attend school every year after our departure from Priisk Konstantinovskii in Siberia. That was not the case with the other teenagers. Gienek, and later one other Polish boy, were my only fellow students during the time we lived in Splavnuha.

Although in theory we had equal rights with the Russians, most of our people felt far removed from them emotionally, spiritually, and culturally. All Russian institutions seemed foreign, abhorrent, and irrelevant to our future lives in Poland. The shoddiness of daily life around us made it easy to assume that Soviet education, too, would be inferior. Perhaps most parents did not want their children to be exposed to Russian teaching, which carried the danger of Communist indoctrination. Attending Russian school was not considered quite as disgraceful as going over to the enemy, but to many in our group it represented at least a small step toward conferring legitimacy on a Communist institution. But my father did not share these negative views. He felt that the schools maintained high educational standards, and even though the curriculum was designed to indoctrinate students into the Soviet way of thinking, he knew the studies would not change my fundamental outlook on life. Not only did I acquire knowledge of Russian history, literature, and language that was unusual for a westerner, but I also made numerous local friends and absorbed many aspects of Russian culture. Perhaps equally important, by diligently attending school I did not lose the habit of learning.

The war ended that summer. We had followed the war news closely, rejoicing at every new Allied advance, but we were not quite sure what an Allied victory would mean for us in our remote village. The news of the German surrender was received with great joy in Splanvnuha. Within days of the war's end, we were asked to assemble in the village center to hear a Party representative from a nearby town. He mounted a cart and made a short speech praising the glorious Communist Party and its great leader, Comrade Stalin. "Our task now," he said, "is to work even harder to rebuild the Motherland."

In fact, no visible changes took place after the end of the war. We followed the same daily routine, had the usual shortages, and obeyed the same people—the manager and the Communist Party secretary who had always run our farm. Nor did the men who had been drafted into the army from our district return home at the end of hostilities. We didn't learn the reasons for this delay until later. There was no general demobilization at first because after the defeat of Germany, Russia declared war on Japan. But even after that conflict, the soldiers did not return home. In the year after the war, the people discharged from the armed forces were primarily those needed for critical civilian jobs or students completing their studies. Peasants recruited from farms evidently did not qualify for that treatment and were not released. Similarly, Russian prisoners of war liberated from the Germans were never repatriated; instead, they were interned in Soviet labor camps. Evidently, they had become "enemies of the people" because of their exposure to foreigners, or perhaps because it was assumed they preferred German captivity to death for the "Motherland" and Stalin. One can only feel sorry for those unfortunate souls. Of all their prisoners of war, Germans had reserved their harshest treatment for their Russian captives. The survivors of Nazi camps must have been yearning for the day of liberation, only to find that they were simply transferred from one form of harsh captivity to another.[28]

Women remained in the considerable majority in our village. As in Siberia, the only Russian males were children, old men, and a few Communist and NKVD operatives. This did not mean that the women were in charge. Even though the Communist Party had proclaimed that women had equal rights with men in the Soviet Union, I never saw women invested with any authority except as teachers or managers of village stores.

The absence of Russian men in Splavnuha had the additional effect of precluding romantic involvements or marriages among the villagers. This was not the case among our emigrant community. A few of our men were drafted into the Polish Army, but most stayed behind. There were no weddings, but we did have romances, and at least one scandal, when the baker, a married man, had an affair with his female assistant. They worked long hours, mainly at night, to prepare bread for morning delivery. As is often the case in illicit romantic involvements, the helper was an attractive young woman, while the baker's wife was well past her physical prime. The baker and his assistant both worked for my father, and when the affair was discovered, they turned to him to mediate the situation between them and the baker's wife. The matter was resolved amicably, with the amorous couple promising to maintain a platonic relationship as they continued to work in the bakery. I don't know if the trust of the married woman was restored, but she was surely aware that her husband's position in the bakery was precious, providing easy access to food and guaranteed freedom from hunger. Too much fuss over the affair could have cost the baker his job.

It was not only love affairs that became known throughout the vil-

---

28. Stalin's paranoia did not result only in the incarceration of Russian soldiers who has been captured by the Germans. For years after the end of the war, he hounded friends, associates, and families of those unfortunate people. A friend who now lives in Boston barely escaped arrest by Stalin's KGB: His name has been found in the address book of one of the returning Russian prisoners, and he was accused of past "criminal associations" (see page 54). Stalin's death saved him from arrest; evidently Stalin's successors did not consider association with former prisoners of war to be a major crime.

lage. Families shared small quarters and had little privacy, and everyone knew almost everything about everyone else. Surprisingly, this was not an impediment to marital bliss; just the opposite. Boorish behavior at home was immediately broadcast throughout the village and brought the risk of censure by others. But of course this transparency could not prevent quarrels. There were, for example, many disagreements about card games, and, surprisingly, my father became involved in one of the longest-running feuds in the village. Most men played two card games, called "sixty-six" and "one thousand." Like bridge, both games involved partnership play, but the cards were never shown face-up on the table. In any joint venture it is easy to blame a partner for lack of success, and I found it comical to listen to adult players shout at each other in criticism of supposedly stupid moves. They filled the air with insults, shouting *"Fuszer"* at one another—a Polish term that combined ineptness, stupidity, and probably other disparaging traits. My father and his adversary in the longstanding quarrel were recognized as two of the best players, and before the feud they had frequently been partners. Inasmuch as I was not a disinterested observer, I am disqualified from passing independent judgment on the causes of the disagreement, but I remember my father's opponent engaging in excessive and crude criticism of my father's every move. After a while my father decided that they should not participate in the same games. Both men had their allies, but my father's supporters outnumbered the opposite ranks by a wide margin. Human conflict can spring from deep roots unrelated to the issue at hand, and my father's appointment as the head of the local branch of *Gortorg* had provoked envy among some of our compatriots. Although it was not a large organization, his management position carried considerably more prestige and material reward than working in the fields.

Around that time I inadvertently contributed to our neighbor's marital problems. An illiterate young woman lived next to us with her mother and a small child. One day she asked me to read a letter from her husband, who was serving in the Army—not an easy task, because her husband found it hard to express his thoughts in writing. Basically, he said he was looking forward to the end of the war and returning home. The woman asked me to write a reply, but she was not very specific about the intended content of the letter, insisting simply that I include the news that her cow had recently given birth to a calf. I did my best, but evidently I did not know how to write a sufficiently romantic letter. His prompt reply conveyed the accusation that her letter's coldness meant that she had met someone else and no longer wanted him. I tried hard to make amends in her next letter, explaining that any apparent coldness was my fault, since I had been the writer. I pumped her for her feelings or any intimate thoughts, but the only instruction I could elicit from her was that I should once again write about the farm animals and tell her husband she was waiting for him. She never heard from him again and assumed that he had decided to live with another woman. If only I knew then what I know now about expressing affection! If I had had the ability to write passionate letters, I might have helped to maintain a long and happy relationship between those two innocent souls.

The school I attended in Krasnoarmieisk, photographed in 2005, by Sergei Boyko.

HIGH SCHOOL

IT WOULD BE an exaggeration to refer to Krasnoarmieisk, where I attended school that fall, as a town. The houses did not differ materially from those in our village of Splavnuha, and the streets were not paved, although they were laid out in an orderly square grid. Still it was a much bigger settlement than Splavnuha. The seat of the district (*rayon*) government, it had a population in excess of twenty thousand. In that part of Russia, Krasnoarmieisk's relative size and the fact that its citizens were not involved in farming probably earned it the designation of "town." The distance between Krasnoarmieisk and our village of Splavnuha was about sixteen miles, too far to walk home to be with my father on Sundays, so I returned home only on school vacations and national holidays. My father, still driving his faithful grays, came to Krasnoarmieisk on official business once or twice a month, making our separation less painful. He arranged for me to stay with a Polish family, a mother and three daughters. The mother was a strong-minded woman who dominated the household. The two older daughters worked in offices, while the youngest, Basia, was my age. She neither worked nor went to school, but helped her mother at home. In those days young people in Russia did not mature as quickly as they do currently in the West, and my interest in girls was not yet fully developed. As a result, Basia and I had more of a sibling relationship than a romantic one.

Conversely, my classmates were treated almost as adults. Tenth graders, like upperclassmen in the United States, were expected to provide student leadership and set the tone for the schools. I was lucky to be one of the best students and to enjoy the respect of both the teachers and my classmates. I developed a particularly close relationship with the mathematics teacher, Lia Eveleyevna Maizlish. An older woman who lived alone, she occasionally invited me to her home, and we had long conversations about our pasts. She was born long before the 1917 Communist Revolution and at one time had translated Hebrew texts into Russian. She was curious about the history of my family and the Jewish communities in Poland. Despite our friendship, however, she was my severest academic critic. I seldom received the highest mark of five from her, even though mathematics was my strongest subject and I had fives in other disciplines. She sensed that I did little work and told me she would evaluate me not only on what I knew but on how closely my mastery of the subject approached my learning potential. Many people have had a particularly remarkable teacher in their lives, and Mrs. Maizlish was mine—both my idol and the only teacher I remember well.

Tenth-grade students were expected to enroll in KOMSOMOL, the Young Communist League, and I was pressured to become a member. However, my father and I were both against this commitment, and I did not join. As a foreigner, I had an excuse to stay out of the organization, whereas it would have been dangerous for a Russian to refuse. Even as a nonmember, I felt no discrimination and was encouraged to participate in all school activities, including those directed by the Young Communist League.

In 1946 the Government authorized a general election to the Supreme Soviet, theoretically the Communist equivalent of the U.S. Congress. The Soviet met about once a year; the election of deputies was a mere formality, since all candidates were appointed by the Communist Party and there was only one candidate for each seat. In our town, the task of mobilizing people to vote was entrusted to the tenth graders of the town's two schools. The process started with a class presentation by a KOMSOMOL agent, and although I was not a member, I was asked to attend that meeting and to work for the election.

We were organized to work in pairs. Each pair visited an allotted number of people, asking them to come to the school on certain dates to register for the election. We were also instructed to tell the voters that special snacks would be served on election day. With the prevailing food shortages, this was not a trivial enticement.

At first, my partner and I felt embarrassed going from house to house disturbing people to check off their names and ask them to register. But gradually our attitude changed. We were surprised to find the potential voters frightened by our presence. Usually visits from strangers brought little good, and we were treated with deference and even fear. A couple of weeks later, the Young Communist League held another meeting at the school for all solicitors. This time we were presented with the names of people who had ignored our request to register. We were told in no uncertain terms to lean hard on our constituents and ask why they did not want to vote. Could it be that they did not approve of the process, or perhaps they did not like the Soviet Government? Our return to their houses produced near panic and obsequious assurances that they would register immediately. Their apologies and entreaties had an interesting effect on us. We now felt that we had been promoted to a position that carried a considerable degree of authority. I hope we did not behave arrogantly, though I can see now that we were not nearly as careful and considerate as we had been on our initial visit. It became quite clear to me how corrupting a sense of power could become.

The voter turnout on election day was most gratifying, at least to the authorities, with almost 100 percent participation. Since there was only one candidate on the ballot, the outcome was never in question. Theoretically, of course, the voters could have crossed out that candidate's name in the privacy of the voting booth, but no one did. Not only were snacks provided, but there was also, at the end of the day, a big party for all solicitors. None of us regretted our participation in this charade, and many were proud of having been placed in a position to intimidate adult voters. I learned another lesson from that election: Low voter turnout may be indicative of apathy, but near 100 percent participation is often an excellent indicator of repressive government.

During the last term of the academic year we were expected to write a major essay on a given theme. The teacher assigned each student a literary, historical, or political subject. I was given what was considered the most challenging topic: "Theory and Tactics of Proletarian Revolution." My task was to discuss the ideological tenets of communism and to provide examples of strategies used by communist thinkers and tacticians to overthrow capitalist governments and usher in the new "peoples' order." The subtitle of the second part of my essay could have been "The Ends Justify the Means," to give the true flavor of what was done to create the ultimate communist paradise.

I had seldom done any homework, so doing a lot of research for the essay was a new experience, which, to my surprise, I greatly enjoyed. While there were shortages of almost all types of books, the library shelves were well stocked with the writings of Marx, Engels, Lenin, Stalin, and other Communist leaders. I started my survey with Marx and Engels, quoting what are probably the most famous lines of the Communist Manifesto: [29]

> The history of all hitherto existing society is the history of class struggles. Freeman and slave, patrician and plebeian, lord and serf, guild-master and journeyman, in a word, oppressor and oppressed, stood in constant opposition to one another, carried on an uninterrupted, now hidden, now open fight, a fight that each time ended, either in a revolutionary reconstitution of society at large, or in the common ruin of the contending classes.

In other words, the history of mankind has been characterized by a struggle between the exploiters and the exploited. In Marxist dogma these historical forces inevitably led to communism "and communism would remain mankind's ultimate social order."[30] Capitalists unwittingly created favorable conditions for the arrival of socialism and communism: In order to satisfy the markets unleashed by the Industrial Revolution, they gathered dispersed rural craftsmen and peasants in giant factories.

---

29. Karl Marx and Friedrich Engels, *The Communist Manifesto*, 1848.

30. This understanding of history was most closely associated with the great German philosopher G.W.F. Hegel. Both Hegel and Marx believed that the evolution of human societies was not open-ended, but would end when mankind had achieved a form of society that satisfied its deepest and most fundamental longings. Both thinkers thus posited an "end of history": for Hegel this was the liberal state, while for Marx it was a communist society. Francis Fukuyama, *The End of History and the Last Man* (New York: The Free Press, 1992), p. xii.

This action established the viciously exploited working class, which was easier to organize than the scattered, downtrodden, feudal masses. However, the workers were not politically astute, and had to be educated and led toward revolution by the Communist Party, "the vanguard of the proletariat." After revolution, the communists would not allow the capitalists to appropriate the fruits of the toilers' labor, but would distribute the generated wealth equitably among all people. The greedy capitalists, I wrote, were expected to mount vigorous resistance to such a redistribution of income. They had set up the police, the army, bourgeois governments, churches, and other vehicles of suppression to control the workers. Those institutions would have to be liquidated, if necessary by violent means, to achieve the liberation of the people and installation of the new order.

In the second part of the essay I gave two examples of the tactics used by communists. The first was the strong support of capitalism by Marx and Engels, even though they were implacable foes of that order. Capitalism suited their long-range goals: Let the capitalists destroy the feudal system, then the communists would eliminate their recent allies. Clearly Marx and Engels were admired not just for their theoretical contributions to communism but, at least in the writings of their followers, for their wily tactical sense unencumbered by moral considerations.

My second example was Lenin's "selfless" effort to fight enemies of the Russian Revolution. I described his effective strategy of pitting one faction against another, such as monarchists, social revolutionaries, and Western imperialists. Western imperialists, in particular, supposedly conspired to restore the Tsar's rule and deprive the workers of their newly won freedoms. I described Lenin in glowing terms, praising his eternal vigilance and his devotion to the workers and peasants.

Even as a former Siberian prisoner, I did not fully appreciate the horrible reality of Lenin's regime until the opening of the Communist Party archives after the fall of the Soviet Union. Shortly after the Bolshevik Revolution, Lenin sent armed thugs to the countryside to confiscate food from the peasants and to distribute it among his followers in the cities and in the army. In many cases this lawless action resulted in armed resistance, which was brutally suppressed by every means, including the occasional use of poison gas. One of the better organized peasants' attempts to safeguard food and seeds for the next harvest was led by Antonov. In his book *Lenin: A New Biography*, Dmitri Volkogonov quotes from the previously secret Soviet archives the following order issued by Lenin on June 11, 1921, with the approval of the Politburo:[31]

> Antonov's band has been smashed by the decisive action of our troops, it has been scattered and is being captured piecemeal. In order finally to tear out all the SR-bandit roots . . . the All-Union Executive Committee orders as follows: 1. Citizens who refuse to give their names are to be shot on the spot without trial. 2. The penalty of hostage-taking should be announced and they are to be shot when arms are not surrendered. 3. In the event of concealed arms being found, shoot the eldest worker in the family on the spot without trial. 4. Any family which harbored bandits is subject to arrest and deportation from province, their property to be confiscated and the eldest worker in the family to be shot without trial. 5. The eldest worker of any families hiding members of the family or the property of bandits is to be shot on the spot without trial. 6. If the bandit's family flees, the property is to be distributed among peasants loyal to the Soviet regime and the abandoned houses burnt or demolished. 7. This order is to be carried out strictly and mercilessly. It is to be read at village meetings.

Naturally, even if I had been aware of Lenin's vicious methods, I would not have discussed them in my essay, nor did I raise any moral issues. There was little talk about morality in Russia except occasional mention of "Revolutionary morality." By definition, everything that promoted progress toward communism was moral; everything that impeded that progress was immoral. No one debated either the ethical or practical implications of the eventual communist system. That communism would automatically lead to universal bliss was, officially at least, a self-evident truth.

My essay was judged to be the best in the tenth-grade classes in both schools, and was sent to regional authorities as an outstanding example of research and writing. I had worked hard on the essay, but it was more remarkable as an example of "playing" the Soviet system than as

---

31. V.I. Lenin, *Polnoe sobranie sochinenii*, fifth ed. (Moscow, 1958-1965), vol. 41, p. 383.

a serious piece of work. Two-thirds of it consisted of quotations from eminent authorities of communism and documentation of the sources. The "original" third could best be described as smooth transitions from one quotation to the next. My conclusions were in full agreement with all my sources; I even "borrowed" my writing style from the orthodox communist literature. Anyone who read Pravda editorials during the decades of the Soviet Union is familiar with that style: long, obscure sentences sprinkled with terms like dialectical materialism, progressive, imperialists, oppressors, brotherhood, freedom, Great Leader Stalin, and similar jargon. I suspected that my teacher had to give me the highest grade or risk being accused of not appreciating such exalted thoughts.

Did I believe the conclusions of my own essay? I certainly did not think so at the time, but then how could I present them so convincingly that the essay was chosen as an outstanding example of correct political thinking? With the long passage of time, it is hard to remember my state of mind, but I probably regarded my composition as an effort to describe what Richard Pipes called "surrogate reality." Studying philosophical Marxist texts printed in attractively bound books was far removed from our everyday shoddy life in primitive, isolated villages. Analogies are seldom perfect, but I may have viewed the presentation and conclusions of my essay as an exercise similar to proving a geometrical theorem whose premise may, in fact, be irrelevant or illogical. In both cases there is a body of given assumptions, which, once accepted, can be built upon to bring us to a desired "proof." In the same way, once the assumptions of Marxism-Leninism are accepted as facts, certain political and economic conclusions inexorably follow, and producing the proof becomes a technical matter that does not necessarily correspond to reality. In the Soviet Union, Marx and Lenin had been elevated to saintly status, and their words, like the rules of Euclidean geometry, had to be treated as gospel truth. I was able to prove this truth without accepting any of it.

For a long time I believed that my exposure to Soviet propaganda and my study of communist theory had had little effect on my teenage mind. The Soviet reality should have undermined the propaganda: we certainly could not reconcile our daily misery with the promised ideal system. Or so I thought. It turned out, to my chagrin, that I was wrong. After we left Russia, I found that many of the ideas had been pounded so deeply into me that they were still embedded in my habits and responses. It took several years of conscious effort and observation of life outside the Soviet system to purge them completely.

WE LEAVE RUSSIA

By THE MIDDLE OF 1946, with the Russians firmly entrenched in Poland, Polish communists loyal to Stalin were installed to run the government. Former Soviet officers held key command and "advisory" posts in the Polish Army. The UB—a security service modeled after the NKVD—enforced adherence to the Soviet Communist Party line in all aspects of everyday life. The presence of the Soviet garrison and the country's geographic confinement between the Soviet Union and the huge Russian occupation force in East Germany would have doomed any armed Polish uprising. Large commercial enterprises were nationalized, leaving only small businesses and farms in private hands. Export industries were being integrated into the Russian economy.

The Poles, of course, felt that the Soviets were plundering their country. According to a popular and essentially accurate joke, Soviet scientists had succeeded in crossing a giraffe with a cow, producing a beast that was able to graze in Poland while being milked in Russia. Russia, with the complicity of the Western powers, had brazenly taken Poland's eastern lands, giving Poland in return the eastern part of Germany. The Poles living in the territory which had been ceded to Russia were allowed to stay in place (though many chose to move west

Map of Poland showing territories before and after World War II.
Courtesy of the Encyclopedia of the Holocaust.

to avoid being trapped in the USSR), but the Germans were expelled from the territory ceded to Poland. When the Soviets allowed several hundred thousand detainees, including us, to return to Poland, many were directed to the newly acquired and now largely vacant western territories.

In May 1946 we were notified that we would soon be allowed to return to Poland. We did not yet understand how firmly our country was now held in Stalin's grip, and we felt nothing but infinite joy when we heard that announcement. We talked of little else and made plans for what we would do on our return. It was also the time for remembering those who were no longer with us, and once again my father and I felt the pain of my mother's death. When our departure was set for a date before the end of the school year, several of my teachers and the head of the school tried to persuade me to stay until graduation. Their arguments were compelling: They said I was a good candidate for a gold medal and that, with such an awards I could go to any university in the Soviet Union. Indeed, the medal would be helpful even if I later decided to go to Poland. But there was no question in my mind or my father's about what we would do. In those days, when you had a chance to leave the Soviet Union, you went as soon as possible, before the authorities could change their minds.

In retrospect we made the right decision. The gold medal—assuming I earned it—would not have made the slightest difference in Poland, or later in the West. And the risk of staying would become even greater than we had imagined, as Stalin, with the developing Cold War, steadily tightened his noose around the people's freedoms.

On the day of departure, shortly before my sixteenth birthday, we loaded our belongings onto a cart and began our trip to the nearest railroad station. Once again we were crowded into cattle cars, but this time they did not seem uncomfortable. We did not know our exact destination, but we knew—or hoped—we were truly going home. The sights along the way were not happy ones. Traveling through areas completely devastated by the war, we saw hundreds of people—mainly women—trying to hitch rides on freight trains in search of food. These were two types of travelers: the lucky ones who had already made their purchases, and others who carried boxes or bags of belongings to be exchanged for staples at unknown destinations. These poor women were everywhere, boarding freight cars bound in all directions in what appeared to be total confusion. Occasionally we talked to these bewildered souls. It seemed that those in search of food traveled east hoping to reach areas not completely devastated by war; they boarded trains in a haphazard way, not caring exactly where they were going as long as they were moving eastward. The women carrying food were traveling westward, again not in a direct route, but boarding trains they thought would deposit them closer to home.

On one occasion we saw several women struggling with heavy bags, trying to board a freight train. They could barely lift their load, much less place it high above their heads into cars whose floors were four to six feet from the ground. Struggling with their own bags, they made no

Polish exiles on way to repatriation, 1945

attempt to assist one another. We could not help but feel compassion for these wretched, exhausted people desperately trying to safeguard their precious food and bring it back to their families. The lack of physical activity on the long train trip had made us restless, and with our extensive field experience in handling bags of grain, we were eager to help them. We approached the women and split into three-man teams. At first the women recoiled in fear at the sight of the tall young men approaching them, obviously worried about the safety of their cargo. But their initial fright turned into cries of delight when we started loading their grain. Two of us gripped the top and bottom of each bag, swung it back and forth a few times, then tossed it upwards toward the interior of the vehicle. As it rose on its final swing, the third man pushed the middle of the bag sending it flying, as if weightless, into the waiting freight car. It took just a few minutes to accomplish what most of these women could not do by themselves.

We approached the Polish border with a great deal of trepidation. The closer we came to our homeland, the more we worried that something would go wrong. We had heard rumors about the unpredictability and crudeness of the Russian *pogranichniki* (border guards), who apparently were organized into a special section of the NKVD Army. The rumors turned out to be true. When we reached the border, the train was surrounded by soldiers armed with submachine guns and, even more frightening, seven-foot-long iron bars ground to sharp points at one end. They rudely and impatiently ordered us out of the trucks and confiscated our Soviet documents. We all passed nervously in front of the armed soldiers, especially the bearers of the pointed rods, which looked like medieval lances designed to pierce human bodies. We learned, however, that they had a different, though still loathsome, purpose. After checking our documents, soldiers climbed into each railway car and forcefully plunged the sharp tips of their spears into our luggage. The intent, of course, was to discover any stowaways who might be trying to cross the border illegally. They did not find anyone, but we shuddered at the possible fate of anyone who tried to evade them. In a few hours, the checking process by these masters of intimidation was over and we were allowed to proceed, but only after being told that Russia was better off without us. I have heard people say, rather proudly, "I've been thrown out of better places than this," but I gained a real-life appreciation for that sentiment when I was thrown out of Communist Russia.

It is hard to describe the feeling that came over me when we finally crossed the Polish border. Something we had dreamed about for six years, but were never sure could happen, had at last become a reality. I shall never forget the first small Polish town. We now had a Polish train crew, and the conductor announced that we would stop there for a few hours. Gienek, my friend from Splavnuha, and I, and an adult woman from our group decided to explore the town. The streets were clean, the people friendly, and the sound of the Polish language was everywhere. We still spoke Polish fluently—a result of living in our closely-knit emigrant community in Russia—and felt completely at home. After initial hesitation we entered a small bakery, where we were greeted with a smile, a cheerful "good morning," and an offer to help with anything we needed. The contrast to the gruff Russian shopkeepers made us feel as though we were on another planet. There were white rolls, white bread, and pastries—all items we had not seen for years and barely recognized.

We looked at each other and realized we had to buy something and leave before our laughter offended the shopkeeper. We paid with Russian money, left quickly, and broke into euphoric laughter in the street. We laughed for a long time, exploding at the sights around us and finding Poland so much more genial and civilized than the pathetic Communist Russia we had finally left behind.

The stark contrast between Russia and Poland was not confined to the attitude of shopkeepers. The Polish town was clean and bustling, and its shop windows displayed consumer goods. The Russian settlements on the other side of the border, barely a few miles away, were stark and oppressive, their people deprived. The border between Poland and Russia had been redrawn only about a year before our arrival. Both sides had suffered equally from the same horrible German occupation and the same furious battles between the opposing armies, yet the Poles, still enjoying the vestiges of prewar freedoms, managed to recover from the war and cultivate comfortable living conditions. For their part, the Russian occupiers of previously Polish lands succeeded only in imposing their heavy-handed regulations on their new domain and, in the process, fomented disaster and famine.

After a few days, I had a strange feeling of regret about leaving Russia. I know Gienek and other friends shared that emotion, because we discussed it with some degree of embarrassment. Despite the hardships, there had been many pleasant experiences and, for us youngsters, much growth. We had left behind good friends and happy memories. Yes, we had been underprivileged foreigners in that land, but most of the native population was underprivileged, too. In the face of the common enemy, the Communist regime, we had formed strong ties of friendship with many Russians, as well as with our fellow Poles. While traveling west on our train, we discussed our mastery of the Russian language and realized we would no longer be able to use it in daily conversation to crack untranslatable jokes, refer to proverbs without having to explain their meanings, or quote well-known literature passages just by uttering a few words. It was as if someone had just removed a big chunk of our past and pared down our personalities.

Books have been written on the depth of Russian culture (one of them, *Mother Russia: The Feminine Myth in Russian Culture,* by my cousin, Joanna Hubbs), and we certainly felt its effects that day in June 1946. My love of the Russian language, literature, and certain aspects of the Russian personality have stayed with me to this day, and I expect will remain forever.

There was also a feeling of uncertainty about Poland. In Russia, our overriding objective had been to return home, but now, as we rode farther into the country, we found growing evidence that our home was imprisoned by a totalitarian regime. Poland, like Russia, was now a communist country, and we harbored no illusions about the source of authority. We began to realize that the top positions in the army and government were held by Soviet nationals or by Poles loyal to the Soviet Union. That fact was officially presented in the press, which proudly proclaimed that the authorities in Poland consisted of "democratic and progressive" elements. It seemed as though we had exchanged one communist country, where there had been hope of departure, for another country whose oppressive political system we could not escape. Those of us who were Jewish worried about anti-Semitism. Before the war, many Polish Jews felt like second-class citizens in their own country. Now we heard rumors of renewed anti-Semitic outbursts and even occasional pogroms. Would the Jews sink back to their former status? Despite these doubts and misgivings, however, we were still overjoyed about our return to Poland, and I'm sure that none of us would have considered returning to Russia.

We had been aware of the Holocaust but had not comprehended its scale or the total number of Jews systematically killed by the Nazis. Most of our information came from the Soviet press, but there were those among us who, even on the eve of World War II, foresaw the coming disaster. Hitler's pronouncements and information filtering through from Dachau, a concentration camp established in Germany in March 1933, had made the Nazis' intentions abundantly clear. Most people, however, had considered Hitler's speeches to be ranting fantasies and gross exaggerations—and who could blame them? It was hard to imagine that any nation, least of all a European country steeped in rich culture, would be capable of such atrocities.

We were hoping against hope to find relatives and friends who had survived the Nazi occupation, but in many communities Jewish homes had been demolished, possessions appropriated, and neighborhoods destroyed. Yet, as I look back, I don't remember any handwringing or much conversation bemoaning the fate of the Polish Jewry. Of course, in our hearts we suffered pain at the horrible deaths of so many of our compatriots, but the atrocities of the war and our six years of Soviet exile numbed our feelings and made disasters seem almost commonplace. We were also preoccupied with the struggle for our own survival. For Americans and most Europeans, the end of the war constituted the closing of a terrible part of their lives. But they could go home to their families, rejoin their communities, and resume their lives. For them it was time to take stock of their situation, mourn the past, and tackle a stable future. Not so with us: We had no home, no surviving families among those who had remained in Poland, no community to fortify us, and no reliable political order. Military action was over, but we still had to find our place in the war's uncertain aftermath. That situation, not the tragedy of the Holocaust, occupied most of our thoughts upon our return from the Soviet Union.

Our final destination in Poland was a beautiful small town called Kłodzko (Glatz in German). It was located near Wrocław, formerly Breslau, in the part of Germany given to Poland in the Yalta-Potsdam agreement as compensation for losing its eastern lands to the Soviets. Located in the hills of Silesia, the town had been untouched by the fighting. We were given a furnished apartment that must have been abandoned by German tenants who had either fled the advancing Russian Army or been forcibly resettled into Germany after the war. My father found a job as an accountant in a small cooperative that produced men's clothing. His position allowed him to buy men's trousers at deep discounts, and I was able to sell them in the farmer's market. Unlike our little commercial adventure on the trans-Siberian railroad, this trade was serious business. I was never good at haggling, but I tried to get the best price possible. I can't remember what our costs were, but my bottom price was 850 złotys, and I frequently received my asking price of 1300 złotys (the average sale price was about 1100 złotys). On market days, I started with eight pairs of trousers of various colors, sizes, and designs, and demand was so great that I could sell them all within two or three hours.

Despite our initial misgivings, it did not take us long to adjust to our new life in Poland. A postwar euphoria still filled the air. We were all new to the area, giving all of us something in common. Unlike the Soviets, the Polish communists did not eliminate private enterprise, at least not small businesses and farms. That policy led to a vigorous flourishing of the simple shops and small workshops reminiscent of prewar Poland. The Jewish community coalesced quickly to set up mutual aid organizations, helping all its members cope with the new conditions and forming a wide, inclusive social circle.

The main worry was the persistent anti-Semitism and the uncertainties of our long-term future in a communist country. When we arrived in Poland about a year after the end of the war, the communist government was not nearly as dictatorial as its Soviet masters in Russia, but already we could discern early signs of stricter control. We witnessed arrests of partisans who had fought the Germans during the war and who had also bitterly opposed the virtual annexation of Poland by the Soviets. One evening, I was particularly shocked by the brutal abduction of a drunken man who made the mistake of uttering an unflattering remark about the current state of Poland. He was unceremoniously grabbed by two policemen and dragged into a side street. When he reappeared a few minutes later, still flanked by his pursuers, his left arm was hanging helplessly by his side; we suspected that the policemen had broken his collarbone. As unpleasant as these conditions were, they were considerably better than those of our six-year internment in Russia. Having no other choice, we learned to cope with them.

My social life blossomed as I turned sixteen. I attended dances at the newly established Jewish Community Center every weekend, where we also gathered to play ping-pong and discuss Zionism. My immediate social circle consisted of four girls and four boys. We always met as a group, although each one of us had a special partner. My first steady girlfriend was beautiful Stella Wasserman, a tall, dark, slim young woman. We lost contact after my departure for England, but I understand that she emigrated to Israel, where I hope she is still leading a happy life. Even though my father and I were very close, we did not discuss my feelings toward girls, which I considered an embarrassing subject.

The Zionist political parties ranged from those of the extreme right, which stayed underground, to various types of socialist parties. I was tired of socialism and ready for change. I thought that the only way to expel the British from Palestine was through armed insurrection. While I did not join a political party, my leanings were close to the right side of the political spectrum. Most of the teenagers in my circle had grown up together in Siberia and felt free and easy with each other. We had celebrated the end of the war and the end of our Russian exile. We also felt we were in a transition from the war to a more normal and peaceful existence, and like passengers who relish their temporary status on a vacation cruise, we enjoyed the present state of affairs. We thought that the serious business of life still lay ahead of us.

In the fall I enrolled at the University of Wrocław, about fifty miles from Kłodzko, along with Gienek and Adek, a new friend. Having left Russia before graduating from tenth grade, I did not have a high school diploma, but at that time the rules of university enrollment were flexible enough to accommodate students whose studies had been interrupted by the war. I attended classes in the Department of Mathematics, Physics, and Chemistry, with the understanding that at the end of that academic year I would also have to pass a high school equivalency exam.

Wrocław had been almost completely destroyed during the fighting, but the university, which was on the town's outskirts, survived unscathed. Subjected to incendiary bombing, the city was largely burned out. Its streets were lined by walls six stories high, with gaping holes where windows had been, giving the walls an impression of a ghostly labyrinth. There were no roofs or floors. The apartment building where I lived had been rebuilt and now housed about sixty Jewish university students, but there were no other occupied buildings for a couple of blocks in any direction. At night the streets were dangerous, and despite the discredited Nazi philosophy, anti-Semitism still existed in Poland. Two of our students took turns guarding the building each night. We were issued Russian rifles with live ammunition, and we guarded the only entrance to the building from behind locked doors. No serious attempt was ever made to enter the hostel by force, although there were a few incidents of name-calling and threats to storm the building.

The Jewish community of Wrocław consisted almost entirely of returnees from the Soviet Union, and, though scarcely one year old, was well organized. I frequently attended its various recreational facilities where, in addition to social activities, we continued our Zionist debates. I also took advantage of money the Jewish Committee offered for adult education. I imagine the funds came from American Jewry, although at the start of the Cold War, the source was not widely advertised. One could learn a trade free of charge, but instead I took driving lessons and obtained a driver's license. It was much harder to qualify for a Polish permit than it was to earn a British or U.S. license later on, for we had to be proficient not only at driving but also at engine operation and car mechanics.

The war had interfered with my father's plans to send me to study in England, but our current situation under communist rule strengthened his determination for me to join my uncle in London. He investigated several possibilities for my departure, but initially none of them looked promising. Then he became aware of a 1945 British government program that authorized the entry of up to one thousand East European orphaned Jewish boys under eighteen. I did not, of course, exactly fit that description, but my father obtained a document that implied I was an orphan. A Rabbi Schonfeld was gathering a group of sixty boys for emigration to England, and I was fortunate to be included among them, but I still needed documents to exit from Poland and enter Britain.

Father mounted a campaign to obtain those papers. His letters to my cousin Bronek and Uncle Ilya in England gave a detailed description of documents required to obtain the necessary travel permits. He also discussed the excellent results of my informal examination for admission to a Polish university and sang my praises with paternal pride as someone who was "passionate about learning." In one of his letters he wrote, "I am delighted that, in spite of the war and our exceptionally difficult circumstances, Bronek (referring to me) continued his studies and achieved his initial goal." By "initial goal" he meant admission to Wrocław University.

By then, however, the Iron Curtain had already been drawn around the lands dominated by the Soviets, and I had little hope that my father's plans would succeed. People were escaping by illegally crossing the Czech border and then proceeding to Austria, but those were hazardous undertakings and, even if successful, unlikely to lead to a British entry visa. Accordingly, my father kept trying to obtain an official permit for my journey.

The pace of correspondence with my western relatives and government officials was slowed by the inefficiency of the Polish Post Office and by the bureaucratic delays inherent in dealing with ponderous emigration authorities. The exchange of correspondence lasted for months, creating anxiety and fear of retribution from Polish officials, but eventually my father's persistence paid off. My uncle decided I was worthy of his support, and the authorities of England and Poland promised to issue the necessary papers.

Once all the preliminary formalities were behind us, we applied for a Polish passport and a British visa, which arrived sooner than we had expected. My date of birth was listed as June 19 instead of 15, but we were certainly not going to ask for a correction. You don't let go of the passport that enables you leave a communist country. In May 1947 my father and I left Wrocław for Gdynia, the port where I was to join the other boys traveling to England.

Stopping in Warsaw on our way, we decided—with some trepidation—to explore the city. After a six years' absence, we did not know what to expect. We found the center of Warsaw partly restored, with traffic in the streets and stores selling goods, but when we visited our former neighborhood, Karmelicka Street, we faced a daunting sight. This street had been in the center of the Warsaw Ghetto, and now there was nothing but rubble as far as the eye could see—not even a remnant of walls to remind one of the tall residential buildings that once stood there. Our neighborhood had been totally devastated during the six-week uprising in 1943. The only way the Germans had been able to subdue the Jewish defenders in the urban street fighting was to destroy every structure in order to deny the insurgents a place to hide. Rubble completely covered the area, piled higher on the sites of former buildings than in the streets, helping us find the remains of our building.

We seemed surrounded by an eerie silence, but when we stopped, we realized that the noise of our footsteps had obscured an even fainter, slow, rhythmic sound. Then we saw dozens of bent-over figures, well separated from one another, digging in the rubble. It was a surrealistic scene. These shabbily dressed humans did not speak to one another, did not even stand as they foraged slowly like giant birds seeking worms, doggedly turning over stones with small hoes as they searched for abandoned treasures. I instantly resented their presence, which disturbed the peaceful silence. Rather than respecting this scene of horrible slaughter, they violated the site by trying to enrich themselves at the expense of Warsaw's former residents.

We said our goodbyes on the platform of the Warsaw railroad station. The parting was brief, as it had to be for us to maintain the pretense that we would soon see each other again. We embraced, kissed on the cheeks, exchanged good wishes, and in a minute I boarded the train. As we pulled out of the station, I watched my father standing motionless, except for tentative waves of his hand, until he disappeared into the distance. I assumed that he did not accompany me to Gdynia, the port of my departure, because he had to return to work in Kłodzko, but now I know that he simply could not prolong his agony; the pain of my departure was too strong to bear for one more day.

In Gdynia I joined the group of sixty other boys in preparation for boarding a British troopship. One hurdle remained: we had to pass through Polish Customs and Passport Control, and in a communist country one could never be certain of the outcome of such an encounter.

In my case there was an added difficulty. My father had insisted that I carry something of value to use in case of need. We settled on the ring that the hapless watchmaker had made for us in Siberia from gold

The remaining rubble of the Warsaw Ghetto.

I panned. Although we had no information about customs regulations, we felt that valuables would most likely be confiscated. Accordingly, we sewed the ring into my jacket, hoping it would not be detected at the checkpoint. Unfortunately I attracted the attention of one of the officials, who, rather than embark on a thorough search, told me to declare all my valuables, explaining that such a declaration would result in a mere confiscation of the property. He pointed out that they were experts at finding hidden objects and that discovery of an undeclared item would result in cancellation of the exit visa and a severe penalty. When I denied having any valuables, he asked me to step into a private room.

I didn't know what to do. A rigid ring sewn into clothing would not be hard to find, and it would be obvious that I was trying to conceal it. Giving it up would mean the loss of an object we had worked hard to acquire and took considerable risk to retain, while remaining silent could jeopardize the entire trip my father had taken so much trouble to arrange. Immediately I was plunged back into the old world of danger and fear, and once again the course of my life seemed to hang in the balance.

The stroll to the back room was too brief for me to make up my mind. My escort was most pleasant, and when he had closed the door behind us, he became almost brotherly. "Let us wait here for a while so they think I am searching you," he said. "I understand that everybody wants to take something with him into a foreign country and I would not begrudge you that opportunity." His tone was so friendly that I could almost believe he understood my plight and even disliked the regulations he had to enforce. He was so persuasive, in fact, that I almost blurted out the information about my ring. Fortunately, I remembered what I had heard about the tactics of interrogation, and I remained silent. After a few additional amiable remarks, and no physical search, I was freed. Greatly relieved, I returned to my companions, feeling once again that I had come within a whisker of disaster, but managed to escape unscathed. After a head count, we were led outside the customs house and boarded the British ship *Eastern Prince* bound for Edinburgh. By coincidence, *Eastern Prince* had been the first ship to carry American cargo to Europe under the Lend-Lease program.[32]

I did not realize at the time what a sacrifice my father was making. Only when I had my own children could I fully appreciate how painful my departure must have been for him. Our wartime struggle had created a strong bond between us, and he must have suspected that he would never see me again. He had no family left in Poland: Most of his relatives had been killed by the Nazis, and his two cousins whom we found after the war had already left Poland illegally. He believed there was no future for me in our native country, but that in England, under my uncle's guidance, my prospects would be most auspicious. He had taken these actions against the advice of all his friends, who refused to part with their own children. Fortunately, two years later he was able to emigrate to Israel, where I saw him a number of times, but before his departure his letters to me were melancholy. He had lost his wife, and now he was voluntarily giving up his only son. We discussed his worries, and before my departure and in my subsequent letters I assured him that we would be together soon. He probably believed otherwise and was skeptical about that prospect.

Given his profound influence on my life and his contribution to whatever success I have had, I shall digress to give the reader a better understanding of the man I called "father." I have already described the

---

32. "Lend-Lease . . . was a program of the United States during World War II that allowed [it] . . . to provide Allied Powers with war material without becoming directly involved in the war." See Wikipedia, *The Free Encyclopedia*, at:http://en.wikipedia. org/wiki/Lend-lease.

My father and I just prior to my departure from Poland.

example he set in his leadership role in our exile community: his ability to analyze a situation, take proper action, and offer useful advice. When I left Poland after the war, he was still strong and healthy, though he had by then acquired a sprinkling of grey. The events of his hard life, during which he lost everything more than once, were etched in his face. Two Siberian exiles, two world wars, and the early loss of his wife made him a confirmed pessimist. He feared the future, and often, toward the end of his life, had the appearance of a broken man. Throughout our exile and after our return, my future became his top priority. In Russia he was a good provider of food and clothing, insisting that I attend school and never losing hope of our return. When we came to Poland, he did everything possible to send me to England—a sacrifice that others in our group either were not willing to make or did not know how to achieve.

He and I always had a close, if not overly demonstrative, relationship. He was not judgemental, and any direction he gave me was in the form of quiet counsel rather than instruction. In fact, the only specific advice I remember him offering just before I left Poland was *Nie rozmieniaj się na drobną monete*–literally, "Don't exchange yourself for small coins." (The actual meaning was, "Marry a person of substance.") He did not speak of the need for hard work, the importance of honesty, or the debt of gratitude I would owe my uncle, for those values were understood.

As I looked forward to my future in England, I thought of those who did not have such an opportunity. Many of my contemporaries had perished in Russia; many of the survivors did not have the running start that I was lucky enough to achieve after liberation. I was launched on a fortunate course, thanks to the direction set by my father, and it is largely to him I owe my present good life.

ENGLAND

Listening carefully to the captain's orders, I watched the ship's lines being removed from the mooring posts on shore. Gently nudged by a tugboat, the vessel slowly glided from the dock and then gathered speed toward the open sea. I felt a sense of exultation exceeding even my previous joy at leaving Russia. Having survived the war and the trials of Siberia, I was finally leaving the odious world of communism for the promised land of the West. My father had dreamed of this trip for years—since long before the war—and now this dream, so violently interrupted, was becoming a reality. Still young and immature, I had nothing in my background that would enable me to visualize England. I think I may be forgiven for conjuring up a hazy, almost heavenly universe populated by prosperous, competent, and benevolent people. Such fantasies are easily shattered, of course, especially when my expectations were so high. England certainly shimmered in stark contrast to Siberia, where our ambitions could not have been lower. In a way, those low expectations eased our plight: All we wanted was to survive, and achieving that limited goal was sufficient to make us happy. Standing on the deck of our ship that day, I could not have imagined that in London—which I thought of as the center of modern civilization, populated by the world's most educated and successful people—there would be times when I would feel more miserable than I had in Siberia. Certainly it was a shock to discover that I was not entering a paradise, and it took months to discard the fantasies and years to accept the reality that the level of kindness, generosity, and support amid our small band of exiles in the stark environment of Siberia was often higher than I would encounter in the West. Perhaps the survival instinct I honed in Siberia plus natural genetic characteristics allowed me to take my disappointment in stride. In future years I would find that the gap between my unrealistic expectations and reality would not interfere with my ability to function in the West.

Eastern Prince was the first ocean-going vessel I had ever seen. She was painted battleship gray, and the huge open space below deck was crisscrossed with girders in every conceivable direction. There were no portholes, and the darkness was thinned by dots of dim electric bulbs, superimposed on the eerie pattern of the steel beams. Dozens of hammocks hung from the metal members in jigsaw-puzzle fashion at different levels and at a multitude of angles. During the war the ship had transported troops; later it had carried the Polish soldiers who had served in the British Army from Edinburgh to Poland. Now, on this return trip to Scotland, we were her only passengers.

On the way we passed through the Kiel Canal and stopped at the German port of Cuxhaven. That day in May of 1947 was the first time I saw German civilians or any part of Germany. Not allowed to leave the ship, we could not view the results of the Allied bombing, which had largely destroyed the port. The aftermath of the war for the civilians was obvious, as they swarmed toward the ship in small boats and tried to trade household items for cigarettes and nylon stockings. They looked dejected and powerless, but our emotional war wounds were still fresh and we did not feel sorry for them—only curious at how these pitiful people could have organized the powerful German military machine.

During the crossing I explored the ship, watched the grey, rolling sea, and studied the mysterious British sailors. No one in our group spoke English and the crew did not speak Polish, making communication difficult. That situation led to a few comical incidents, especially regarding food. In the morning we received big boxes of cornflakes, bottles of milk, bowls, and spoons. Someone tried to pour milk into the bowls with flakes but decided the combination lacked flavor, and we simply ate the dry flakes from the bowls with spoons. The problem remained of how to consume the milk without glasses, since drinking from a common bottle seemed unhygienic. We solved the problem by finishing the cereal and then pouring the milk into empty bowls. We assumed that glasses were frowned upon by English gentlemen, or at least by English seamen, and that bowls, though inconvenient, were the preferred drinking vessels in that strange country.

I felt no anxiety as we approached Edinburgh. Today, I am surprised at that carefree attitude: I was, after all, traveling to a completely different world whose language I did not understand, and I was going to live with people I did not know. Whether or not I could cope with my new surroundings did not even enter my mind. And yet at seventeen, I was ill-qualified to fend for myself. The only item of value I had was the gold ring. Families, I thought, existed to provide support, and it was inconceivable that my "famous" uncle would not take excellent care of me. I was curious, but not nervous about finally meeting him.

I don't remember much about our arrival in Scotland except that we were transported by buses driving on the "wrong" side of the road to a train station. The bus carried us past Edinburgh Castle and we disembarked to board a comfortable train. The English countryside made no impression on me whatsoever; there was simply too much happening to pay much attention to the landscape. The train trip lasted all day, and darkness was falling as we rolled into a railroad station in London. We exchanged addresses of our London relatives and wondered how we would recognize our hosts, who would surely be waiting for us.

As we walked toward the end of the platform, we were struck by the sight of two women standing behind the railing at the open gate. One was very tall, the other almost a midget, and several of us cracked jokes about the height extremes of English women. As we approached the entrance, the short woman became agitated, seized the tall woman's hand, and pointed at me with her free arm. I was surprised to discover that the smaller woman was my uncle's wife, Zhenia, and the tall woman was my cousin Stella! Zhenia had recognized me from my photographs, and Stella had seen me in Poland the previous year, just before coming to England herself.

I looked around for my Uncle Ilya. In my mind he loomed larger than life—a beacon of hope that had sustained us for so many years and taken many forms in my childish imagination. Sometimes he appeared to me as a heroic monument, occasionally as a bomber pilot destroying German cities and changing the course of the war, but always as an all-powerful individual who took charge of every conceivable situation and was capable of handling any challenge. I was looking forward to seeing in the flesh what must surely be an imposing and dynamic figure, and was disappointed at his apparent absence. When I mustered the courage to ask my aunt about the whereabouts of her husband, she pointed to a man standing motionless and silent only a few yards away. He made no movement toward us, but waited for us to join him. A dignified-looking gentleman, he was nearly six feet tall, with a somewhat portly shape. Although I did not know it at the time, he was fifty-four years old, but his thin, gray hair and long, sharp-featured face made him look older. He was impeccably dressed in a striped three-piece suit of dark blue and highly polished black shoes.

On seeing me, his face remained impassive, offering no sign of welcome or recognition. My father had given me detailed instructions on how to behave during my first meeting with the relatives. Following an accepted Polish custom, I was to kiss the ladies' hands and hug and kiss my uncle on both cheeks. By the time I spotted him I had already greeted the ladies in the prescribed fashion; now I advanced toward my dignified, stationary relative. He sensed that I was about to kiss him, however, and quickly stepped back, leaving me somewhat bewildered. This was his first reaction to my arrival. Instead of hugging and kissing, we shook hands and exchanged a few words. The ladies joined us and we moved toward the exit in total silence. I followed my relatives, carrying the one small battered suitcase that contained all my worldly possessions.

It was dark outside as we made our way to my uncle's car, a blue 1939 Dodge. I had heard so many heroic stories about my uncle that I expected everything about him to be superhuman, and it did not surprise me that his American-made car was considerably larger than the British vehicles. I knew nothing about cars then—it might as well have been a Rolls. Of course I also expected him to have a uniformed chauffeur and was quite disappointed when he took the driver's seat himself. During our drive from the station, I was his front-seat companion, while the two women sat in the back. We first dropped off Stella and then drove to my uncle's house. The conversation during the trip did not flow easily. My uncle's thoughts seemed to be far away. I was most anxious to express my happiness at finally meeting my London relatives, but I elicited only a restrained reaction: a poker face from my uncle and uncertain replies from my aunt.

I had expected them to live in a palace, so again their house was a disappointment. I was not aware that they lived in one of the best parts of London, their apartment occupying the fourth and fifth floors of a building they owned on Devonshire Place, WI, next to Harley Street, famous as the location of the most renowned British physicians. The first three floors of my relatives' building were devoted to doctors' offices, including my uncle's professional quarters. We entered the building through a door that was kept locked, crossed a small, neat lobby, and rode a modern elevator to the third floor. After ascending a flight of stairs we finally arrived at my relatives' apartment. Despite my initial surprise at not being ushered into a castle, I liked the place immediately. I found out later that the apartment—and for that matter, the entire building—had been remodeled under the supervision of my cousin, Bronek Katz. Bronek, on my father's side of the family, was a well-known architect in London who had managed to combine the features of the old English building with contemporary touches to produce a delightful modern dwelling. The front door opened onto a well-lit corridor with a deep blue Chinese runner rug leading to an area with entrances to a kitchen, a dining room, and a living room; a curved staircase rose to the upper floor. There was a large table under the stairs and a built-in bench that curved three-quarters of the way around the table. The kitchen was directly in front of the corridor, but at least twice its width, and the dining room was adjacent to the kitchen. Both rooms faced the street, and between them they occupied the entire width of the building. The living room shared the wall with the corridor and was the biggest room in the apartment. My uncle invited me to join him there while my aunt prepared tea.

It was a new experience for me to step on a large, plush carpet that covered most of the living room floor. The carpet, like the corridor runner, was an antique deep blue Chinese rug that dominated the entire room. I took short, careful steps, as though walking on a well-manicured lawn that I didn't want to disturb, and sat in an armchair facing my uncle. The room had display cabinets attached to one wall, a grand piano, and a second sitting area with a table, a long, L-shaped, built-in bench, and a music console.

After our tea and another brief, unemotional conversation, we retired upstairs where there were four bedrooms and a modern bathroom. My bedroom was inviting and cozy. Besides a comfortable bed, it had a big wardrobe almost completely filled with my aunt's clothes and a beautiful kidney-shaped antique English desk with a leather inlay top. I was to spend many hours behind that desk, and years later I bought a similar piece of furniture in Boston. Facing the street, my room was more than adequate for my purposes. For the first time, I had a room of my own, although I never felt that it was really mine and never gained that wonderful feeling of privacy that one has in one's own home.

My aunt and uncle had no children. A forty-year-old woman, Edna Lucie, occupied one of the bedrooms. She had been my uncle's secretary before the war, and during the London blitz she had been hit by a bomb fragment that penetrated her skull, sending her to the hospital in serious condition for many weeks. She emerged from that ordeal with a slight speech impediment and a pronounced limp. Edna was a kind, honest, and pleasant person, but poorly educated and of simple thoughts and needs. She revered my uncle, always referring to him as "the doctor." She and my aunt were practically inseparable, seemingly always engaged in quiet chatter and household activities.

Another woman named Dorothy Fothergill, around the same age as Edna, was a frequent visitor. Short and slight in build, and a self-proclaimed connoisseur of the English language, she was a writer and illustrator of children's books. She came to the apartment every weekend and many evenings, traveling by bus from her house in the London suburb of Golders Green. She spent all her time entertaining my uncle in an incessant and usually one-sided chatter, offering him tales and accounts of various exploits that I could not understand for several months, until I had picked up a working knowledge of English. The relationship between Dorothy and Edna was clearly a cool one. Dorothy initiated occasional conversations with Edna, using a less-than-literary style of speech to discuss topics that she thought Edna could follow. Edna, while civil and polite, understandably resented Dorothy's condescending and patronizing attitude. These conversations were brief and rare.

I don't remember my aunt and uncle talking to each other except for occasional functional exchanges, such as "Shall we go to the movies?" or "Let's have dinner." Dinner was the only occasion that brought my relatives, Edna, and me together, and it fell to me to promote the conversation, which seldom flowed easily due to my uncle's sparse responses and the virtual silence of Edna and Aunt Zhenia. Many years later I learned from my Australian aunt that my uncle did appreciate my efforts—apparently even lavish with his praise of me—and told his sister that I always "entertained" them at the dinner table. When Dorothy was with us, conversation was not a problem, for she was a lively companion. But initially I could not take part in her discussions because of my inadequate knowledge of English.

A man of action, my uncle immediately began mapping the course of my education. He wanted me to study at the University of London, which meant that I would have to pass the London matriculation examination, which was essentially a test of high school education. The examination was given in five subjects: There were compulsory tests in English and mathematics, a third in a major foreign language, and two other electives from a wide range of disciplines. Fortunately Russian

Uncle Ilya, Dorothy and Aunt Zhenia.

was considered to be a major language, and I chose Polish and mechanics for my electives. The two foreign languages did not present a problem, and the quantitative subjects turned out to be easy for me to master against my background of a good Russian education in physics and mathematics. Thus I could devote most of my time to the study of English, although I realized I would have to learn English terminology in mathematics and mechanics as well as fill in the gaps of substance that may have existed due to differences in the two countries' curricula.

With his usual efficiency, my uncle arranged for Dorothy to be my private English tutor and also enrolled me in a six-week summer course in introductory English for foreigners at nearby Regent Polytechnic. In September I began a full-time course of study in English and mathematics at City of London College. Despite the word "College" in its name, the school did not award degrees; it offered, among others, courses leading to matriculation diplomas needed for admission to London

University. To cover the other subjects, I attended a night course in mechanics at Regent Polytechnic. Clearly I did not need coaching in Polish and Russian. The goal of all that activity was for me to take a trial examination the following June, a year away, and pass the test six months later, in January 1949.

The lessons with Dorothy started immediately. I used my uncle's old bicycle to travel to Dorothy's house in Golders Green two or three times a week. She was a good teacher and gave me plenty of homework. My progress received a practical test just a month later when my aunt, uncle, Dorothy, and Edna left for their annual six-week car tour of the continent. In their absence, they arranged for me to stay with an English family, the Metcalfs, who also lived in Golders Green. They were delightful people, and despite my initial misgivings, I enjoyed my stay with them. Mr. Metcalf was a solicitor; Mrs. Metcalf stayed at home. They had a daughter, Leoni, who was an aspiring actress, and a son, Peter, who was around twelve. Mrs. Metcalf extended warm hospitality and did her best to teach me conversational English by talking to me at every opportunity. She also introduced me to many local customs and practices, especially to the big English breakfast and afternoon tea.

I tried to be helpful wherever I could, but I was able to make a contribution in only two areas. One was my daily excursion to the fishmonger's, where I bought fish for my hostess to cook for her cat. (Canned cat food was not available in England at that time.) I was proud to be able to negotiate that purchase in English, but it was clear that Mrs. Metcalf had less confidence in my competence to buy other food items at the greengrocers; for those expeditions, my role was to carry her purchases. My second contribution was to meet Leoni late at night at the tube station when she returned from her daily trips to London, presumably for rehearsals or auditions. Leoni was an attractive girl, and I felt frustrated that my English wasn't good enough to carry on a normal conversation on our way home. It's not that I wanted to be romantically involved; she was a few years my senior and much more mature. I just felt that a young lady should not walk alone late at night, even though that part of suburban London was completely safe.

On one occasion the Metcalfs took me to see the American musical *Oklahoma*, my first musical play. Before the war, I had seen a few children's plays in Warsaw, but otherwise I was a complete theater novice. I could not understand the language, and the songs and dances seemed not only frivolous but silly. I don't even think I realized that the action took place in the United States. It sounds strange now, but as the play progressed, I found myself sinking into deep depression. Without understanding the language, I could not appreciate *Oklahoma,* and my thoughts strayed to other topics—the horrors of the war and the sufferings we endured in Siberia. The contrast between those events and the gaiety of the performance was stark and incongruous. A starving beggar watching happy diners consuming vast quantities of food feels deep resentment, which sharpens his hunger. I became indignant at the audience and the entire Western attitude toward life. How could these people take part in such frivolous pursuits when in Eastern Europe the effects of the war were still rampant and entire nations were suffering under the Communist yoke? I felt uneasy at participating in this charade, and my face must have shown it. Mrs. Metcalf asked if there was something wrong. My rudimentary English was insufficient to explain my feelings, and in any case it was not a subject I was prepared to discuss. My hosts had gone to a great deal of trouble to entertain me and I didn't wish to appear ungrateful.

Since that time I have, of course, realized that life should not always be serious, nor do I feel that suffering in one place should preclude entertainment in another. Some Holocaust survivors harbor a feeling of guilt about being spared while so many others perished. I never shared that feeling, but perhaps on that evening at the theater I felt uneasy at being entertained in London while my father and friends still languished in Poland.

Moving in with the Metcalfs did not interrupt my studies of English at Regent Polytechnic. Sad to say, I felt much more at ease with the Metcalfs than with my aunt and uncle. The daily contact with foreign students at the school put me among people who were also new to the country and with whom I had a lot in common. I met no one from

Siberia, but a few Europeans had survival stories no less harrowing than mine. I also saw, for the first time, people from other lands: South Americans, Indians, and Africans.

I almost made an enemy of one of my fellow students, a Cypriot whom I mistook for a Jew. Until my arrival in the West, the only people I had seen with what I thought were Semitic features were Jews, and it did not occur to me that other nationalities—including those from the Middle East—would also have dark skin and black, curly hair. I don't even know if the Cypriot was of Turkish or Greek descent, but he became indignant that I dared to mistake his ethnicity.

My closest companion at Regent Polytechnic was a banker named Louis Alberto Mejia from Lima, Peru. Despite our mutual lack of English fluency, we managed to communicate well. The day before our "graduation" we held a small party, and one of the Indian women read everyone's palms. I watched her carefully to see if she would tell all students the same general story one normally hears from palm readers, but she seemed to be a genuine believer in palmistry and had a different reading for every student. When my turn came she took a long look at my hands and emitted something resembling a "wow" sound followed by an admiring smile and a verdict: I was not an independent person right now, she said, but I would become fully self-reliant in the future. Sitting there in my ill-fitting clothes, speaking poor English and unable to disguise my youth and inexperience, I did not seem a likely candidate for such a prediction. My dependence on others was apparent, and any independence I might achieve surely lay far in the future. But her promise made me feel good—and her prophesy eventually did come true. Although I had no way of knowing it at the time, I would eventually move to the United States, raise a wonderful family, and achieve financial independence.

At the ceremony following the final examination, we all received formal certificates, which were much bigger and more ornate than the diploma I was later awarded on graduation from the University of London. I had now been in England for three months, and my knowledge of English was improving rapidly. My youth, total immersion in my studies, help from the Metcalf family, lessons from Dorothy, and stimulating coursework at the Regent Polytechnic were having their desired effect. When I entered the City of London College in September 1947, I could follow the classes designed for English students, although the standard of my writing must still have been pitiful.

In December I had a chance to review my achievements in the English language. The English teacher at the City of London College gave us a test similar to the one we would take at the end of the year. Based on our results, she divided the class into four categories. The first one was almost guaranteed to pass the examination in June; the second might succeed if they studied hard; the third had little chance of passing and consisted mainly of foreign students in the class. And I was a member of the small fourth group—which she simply ignored. The teacher's evaluation did not surprise me. After just six months in England, I could not hope to reach the writing standards expected of English secondary school students. Despite her pessimistic prognosis, however, I decided to take the examinations in June, just to practice taking written tests in my new country. It became clear that my main problem would be the two compositions, and my uncle devised a strategy to help me pass the test. He asked Dorothy to compose several essays on subjects likely to be given during the examination and told me to memorize them word for word. It was just possible, he reasoned, that those topics would be given during the test in which case I would simply reproduce Dorothy's composition. If they were not given, as was more likely, Dorothy would have set an example of good writing and I would retain the lessons if I learned her work by heart. Although I doubted the morality and effectiveness of this approach, we carried out his plan anyway. When I eventually took the examination in June 1948, the topics required for the two essays bore little resemblance to any of Dorothy's chosen subjects.

Around that time, despite my poor showing in December, I began discovering the joys of the English language. The first books I read were by Jack London, Arthur Conan Doyle, and Jules Verne. I had read Russian or Polish translations of works by those authors, and I was familiar with the contents. Remembering the texts helped to make up for my poor command of English and decreased my dependence on dictionaries. Later, as my language skills improved, I read short stories by Somerset Maugham. I liked Francis Bacon and thought his short essays would be particularly useful as examples of good writing for my exams. Francis Bacon opened up the world of the English essay, a medium that was new to me. Russian literature has a number of superb short story writers, but I realized that it was the English who had developed essay writing to a fine art.

One day I found a particularly good book in our library: a collection of essays by Lin Yutang, on a large variety of topics. I studied them assiduously; they were easy to understand and I hoped to imitate the author's style in the compositions set for my impending exams. I was very excited by my find and showed it to Dorothy. Her reaction was strange. She told me she was familiar with the book and that I should concentrate only on certain parts, because reading all of it would interfere with my other studies. She carefully listed the pages I should read and isolated chapters for me to ignore. I took her advice at face value until I found that she wanted me to avoid an essay on travel. The reason was obvious: She had copied that same essay almost verbatim and presented it as an example of her own good writing in an attempt to fulfill my uncle's request! I was disgusted. Here was a woman I respected as my teacher, a good writer who felt she had to resort to plagiarism. I had memorized several of "Dorothy's essays" and could have reproduced them during my exams. Those copied from Lin Yutang might well have been recognized and I could have been barred from entering London University. That possibility did not seem to bother Dorothy; her sole motive had been to impress my uncle. I think she may have been in love with him. I don't know if he responded to her feelings. Although I eventually told my uncle of her duplicity, that revelation did not alter their relationship.

On the day of the big test in June, twelve months after my arrival in England, I walked through the long underground tunnel connecting the tube station to the exit near Imperial College in Kensington where the matriculation examination was administered. During that walk I asked myself, "Where are you going? You know this is just a dry run, but is it really worthwhile to make a fool of yourself just to practice taking the exam?"

Unexpectedly, however, I felt quite comfortable during the tests. As I had anticipated, I finished the Polish and Russian examinations in less than half the allotted time. Mathematics and mechanics were easy, although I still had some doubts about my mastery of inches and pounds. The two topics I chose for my English essays were "Plans you would make for a friend visiting London over a weekend," and "The speech you would make upon the departure of a member of your club or a society." I had recently visited many interesting places in London and remembered them well, which gave me ample material for the first essay. In Russia, we had to read heroic speeches about great achievements of communism and its leaders, and that came in handy for tackling the second topic. Of course I was not confident about my overall command of the language, and did not expect to pass the examination.

Six weeks later the results were posted on a university board, and I examined them "just in case." There were two categories of successful candidates. I looked for my name in the Second Division, and, as I expected, my name was not there. I then studied the much shorter roster of the First Division to see which of my classmates had achieved that distinction. Incredibly, that is where I found my name. Needless to say, I was proud of my achievement—my test results were better and I passed the test sooner than anyone had expected. But the triumph elicited a remarkably muted reaction from my uncle. Since my arrival in England, he had been highly critical of all my efforts, so my placement in the First Division must have come as a shock. I am sure he was happy for me, but he did not like to be proved wrong in his prediction that I "would never amount to anything." He tried his best to show pleasure, but quickly changed the subject and left the room.

LIFE WITH UNCLE

DURING MY FIRST YEAR in England, I was preoccupied with studying for the London matriculation certificate, but despite my excitement, hard work, and eventual achievement of that goal, I remember that time as one of the unhappiest periods of my life. In view of my Siberian exile, that might appear surprising, but a description of my relatives' background and personalities might shed some light on my feelings.

The extent of my uncle's talents and achievements was almost incredible. At the vocational level, he was one of the best—if not the best—ear, nose, and throat surgeons in England. Before the Second World War, his patients included those members of the Tsar's family who managed to escape to England and lived there with the help of British royalty. After the war he went to the United States to learn a new operating method: on his return, he was the only British surgeon who could restore hearing in the case of a disability previously considered to be incurable. He was on the staff of two prestigious hospitals, received patients in a private office in his building, and had a small laboratory in the basement where he occasionally practiced operating procedures on inner ears he received from organ banks. He was a person of remarkable intellect and had an unusually wide range of interests.

At home I never heard him talk about medicine. He was bored by small talk but could, and often did, recite long monologues on many serious topics. He was interested in foreign affairs, especially as they related to the Soviet Union, but he was also well informed about other parts of the world. He was a student of literature and well versed in the world's major religions, art, psychology, philosophy, and history. An avid reader, despite having only a small reference collection at home, he borrowed books from public and private libraries. In his younger days he had been a passable violinist. He was fluent in German, French, English, and Russian, and had a working knowledge of Italian and Spanish. He was an organized, systematic gatherer of knowledge, and before taking his yearly summer trips to the Continent, he studied the background and language of the countries to be visited and did research on the sights they would see.

Unfortunately, his prodigious abilities were accompanied by less agreeable qualities, especially a lack of patience with others and an abrupt manner of dealing with people, including members of his family. My aunt told me that during his travels, he frequently quarreled with native guides when they could not answer his questions. Apparently he did not hesitate to lecture them on their inadequate knowledge of their subjects. A man of iron will, he was apparently incapable of any compromise. A person might be dismissed as purely obstinate when he refuses to change his mind once proved wrong, but my uncle was rarely wrong. He just saw everything in black and white, and delivered his opinions accordingly. I seldom saw him in action outside the house, but I formed an opinion about his attitude toward his hospital coworkers and subordinates by listening to his end of a few telephone conversations. I was not eavesdropping, but even in such a large apartment it was impossible not to hear his angry outbursts. Any hospital request to reschedule an operation or change the operating room, for example, was met with indignant refusals, statements that such requests did not qualify as topics for discussion, and instructions never to bring up similar points in the future. At that time, doctors in England wielded a lot of power in hospitals, but my uncle seemed to take his authority beyond reasonable limits.

At home he was an absolute dictator and created what I think was an unhealthy atmosphere. Of the three women who were usually present, only Dorothy attempted to communicate with him. Edna was happy just to be there, and remained quietly in the background since she had nothing "worthy" to discuss with my uncle. My aunt seemed to be content to run the household and, at least outwardly, never opposed her husband. He largely ignored her, but I noticed that he became especially irritated when, on a couple of occasions, she tried to pay for tickets at the movies. He angrily grabbed her money, shoved it aside, and paid out of his pocket. Much later I learned that she came from a wealthy pre-Revolutionary Russian family, and that my aunt and uncle maintained separate financial accounts. At the same time, it was apparent that my uncle could be most charming and gallant under the right circumstances, and he was greatly admired by a wide circle of friends. He was an honest, compassionate, and honorable man, but his brusque manner and rough, though always politely worded, talk often made him hard to bear.

Over the years I tried to learn the details of my uncle's early life, but he refused to discuss them. He remained aloof, probably considering the matter too intimate to share, even with his own nephew. I pieced together most of what I know from conversations with his sister, my Aunt Rosa, when I met her in New York many years later.

My Uncle Ilya was born into a large family in the Siberian town of Petropavlovsk in 1891. As far as I could determine, his grandfather, named Naum Vitenson, had moved or was taken to Siberia under mysterious circumstances. The patriarch never confided to his children the reason for his departure from his original home in the European part of Russia. At that time, as my Aunt Rosa put it, "It was easy to be sent to Siberia for all kinds of reasons." Or, he might have elected to go there to escape the pogroms in the western part of the Russian empire.

The old man's family managed to stay together and thrive, and by the time my uncle was born, the clan consisted of many relatives all living in one house. The Vitenson family was in the steel distribution business, importing prefabricated rods and other raw stock from the European part of Russia for local sale. According to Aunt Rosa, the youngest sibling of my uncle's generation, every member of the family worked together in the uncovered, fenced-in space where the steel was stored. The work was hard and especially hazardous in the winter, when any contact between the metal and bare hands resulted in skin "burns" that would take weeks to heal. Otherwise, life was good, and lack of privacy was offset by the warm camaraderie, especially on religious and national holidays and during family celebrations.

The Vitensons, following the trend of the times, believed in having large families. My uncle's grandfather had five sons and four daughters, one of whom, Nicolas Vitenson, was Uncle Ilya's father. Each of them in turn had at least seven children, with one of them raising a family of ten. It was not unusual for celebrations in my uncle's Siberian household to include over two hundred family members. Ilya was the eldest of five brothers and two sisters, one of whom, Miriam, was my mother.

The grandchildren of the patriarch, including my uncle, attended a local school, but their mother—my grandmother—was for a long time illiterate, like many women of her generation. But despite her lack of formal education, she was a remarkable woman. As soon as Ilya learned to read and write, she acquired those skills from him and then proceeded to read most of the Russian classics on her own. She also insisted that her sons obtain a college education. The quotas at Russian universities did not allow more than a certain percentage of siblings from one Jewish family to attend, but she successfully pleaded with the governor of the local province to have the rule waived, with the result that four of the five brothers were accepted for undergraduate studies at the university in the Siberian town of Tomsk.

It is not clear what professions Uncle Ilya and his brothers wanted to follow, but again the Jewish quotas for most desirable fields such as law or engineering were tiny. Medicine was not as popular with most Russians, consequently quotas for medical studies were much more generous for Jewish students. My uncle and three of his brothers studied medicine at Tomsk University and eventually became practicing physicians. The fifth boy stayed home to help in the family business and provided early financial support to his more fortunate brothers. Before the

First World War, my uncle transferred from Tomsk to a school in Germany to finish his medical studies. After the war he returned home and served (or was drafted) into Kolchak's army, which fought against the Bolsheviks during the civil war unleashed by the 1917 October Revolution.

After the civil war, my uncle, his parents, two sisters (Aunt Rosa and my mother), and one brother escaped to China. Following World War I Uncle Ilya made his way from China back to Germany, where he practiced medicine and helped support the family members who remained in China. Aunt Rosa managed to settle in Australia a few years after Mao's revolution.

In China my uncle had initially settled in Harbin, where he met his future wife, Zhenia Tonkonogoff. The Tonkonogoffs originally came from the Siberian town of Eniseisk and were among the wealthiest Jewish families in pre-Revolutionary Russia. They traded furs in Russia and Europe and had warehouses in Moscow and St. Petersburg, as well as in London and Frankfurt. During the Revolution, they were able to rescue enough wealth— most of it just the value of the inventory stored in their foreign warehouses—to support the entire family in the West for the rest of their lives. It was a large family, consisting of twenty-six people. None of

Uncle Ilya in the uniform of Kolchak's army.

Aunt Zhenia's parents, pre-World War I.

them worked or engaged in any kind of business after leaving Russia, and they all lived well, though not extravagantly, in Nice, Paris, London, and New York. As far as I know, no children were born to any of them. In many ways, the clan was typical of emigré society from Tsarist Russia. To the end of their lives, many of them believed that the Communist government was a temporary phenomenon, and that they would all eventually return to Russia, resurrect the old order, and have their property restored. Few of them integrated into western society or set down roots in their new countries. The family gradually died out, most having lived comfortably to an old age, with Zhenia surviving them all until her death at 95 on July 1, 1990.

When my uncle met Zhenia, she had already graduated from a dental school in St. Petersburg. They were married in Harbin and later settled in Germany. Part of her "dowry," my Aunt Rosa told me, was a commitment by Zhenia's father to help the rest of my uncle's clan. That apparently never happened, creating bad feeling among the Vitensons toward the Tonkonogoffs. In the early 1930s Ilya and Zhenia visited London and decided to move there permanently if my uncle could pass the British examination required to practice medicine in England. He accomplished that task with his usual determination, and they then settled in England, became British subjects, and lived through the London blitz during the Second World War.

The little I did learn makes me yearn for more of my uncle's story. For example, an event he described from his early life illustrates the effect of indecision on a person's fate. The incident took place during the civil war that followed the Communist revolution, when Siberia was still under the control of anti-Soviet forces commanded by Admiral Kolchak, in whose army my uncle had been serving. Early one morning, he was awakened by loud knocking on his door. The soldiers outside told him to report to the local commander, who was forming a firing squad to execute two "Reds." My uncle was needed to certify the eventual deaths of the prisoners.

He dressed quickly and reported to the command post. There several soldiers ordered the two victims into the back of an open truck and asked my uncle to accompany them. It was a fairly long ride, during which the two condemned men pleaded for mercy. "Brothers," they kept repeating, "we did absolutely nothing wrong. Why would it bother you if we stayed alive?" The soldiers not only ignored their pleas, but behaved as if they were going to a picnic. They joked, sang songs, told stories, and generally enjoyed themselves. Upon arriving at the edge of a forest, the site of the intended execution, they ordered the two prisoners to dig their own grave. One of them was a frail old man, the other a young person, tall and strong. After digging the grave, they were ordered to stand in front of the hole.

At that point the young prisoner suddenly dashed into the forest. The soldiers, taken by surprise, shot at him unsuccessfully, and he disappeared among the trees. They all ran off after him into the woods, leaving my uncle and the other condemned man behind. The old man just stood at the edge of the grave, too paralyzed with fear to escape. My uncle was reluctant to encourage him to leave the scene for fear of being overheard and accused of treason by the returning soldiers, but he did walk away, turning his back toward the old man and to give him a clear opportunity to save himself. It did no good. After about half an hour, the soldiers returned empty-handed and shot the old man. My uncle verified that the prisoner was dead, and after burying the body, they all returned home.

Why was I so unhappy during that first year in England? Undoubtedly the shock of being separated from my father and everyone I knew strongly influenced my attitude. The change in surroundings from Siberia and post-war Poland to England, especially my uncle's England, was also unsettling. But it was the way my relatives treated me at home—the humiliation—that disturbed me most. The first incident took place scarcely a week after my arrival. With Dorothy's help, I had plunged into my study of English. After doing my homework, I came downstairs into the living room where my uncle was examining a newspaper and started reading a book. He said nothing, but became indignant when the same thing happened the following day. At first there was silence, but then I was treated to a haughty outburst: "You shouldn't be here; you should be studying upstairs. You are not going to achieve anything with your head. It is your behind that has to work for you. Only by sitting on your behind at your desk will you learn anything."

No one had ever spoken to me in quite that tone of voice. I was bothered by his attitude, and probably even more by his implied lack of confidence in my desire to study. "Different people use different parts of their body for the same purposes, depending on what those parts contain," I thought irreverently. "If you have more brains in your behind than your head, then you should use your seat where others might use their heads to do their thinking." Still seventeen and clearly defiant, I was also quite helpless. I went up to my room and continued to read the book at my desk. After that incident, I seldom left my room except for meals. The relationship between my uncle and me was changed permanently by this outburst, and even in later years it was never as close as I wished it to be.

He was critical of everything I did and applied what I can only describe as shock treatment to make a sophisticated man out of me. For example, shortly after my arrival, he inquired about my interest in art. My previous exposure to painting had been limited to Russian Revolutionary art, which consisted mainly of portraits of Lenin and Stalin or depictions of the achievements of the Bolshevik Revolution. "I want you to visit London museums and art galleries on Bond Street," he announced, insisting that I start my tour the next day. Naturally I complied with his wishes. Bond Street was within walking distance, but I think the sudden, mandatory nature of the assignment set back my interest in art by a few years. To this day I feel uncomfortable browsing through galleries with no intention of buying anything. At that time it was a scary experience for a boy who knew nothing about the content or etiquette of the London art world and did not speak the language. I might have felt differently if he had spent at least a couple of hours with me during my first museum foray, instead of expecting a detailed report of my impressions. He was never satisfied with the descriptions of my visits, with the result that I went through the motions but hardly absorbed anything.

Occasionally, his attitude bordered on the ridiculous. A few months after my arrival in England, my father sent me a small parcel through someone who lived outside London but was able to visit Poland. Such visits were rare, since the Communist government issued few visas to outsiders. We had corresponded several times to establish what my father should send me, but the parcel was less important than meeting the person who had actually seen my father. All correspondence between

Poland and England was likely to be censored, and I was most anxious to hear any verbal message my father had sent by way of this visitor. It turned out that he had no new revelations, but it was reassuring simply to see a man who had just met my father in the flesh. The conditions in Poland had not changed since my departure, but my father still hoped we would be reunited in the near future. The parcel contained a few photographs and a booklet with a cover made of Polish amber. Between travel time and the detailed discussion, the trip to retrieve my parcel took several hours, and this provoked an angry outburst from my uncle, whose view was that that time would have been better spent studying.

He also decided that I should meet young English people, and he arranged for me to attend Sunday afternoon teas that a Protestant minister was holding for his congregation's youth. The minister received me with open arms and his other guests were most gracious, but I felt like a fifth wheel at those small, sedate gatherings. I did not speak the language and felt I was ruining their afternoons by forcing them to abandon their usual conversation and try to communicate with me. Somehow the message (or perhaps complaints) must have filtered through to my uncle, because after just a few Sundays I was able to discontinue my visits.

My uncle clearly sensed that I did not agree with his extreme policies, although I was always polite and never raised my voice to him. On one occasion I even broke into tears, something that had never happened in Siberia, except after my mother's death. A seemingly innocuous occasion, it made clear my real status in that household. It was a foggy London Sunday, with the air so thick that it obscured the other side of the street. As usual I was studying at my desk when, following my uncle's instructions, Edna came into my room and announced that I had the doctor's permission to come downstairs. That little phrase crystallized in my mind the fact that I was almost under house arrest—in effect, prohibited from going from one room to another without permission. I remained at my desk despite another summons from Edna, and about half an hour later, sensing that something was wrong, my uncle came to the door of my room. He did not inquire about my state of mind, but, in a voice that for the first time showed a measure of concern, simply said, "I hope you have been watching the fog."

My aunt did not make the situation any better. I think she was an unhappy woman. She told me later that her husband had never wanted children, a sentiment she probably considered an insult. My aunt supplied my clothing and provided the cash allowance, which she dispensed in small amounts, usually by the ten-shilling note (equivalent to about $1.50), but only after I was forced to ask for it—something I found extremely unpleasant. Each such transaction was accompanied by frowns, derogatory grunts, and the observation that I was spending too much. I did not suffer this indignity gladly, but I did my best to minimize expenses. Those ten-shilling alms—which is how I looked at them—usually lasted a couple of months. I spent the money primarily on school supplies and did all I could to postpone the next humiliating request for funds. My school courses were free, Dorothy's private lessons were either free or she was compensated directly by my uncle, and I used my uncle's old bicycle for all my travels. I ate every meal at home and bought no clothes.

To add insult to injury, there were several occasions when my aunt appeared to take delight in making fun of me in front of others. A prized possession at that time was a coupon used for buying sweets, which were strictly rationed. Naturally, I considered such purchases to be luxuries I could forego in view of my limited funds. In my presence, my aunt told several people I was so tight-fisted that I would let those coupons expire rather than spend them. Of course she did not offer the additional funds or use my coupons to buy the sweets for me.

I had arrived in England with few possessions. I had one new suit and a good pair of shoes, but the suit was of poor quality and soon became useless. My aunt did not buy any new clothing for me. Instead I inherited one of my uncle's old suits and a few shirts. It was embarrassing to wear those garments: the suits were too large at the waist and not quite long enough at the arms and legs. They were also too formal for a boy my age. Socks presented no problem, because in Russia and Poland I had learned to darn quite well. I think the only clothing I bought that first year in England was a pair of shoes, since my uncle wore a different size. By the end of the year I understood what it meant to be treated like a poor relation. In all fairness, my aunt's tight-fisted attitude was not restricted to me; she was equally stingy with laundry employees, the cleaning women, and Edna. But these people were not totally dependent on her for their support.

In Russia I had become accustomed to living with shortages of essential items, including food, but somehow my life as a poor relation in London was often more traumatic than life as a prisoner. Poverty in Russia was imposed on many; it wasn't personal, but it was the general condition of the country. The Communist regime was a distant though pervasive authority, and we accepted that, too, as an inevitable hardship, just as we accepted the severe climate. We knew we could change neither and grudgingly came to terms with both. On the other hand, I found my uncle's harshness offensive and my aunt's parsimony capricious—perhaps even malicious. In Russia I could obtain extra food by collecting berries, panning for gold, or working in the mines. In London, I felt completely dependent on one woman and totally without alternatives. I envied those around me who could afford to take buses or subways. In that connection, one thought kept recurring, "There are so many people here who would not miss half a crown (about a quarter)—a modest sum of money that, in my hands, could be used for bus fares when it rained heavily or to go places too distant to be reached on a bicycle."

I did the only thing I could to raise additional funds: I sold my only valuable possession other than my gold ring, which was too precious to part with. Over a number of years in Russia, I had laboriously assembled a collection of Soviet stamps issued to commemorate important national, sporting, and artistic events. One day I visited several philatelic shops and sold my treasured collection of several hundred pieces to the highest bidder for seven shillings and sixpence, a sum equivalent to approximately one dollar.

Curiously, I did not develop any hatred toward my aunt—only lack of respect. In fact, although we were never close, I felt strong family ties to her. Many years later in New York, when she became totally disabled, I did my best to ease her pain and provide her with good medical care. When at the age of ninety-five she finally passed away, I felt a sense of deep personal loss.

The transition from life in Eastern Europe, where I was treated like an adult, to my frustrating dependency in England was not an easy one, but I drew on several sources of strength. I had two cousins and an aunt from my father's side of the family who had also settled in England and who seemed genuinely interested in my progress. The cousins were almost my father's age, and their encouragement helped me to live with my uncle's continual criticism. My cousin Bronek Katz and his wife, Janna, were especially helpful. The other cousin, Stella Tohari, and her husband were also most hospitable. My Aunt Dora served me old-fashioned Polish meals.

But the main source of encouragement was my father. We wrote each other at least once a week, and those letters formed a vital lifeline. He understood my problems, expressed full confidence in my judgment and ability to cope, and tried to put the situation in proper perspective by occasionally comparing my circumstances with the major difficulties we had overcome in Siberia. He commented on most of my complaints and helped nurture my spirit and preserve my confidence. At the same time, he frequently reminded me, without undue pressure, that I should concentrate on my studies and not abandon my goals. That he was able to give me such support was impressive, for not only was he alone in the world, but his own future was uncertain. On rereading his letters recently, I saw many allusions that escaped me when I was seventeen. He was trying to tell me that I was the only person he had in the world, and that my future was also his future. Two Siberian exiles and two world wars had wrought their destructive effect on him, and he, too, occasionally felt the need to cry for help. But at the time I was too preoccupied with my own problems to notice his pain.

Since it was not safe for Poles to communicate with relatives in the West, he destroyed the letters I sent to him in Poland, although he kept everything I subsequently mailed to Israel. I wish I could reread those Polish letters today, for they would remind me most accurately of my state of mind. But his letters to me, which I preserved, give a reasonably close approximation. I must have sounded discouraged and bitter about my relatives and Dorothy.

Gradually I became more comfortable with my new surroundings, and my English improved markedly. I made a number of good friends in school, both foreign and English, with the latter not at all conforming to the stereotype image of the cold English person. About three months before matriculation, my uncle came to the conclusion that I would never amount to anything—at least, that is what he told me. As a result, he said, he had lost interest in my studies and my general development, and I would now have to cope without his help. I could hardly contain my joy at this pronouncement. He did, in fact, change his attitude toward me by ceasing to interfere with everything I did, thereby making my life much easier. Toward the end of the year, I believe he understood for the first time the miserly way in which my aunt supplied me with money. He opened a bank account in my name with an initial deposit of ten pounds, which seemed enormous to me. He also gave me a modest but adequate budget and asked that I inform him when I ran out of money. I did not abuse the privilege, and he never made me feel bad when I requested additional funds.

I have occasionally asked myself whether the harsh treatment I received that year helped build my character. My uncle's attitude was certainly tough. It was probably best summarized by my father in one of his letters. He described a conversation between my mother and my uncle during his trip to Poland when I was two years old. They were discussing the way children should be brought up, presumably with my future in mind. "You have to bring up these kids with a stern hand," he told her. "Keep them on a short leash, do nothing to spoil them. Then they will grow up to be good, respectable people. But what are your chances of doing it? You are a weak woman."

That philosophy was probably not unique at the time, and my experience with my uncle did me no lasting harm. Indeed, it would even be possible to argue that my relatives were motivated strictly by their idea of what was good for me. My uncle might have insisted on the long hours of study so that he could convince himself of my sense of responsibility. He might have stepped back and said he had lost interest in my progress, knowing that his withdrawal would encourage me to study harder in order to refute his low assessment of my abilities. My aunt's frugality might have been well meant, intended to teach me the value of money. So, their every action might have been carefully planned to build my resilience and teach me to overcome difficulties—I'll never know for sure.

Whatever my uncle's motivation, he, like my father, had a profound influence on my life, but the two men could not have been more different. My father always treated the people around him at least as equals, while my uncle invariably asserted his superiority. Ilya had to be in charge of every situation to the point of micromanaging his relatives' lives, and he demanded absolute obedience, both at home and at work. He believed that his knowledge of his chosen subjects—and that included practically everything—and of life in general was superior to almost anyone else's. He was a poor listener, and discussions with him usually degenerated into silence or a one-sided pronouncement of his views. By the time I arrived in London, my uncle and Zhenia had grown apart in an unhappy marriage. Their personalities must have developed at a different pace, and they formed an unlikely couple. He was an inquisitive, tall, distinguished, handsome, and elegant man; she was a socially awkward woman with limited horizons, of small stature, and spoiled by her wealthy upbringing. However, they had learned to live together in their different worlds, and I never witnessed any quarrels or even loud arguments between them.

Ilya must have sensed my quiet defiance and perceived my ability to function without his advice. He probably envied my youth and my future in a free country, so different from his prospects at my age in Tsarist Russia on the eve of World War I and the Soviet Revolution. Perhaps that was one reason for his need to assert himself in our relationship. Even when I had considerable achievements behind me later on, his letters to me were usually full of criticism. In one of them, discussing the differences in our mental capabilities, he claimed that he was an intellectual giant and I was a pygmy. I had always deferred to what I had considered his superior intellect, but it is significant that he felt the need to compare our abilities. In another telling incident, after I had raised capital from an independent source to start my first company in the United States, he told his relatives in New York that he had provided the funds. Perhaps, like many parents and guardians, who feel the need to participate in their former charges' future, he still wanted to rule my life, and he lashed out at me when his help was no longer needed.

It would be tempting to explain my uncle's overbearing traits by the difficulties of his early life, but it is more likely that the troubles he had encountered in his youth simply reinforced his inbred authoritarian character. His mother, who had died before I was born, seemed to have been the pillar of the family. His father, who came to England from China after Mao's Revolution and lived with us for a year, was a wonderful, but weak, man. Upon his return from Germany during the times of trouble in Russia, Ilya, the oldest sibling, became head of the family. He performed that role well, looking after those family members—his parents, his brother, and his two sisters—who had escaped to China. He also provided financial help to more distant relatives and, of course, took it upon himself to bring me out of Poland. Having the most resources in his family and successfully navigating the most disruptive events of the first half of the twentieth century must have boosted his already strong ego and, in his view, justified his haughtiness and demands for obedience and admiration from those around him.

In many ways I was the beneficiary of my uncle's fiery ambition and drive. Had he been a person of average ability, he would have remained in Siberia instead of becoming a respected London doctor and a person of extraordinary erudition. Without my uncle my life after the war would have been very different.

SUMMER 1948

WITH THE MATRICULATION examination behind me and the Vitensons embarking on their annual six-week tour of the Continent, I looked
forward to a summer of well-deserved rest. I relished the thought of
having the apartment all to myself and being able to explore London.
It was one of those times that follow the completion of a difficult task
and precede the beginning of a new endeavor, a wonderful opportunity
to catch one's breath, renew acquaintance with one's surroundings, and
simply spend some idle time. The only urgent task facing me was to apply to college, but in England that was a relatively simple procedure.

I had plenty of time to describe my new world in letters to my father
and an eager audience of Polish friends. Sharing my experiences with
them made the exploration of London and the study of its inhabitants
all the more enjoyable. The entire atmosphere of England was so radically different from my previous surroundings that almost everything
seemed exotic, even eccentric. Initially, at least, I could not tell the difference between the traits and behavior that were peculiar to the British
and those that were found in the rest of the civilized world.

The passage of time has blurred the memory of my initial reactions,
but I still remember my wonder at the British sense of honesty. I saw
the stacks of newspapers left unattended on sidewalks and the people

leaving coins in payment. No one cheated and no one stole the money. On those wonderful, red, double-decker buses—that seemed like moving apartment buildings that could surely topple at any time—when a passenger reached his stop before the conductor came by, he simply left the correct fare with another passenger, who passed along the payment for him. Such behavior was almost incomprehensible to a recent arrival from Eastern Europe. In the same way, the British practice of forming queues if several people were waiting for a bus or to buy tickets contrasted starkly with the pushing and shoving crowds in Poland and Russia. Sometimes I saw just two waiting passengers form a queue, a habit that struck me as pleasantly eccentric. I found these law-abiding habits most attractive and quickly adopted them for my own behavior, but I was steered in this direction by an angry—and in this case fully justified—outburst of criticism from my uncle. A few weeks after my arrival in England, we went to the movies. When the ticket line passed in front of an open and unattended exit door, I suggested we enter there instead of paying the price of admission, as would have been standard practice in Russia—an influence still with a strong hold on me. "Just because someone is not looking is not a reason to steal his money," was his stern reprimand.

Looking back at that summer from the perspective of my subsequent fifty years in democratic countries, I now realize what a strong grip the Soviet propaganda had on me. I was no friend of the Communists, yet I found myself defending many of their practices. I also misinterpreted things. When I first saw British policemen, my immediate reaction was that they were most likely sons of wealthy capitalists organized to control workers. Nor was it easy to appreciate the meaning of free speech. London had a delightful collection of speakers who gathered at the Marble Arch section of Hyde Park. Holding forth primarily on political subjects, both domestic and foreign, they usually drew a sizeable audience. Most of the listeners were serious, while others attended just to heckle the orators. I was a frequent visitor to that speakers' corner because I wanted to improve my English, learn the technique of public speaking, study British politics, and participate in these new and exciting public debates. But even in that free-for-all forum, it took me a long time to realize that the speakers were private citizens and had not been sent there by the government to influence public opinion.

Two books that helped dispel my lingering doubts about the West and any remaining illusions about the Soviet Union were *Darkness at Noon* and *The God that Failed,* both by Arthur Koestler. In the first book the author, who for years had been a devoted German communist, described chilling scenes from Soviet prisons and detailed the Bolsheviks' favorite method of executing their prisoners: a single gunshot to the back of the head. In the second book Koestler edited a collection of essays by previously eminent but now disenchanted communists from several European countries. They described their blind, illogical faith in the system and told how long it took them to shake it off, despite clear evidence and inside knowledge of its evils. I knew the practical reality of Stalinism, but my years of indoctrination had left a deep impression that was not easy to dislodge. I still believed in many of the theoretical assumptions of Marxism-Leninism, but those books gave me an intellectual basis for rejecting communism, at least in its Soviet form. Reading the two books was not easy. They were the first anti-communist works I had ever seen; holding them, I felt like a medieval monk fearfully exploring heretic literature. I did not expect a bolt from heaven, but I did have the sense that I might be committing a major transgression against an immensely powerful and vengeful force.

Around that time a friend took me to a lecture by the prominent socialist academic, Harold Laski, at the London School of Economics. His lecture was similar in content to many talks I had heard in Russia, although much more elegant in style, and I was by then horrified and angry that such near-communist ideas could be legally aired in England. Clearly I had made the transition to the Western philosophy of government, if not entirely appreciating the value of free speech.

Although I thought I would have my uncle's apartment to myself that summer, I unexpectedly acquired an interesting companion. A few months after the war, my aunt decided to bring an au pair from Europe to help her with the household duties. After a long waiting period, we received a letter on the eve of my relatives' departure to the Continent announcing the arrival of a Finnish girl within a week. A refusal to accept her would have resulted in another long delay, and a postponement of my relatives' trip would have been inconvenient. So off they went, leaving me to settle the girl in London.

I made elaborate preparations for welcoming our new tenant. I tidied up her room and found a Finnish-speaking student at an International Student Club I had recently joined. On the appointed day the two of us went to the train station to meet the new arrival. I had no idea how old the woman would be or whether she would have a working knowledge of English, but I remember my rising level of excitement as the train pulled into the station. Just a year earlier I had arrived in London myself, and I recalled my anxiety about meeting my relatives. Now I was in a position to welcome a foreigner.

I don't remember how we found her, but we had no difficulty identifying our guest. Her name escapes me, but she was a very attractive young woman, about twenty years old with traditional Scandinavian features, though not very tall. She had blonde hair and blue eyes, and her figure was full but not plump, while her gait, broad shoulders, and facial expression were somewhat reminiscent of Russian peasant women. She seemed subdued, but I ascribed that to her initial cautiousness about the new country and her inability to speak English. The first couple of hours with her were easy because we had an interpreter, but when the Finnish student departed, the au pair and I were left to our own devices.

In the preceding few days I had mapped out a program for the new arrival. On the assumption that her knowledge of English would be rudimentary, I had decided to give her English lessons, emphasizing terms she would need in her future domestic duties, and to introduce her to the neighborhood shops where she would buy food and household supplies for my aunt. We got along very well. Fresh from my own introduction to the English language, I found it enjoyable to pass my knowledge on to her, using Dorothy's early lessons as my model. In those days it was strange and inappropriate for two single young people of the opposite sex to share the same apartment, but she did not object to this arrangement. Despite some early misgivings, I enjoyed having a companion, especially a pleasant, attractive young woman who cleaned the house and cooked for me.

Two big surprises came when my aunt and uncle returned a few weeks later. I was still having some difficulty communicating with my new pupil, but we could understand each other well enough to convey simple thoughts. To my embarrassment, she could not make anyone else understand her, nor could she follow my aunt's instructions. I therefore had to act as interpreter until our Finnish visitor became more fluent. The second, even more embarrassing surprise, which was recognized only over time, was that she was becoming visibly larger around her waist. At first, Zhenia assumed that the weight gain was due to a better diet, but she soon suspected her au pair was pregnant—a condition the Finnish woman strongly denied. Then, remembering my previous seclusion with her, my relatives began casting accusing glances in my direction. The bigger my summer companion grew, the more suspicious my aunt became of my culpability, and soon Edna and Dorothy joined her in the chorus of humorously reproachful remarks. It did not take long before the girl admitted she was carrying a baby. She had become pregnant before coming to England and, fortunately, the baby's expected date of birth confirmed her claim. I don't remember whether she knew of her condition at the time of her departure from Finland, but she said that the father was an American soldier who was living in Helsinki. She decided to put the baby up for adoption, but when her daughter was born, she changed her mind and returned to Finland, taking the infant with her. We were all pleased that she decided to keep the baby. She was a pleasant young woman, and we had grown fond of her and wished her well, but we never heard from her again. For me, the only legacy of that whole episode was two Finnish words she taught me: *lentokone* and *kiitos*,—"airplane" and "thank you."

My hosting duties temporarily took my attention away from matters of education, but after settling the au pair in our apartment and establishing her routines, I returned to my pursuit of higher education. I knew of only three English universities: Cambridge, Oxford,

and London. It was 1948, and British universities were giving preference to ex-servicemen whose studies had been interrupted or delayed
by the Second World War and who were applying in record numbers.
The second priority was given to other British citizens, while foreigners
came last. Dorothy and several other people suggested that the first two
institutions were beyond my reach and that I should concentrate on securing a place in London. The tall building in Russell Square, which I
thought housed the entire University of London and was within walking distance from our house, turned out to contain only administrative
offices. The university consisted of a number of separate colleges, and
applications had to be directed to them individually. Some of those colleges were part of the University of London system and had courses for
so-called "internal" students. Additionally, the university thoughtfully
made it possible for "external" students to obtain London degrees by
pursuing courses of study at specially approved colleges in many places
under the British flag.

I soon discovered that none of the local colleges, whether serving
internal or external students, was interested in having me as a student,
and I applied to what I hoped would be more receptive provincial institutions. While the rejections were arriving, I had a few anxious moments. I remember passing the Russell Square university building on
several occasions and looking with envy at the young men and women
who, I assumed, were students on some errand at the administrative
offices. They seemed very privileged, and I wondered whether I would
ever join their ranks. Fortunately, I was accepted as an external student
by two colleges, and I chose the Leicester College of Technology for its
proximity to London.

Toward the end of the summer, I realized that the term of my Polish
passport had expired, since it had been issued for only twelve months.
When I went to the Polish embassy to have it renewed, I was met with a
rude and hostile reception; in fact, the officials treated me like a traitor.
Eventually they gave me a long form to fill out and told me to return
with twenty pounds. I was glad to get out of there. Even in London,
the Polish clerks managed to reproduce the atmosphere of Communist

Poland. Before the visit I had had little desire to remain a citizen of a Communist country and the reception at the embassy did nothing to change my mind. In any case, the fee was beyond my means, and I decided to apply for what is sometimes known as a stateless passport. Many countries issued such documents to people having the right of residence but not qualifying for citizenship. In England the "passport" was known as a "travel document," and, as the name suggests, it could be used for obtaining visas for foreign travel. The British Home Office, also in charge of immigration matters, issued such documents.

I went through a lot of soul-searching before embarking on that course. I still retained my old fear of government officials from my time in the Soviet Union, and I worried that drawing attention to myself might result in my being expelled from England. The Cold War was at its peak, and I anticipated a grueling interview designed to test my loyalty to the British Crown. Accordingly I spent several days preparing myself to answer the toughest questions imaginable, rehearsing elaborate explanations for my desire to stay in England, and providing evidence that I did not pose a threat to the country despite my father's residence in Poland.

I finally gathered enough courage to present myself at the Home Office in Holborn and told the porter at the small entrance hall the purpose of my visit. He handed me several small forms and suggested I return the completed blanks with two recent photographs and my Polish passport. I was happy the examination had been postponed, giving me time for further preparation. The forms were simple to fill out. Hoping for a reasonably quick response, I was not disappointed. Exactly one week later a thick envelope arrived from the Home Office. When I opened it, I could hardly believe my eyes: The envelope contained my travel document. Another shock was yet to come. When I opened my new passport, everything inside was in my own handwriting. It took a few moments to realize that the passport office had merely cut up the completed forms and pasted them, along with my photograph, into the new document. Such efficiency and trust alone, especially in contrast with my recent experience at the Polish embassy, should have been enough to make me a British patriot. But the effects of my years of Soviet Communist indoctrination had not yet disappeared. Because the British authorities had kept my Polish passport, I was convinced they would give it to a spy who would operate in Poland. Thirty years later, when I needed to demonstrate my past Polish nationality for another purpose, I found that I had been mistaken. Acting on my behalf, a friend visited the Croydon branch of the Home Office, where old documents were filed. It took the clerk only a few minutes to retrieve my original Polish passport and exchange it for the by-then-obsolete travel document.

My description of the English sense of order might imply that Londoners were dull, humorless, or blindly obedient to regulations, but I found the reality to be quite the opposite. They followed rules not to conform, but out of consideration for others. They did break regulations, often with gestures of great playfulness and humor, when the practice did no harm. I saw a good example of that at the Royal Albert Hall. London was a wonderful place for music and boasted several world-class orchestras. Each summer, the Albert Hall scheduled an eight-week series of classical music programs called the Henry Wood Promenade Concerts—the "Proms." In addition to reserved seats, the box office sold standing-room tickets on the day of the performance. The price of admission for standing listeners was two shillings—roughly a quarter. This attractive deal made it possible for me to attend concerts quite frequently. Tickets were sold with the strict understanding that we would stand in the center arena during the performance, but as soon as the orchestra started to play, we defiantly sat on the floor—probably in violation of fire codes or, perhaps, pricing regulations. This strategy rendered the attendants helpless, since any reprimand would break the silence required during the concert. During the intermission, we were forced to stand, but we sat again at the first sounds of music. We repeated this charade throughout the season, producing no anger but a great deal of enjoyment on the part of the listeners and even, I suspect, the attendants, who tried their best to look stern in the face of such flagrant behavior.

The summer of 1948 was another milestone for me. Now settled in England, I had managed to understand and adopt many of the ways of my new country, and I was about to embark on a new stage of life as a university student. True, this new degree of maturity did not yet include financial independence, but at least I had a dignified arrangement with my relatives and would no longer live with them. Toward the end of the summer, I collected most of my belongings, including my trusty bicycle, and took a train to Leicester. It was only a two- or three-hour journey, but it was a world apart from my previous surroundings, at least psychologically.

UNIVERSITY YEARS

My EXPECTATIONS and concerns during the trip to Leicester were different from those of most American or English students upon entering college. I did not ask myself whether I would make new friends or like my roommates, whether my teachers would be competent, or whether I would make a sports team. All those considerations were secondary to the prospects of learning a profession that would provide a means for making a living. A few years later, in England and in the United States, I became familiar with others' expectations of the university experience. "If a practical end is to be assigned to a university education," I read somewhere, "it is surely to train good citizens." Such ideas were completely foreign to me at that time. I was brought up under difficult conditions and it never occurred to me that the purpose of education was anything but learning a trade or a profession to earn money. While I now agree that a university should not be a "trade school," it still strikes me that good citizenship, no matter how well taught, would be difficult to practice on an empty stomach or in a dull, demoralizing job.

I decided to become an electrical engineer, which I supposed would probably mean a radio engineer. The ability to transmit information through the air had always intrigued me, and I thought it would be fascinating to be involved in a technology that allowed remote control of airplanes, ships, machinery, and appliances. An early working television set that I saw at a London museum increased my curiosity about the field of broadcasting.

First-year students in my program did not have to choose between science and engineering. The course at that level was still broad, and offered four subjects: pure mathematics, applied mathematics, physics, and chemistry. To qualify for a bachelor's degree in science, students had to pass three of those courses, but a successful completion of all four subjects was required to continue engineering studies. With my professional goals set, I took the entire curriculum. I soon found that the first three disciplines came relatively easily to me, while chemistry proved to be much more difficult. Even though I spent more time studying that troublesome subject, it was there I got my lowest grades.

In Leicester, I discovered English "digs," which usually consist of room and board in a private house. The term is probably as famous as the "artist's garret" of Paris, though the image is surely not as glamorous. I shared my digs with an English architecture student named Peter at the home of a gracious, hospitable English family. They lived in a village with the colorful name of Kirby Muxloe—which we promptly renamed Murby Kuxloe—about four miles from Leicester. We shared an upstairs bedroom and a downstairs study. The landlady served us breakfast and dinner on weekdays, and on Saturdays and Sundays we had breakfast and lunch. English food does not enjoy a good reputation, but after Siberia and even after my aunt's cooking, it tasted just fine, and the quantity was more than sufficient.

Three walls of our bedroom had windows, and Peter insisted even on the coldest days that they should be partially open. Following the fashion of most English houses, the bedroom was unheated, and on a few occasions during particularly cold and windy weather, snow drifted onto our beds—an incursion I was spared even in Siberia. The fireplace in the study seemed to generate a lot of heat, but on most cold days it did not keep the room warm. Our favorite method of studying was to sit close to the fireplace, initially facing the fire, then turning around every few minutes when that side became unbearably hot.

The academic year in Leicester passed quickly. I enjoyed the studies and, for the first time since my arrival in England, I could lead my life without supervision and criticism from my London relatives. I spent most holidays and school vacations with them, but I also used my free time to explore areas adjacent to Leicester. There was a good-sized Polish population in my new town, mainly former soldiers who had served in various armies during World War II. They organized the Polish Veterans' Club, which, rather comically, accepted Polish fighters from both sides of the recent conflict. I occasionally visited the club, but I spent most of my time with English friends, even acquiring an English girlfriend, Margaret. We were too young to make a permanent commitment for the future, but the relationship confirmed the fact that I felt at ease in England and could have stayed there for the rest of my life. Our friendship lasted a few months, then we parted company at the end of the year, when I returned to London.

After passing the first-year final examination, I transferred to Battersea Polytechnic, which was primarily an engineering college for internal students in London. I preferred London with all its cultural offerings to the small town of Leicester, and Battersea, which specialized in technical subjects, offered a more advanced curriculum. During the summer before transferring to Battersea, I also worked at my first job—if only for six weeks—at a power-generating station in the Cornwall town of Hale. Cornwall, at the extreme southwest of England, is a delightful part of the country, and I spent many hours exploring seaside towns, villages, and picturesque ports on my bicycle. I also discovered how various parts of England differed from each other. Cornwall had its own local dishes, unique heavy cream, and distinct brands of beer. I found digs in Hale, but by the end of my six weeks I still could not understand a word my landlord said, although I had no difficulty following his wife's speech. He was not using a different language or even an English dialect; he simply had a thick, local accent that I found incomprehensible.

My primary work at the small electrical power station was to maintain the rotating machinery and clean the huge steam boilers. Occasionally, I was allowed to manage the control room, which was studded with many instruments and supervisory panels. I enjoyed my direct exposure to those wonderful machines, which generated tens of megawatts of power. The big rotors, which turned at 3,000 revolutions per minute, had to be perfectly balanced, because the slightest vibration would cause them to tear the equipment from its foundation. The mechanics proudly displayed the stability of their generators by placing an English penny on top of their machinery; the penny, which despite its low value was by far the largest coin of the realm, stood still on its edge without falling. I left Hale with my interest in technology enhanced and my desire to become an engineer confirmed. The job also helped me widen my technical interests beyond radio.

I rejoined my aunt and uncle in their apartment at Devonshire Place. I was nineteen and our relationship had improved appreciably; they now treated me with much more consideration and respect. Devonshire Place was a reasonable thirty-minute bicycle ride from Battersea Polytechnic, which was located south of the Thames in London. To reach my destination I passed through several of the better-known parts of London. I often rode on Baker Street, of Sherlock Holmes fame, to Oxford Street, with its many shops and department stores. Oxford Street led to Marble Arch, so named for the arch that forms one of the gates to Hyde Park. The gate was closed to all but the Queen, and I saw it opened only once to allow the royal car through. On that occasion, before the motorcade entered the gate I was riding my bicycle not more than a couple of feet from the Queen's car. Our eyes met, but her expression did not change, and I don't think I reacted in any way. London was a peaceful city in those days, and clearly no special precautions were needed to separate the Queen from her subjects.

After Marble Arch, my path to Battersea led through Hyde Park to Hyde Park Corner, a busy intersection with fine monuments, and then on to Knightsbridge. Hyde Park offered a pleasant ride. The road, bordered by greenery on both sides, ran for a stretch next to Park Lane, with its grand hotels, then alongside a bridle path. Mostly on weekends, but also during the week, one could admire well-attired riders of both sexes on their beautiful, well-groomed horses. I could not help comparing that refined equestrian display with my own experience of working with those sturdy little grays on the Russian steppes. It felt good to be part of the English civilization, and to think of Russia as my distant past. The road I traveled also passed near the "Serpentine," a body of water where one could rent sculling boats, but which tended to attract fog. It is much easier to see through fog on a bicycle than in a car, where the windshield forms an optical barrier, and on especially turbid days a long snake of vehicles would form behind me, the drivers using me as a moving beacon. It was astonishing to think that my hand-me-down bike had at least one advantage over the modern motorcar.

I would leave the park at Knightsbridge, not far from Harrods, probably the best-known department store in London. Legend had it you could buy anything there, including elephants, which I assumed were not held in inventory but would involve a special order. I went from there along Sloane Street through the Bohemian district of Chelsea and finally crossed the bridge that spanned the Thames next to Battersea Power Station. From there it was just a few minutes to my destination, along a nondescript gray street known appropriately as Battersea Road.

The subjects studied during the first five trimesters were the same for all future mechanical, civil, and electrical engineers, allowing us to postpone the choice of our specialty for almost two years. The system actually made my decision more difficult, because in many ways I enjoyed civil and mechanical engineering more than some of the electrical subjects. The first two specialties produced more tangible signs of progress—for example, we designed interesting structures such as bridges and roof trusses and calculated their endurance against loads of rolling traffic and hurricane winds. In mechanical engineering we designed and tested machinery with cylinders, pistons, flywheels, and other intricate moving parts, whereas in electrical courses and laboratories our satisfaction came from watching passive instrument needles arrive at a prescribed line. The moving generators and motors were so well enclosed that the rotation manifested itself only in the murmur of the armature, with little physical evidence of motion. Still, when the time came to make the decision, I retained my original convictions and chose electrical engineering, which in retrospect was the right move. Not only was this field where my real interest lay, but the electrical degree made it easier for me to join a new and fast-expanding industry.

As I have already explained, my first "academic" contacts with electrical phenomena occurred in Siberia, where I procured a battery that made it possible to perform simple laboratory demonstrations in my school. Even then I marveled at the uncanny properties of electricity. For instance, a copper wire did not change in appearance while conducting current and producing spectacular results, such as lighting a bulb, turning a motor, or even causing an explosion when connected to a proper output device. To me this phenomenon seemed to be pure magic. My interest was further enhanced when I studied radio, especially the science of remote control. At that point, my intrigue with "magic" was replaced by admiration for the human mind, which seemed able to accomplish such seemingly impossible tasks. Although I was interested in all areas of technology, electricity, with its underlying mathematics, held a special appeal as being more cerebral and more dependent on human imagination than sciences dealing with tangible objects.

Not all my college days were spent studying. Battersea Polytechnic did not have as many extracurricular activities as most American universities, but there were enough student clubs to satisfy my intellectual interests. There were no sport clubs or playing fields (and no one seemed to miss them), but there was a drama society, a debating club, and ballroom dancing. Having played chess in the past, I eventually joined the chess team that represented our college in the London University league. I also attended all our formal debates and some held at other colleges. The English had developed debating into a fine art. The content of one's opinion was less important than the way it was presented, and it was not unusual to take a position in one debate and defend the opposite viewpoint in the next. Much as I admired the practice of debating, I was too unsure of my newly acquired English skills to join the club. To overcome my nervousness, I decided to participate in the debates by speaking from the floor. The debate in which I first took part was held shortly after scientists, using the latest instruments, had discovered that the speed of light had been understated by a small amount. It was not an earth-shattering event even in the world of science, but our next debate was devoted to the proposition that "This house considers the speed of light to be excessive." I think I spoke in favor of the proposition, but I don't remember much about my presentation. I worked hard preparing the text and committing it to memory. I was not sure until the very last minute that I would speak, but I forced myself to stand and for the first time present my views to an English audience. After surviving that test, I found it much easier to take part in subsequent debates.

Many of those forums dealt with seemingly frivolous topics designed to hone presentation and verbal skills, but there were also serious themes. The Cold War was intense, and East-West political topics were of great interest to English students. Over the course of my studies my political views drifted from left-of-center toward the right. My Siberian background made me something of a rarity, and I found myself involved in vigorous late night discussions with fellow students primarily at the International Students' Club in Gower Street, not far from London's University College. But those sessions turned out to be much milder than the fiery arguments I was plunged into when one of my classmates introduced me to a group of activists at the beginning of my sophomore year.

Tony Hewitt-Emmett was markedly different from the other students in my class. Tall, wiry, and blond, with long wavy hair, he looked a few years older than the rest of us. We all studied technical subjects, but Tony's main interests lay elsewhere. He often questioned me about my Siberian experience and solicited my political views. I must have impressed him with my theoretical knowledge of communism, because just a few weeks into the academic year, he invited me to join him and a few of his friends for late coffee at a small restaurant in Edgeware

Road near Marble Arch. Arriving a few minutes late, I found Tony and his companions already engaged in vigorous debate. There were six of them—young, unkempt intellectuals—and unlike most English conversationalists, they reinforced their arguments with expressive gestures. They fell silent on my arrival, flashed admiring glances in my direction, as if I was a celebrity, and immediately started questioning me about the Soviet Union. At first the conversation revolved around my personal history, but then it turned toward political topics, and here their attitude changed from admiration to disappointment. I think I embarrassed Tony. His friends were a mixture of Stalinists and Trotskyites, and he had not realized that by then I held strong anticommunist views. Nevertheless, we spent a stimulating evening. Two of my companions advocated Trotky's views, the rest admired Stalin. The fact that Stalin expelled Trotsky from Russia and then had him murdered in Mexico did not divide my interlocutors. My companions' idols had been bitter enemies, but it seemed they were both preferable to the dirty capitalists who were exploiting the world. I enjoyed our debate, though I made no headway in persuading my companions that their prescriptions would not create the paradise of their dreams. I was in a minority, one against six: Tony's friends were well-versed in communist theory and had closely followed and absorbed the rhetoric of communist propaganda. The evening ended on a cordial note, but not before the most outspoken member of the group accused me of being a liar and a pretender who had never been in Russia. Over the next few weeks, we held similar late evening sessions, but gradually the group decided that my misguided attitude did not suit their purposes and no longer wanted to see me. Tony and I remained friends, but he dropped out of school at the end of that academic year, presumably to find more rewarding ways to serve humanity. I never heard from him again.

I was not overly surprised by the naïve beliefs of my companions. They were by no means unique, for there were numerous groups with extreme left leanings in England after the war. The country had had a long tradition of free political discourse, with strong support for socialist views. Karl Marx conducted much of his research in London and, in fact, lies buried there. The Fabian Society, with George Bernard Shaw as one of its most prominent members, helped shape the program of the British Labor Party, which began nationalizing British industry during my stay in England. Little was then known of the atrocities committed by Stalin's regime, and many people regarded Russia, a recent ally and supposedly the first truly socialist country, with a great deal of sympathy. Capitalist America, on the other hand, with its atomic weapons and loud criticism of the Soviets, was perceived as an aggressor and warmonger. This atmosphere formed an interesting backdrop for intense debates and discussions, which provided a great deal of intellectual stimulation. In contrast, when I came to the United States in 1956, I was surprised to find American students uninterested in the world beyond the country's borders; the main topics of conversation seemed to be sports and dates. Only ten years after the war, several students I met in Boston did not even know which side the Russians had fought on. The political apathy of young Americans and their ignorance of world affairs was most discouraging, but, of course, all that changed in the sixties.

In addition to the East-West controversy, I was keenly interested in the developments in Palestine. It was difficult to debate those sensitive issues in England, because the British, as holders of the United Nations Mandate, were involved in an often violent struggle with Palestine's Jews, who were fighting for their independence. The United Nations' decision to partition the country into Jewish and Arab sections and the subsequent British withdrawal, finally resolved that issue and resulted in the establishment of the State of Israel in 1948. While that event was a source of almost indescribable joy for most of the world's Jews, it would have an especially strong impact on the lives of the remnants of Eastern European Jewry.

The creation of Israel and a change of heart by the Communist Party authorities made it possible for Jews to emigrate from Poland. Initially, my father did not trust the government's new policy and feared that it was a trap to identify people who were dissatisfied with the Polish regime. I did not realize it at the time, but his letters to me were crafted to build a case with the authorities, who, he was certain, were censoring his correspondence. He wrote that he was a loyal Polish citizen and had great doubts about leaving the country. As a working man, he wrote, he was happy in Poland, but he was alone there and contemplated a new life in the Middle East only because he had relatives and friends there. I did not understand the reason for his apparent hesitation and I did my best—taking care not to incur the wrath of possible censors—to persuade him to leave. The idea that he might remain in Poland despite the opportunity to escape filled me with horror. One of the happiest days of my life was when I finally received his postcard from Venice on August 10, 1950. It contained just a brief note stating: "I am writing this card from Venice. Thank God all that is behind me."

My joy was soon tempered by father's first letter from Israel, dated August 29, 1950. Here are some excerpts:

> My dear Bronek!
>
> It is very bad here. The country is extremely poor. The intense absorption rate of new immigrants is heavily burdening this poor, young country. No wonder we live in tents and there is no work. Those over 45 cannot find work, over 50 are worthless. The climate is terrible and, in our view, there is little to eat. We had meat, butter [in Poland] but there is nothing like it here. I made a big mistake. I had an apartment, I commanded respect, I was a valued employee, I earned a good salary, and here I am nothing. My dear Bronek, my situation is hopeless without even the slightest prospects for the future. I am not the only one. Yesterday I saw Jakubowicz, and he cried like a baby. It is so hard, old people like us should not have abandoned our old place. Only God knows what will happen to me. I wonder, my dear Bronek, what you think about all this, is there a solution to my problems? Jakubowicz wants to return to Poland, what do you think I should do? Please forgive me, my dear, for poisoning your peace and your life, but I tell you, if I did not have you I would have long departed this world. I am facing a period of terrible suffering. My life was better in Vasilevskii [in Siberia]. Please don't abandon me. Write as often as you can.
>
> With best wishes and kisses your father.

I was devastated by his anguish. But I hoped that his extremely pessimistic attitude was partly the result of unrealistic expectations. After his terrible wartime trials, he finally escaped to freedom in a country he could call his own, only to find himself herded into camps with no road map for the future. I sensed that tough as things were for him at the time, his life in Israel would eventually be brighter than in Communist Poland. The prospect of his returning to Poland and my never seeing him again was horrifying. I could not travel to Israel to ease his pain, for I did not have the money and my uncle refused to advance the funds during the academic year. Not able to help him immediately, I felt guilty and helpless. I did the only thing I could: I set about to lift his spirit by correspondence. I don't have copies of the letters I sent him, but evidently my efforts were not in vain. Following are excerpts from my father's letter of September 24, 1950:

> My dear Bronek!
>
> It is hard for me to describe my joy after I received your telegram and your letter yesterday. Perhaps I exaggerated my difficulties, but I have been so depressed that I see everything in black colors. I assure you that only your letter lifted my spirits. I realize that my departure from Poland was the only way out. I don't want to be a burden to you, but I expect that, once we are reunited, I'll gain a new lease on life and will again become a productive person. . . . You wanted to know details of my journey from Poland. I left my job on 8.4.1950. Before leaving I was visited by several Kłodzko dignitaries. They tried to convince me to abandon my plans to leave Poland. Fortunately neither the UB [Polish equivalent of KGB] nor Special Commission agents came to see me. They interrogated all other travelers to Israel, often with sad results. I left Kłodzko on the 5th, stayed in Warsaw overnight and left Warsaw on the 7th. We were delayed for 24 hours at the Polish border. I was the first one to be summoned to the customs and passport control. The guards confiscated 3 kg of sausages, a bed sheet, a shirt, an abacus, a slide-rule, and an attractive cigarette case. I lost all those items but, thank God, I did not have to pay a fine.
>
> Our trip was very pleasant. We traveled in special sleeping cars but with no right to leave the train. We saw the beautiful alpine scenery; I cannot find the words to describe it. We arrived in Venice in the morning and stayed for the whole day but only in the port. We were in the free world! I was allowed to take only $12.00 out of Poland, and I spent part of it buying a few minor items which I sold here for over 20 Israeli pounds. Life is terribly hard here. We were taken to quarantine for various medical tests. Afterwards we were settled in "Beit Olim"—an immigrant camp. We live in tents. Flies are torturing us during the day, mosquitoes are making life impossible. The sun is so hot we cannot catch our breath. The worst part is that I don't even have a roof over my head and no prospect for earning a living. To make things worse, I don't speak the language. Bokser and Esther live nearby, they are in a work camp. So far I am getting my food free, but he has to work, carrying stones and working in the fields. The work is extremely hard in this hot climate. . . . I am supposed to get an interview for a job as a bookkeeper, but it will be harder

Father's first letter from Israel.

to qualify without the abacus the Polish guards confiscated at the border. If you can buy an abacus or a mechanical calculator in England, would you send it to me?... My dear Bronek, your letter took a load off my heart. I see your image everywhere; I am not alone, we will be together. As of yesterday, I became a man full of hope and courage. I believe that somehow things will work out. . . .

Wishing you all the best, your loving father.

He was right; things did work out. He got the bookkeeper's job at a primitive agricultural village. Not stellar surroundings, but at least he did not have to live in a camp.

I wanted to see him as soon as possible, and I took a ship to Israel during my 1951 summer vacation. We met on a dock in Haifa and had a very emotional reunion. Not only had we been separated for four years, but as the Polish Communists solidified their rule, I had become convinced we would never see each other again. Our reunion seemed nothing short of a miracle. Most of the students from the Wrocław hostel had also emigrated to Israel, and about ten of them were with my father to greet me on my arrival.

Until the ship docked in Haifa, I had always seen Jews as a minority—usually a persecuted minority—and it was most gratifying to be in a Jewish State. For many years it had seemed all but impossible that Israel would ever become a reality. I was used to seeing Jews in professions requiring mental rather than physical effort, but in Haifa the first spoken words came from Jewish stevedores speaking Hebrew and Yiddish but swearing in Russian, a language particularly rich and expressive when it came to cursing. Later that day, I saw a Jewish shoeshine boy cleaning the shoes of an Arab in traditional Bedouin attire, and to top it all off I saw American sailors from a visiting destroyer looking for—and finding—Jewish prostitutes. "Israel is a normal country," I said to myself in astonishment and satisfaction; "The Jews are just like everyone else!"

After exchanging addresses with my Polish friends, I rode with my father on a bus to his village. He lived in a *moshav* called Kfar-Pines, between Tel-Aviv and Haifa. A *moshav*, a less-familiar form of agricultural settlement than the *kibbutz*, is a village where the farmers have

247

their own houses and fields but the machinery is owned in common, and both the purchasing of seeds and the selling of the harvest is the responsibility of a central organization, with the proceeds distributed in proportion to each farmer's harvest. A primitive village, it had only one partially paved, dusty road. The paving was narrow, with two dirt strips on each side. The farmers' houses and fields lined both sides of the central artery. The houses were small and of simple construction, but had electricity, running water, and adequate plumbing. It was always hot, and working in the fields or even just walking was uncomfortable in the middle of the day.

My father rented a small room from one family of friends and ate all his meals with another family. His quarters had just enough room for a chair and a bed, which we shared. He worked in a small office as the *moshav* accountant. I watched him walk to work in the morning. He was a kind man and on most summer days a small group of children waited in front of the house to accompany him to the office. He proudly introduced me to his followers and then engaged in a lively conversation with them in Hebrew, which I did not understand; one word, *boolim*, cropped up frequently. My father explained that the word meant "stamps", and that he often gave the children the stamps from my letters.

I couldn't help feeling sorry for my father, living alone in his tiny room and relying on meals at another house. He had known both families in Poland before the war and was treated respectfully by them, but he had no close relatives there. He seemed almost as much out of place in semi-tropical Israel as he had been in frigid Siberia. A town dweller for most of his life, he did not adapt well to the hot climate and life of the primitive village. Like many immigrants his age, he often dressed as if he were still in Europe. For example, he wore heavy trousers, which he no doubt brought with him from Poland, and I discovered that he still supported his socks with garters strapped below the knee. Upon seeing that the elastic bands made his legs perspire heavily and produced an uncomfortable skin rash, I immediately talked him into abandoning the garters; he found that the socks stayed up without external help, and the rash quickly disappeared. But that was just one small physical improvement. He looked like a dignified but somewhat bewildered European gentleman transplanted to a foreign world. Nor was his workplace comfortable or inspiring: He sat in a tiny, sweltering room all day, making entries in books and presumably producing various financial statements.

Like every man in the village, my father served on a paramilitary night patrol a few times a year. The patrol usually consisted of two armed men whose duty was to protect the village from the Arab infiltrators who occasionally crossed the Jordanian border to steal animals. My father's *moshav* was located in a narrow part of the country, a ten-mile wide strip between that border and the sea, and thus was easily penetrated by foreigners. Israel's small size gave rise to a number of ironic jokes. A typical story related that the sign on trains, instead of saying, "Don't lean out of the window" proclaimed, "Don't lean out of the country." Another joke about public transportation had to do with buses: Instead of the sign seen in other countries, "Don't talk to the bus driver," the sign in Israel read, *"You have no one else to talk to except the driver?"* Naturally, the joke had to be told with a heavy Yiddish accent to be fully appreciated.

On weekends my father always went to Tel-Aviv to stay with friends. He was a reserved but amiable man whose sense of humor always contributed to any social gathering, and he was eagerly welcomed at many households. He invariably brought food for his hosts, usually chickens split in two and safely wrapped and concealed in his pockets. At the time of my first visit, food—even the abundant oranges—was rationed in Israel, and it was illegal to bring supplies directly from the villages. Buses going to major towns were often stopped and luggage examined to prevent illicit trade, but the police did not go as far as conducting personal searches, and his concealed chicken parts were never discovered. I accompanied my father on his weekend visits and met a number of his friends.

After a couple of weeks, I set off on my own to explore Israel. Most of my fellow students from the Wrocław academic hostel were now dispersed throughout the country. One of them gave me a list of their addresses. It was quite normal among this crowd to arrive without warning at a friend's doorstep and stay the night. Where I knew no one, I stayed at *kibbutzim,* which always welcomed guests, occasionally for a small fee but usually without any charge. On a few occasions I simply slept on the floor in a schoolhouse or another public building.

In retrospect I wish I had been better prepared for that sightseeing trip. With my Soviet primary education and English technical studies, I had little knowledge of Middle Eastern history and the achievements of the Zionist movement. I spoke English, Russian, and Polish, the last two languages being more helpful than English. Many Israelis were emigrants from Russia and Poland and were fluent in those languages, but I felt like a foreigner because I did not speak Hebrew. I admired the ruins of ancient Jewish and Roman edifices and marveled at the modern green Israeli settlements amid the arid surroundings. I came back from my excursion with many impressions, but perhaps the strongest images were of Sbeita, a long-abandoned Roman town at the outpost of the Empire in the present Negev, and of Kibbutz Degania, near the Sea of Galilee in Northern Israel.

Sbeita was a town in the desert where, in Roman times, caravans could replenish their supplies of water and food. Water was collected in primitive underground tanks during the rainy season. So efficient was the rain-gathering apparatus that during my visit at the peak of the summer, this two-thousand-year-old system still performed well. Though the tanks had lost their covers and were effectively open vessels, they still contained a lot of water, gathered unattended during the rainy season.

In the northern part of the country I was graciously welcomed at the modern Kibbutz Degania. Several of the founders were Russian Jews who still spoke the language, so it was easy for me to communicate with them. Directly in the path of the Syrian invasion of 1948, this kibbutz bore the brunt of the attack. The farmers of the village defended their homes with handguns and Molotov cocktails. It was a tough fight against the invading tanks, but the Israelis stood their ground and the Syrians retreated. A disabled Syrian tank was preserved at the edge of the village to commemorate the victory.

I could not visit East Jerusalem and the Wailing Wall because at that time the area was under Jordanian control and inaccessible from Israel. But I spent a lot of time in the modern, western part of the city, staying with my old Polish friend Adek, who was studying medicine at Hebrew University in Jerusalem. He lived at an academic hostel reminiscent of our Wrocław building, along with several other students with whom we had shared quarters in Poland. It was wonderful to reunite with all of them and share our experiences of the previous four years. I was especially glad to be of use to Adek. His English was poor and many of his medical textbooks were written in English, so he had been struggling to read several texts with a dictionary—a time-consuming process. I translated the texts for him, accelerating his learning considerably.

Life in Israel was difficult, but most people—despite their grumbling—had a feeling of excitement and patriotism about building the new Jewish state. My father and I spent many hours discussing our future. One thing was clear: We wanted to live in the same place, and the best way to accomplish that would be for me to finish my education in England, obtain practical experience, and then emigrate to Israel. We felt it would be difficult for my father to start a new life in England, and besides, we identified with Israel and wanted to contribute to the development of the Jewish state. I left Israel with a promise to visit the following summer, which I was able to do.

On my return journey to England, I traveled to Nice by ship and then by train to Paris. In London I had bought a guidebook, *Eight Days in Paris and a Day in Versailles,* and for the first (and last) time in my life I followed the advice of a guidebook almost to the letter, exploring various neighborhoods and restaurants in the prescribed order. I left Paris feeling that I knew the city well—an exhausting visit, but one that provided me with a good background for subsequent trips.

It felt good to be back in London. Only when I returned did I realize how much at home I felt there and how much I had adapted to the English way of life. Two new developments had taken place in my absence. One was my uncle and aunt's decision to emigrate to Canada, with subsequent plans to move to the United States. Their desire to leave England was not entirely unexpected; they had first discussed a move during the Soviet blockade of Berlin in 1948. As the relationship between Russia and the West deteriorated, my uncle decided that he had lived through enough wars in Europe; he had narrowly escaped with his life during the London blitz and he didn't want to be caught in another conflict. The waiting list for Russian-born immigrants to the United States was long, and he decided on Canada as an intermediate stop.

The second family event was the arrival of my Uncle Joseph, Uncle Ilya's brother, from China. Like his older brother, Joseph was also a prominent ear, nose, and throat specialist. He had lived in China after escaping the Bolsheviks following the Russian Revolution. Unfortunately, he was caught up again in turmoil during the Communist Revolution in China. He had tried hard to move to France, England, or the United States, but none of them was hospitable to immigrants; at best, he would face a waiting period of many years. His strategy, not uncommon among emigrants, was to secure the right to settle in another country, in his case Bolivia, and then acquire transit visas through England and France. He hoped that once in London, he would be granted the right of permanent residence in England, a task that seemed easier than negotiating similar arrangements with the British consular authorities in Shanghai.

Since Ilya had sold the building on Devonshire Place before departing for Canada, Joseph rented a pleasant apartment in Portland Place. With my more modest resources, provided by Uncle Ilya, I rented a small room in a boarding house not far from Joseph's flat. The rooming house had about ten boarders, and we ate our meals together in a common dining room. It was a modest lifestyle, but I enjoyed sharing meals with Englishmen of different backgrounds. Each room had a coin-operated gas heater, which accepted, if I remember correctly, one-shilling pieces (about 15 cents). This heat-for-coins arrangement seemed comical to me, until I ran out of shillings on a cold day and the room temperature plunged. I was reminded of the stories of my cousin Bronek Katz, who had come to England before the Second World War. He, too, had rented a room with a coin-operated gas heater and found that he could save money by attending double-features at movie theaters. The shows lasted about four hours—less than the cost of feeding the gas meter. He spent a lot of time in theaters and quickly became an authority on good films for many of his friends, including my uncle, who always consulted Bronek before deciding whether to see a new movie.

My aunt and uncle left London at the beginning of my last academic year at Battersea Polytechnic. Shortly after their departure, Joseph developed colon cancer, was hospitalized, and despite having several operations over a period of weeks, he visibly deteriorated with each passing day. He knew no one else in London, and Ilya insisted in his letters from Canada that I visit Uncle Joseph every day. The visiting hours at St. Mary's Hospital in Paddington were limited, but because both my uncles were doctors, arrangements were made for me to spend entire evenings with Joseph during the week and almost all day on Saturdays and Sundays. I had not known Joseph before his arrival in London, and we did not have much in common. He was not an easy person to be with and, sadly, his illness did not make him more agreeable. Conversation, never easy between a patient and a visitor, was usually quite strained in our case. It was a depressing year for me, since my social life was completely ruined and I had little time to study. As the final examinations approached, I worried about my ability to graduate that year. At the same time, I felt guilty for harboring such selfish thoughts and for not being more compassionate toward my sick uncle, whose chances of recovery seemed slim.

Toward the end of the academic year, Ilya returned to London for a visit, notifying me of his plans a few weeks before his arrival. It was wonderful to see Joseph's reaction to this news: His mood changed instantly, and he talked mostly of his hopes of speedy recovery once his brother arrived. It was his belief that Ilya would check the diagnosis, change the treatment, and force the hospital to provide better care. He was confident that his chances of being cured would improve considerably and that his discharge would be imminent.

I met Uncle Ilya at the airport and accompanied him to the hospital. Joseph's joy was in stark contrast to the sadness that came over Ilya at seeing his brother's pitiful state. Within minutes, Joseph became completely relaxed for the first time since his admission to the hospital. After a couple of hours, Ilya and I left the hospital, he going to his hotel and I to my room. I was awakened at about four in the morning by a policeman who came to inform me that Joseph was dead.

Despite our strained, unnatural relationship, I had grown attached to my sick uncle. Like his brother, he had a strong personality and a wide range of interests. He was a reasonably good artist and painted in his hospital bed. You could almost gauge the state of his health and his mind by the nature of his paintings, which became progressively more depressing with his deteriorating health. When he was admitted to the hospital, his painting resembled Cezanne's work, tending toward realism and bright colors. As illness robbed him of energy and weight (he died at barely 90 pounds), his paintings became progressively more abstract, with dark and gloomy hues.

I did not have much time to brood over his death, which occurred two weeks before the final examinations at Battersea Polytechnic. The examination would be the culmination of four years of study—the freshman year at Leicester and three years at Battersea. Fortunately I had spent the previous year and a half majoring in electrical engineering, and I felt comfortable studying the subjects leading to that specialty. Therefore, I reasoned, if I worked hard for the two remaining weeks, I still had a chance of earning my degree. Also, Jim Foster, my close friend and probably the best student in our class, came to my rescue. He invited me to spend the rest of the time before the examinations at his parents' house in Sheerness, a small town on an island in the Thames estuary. We both studied intensely, helping each other when we came to points that were difficult to understand. The peaceful atmosphere of the island, the Fosters' hospitality, and Jim's good will made a tremendous contribution to my ability to absorb the material. It was not all work, for in the evenings we enjoyed the wonderful atmosphere of local pubs and occasionally went to the movie-theater. After two weeks we returned to London to take our examinations.

It seemed unlikely that in two weeks I could make up for an entire year's neglect of my studies. The University of London maintained high academic standards. We had to pass ten three-hour written tests, and the technical problems required precise answers. If I remember correctly, we were expected to answer ten out of twelve questions in all our tests. I ran into difficulties almost immediately. I tackled the first problem and had to abandon it for lack of knowledge. The same thing happened with the following three questions. My chances of graduating were slipping away fast. Half an hour of my first examination had passed and I had accomplished precisely nothing. Stopping to collect my thoughts, I started again at the beginning, and the second time around I made better progress. My performance at the remaining nine examinations was less dramatic, but it was hard for me to judge the outcome. My father was anxious to follow my progress, and I sent him postcards after every test. I think he had more confidence in my abilities than I did, and he probably attributed the uncertain nature of my reports to excessive modesty.

As in the case of the matriculation examination, the results were posted on the university boards six weeks later. On that fateful day, a long line of hopeful students formed to read the announcement. There were three groups of successful candidates: The lowest was a "pass" grade, then "second class", and finally "first class" honors. Four years earlier I had looked for my name in the lowest section, and that is where I looked first this time. It was a long list and it took a while to realize that my name was not included in that part of the roster. To my dismay, I could not find my name in the shorter Second Class Honors division. In desperation I turned to the much shorter highest category. The names were arranged in alphabetical order and, as I expected, Jim Foster was featured near the top of the roll. The heads of other students in front of me obscured the lower part of the list. I moved to a better position, and there it was, in full glory—Frusztajer. I had not only passed, counter to my own expectations, but I had passed with flying colors!

Early British transistors, Rugby, England, 1954

RUGBY

SEVERAL MAJOR INDUSTRIAL COMPANIES sent representatives to Battersea Polytechnic to interview members of our graduating class. They gave us two choices: accept a position as an engineer, or join a two-year "graduate apprenticeship program," a situation roughly equivalent to becoming a trainee in an American company. The first alternative offered a higher salary, but it required an early commitment to a particular field. Compensation for graduate apprentices was considerably lower, but the program had significant advantages: It did not force us to choose a specialty at once, and it allowed trainees to work in several departments of their chosen company, including sales, design, research, and manufacturing. Equally important was a requirement for apprentices to function not just at the professional level but also in the capacities of assembler, machinist, and other similar occupations, which developed hands-on working skills and gave the future engineers a feeling for the reality of the production floor. To me, the value of the opportunities offered in the apprenticeship program was clear, and I did not hesitate to choose this option. Most of my fellow students chose the same path. The others, presumably sure of their primary interest or needing a good salary at once, accepted engineering positions.

The average length of training in each section was three months, exposing us to eight different aspects of the industry over a two-year period. Because I wanted to explore my new field from the bottom up, I was reluctant to choose a specialty without being able to examine it in great detail. To the uninitiated, electrical engineering might appear to be a narrow field, but in fact it covers a wide range of activities, including generation and transmission of power, motors, electrical equipment for ships and aircraft, radio, radar, television, telecommunications, and the manufacture of electronic components, to list just a sampling.

My employer was the British Thomson-Houston Company, whose main facilities were located in Rugby. I reported for work in the autumn of 1952, after once more spending most of the summer in Israel. For the first three months I was assigned to a small factory in the nearby town of Coventry, where I worked on electrical equipment for aircraft. Although the work was not particularly exciting and consisted primarily of testing small high-speed generators, I was thrilled to be in the real world, hopefully making practical contributions. It also felt good to be financially self-supporting. My salary before taxes was seven pounds a week, about seventeen dollars back then, but my expenses were comfortably lower and I was able to start a modest savings program.

Coventry had been a major industrial center before the war, but was almost totally destroyed by German aerial bombardment. The devastation in Coventry was especially notable because much of it could have been avoided. The British had deciphered the German military codes and had prior knowledge of the raids. That knowledge presented Churchill with a moral dilemma: either order an evacuation of the town, most likely signaling to the Germans that their code had been broken, or refrain from any action, endangering the town's population in hope of shortening the war and saving many more lives. Churchill's decision not to act must have been an extremely difficult one, but it has subsequently been endorsed by many experts as necessary for shortening the war.

By the time I came to Coventry in 1952, the town had been largely rebuilt. I found accommodations in a big complex of temporary, single-story structures erected during the war to house the employees of military industries. My room was scarcely wide enough to contain a narrow bed. A chest of drawers stood at the foot of the bed, and a small sink with hot and cold running water was attached to the opposite wall. Next to the head of the bed and facing the window was a night table that doubled as a desk. Dozens of identical rooms lined both sides of a long corridor of our building, which was similar to several other barracks of the sprawling complex. The shoddy construction materials and dull colors of the utilitarian structures, hastily thrown together to support the war effort, were hardly inviting or inspiring, but that was a small matter compared with my sense of pride at finally having—and paying for—my own dwelling.

The complex was not, however, totally devoid of conveniences and opportunities for entertainment. Morning and evening meals, which were included in the rent, were served in a big dining room. There was a recreation hall with ping-pong tables, where I met several Poles who lived in the same complex and excelled at the game. Many of my countrymen lived in England at that time, having come as members of the Polish army that had escaped from the Germans to the Middle East in 1939. They were later joined by arrivals from Russia in the early 1940s. These Poles had fought alongside the British in Italy and Germany, and after the war they settled in England. I played ping-pong with them several times a week, but most of my social life revolved around activities with fellow apprentices. We attended movies, dances, and a local theater called the Hippodrome, which produced good plays and musicals. I had already seen American-style musicals in London; the Hippodrome introduced me to German operetta with a performance of *Die Fledermaus* in English.

After three months I moved to Rugby, a town smaller than Coventry but from my point of view much more exciting. The large installation of the British Thomson-Houston Company in Rugby employed around ten thousand people. The facilities housed the company's headquarters, marketing department, main research laboratories, engineering design, and manufacturing plants. There were several hundred graduate apprentices, primarily from the British Isles, but the trainee group also included young men from all parts of the British Commonwealth and other countries, including the United States. I settled at The Laurels, a hostel built especially for graduate apprentices. Most of the rooms were doubles or triples, and I shared my quarters with Dick Garside, who had been a fellow student at Battersea Polytechnic. About sixty of us lived at the hostel, all men; in those days very few women entered the engineering profession.

I look back at the years I spent in Rugby as one of the most enjoyable periods of my life. The graduate apprenticeship program was a pleasant interlude between the intensive academic requirements of college and the real responsibilities of professional life. The focus was on practical experience, and except for a couple of company-sponsored theoretical courses, we were not immersed in technical studies. Our evenings were free from homework and we did not have to worry about examinations. Our duties at work were simple, and we were not expected to make any major decisions. The sheer size of the B.T.H. complex and the great variety of products manufactured in Rugby and neighboring towns provided ample exposure to the opportunities available to electrical and mechanical engineers. The company was most helpful in trying to accommodate our interests by scheduling the training program in the departments of our choice. The Apprentice Association, run by the trainees and supervised discreetly by the company, created a pleasant social atmosphere, offering club facilities, organized dinners, dances, various meetings, and other events designed to promote social interchange and a spirit of camaraderie. The presence of apprentices from many parts of the world lent a cosmopolitan air to most of those gatherings. In addition to social events, we often invited speakers prominent in various technical fields and occasionally held one-on-one discussions with the top executives of the company. At one of the annual dinners, attended by several hundred people, we heard after-dinner speeches by senior B.T.H. executives and a prominent visitor. On this occasion, I had the privilege of "answering for the association," a task I found most enjoyable in that the requirements were to deliver a half-serious, half-humorous talk that allowed me to make irreverent comments about our training program and also poke fun at our supervisors. Following an old English tradition, those officials were humorless at work and did not tolerate any nonsense from apprentices during business hours, but they were much more forbearing at social occasions.

While the formal programs and top-level contacts were valuable, the knowledge we gained by working with our hands, alongside line workers, was equally important and in many ways more pertinent to our future progress. At the beginning we were taught to use hand tools, starting with a simple file. We received a block of steel about three inches long, one and a half inches wide, and three quarters of an inch thick. After clamping the block in a vise, we had to file all six sides flat and parallel to the opposite faces and perpendicular to the adjacent sides within one thousandth of an inch—about one third the thickness of a human hair. It was a most frustrating task, because even a single light, careless stroke with the crude file could remove several thousandths of an inch of metal from one spot and require many hours of repair. The task took most of us about a week, but at the end of that period we had a good appreciation for the skills of workmen using hand tools and a firsthand understanding of what one-thousandth of an inch really means—important knowledge when it came to specifying dimensions in our future design work.

I then spent three months working with a fitter, carrying tools for him and helping with final assembly of huge generators, motors, and electrical transformers. He was a demanding but fair taskmaster, and I learned a lot from him. My first task was to work on the rotor, the rotating part of a big motor-generator set, which was one of the last ones made before newer technology superseded its function of converting alternating current to direct current. Part of the rotor was a large horizontal cylinder, or commutator, six feet in diameter and six feet long, whose surface consisted of shiny, wide copper segments. It took several weeks to balance the commutator and tune it to the required accuracy, and I had to work a couple of feet above the gleaming surface of the machine. Before dispatching me to my task, the fitter used his own mode of expression to clarify the need for care in bringing the copper cylinder to the required dimensions. "If you drop a spanner (wrench) on that commutator, I am going to kill you," he said, "so you'd better not do it." His tone left little doubt that he would gladly wring my neck if such an accident occurred. On another occasion I worked twenty feet above floor level on a transformer that would eventually be lowered into an oil-filled container with an opening about six by six feet square and perhaps ten feet deep. As I took my position above the oil-filled box he warned me, "You better not fall into it, because nobody can swim in oil." Oil, of course, cannot support a swimmer because it is lighter than water. I glanced into that forbidding vessel, filled with black, viscous liquid, and it did seem to be waiting to swallow me at the slightest opportunity—a frightening thought, but appropriately planted in my mind by a caring supervisor.

A few months later I worked in a research laboratory, assembling a large electronic instrument full of vacuum tubes intended to detect flaws in high-voltage insulation. Many laboratories faced one another through glass windows across the long corridor of our modern building. One of the groups in a room on the way to my workplace was engaged in metallurgical research. The workers examined polished samples of various alloys by studying them under a microscope; they measured angles of metal grains by shining lights of three distinct colors from different elevations. Instead of mounting separate light sources, they used one long vertical fluorescent tube which, strangely, was red for one third of its length, then white for another third, and finally yellow. Although I had seen fluorescent lights of various colors, I did not understand how one tube could have three different hues. Having studied lighting in our final year in college, I remembered that placing sodium inside the tube would color the light yellow, and that argon would produce red illumination. To maintain a sharp delineation between colors, the various gases would have to be prevented from mixing with each other, but I could not see any internal barriers between different sections of the tube. After devising several highly scientific hypotheses, none of which was satisfactory, I finally asked the researchers how they were able to produce the multicolored tube. "Oh, it's very simple," they said, "we just painted the three sections with different colored paints."

Once a year the apprentices organized what we called a Rag, which was a fundraising effort for charity. Normally the activity included a dance and a procession with floats built by different departments of B.T.H. and several other local companies, as well as clubs and municipal organizations. Toward the end of my apprenticeship period I met Norman Chigier, a trainee from South Africa, who directed the effort for the current Rag. He formed a small committee, of which I became an enthusiastic member. Not content with previous efforts, we decided to expand the activities of our Rag. Norman's drive and enthusiasm were infectious, and under his direction we planned and organized many new events. We still had the dance and the float parade, but we made sure that both were on a much larger scale than in the previous years. Instead of merely hiring a local band, we booked one of the best-known orchestras in England, the Sid Phillips Group—a calculated risk, because the orchestra's fee was high, but one that paid off handsomely.

We also made elaborate plans for using the float procession to attract new participants, hoping especially to involve the nearby American Air Force base. They were, indeed, happy to participate, and they built an attractive float. The American participation encouraged others to build new entries, including a B.T.H. department that employed many women, who pressed us to place their float next to the Americans. Another new idea was to roast a cow in an old-fashioned English barbecue. We could find only two individuals in all of England who knew how to do this cooking, and one of them agreed to travel over a hundred miles to be our chef. We asked several local farmers to donate a cow, but secured only vague promises of a big pig. As the time of the Rag approached, we still had no definite commitment of an animal, but our redoubled soliciting resulted in not just one but two enormous pigs, which we roasted on two consecutive days. The barbecues attracted huge crowds and substantial revenues, with the first slice of each pig being auctioned for a healthy sum to the highest bidder—who turned out to be the Mayor of Rugby. We also organized a parade with American-style drum majorettes, who had to be specially trained for the occasion. We had a theater, a nightclub with a reasonably good amateur show, a sheepdog-herding demonstration, and a widely publicized event of a man being "shot" out of a cannon. All in all, the Rag was a huge success, and we beat all previous fundraising records by a large margin.

In the summer of 1953, three friends and I toured Europe on two motorcycles. The reason for taking motorcycles rather than a car was strictly financial: we could afford a used motorcycle but not a used car. We explored several European countries and encountered few mechanical problems, except in Spain. In those days, Spanish roads were terrible and it was not unusual for the two bikes to have one or more flat tires every day. The gasoline in that country was of poor quality and most likely contributed to the valves burning out on one motorcycle. We were good at patching inner tubes, but repairing valves was beyond our capability. A Spanish mechanic at a primitive workshop in a tiny village made a new valve for us by using an old part from a different engine. I remember Spain not just for its roads but also for the contrast with France. Having admired the attractively dressed French girls, we were disappointed to find Spanish women of all ages wearing long black dresses with long sleeves, leaving little skin exposed despite the hot summer weather. We were also amused by the slogans that greeted us on both sides of the border. The French customs house proudly heralded, *"Liberté, Égalité, Fraternité,"* while the corresponding three-word sign chiseled into a stone wall on the Spanish side of the border proclaimed, *"Franco, Franco, Franco."*

As the end of my apprenticeship drew near, I identified several fields that I did not want to enter. I was not comfortable being part of a big technical team designing large machinery—a feeling that was the direct result of three months spent in an office with about a hundred engineers, each of whom was charged with performing calculations on a slide rule and compiling masses of numbers. Every day there we followed the same routine: At eight-thirty we took our places behind rows of desks and, for a few minutes, exchanged the usual remarks about the weather before plunging into our calculations. At ten-thirty we had a ten-minute tea break. Without leaving our desks, each engineer ate a few cookies ("biscuits" in England) brought from home and drank a cup of tea provided by the company. At twelve-thirty we departed for lunch in the cafeteria, returned to our desks an hour later, and repeated the tea ritual at three-thirty, going home at five-thirty in the afternoon. I am sure senior engineers had more interesting tasks, but the thought of leading this existence for decades before doing something original was more than a bit unsettling. Much had been written about production workers becoming automatons on an assembly line, but I did not realize until coming to Rugby that the same fate might be in store for design engineers.

Nor was I interested in a number of other opportunities. One was sales, which I considered (wrongly) totally unproductive and unworthy of an engineer whose calling, I thought, should be the production of goods rather than their dissemination. Another possibility was so-called "construction," which involved delivering and commissioning machinery at the customer's site. I did not yet realize the importance of that activity, which seemed vastly beneath the process of creating the products. Advanced research appeared interesting, but was too slow for my liking.

Fortunately, I did not have to do much agonizing. It was the beginning of 1954, and there was much talk about a new American invention, the transistor. I heard that the B.T.H. research laboratory had reproduced some of the American results and that the company planned to manufacture the semiconductor devices. The transistor seemed attractive from several points of view. Most important was that it had the potential to change the electronics industry by replacing vacuum tubes with far more efficient solid-state switches and amplifiers, although few people then realized how revolutionary this change would be. It was a new field for everyone, so I would not be at a disadvantage compared with other practitioners.

The device held an additional, personal attraction: It seemed to offer a practical way to satisfy my long-held but still secret desire to start my own company. The transistor was tiny as well as new, and I reasoned that in due course it would be much easier to start a company to supply small devices rather than large ones. The requirements for producing small, new products, both in money and personnel, would be considerably lower than the resources required to compete with established product lines of conventional electrical equipment.[33]

The last four months of my apprenticeship were still uncommitted, so I asked to be placed in the proposed transistor department. My request was not only favorably received, but I was given the responsibility of establishing the entire section. Assigned a few benches in a factory in the neighboring town of Lutterworth, I was told to organize a production line to manufacture transistors. Before accepting the assignment, I requested a four-week vacation period at the end of my apprenticeship, in order to spend time in the summer with my father before taking a permanent job that might not allow me to take long breaks for some time to come. My supervisor agreed to this arrangement, contingent upon my establishing a complete manufacturing line and producing one hundred fully functioning transistors during the four months preceding my vacation.

The optimism and fire of youth, enthusiasm not yet shaken by the vicissitudes of an established professional life, are wonderful! I agreed to his conditions even though, until recently, I had never seen a transistor, had no manufacturing equipment, had never been given responsibility for any business endeavor, and had only a vague idea how the devices were made. But to a young engineer finally entrusted with his first project, four months seemed long enough, and there was no doubt in my mind that I could accomplish the task. Today, with a more seasoned and skeptical mind, I would stretch that time target to at least a year, if not two.

I was not, however, starting completely from scratch. During World War II, the Lutterworth factory had already produced microwave diodes,

---

33. This reasoning was correct in 1954. At the time of this writing (2004), the capital required to build a semiconductor plant (so-called chip factory, or "water fab"), now expected to produce much more sophisticated devices, can run well in excess of two billion dollars.

distant relatives of the transistor that are used in radar. The company also made germanium diodes and, with certain modifications, some of the processes used to manufacture those devices could be used to produce transistors. I began my task by spending a few days at the Rugby research laboratory, where I learned how to make primitive prototypes.

On my return to Lutterworth, one of our company's engineers constructed a simple furnace by winding resistance wire around a quartz tube about two inches in diameter and five feet long. He enclosed the heated portion of the tube in a metal box packed with thermal insulation. I measured the temperature with a thermocouple inserted into the open end of the tube, and controlled the amount of heat with a variable voltage transformer, which fed power to the winding. I then assembled several pieces of test equipment, using electrical circuits shown in American magazines. Two young women were assigned to help me with the initial experiments. The prospect of people working for me was intimidating, but I received timely reassurance from Dick Garside, my roommate and fellow student in college. His final apprenticeship assignment was to run the germanium diode production line, which employed about twenty women. In fact, it was Dick Garside who told me about the transistor opportunity. When I asked how he managed his employees and assigned tasks, he replied, "It is the simplest thing in the world. I just ask them what they are doing and then tell them to do it faster." This bit of humor boosted my confidence in becoming a "boss."

Building transistors turned out to be an exacting task. It required assembly of wires thinner than human hair and had to be carried out under conditions of absolute cleanliness and a high degree of dimensional accuracy. Unlike American companies, which were already busy launching a major drive to produce semiconductors, my company viewed these products as peripheral and did not devote sufficient resources to making them. For example, we had no means of producing high-precision jigs and fixtures, and we had to improvise. It was a challenging task, but at the end of the four months I had managed to establish a small manufacturing line employing half a dozen assemblers and had reached my goal of producing one hundred transistors.

Departing for Israel, I left the head woman in charge of the line, with Dick Garside's promise to help her. Happily, I found the operation in good order on my return.

To the best of my knowledge, those were the first transistors produced in Great Britain, although Mullard, a subsidiary of the Dutch company Phillips, sold similar devices manufactured by its parent in Holland. To market our new product, we teamed up with Hivac, a British company engaged in the production of miniature vacuum tubes that were used primarily in hearing aids. An early application for transistors was the replacement of vacuum tubes, and Hivac was anxious to get a source of transistor elements that they could encase in glass envelopes. After a somewhat rocky start, the two companies developed a good working relationship, and Hivac became our largest customer. Another buyer was Ferranti, a British company which, I believe, used our devices in early digital computers.

The transistor was very much a novelty and attracted a lot of attention. We received many requests for lectures on the theory, manufacture, and applications of transistors. I prepared a talk with just that title and delivered it to a number of organizations, both within and outside the company. The tiny transistor presented a striking contrast to the much larger vacuum tube, which required big batteries to supply it with power. At the end of each lecture, I demonstrated a "spit" oscillator (not my original idea) to show how little current was required to drive the new device. As the name implies, the "battery" I had for driving the transistor, which in the demonstration produced a shrill whistle, consisted of a nickel coin and a copper penny separated by a small piece of blotting paper. I activated this "battery" by simply wetting the paper with saliva. It was not an elegant process, especially for well-mannered England, but a welcome counterpoint to the dense technological content of the lecture and a striking illustration of how little power is needed to operate transistor equipment.

I will not bore the reader by reproducing that lecture here, but the transistor has become such an important device that it merits at least a simplified discussion of its properties. The transistor, at first earning the nickname of "The Mighty Midget," has been at the core of the Information Revolution, often considered to be the second Industrial Revolution. It has become the basic building block of computers, cellular phones, and the Internet, made it possible to fly to the moon, changed the nature of warfare, and improved the efficiency of many professional activities. And yet the functions of the transistor are amazingly simple. In the 1940s and 1950s, its dimensions were measured in small fractions of an inch; half a century later, millions of transistors are embedded in a sliver of silicon the size of a fingernail, and half a billion into a chip the size of a postage stamp. Far from being an exotic material, the silicon itself is, in fact, the most common element in the earth's crust, although to be useful for transistor manufacturing it has to be extensively purified and presented in crystalline form.

The essential, yet simple, function of a transistor is to amplify electrical current. To put it simply, one unit of current fed into a transistor can produce, say, one hundred units of current at the output. Such a trick seems to defy common sense; it is almost like realizing the alchemists' dream of turning lead into gold. How can you invest one unit of current and reap a one hundred-unit bounty? In fact, there are many kinds of equally remarkable "amplifiers" we cannot live without today. For example, the common lever is extremely efficient at amplifying force. Properly placed, a force of, say, ten pounds at one end can lift a hundred pounds at the other. But neither transistors nor levers can generate something out of nothing. With the lever, we have to move the ten pounds force over a distance ten times as great as the load is moved. In the transistor circuit, the extra current must be supplied by an external source such as a battery or an electric utility.

How could a simple transistor create the second Industrial Revolution? The communications industry provides one example, the computer industry another. A microphone generates electric currents, which in amplitude and frequency are similar to the detected sound. Such currents fed into a loudspeaker produce the merest whisper. Transistors amplify those currents, which in turn drive the loudspeaker to reproduce the sound at any desired volume. Similar considerations apply to the radio and television: Transistors select and amplify the tiny signals contained in radio and television broadcasts.

In computers, transistors can be compared to the beads of an abacus. In that ancient mechanical calculator, beads at one end of the frame are said to be equal to zero, but when they are moved along the wires to the other side, they assume a predetermined value, allowing the abacus to perform calculations in a matter of seconds. An abacus, depending on its country of origin, typically contains sixty to a hundred beads. In a computer, a transistor that blocks electric current represents a zero, while a transistor that conducts current represents a one. The change from the zero state to the one state, which takes place at speeds measured in billionths of a second, is accomplished by electric signals sent by keyboard strokes or other input devices. A computer can contain billions of transistors, which, considering their extreme speed of operation, make it possible to perform an enormous number of calculations in a short time. The powerful computation capability of modern computers not only makes it possible to process numerical data but also allows the internal signals to represent letters and numbers, serve as "memories," and provide visual information such as pictures and diagrams. The difficult task of coordinating all these mathematical transactions is left to software. While the computer is vastly more powerful than the abacus, the function of its transistors built into chips is essentially equivalent to the function of the humble abacus beads.

In the mid-1950s, transistors were at the forefront of electronics technology, and B.T.H. was eager to show my production line to customers from all over the world. An endless stream of curious visitors came to see the transistor, and as a young engineer with a foreign accent, I was a suitable host to demonstrate the new invention. In that era, it was not unusual in England to assume that a "real" scientist had to be a foreigner, probably because of the exodus of many top scientists from central Europe, fleeing Nazi persecution. Those refugees made crucial contributions to science and technology in England and the United States, and with their thick foreign accents, they became distinctive members of the scientific community.

I always enjoyed outsiders' visits to our plant, for they gave me a chance to show off my work and were usually followed by lunch at the company's expense at one of the two excellent local country pubs. Contrary to conventional wisdom, English food can be very good. Both pubs produced a variety of tasty traditional English dishes (at least they seemed good to me at that time, perhaps in contrast to my landlady's cooking) and served delicious Stilton cheese. It was fun introducing foreign visitors to the comforts of an old English country inn and ordering drinks for them. Especially intriguing were "Gin and French" (a dry martini) and "Gin and It" (gin and Italian sweet vermouth), both popular drinks in England at that time. On a visit to England twenty years later, I found that the name "Gin and It" drew only blank stares from pub bartenders.

Our visitors were mainly interested in the applications of transistors, and when I informed them that the primary use was in hearing aids and radios, they wanted sample transistors to make those products. I had no difficulty supplying them with devices to make hearing aids, but we had no transistors for radios. After several requests for radio transistors, I decided to end what was becoming an embarrassing situation and see if we could develop components for this new application. I chose my most able assistant, told her to scale down the dimensions of the transistors we were making, and twenty-four hours later we had twelve functioning devices suitable for a radio. I believe they were the first radio transistors produced in Europe. A fellow engineer named Alan Dixon immediately constructed a crude radio set, or "wireless" as it was known in England, consisting of a board with several transistors and other components wired in haphazard fashion. The first devices were good enough to receive only one of the three British radio stations, called the Light Programme; the other two broadcasting stations had wavelengths that our early transistors could not handle. But we remedied that situation within a few weeks by producing devices with higher frequency ranges.

As we increased our production capacity to meet the rapidly growing demand for our products, I was fortunate to hire John Wood as foreman of the operation. Despite having only a rudimentary high school education, John was extremely effective in handling his subordinates and grasping the intricacies of the complicated semiconductor manufacturing processes. We had had great difficulty controlling the number of rejected transistors, but under his direction, efficiency increased steadily and the number of "rejects" dropped dramatically.

Although I enjoyed my job immensely, the contrast between the performance of our products and those made in the United States made me uneasy. One of the main features of the transistor was the voltage it could withstand. American magazines routinely advertised thirty-volt transistors, but hard as we tried, the best we could achieve consistently was ten volts. I did not discover the real reason for our apparent failure until I came to the United States. Our semiconductor department had initially been organized as a section of the switchgear operation, and the test procedures designed for transistors followed the practice for testing switches and contactors used to control currents in traditional electrical applications. To build in a safety factor, switchgear was tested under stresses considerably greater than those expected in the field.

There was little reason to use similar safeguards in testing transistors, but those were the rules we followed, and I never thought to question them. The Americans were not encumbered by these handicaps, and they tested their units under the expected working conditions. Little did I realize that our ten-volt units, which we tested to much higher standards, were not inferior to their American counterparts after all. Had we been able to evaluate U.S.-made devices alongside our own, we would have discovered that they were of comparable quality. But severe import restrictions and bureaucratic purchasing procedures within B.T.H. kept us from obtaining any American samples for testing.

I mistakenly attributed our seemingly inferior performance to the fact that the Americans could do everything better than the Europeans. That certainly was the common wisdom in Europe at that time. I assumed—correctly—that our foreign competitors had large technical teams developing the product, whereas I represented the entire transistor development effort at B.T.H. I also realized that, for what seemed then to be sound commercial reasons, my company was not interested in emphasizing the transistor business. The entire market for my products was smaller than the value of one large electric power generator. My employer was using conventional business sense to maintain just a small transistor effort to learn the technology and be in a better position to make further tactical decisions when the potential of the new field became clear. While that course was probably logical, the situation made me restless, and I started thinking about emigrating to the United States, to be at the center of the semiconductor activity. The magazines that advertised transistor products also solicited applications for engineering positions available at various American semiconductor manufacturers. Despite serious misgivings, I sent my resume to several U.S. companies and applied for the advertised jobs.

I hesitated to leave a good situation and venture into the unknown. My main deterrent was the negative political image of the United States in Europe after the Second World War. Senator McCarthy's hearings received wide publicity in England, and I was worried that, having spent six years in Russia, I would be accused of harboring Communist beliefs and even be arrested or ignominiously deported. I was also concerned that I was ill prepared to keep up with my future colleagues on the other side of the Atlantic, because American science had developed a reputation for being far ahead of its European counterpart. The lure of joining a flourishing and vibrant semiconductor activity and the promise of a much higher standard of living prevailed, however, and I decided to explore the possibility of employment in the New World.

Most of the companies I contacted responded immediately. A few were not interested at all, two others were eager to interview me if I found a way to emigrate to the United States. One company, Transitron, sent me a telegram asking me to call them collect. I did not know what "call collect" meant, but I suspected that it corresponded to the English expression "reverse charges," confirming that theory with an American friend before placing the call. I spoke with Dr. David Bakalar, the president of the company, who offered to pay all my expenses to come for an interview. A few weeks later I picked up prepaid tickets at the Pan American Airways office in London and, without announcing my plans to the people at B.T.H., traveled to Boston, Massachusetts.

My first impressions were different from what I had expected. Logan Airport was not the shiny, gleaming monument I had imagined for an American port of entry. When I took a taxi to Melrose, the Boston suburb where Transitron was located, the driver immediately challenged me to a bet, asking me to guess the fare to my destination. If my estimate turned out to be closer than his, I would not have to pay him. If his guess was closer, the fare would be doubled. Naturally I refused his offer, but I immediately developed serious doubts about the wisdom of coming to such a country. As we drove toward Melrose, I realized what a false picture I had of America. I had expected to see only closely packed skyscrapers and factories, not small houses and open fields.

The reception at Transitron was very cordial, and I spent the whole day talking to technical people and touring the plant. I quickly realized how insignificant our activity at B.T.H. was compared with this company's facilities and their several hundred employees. The engineers and scientists at my interview were much more knowledgeable than anyone I had met, making my own expertise seem rudimentary. But I felt I knew enough to make a contribution to Transitron's effort. I was both a little envious and intimidated.

When David Bakalar asked for my impressions, I told him that the visit had reinforced my desire to come to America. When he asked me what my salary requirements were, I was completely taken aback, because in England one did not discuss such matters in an interview. A professional employee simply accepted or rejected the salary offered by the employer. In short, it was embarrassing for me to talk about money, and I told David Bakalar that I had no idea what my salary should be. He offered me $5,200 a year, which was three times my remuneration in England. When I mentioned that I planned to spend a few days in New York with my uncle, he urged me to return to Boston afterward for another discussion at Transitron before returning to England. That evening he took me to dinner at the Colonial Restaurant in nearby Lynnfield, where I ordered roast beef. I had heard of American portions, but the huge one-inch-thick piece of meat exceeded my expectations, especially when compared with what I would be served in England—a humble portion about one-tenth the thickness and one-third the circumference. Years later, we would be told that such big servings were detrimental to one's health—and even vulgar—but during my first trip from England, where meat was in short supply, the dinner served to reinforce my impression of American bounty. David Bakalar was a congenial companion and generous host, and that evening he even dropped me off at the Copley Plaza Hotel in Boston.

I was eager to explore at least part of that renowned city the following morning. It was a beautiful spring day, and I started my tour by walking through Boston's Public Garden. The famous swan boats moved smoothly and silently along the surface of the small pond without sails or obvious means of mechanical propulsion. With my European awe of American technology, I fantasized that either they had an advanced silent motor or a quiet atomic engine! I had a good laugh when I eventually realized that they were pushed along by good old-fashioned pedal power. After exploring the surrounding streets, I returned to the hotel and made a few telephone calls.

My first call was to Uncle Ilya, who by then had emigrated from Canada to New York. He had encouraged me to come to the United States, although he wrote a long letter expressing his anger when he realized that I had arranged my own interview without asking his advice. He also seemed annoyed that I made the trip without relying on him to pay for my ticket. The second call was to John Harmer, an English engineer with whom I had worked at B.T.H. John had met an American woman in Rugby, married her, and moved to Boston, and he was now working for Raytheon. He was glad to hear from me and immediately offered to contact his employer's semiconductor people to see if they had any engineering vacancies. Within an hour I received a call from George Freedman, one of the best-known executives in the field. He wanted me to come at once for an interview, but after learning that I was leaving for New York that day, arranged to meet me there the following week. I also called RCA, a transistor manufacturer in New

Jersey, which had suggested I visit them if I could arrange a trip to the States. After making an appointment with RCA, I flew to New York to spend a few days with my aunt and uncle.

I received a warm welcome from my relatives, who seemed genuinely happy to see me. Although we had never developed a very warm relationship, they now treated me much more cordially and with more respect than they had in London. My uncle had a wealth of information about the current situation in the United States and was eager to share it with me. He was a wonderful guide, and I probably saw more of New York City during those few days than on all subsequent visits. We explored Fifth Avenue, Central Park, Chinatown, Wall Street, Harlem, Greenwich Village, and several major museums. It was good to see him and my aunt. They gave the feeling that, should I choose to leave England, I would have a base in my new country.

George Freedman called to arrange the final details for a dinner at the Quo Vadis Restaurant on New York's East Side. He arrived with his immediate superior, a Mr. Dukat, whose first name I don't recall. George was clearly a connoisseur of food and wine. The restaurant was much better than any other eating establishment I had ever seen, and we had a delightful dinner. At that time, Raytheon produced more transistors than all other companies combined, and that achievement owed a great deal to George's leadership. We discussed many aspects of the industry, my experience, Raytheon's plans, and the fact that Transitron had brought me over for an interview. At the end of the evening I had an offer to join Raytheon's development team at an annual salary of $7,200. The subject of money was handled in a more elegant fashion than at Transitron, and I was surprised at the $2,000 difference between the two offers—an enormous sum to me. I thanked them for their hospitality and confidence, asked for a couple of weeks' thinking time, and promised to get in touch with them after returning to England.

The interview at RCA was less exciting. I spent an hour with a production manager who seemed to be bored with the whole interview process. At the end of our discussion, he showed me around a small part of the factory, where I saw only basic manufacturing procedures.

He may have been concerned about revealing trade secrets, but I could only assume he was not interested in me as a potential employee. I was all the more surprised when he asked me to stop in at the personnel department, where a written offer of employment was waiting for me. The position would be that of a manufacturing engineer, at an annual salary of $7,200, exactly the same as the Raytheon offer.

Before returning to England I had another meeting with David Bakalar at Transitron. Since that company had brought me to the United States, I had already made up my mind to join them, despite their lower offer and the fact that the Raytheon situation was more enticing. After a few pleasantries, he asked me whether I had visited any of his competitors, and I told him about my contacts with RCA and Raytheon. He wanted to know if I received any offers, then inquired about the salary levels. He became quite agitated when I told him that both offers were for $7,200. "You are not worth $7,200," he said in a very resentful way. I found his remark distasteful and even more offensive than his desire to negotiate the salary during my first visit. My facial expression must have reflected my disappointment, because his next statement was, "All right, we'll pay you $7,200." I thought it over for a few minutes and, having already decided to join Transitron, I accepted the offer.

Back at B.T.H., none of my coworkers initially believed that I had visited the United States. They greeted the news with a knowing smile, assuming that I had just returned from an amorous adventure whose details I wanted to keep to myself. At that time America was a distant, wonderful, but unapproachable country for most of us, and going there even for a short time was nearly as improbable as going to the moon. When they finally accepted the reality of my American trip, their understanding changed to open admiration, followed by questions about my plans. They assumed I would most likely move there, but I was vague about my intentions until I had presented a formal notice to my immediate supervisor a few days later.

The reactions from the division engineering manager and the plant superintendent were diametrically opposite. The technical executive,

Len Rushforth, tried to discourage me from accepting my new position; the general manager, Bill Dawson, seemed happy about my initiative. He felt that my offer would open tremendous opportunities for me in America and that I should definitely go there, whatever inconvenience my departure might cause B.T.H. My coworkers were also very supportive. Each of them brought me the latest data from their area of semiconductor technology to help me with my transition to the new job. They organized a well-attended farewell dinner, with many speeches devoted to reminiscences of our time together. It was an emotional occasion, and I had to call on all my powers of self-control to avoid bursting into tears. It was hard to leave this group of kind and supportive friends. It was also hard to leave England, a country that had given me my education and the opportunity to participate in a new and exciting field. As I pondered the day's events, I realized I felt very much at home in England. Surrounded by genuine friends—and despite the widely held belief that the British are intolerant of foreigners—I had never felt like an outsider, except perhaps for the first months when I could not speak the language.

As I began to focus on the reality of my departure, my old doubts about the United States surfaced again, but I dismissed them quickly. My supervisors assured me that I could always come back to B.T.H., and I knew that with just a few weeks' salary at Transitron I could save enough money to return. Having spent most of my life as a refugee and an immigrant, I tried to anticipate potential problems in a new country. I concentrated on difficulties that might prevent me from returning to England in case I found living in the United States troublesome. Since I had very little money, the main threat would come from unusual expenses. I knew food would account for a small percentage of my salary. I was good at mending clothes, a skill I acquired in Siberia, so tailoring would not represent a significant drain on my resources. The main vulnerability would be footwear, so I planned to buy a sturdy pair of English shoes that, no matter what the weather, would serve me long enough to earn my passage back. I even joked to myself that the worst possible fate was being shot, but I had already faced that threat in Siberia and survived.

Having put on that psychological armor, I decided to visit Israel before my departure for the United States. Norman Chigier, my roommate in Rugby digs, had similar plans for the summer, and we decided to travel together. Norman wanted to visit his girlfriend Jose in Holland on the way to Naples, where we arranged to board a ship for Haifa. We would travel by motorcycle in order to go sightseeing in Europe and to have our own means of transportation in Israel. Norman had never ridden a "bike," as we called them in England, but I quickly dispelled his doubts. We found a medium-sized Norton and bought it for forty pounds, the same price we had paid the previous summer. I gave Norman several driving lessons, we packed a few belongings, including the all-important rain gear, and departed for Holland, crossing the channel in an airplane specially equipped to carry motorcycles and their riders.

We were well received by Jose's parents in Holland, but learned that Jose was staying in a German town near the Dutch border. We made plans to visit her there the following day. Our hosts did not speak English, but Norman, a native of South Africa, had no trouble communicating with them in Afrikaans, which is similar to Dutch. During the course of the evening, we discovered that Jose's father was the retired chief of police of his city and that we were close to Eindhoven, the town where the Dutch company Phillips had its headquarters and extensive manufacturing facilities. On hearing that Phillips was a major semiconductor producer, our host offered to arrange a visit to their factory through the chief of police at Eindhoven. The next day Norman took a train to visit Jose in Germany, while I rode our bike to Eindhoven and stayed overnight in a small hotel. In the morning a police car took me to the Phillips visitors' center. I was given an all-day tour of their facilities, but I did not see the transistor manufacturing plant, which they claimed was in another city. I was introduced to several high-ranking Phillips officials and was treated most cordially. At the end of the day, the reason for the "royal" treatment became clear. My guide confided in me that they believed I was with the British section of Interpol. Why else would a companion and I travel across Europe on a motorcycle and arrive at Phillips with a police escort? I did not have the heart to disappoint him by divulging my real pedigree.

After I picked up Norman in Germany, we continued toward Naples. Southern Germany and the Alps were delightful, but Italy greeted us with torrential rain, which made our progress slow and difficult. We waited in shelters for a while but, pressed for time, we finally had to brave the elements. We could afford only a few hours of rest when we arrived in Rome late at night. Rather than check into a hotel for such a short time, we decided to nap in a waiting room of the main railroad station. The Roman police were not pleased, however, and they woke us up rudely and unceremoniously showed us the door. Our eviction turned out to be fortuitous, for it was still raining hard, and the trip to Naples took longer than expected. Indeed, we managed to arrive at the port just before the ship's departure.

My purpose in visiting Israel that summer was two-fold. Naturally, I wanted to spend a few weeks with my father, especially in view of my pending departure to the United States, whose greater distance from Israel would make visiting more difficult. But I also wanted to explore the possibility of starting a transistor company in Israel after gaining additional experience in America. The primary reason for that ambition was my desire to reunite permanently with my father, but I also reasoned that transistor manufacturing would be welcomed in Israel. The value of transistors was high and their transportation costs low, making the product suitable for export. The country had few natural resources but an abundance of scientific manpower. Locally produced semiconductors would encourage the development of the electronics industry, which, like the transistor, demanded little in natural resources but much in the way of skilled personnel. Transistors could be used for consumer and industrial products, as well as military applications, and were of interest to the academic community.

With that idea in mind, I visited three different organizations: Amcor, one of the largest manufacturers of electrical appliances; the Technion, Israel's premier technical university; and the headquarters of the Israeli Army. Despite the fact that I had no one to introduce me and made "cold calls," I was enthusiastically received in all three places, especially after I explained that my mode of operation would require

only a small investment because I was prepared to build most of the required manufacturing equipment. Amcor promised to offer financial support and manufacturing space; the Army, while somewhat vague, also seemed quite anxious to work with me; and a Technion professor suggested that I use part of his laboratory. The meeting with the professor was the most promising of the three. He suggested I come to his house near the university, where he received me in his underwear—an informality extreme even by Israeli standards. A world-famous scientist in his sixties or seventies, he was probably unaware of what he was wearing.

Before leaving Israel, I spent a lot of time with my father, discussing my new situation in America and what it meant for our future plans. The positive reception I received regarding the establishment of a semiconductor business in Israel had been most encouraging, but since I planned to spend at least a year in the United States, I urged him to join me there. He had not wanted to come to Britain, but he agreed to move to America. New York had a large colony of emigrants from his hometown in Poland, and he felt sure that, even without speaking English, he would be able to make a living by working with his compatriots. I explained to him that my salary was more than sufficient to support us both, but he did not want to be a burden. I knew he understood that I was in a position to provide financial security for both of us when I heard him boast to everyone in the village that his son's salary was greater than that of the prime minister of Israel. We traveled together to Haifa on our faithful motorcycle, and he put on a brave face when we said goodbye. Later, Norman told me about my father's premonition that he would not see me again. Unfortunately, he was right. The last time I saw him alive was from the deck of the ship as it pulled away from the Haifa dock.

BOOK TWO

ADVENTURES IN AMERICAN BUSINESS

ENGINEER
IN AMERICA

IT DID NOT TAKE ME LONG TO WIND DOWN my affairs in England; I had few belongings and no complicated financial entanglements. My first order of business was to visit the American Embassy in London to make final arrangements for a permanent U.S. resident's visa. The procedure at the embassy was quick and efficient, but I was taken aback when, without warning, one of the officials grabbed my hand, pressed my fingers on an inkpad, and reproduced my fingerprints on a sheet of paper. It was a bit of a surprise, since it was something I had seen before in the movies about criminals, but I was reassured that it was a standard procedure. Anyway, in comparison with my humiliations at the borders of Russia and Poland, this experience was harmless enough. The Cold War was in full swing, and I was impressed with America's desire to keep tabs on its immigrants, especially those of Eastern European origin. The embassy informed me that I might be drafted into the U.S. Army at a future date, but that at my age I was old enough to be exempted from military service for the time being.

Having said my goodbyes to friends and my few relatives in London, I returned to Rugby to pack my belongings. Dick Garside and I jointly owned an old manual typewriter we had acquired for the purpose of writing technical articles that we hoped would be accepted by professional journals, and I traded my half of the machine for his sturdy trunk. I packed most of my possessions in the trunk and shipped it by sea to the United States, carrying only a small suitcase with a few necessities.

In 1956, transatlantic flights were aboard propeller-driven Constellations that had to refuel in Shannon, Ireland, and Gander, Newfoundland, before reaching the United States. The Shannon terminal was delightful. An attractive, redheaded Irish harpist was plucking at her instrument, performing wistful, relaxing melodies in a pleasant lounge. I noticed that Irish coffee was being served and, wishing to sample local fare, gave it a try. It tasted somewhat strange, but I enjoyed it nonetheless. Later, when we ran into stormy weather and the plane started bouncing around, I realized that the coffee contained a strong dose of Irish whiskey! Our Pan American airplane landed in New York, where I took an Eastern Airlines shuttle to Boston. Arriving early in the morning, I was tired but eager to start my new life.

The taxi from Logan Airport brought me to Melrose, this time without the driver offering any gambling opportunities. At Transitron, David Bakalar introduced me to several of my coworkers, one of whom took me to the new plant in nearby Wakefield, where most of the research and development activity was located. I was assigned space in one of the laboratories there.

My employer had thoughtfully rented a small, but adequate room in a private house in Melrose, where I spent two weeks before moving into an apartment in Malden. There, one room served as bedroom and living room. There was a small kitchen and a bathroom spacious enough for a bathtub, but the slanting ceiling above it was too low for a shower. The apartment was built into a converted attic in a suburban house whose owners, Mr. and Mrs. Earle, rented out the surplus space. Although modest by American standards and certainly not in the same category as my uncle's apartment in London, my new dwelling fulfilled a long-cherished dream: Finally, I could cook meals in my own kitchen, bathe at my own convenience, and live in almost complete privacy. A young Transitron engineer living in a somewhat larger apartment in the neighboring house drove me to work every day until I obtained a U.S. driver's license and bought a used car. The Earles were caring and thoughtful people and went out of their way to help me adjust to my new country.

Just as I was beginning to feel comfortable, I received a telegram with the terrible news that my father had had a stroke and had been taken unconscious to a Tel Aviv hospital. I could scarcely believe the short, crisp, impersonal message. Since arriving in Boston, I had already started making inquiries about securing a U.S. immigrant's visa for him, and in our correspondence we had agreed that he would join me within a few months. I wired back, hoping he would recover in time to receive my reply, but the next day I received another telegram informing me of his death. It must be that the long years of evolution have equipped us to deal with emotional crises, for I read the message without full acknowledgement of its meaning. Rather than dwelling on the fact of his death, I feverishly began making arrangements for a trip to Israel. I needed a visa, but the main impediment was the money required for plane fare. David Bakalar was kind enough to advance me the funds, and I soon boarded a Pan American Airways plane from New York to Israel.

When we landed in Paris for refueling, we were informed that the plane would not proceed to Israel. It was only a week after the end of the 1956 Israeli-Egyptian war, and while we were over the Atlantic, the U.S. State Department had issued an order declaring the Middle East off limits to U.S. citizens. Because our crew was American, the plane could not proceed to Tel Aviv. My only recourse was to change to an El-Al aircraft, which meant a two-day wait in Paris; the Israeli airline had only two flights a week to Tel Aviv.

I arrived unannounced at my cousin Marek's place of business and spent the next two nights in his apartment, contacting Tel Aviv to inform them of my delay and hoping they would postpone the funeral. According to Jewish religious tradition, a deceased person must be buried within twenty-four hours of death, unless death occurs on the

Sabbath, and I was concerned that I would arrive too late to attend the funeral. Soon after sending my request, I was relieved to hear that a prominent Israeli rabbi had authorized a delay, offering the traditional reasoning that it was more important for the son to offer prayers (Kaddish) for his dead father at the interment than to follow strict rule of timeliness.

As I got off the plane in Israel, I thought I heard my father's voice calling me: "Bronek, Bronek!" At first I thought I was hallucinating, but there was no mistaking those insistent cries, and no other passengers responded to that name. I nearly breathed a sigh of relief, thinking that there had been some mistake and my father was alive and well. But then I discovered that the source of those calls was my cousin, Bronek Altschuler, who had come to greet me at the airport. To this day I don't know if he really sounded like my father or if my imagination had changed his voice to conform to my wishes.

I was devastated by the sight of my father's corpse in the hospital's morgue. True, when I had seen him just a few months earlier, he had looked old and tired. But he had been unconscious for the last three days of his life, and the effects of the coma had altered his appearance. With the lack of nourishment, his face was now ghostly thin. To add to his disfigurement, his beard had continued to grow and his cheeks were covered with thick black bristle. I distinctly remember feeling angry at this impudent growth. While the more important parts of his body had ceased to function, the beard kept growing unbidden, disfiguring his face.

Scenes from his difficult life flashed before my eyes, and I thought of the irony of his death coming just weeks before he was to join me and dramatically change his circumstances. At long last, I had hoped, I would be able to help him, look after him, and remove the pressures of survival and the struggle to earn a living that had plagued him for most of his life. I don't know how long I stood there staring at him, but then I felt myself being led away by two men while someone covered my father's face.

At the funeral in his village, I said the Kaddish and the rabbi performed the service and read the eulogy. He praised my father and added that at this time of trouble he could not think of a better person to intercede with God on behalf of Israel. It was probably a common consolation, but it made me feel better all the same.

I remained in the country for a few more days, seeing a few friends and settling my father's affairs. I also spent several hours with the people who had witnessed his death. During a casual conversation with friends in Tel Aviv, he had mentioned that he was not feeling well. He went out onto a balcony for a breath of fresh air and after just a few minutes he fell unconscious and never recovered. The cause of death was determined to be cerebral hemorrhage.

When I returned to the United States, I felt thoroughly demoralized. My father was my only near relative, and despite the long distance that had separated us since 1947, I still felt very close to him. All my plans regarding the place of my residence had been heavily influenced by the desire to be with him; now they felt pointless. My being in America seemed almost bizarre. What was I doing here, so far from my native Europe? Should I move to Israel, where I had relatives and childhood friends? What did it matter, anyway? My Malden apartment, which until just a few days ago seemed to be the fulfillment of my dreams, now looked irrelevant and even ridiculous. I felt like a lost stranger without a road map. I shut myself in the apartment, which provided the much needed private retreat, staying alone to think and reminisce about the Russian life I had shared with my father and about his sacrifices on my behalf. It was his wisdom that had steered me past so many obstacles in Siberia and had allowed me to reach my current promising situation in the United States.

Fortunately my wretched state of mind was short-lived. Two or three days after my return, I awoke with a completely fresh outlook. Realizing that it was not in my nature to brood over my father's death, and that he certainly would not wish my grief to destroy my future, I applied myself with renewed enthusiasm and a zest for life. With a measure of embarrassment, I felt that my father was looking out for me, or at least that the things I was doing would have made him happy. Those feelings brought me strength and reassurance for several years after his death.

Initially, things went well at work. I developed a new transistor for use in computer memories, a project that was both challenging and interesting. The engineers and scientists around me were eager to share their ideas; the laboratory assistants were intrigued by the new arrival from England and did their best to cooperate. Ed Simon, a wonderful person and a knowledgeable scientist with a Ph.D. in semiconductors, was especially helpful. A lot of my previous work had been based on trial-and-error methods; Ed, well versed in physics, helped me understand the basic scientific principles underlying our development programs. Shortly after I joined the company, David Bakalar mounted a concerted effort to bring new engineers from Europe. England was his first target, and I gave him the names of several of my B.T.H. coworkers who I hoped would also emigrate to the United States. Two of them, David Roberts and Alan Dixon, joined me at Transitron within a few months. Englishmen from other companies also answered Transitron's advertisements in the British technical press, and we soon had a thriving colony of young British engineers. There were also arrivals from Holland, France, and Israel, giving the company's technical staff an interesting international flavor. Most of us were young and single, eager to exploit our new financial freedom and integrate into American life. Like many new immigrants, we formed an intimate social circle and together began the wonderful process of assimilation. Of course, most of us soon ventured outside the limited Transitron expatriate group, and I made a number of friends and acquaintances among the Jewish, Polish, and Russian communities of Boston.

While my social life was rewarding, I soon grew restless at work. In retrospect, my disagreements with superiors were probably as least as much my fault as theirs, but after a year, I found Transitron's atmosphere restrictive and stifling. In England I had been left almost entirely to my own resources, whereas in my new situation I was closely supervised. Formal meetings at B.T.H. had been sedate and polite; at Transitron, participants often behaved in what I considered to be an offensive manner, with superiors raising their voices to their subordinates and ridiculing their performance. I was fortunate never to receive such treatment, but I did not enjoy attending meetings where senior engineers—whom I considered to be much more knowledgeable than I, and whose motivation and dedication were beyond question—were criticized in front of their coworkers.

I stayed at Transitron for a year and a half, but at that point David Bakalar and I both decided that the company was not the right place for me. I left my job without definite plans for future employment. In later years, I came to doubt whether Transitron's management methods were compatible with an orderly development of the organization. Their vigorous—and even aggressive—practices propelled Transitron to early prominence in the semiconductor business, but the company also became one of the industry's early casualties. There was an almost total turnover of engineering talent in the years following my departure. The first engineer Transitron brought over from Europe, I was also the first to leave.

Semiconductor engineers were still in short supply, but rather than apply for a new job of a similar nature, I decided the time had come to explore the possibility of starting my own company. I had saved enough money to last me at least six months, which I thought was enough time to investigate such a venture. I explored two ideas: One was to make a piece of equipment for the processing of semiconductors, the other was to make a communication device for firemen. I did not even consider the logical route of setting up an operation to manufacture transistors, even though that was my specialty, because the investment required in such a venture was well beyond my means and because I did not relish the thought of competing with large, well-established companies in the industry.

The machine for manufacturing semiconductors in the United States was based on a piece of equipment we used in England to slice germanium and silicon ingots into thin wafers. The design required mechanical engineering skills I did not have, so I sought the support of an equipment engineer who worked for Transitron. He embraced the idea enthusiastically, but did nothing about it for weeks, except feed me reassurances of his great interest in the venture.

The speaking device for firefighters was an easier project to put into production. It had occurred to me that firefighters who were wearing masks might have difficulty communicating with one another. If I could build a speaking device that could be fitted onto their existing equipment, it might find a market in the firefighting industry. Army surplus stores carried throat microphones that were used by tank crews during the Second World War. Worn on the neck, they sensed the vibrations of vocal cords in order to recreate a person's voice. One strong feature of the technology was that it did not pick up background noise. I thought that connecting one of those microphones to an amplifier and a speaker contained within a small waterproof box, which could be clipped to a belt, would produce a useful and saleable communication tool. I also planned to add a loud, shrill electronic whistle for the firefighter to activate when in danger. I even devised what I thought was a catchy name, "Firefone," and prepared an outline of a brochure.

I discussed the matter with Alan Dixon, whose expertise would have come in handy in building the electronic circuits for the Firefone. He was most enthusiastic about the project, but just as in the case of the cutting machine, matters never advanced far beyond the talking stage. Building an amplifier was not difficult. I bought an amplifier kit and a miniature loudspeaker in an electronics store. A local sheet metal shop fabricated a small waterproof aluminum box, and I built and tested the finished device. The quality of the sound was not good, but I attributed that problem partially to my foreign accent. When I contacted the Malden fire department, the chief was most receptive and arranged for me to demonstrate my instrument and instruct his men in its use. The result was extremely disappointing: The firemen's voices were even less intelligible than my own. They did, however, promise to try my new invention while fighting a fire, and they proudly displayed it at a town show of their fire equipment. But as far as I know, they never used the Firefone.

And so I learned belatedly the perils of venturing into a technology that was not my specialty. The Firefone required skills in designing circuits and reproducing sound, not the ability to build transistors. I also did not learn until the end of the project that the faulty sound was caused by the throat microphone, which I should have tested before spending time and money to build the electronic portion of my instrument.

Although commercially unsuccessful, my efforts during the months following my departure from Transitron were not entirely wasted. I learned a great deal about many aspects of life. I decided early on that I would work hard to establish my new venture, but I would ignore conventional routines of daily life. I would eat when I was hungry, sleep when I was tired, play when I was bored, and work when the inspiration moved me, without regard to the time of day or day of the week. I soon found myself eating, working, resting, and sleeping at most irregular hours, and I felt elated by the freedom to follow my own schedule rather than keeping to an artificial timetable imposed by the outside world. Unfortunately, my joy lasted for only two or three weeks before I became a physical wreck, often unable to eat or sleep despite hunger and exhaustion. Realizing that convention is not always without purpose, I returned to accepted schedules and recovered immediately. My reliance on others during that time taught me a lot about the choice of partners in business, and I learned hard lessons about designing products for markets I did not understand.

After enjoying my newfound freedom for a few months, I decided to return to my profession and find a job as a semiconductor engineer. The three key geographical areas for that industry were northern California, eastern Massachusetts, and Texas. I ruled out California, explored opportunities in the Boston area and applied to Texas Instruments, which, at the time, was considered to be the most progressive semiconductor company in the world. They responded to my application immediately and offered to pay all my expenses to visit their plant in Dallas. After a full day of interviews, I received the offer of an interesting and well-compensated engineering position. Texas Instruments was a much larger and more diversified company than Transitron, and the offer to join them was tempting. The personnel manager asked for a response in a few weeks, and I promised to give him my decision after returning to Boston. I remained in Dallas for a few days to absorb the atmosphere of the city. Then, rather than flying directly to Boston, I decided to use the opportunity to see other parts of the South.

I cashed in my return airline ticket and took a train to New Orleans. To a young European the place was truly intriguing, with its music, restaurants, nightclubs, friendly people, and French colonial architecture. After a few days I boarded a train for Florida to visit my cousins, Stella and Ed Tohari, who lived just outside Miami in Coral Gables. They owned a small hotel in Miami Beach, where I stayed free of charge. Florida was unlike anything I had seen: the palm trees, rows of hotels, blue ocean, and hordes of vacationers and retirees. Ed and I discussed the possibility of my joining him in his company or starting a new business venture. He owned a good-sized steel fabrication and distribution operation that imported European tie rods and sold them to builders in southern Florida. The company had a fleet of forty or fifty trucks ("furmanki," as he called them—a Polish word meaning horse-drawn peasant carts) and seemed to be doing very well. Ed was intelligent and energetic and his proposal for a joint venture was enticing, but I decided I should remain in my own field.

While in Miami I saw airline advertisements offering attractively priced flights to Havana. There were two choices: Direct flights from Miami cost ten dollars, but a bus ticket to Key West was only two dollars, and from there the flight to Havana cost five dollars. A three-dollar saving was significant, and since I also looked forward to seeing the Keys from a bus, I took the longer route. On the way to Key West I met a young New Yorker, and the two of us decided to explore Havana together.

At Havana airport we were approached by two Cubans who offered to give us a city tour by cab for one dollar. Despite initial misgivings about these strangers, one of whom was a powerfully built man, well over six feet tall, we decided to accept their offer. Our first stop was a rum distillery where, although it was ten in the morning, we were given free drinks and asked to buy some of their products. I bought a bottle of banana brandy. The next stop was an even bigger surprise. We were ushered into a brothel where the madam paraded about a dozen young women in front of us. When we expressed no interest in the activities of that establishment, our guides promised to show us other sights—only to take us to another brothel. They were obviously annoyed when we asked them to find us a hotel, and the atmosphere in the cab became tense. Finally they complied, and although we didn't much care for their choice of hotels, we decided to stay there for one night just to get rid of our companions. The following day, the government tourist office recommended a much better place for a considerably lower rate. To make up for our misadventure, the tourism officials gave us passes which conferred temporary membership in one of the more sophisticated private clubs in Havana, where we were dazzled by the beautifully dressed Latin women and treated to free Caribbean drinks. The club clearly catered to Cuban "high society," and we felt well compensated for the previous day's unfortunate spree.

The Havana we explored on foot was a tense city. Castro had not yet succeeded in occupying the capital, but his forces controlled substantial parts of the island and Havana's streets were filled with armed police and soldiers. Government offices were heavily guarded; pedestrians were not allowed to walk in front of those buildings without first crossing the street, considerably slowing down our progress and making us feel like criminals. There was nervous gaiety in the bars and nightclubs, in stark contrast to the obvious poverty of people in the streets.

We visited a large casino in one of the tourist hotels. Like many casino visitors, I had heard of a system that in most cases is supposed to beat the roulette odds. I learned it from a friend in Boston who claimed he had tested it in Las Vegas with some degree of success. It was a variation on the system in which you bet on black or red, doubling your stakes until your color comes up. The problem with the doubling procedure is that you can easily run into house limits and suffer substantial losses. The system I explored increased the stakes more gradually, but it took longer to produce the desired results. Never quite believing that anyone would be able to beat the casino, I did not bet any real money, but I followed the throws for half an hour with a pencil and paper and engaged in imaginary betting. My calculations showed that I would have won fifty dollars, but hypothetical betting probably brings better results than gambling with hard cash.

We had already seen very poor sections of Havana, so the opulence of the casino was even more shocking. The biggest gamblers appeared to be Cubans, or at least Latin Americans. They literally threw money at the gaming tables, in some cases thousand dollar bills. Seeing this, I could not help feeling sympathy for Castro's revolution. At that time, it was not clear that his goal was to establish a communist dictatorship.

On my return to Boston I contacted George Freedman at Raytheon. He was glad to hear from me, and after a short interview he offered me a job in his company's Advanced Development Department. The choice between Raytheon and Texas Instruments was easy to make: I preferred not to move to Dallas and I liked George Freedman. After calling Texas Instruments to decline their offer, I said yes to George and reported for work a few days later at the Chapel Street Laboratory in Newton, Massachusetts. The atmosphere there was much more pleasant than at Transitron. I had a number of projects, but most of my work was developing techniques for building a very high frequency transistor for the U.S. Army. The task leader was Willy Rindner, and within a few months we delivered working samples to the contractor. I was about to tackle another project, when I saw an opportunity that would have a major influence on my subsequent business life.

CRYSTALONICS

WHEN I JOINED RAYTHEON in 1958, the company was the world's largest producer of transistors. Most of the products in the field were germanium transistors, but Raytheon became the first company to introduce P-N-P silicon transistors, which offered better characteristics and were much more reliable. Silicon, a common chemical element, was more difficult to control in production and, consequently, resulted in more expensive products. Its higher performance had attracted the attention of the defense industry, and Raytheon's silicon transistors were designed into a number of military weapon systems and missiles, where quality was more important than price.

Raytheon had established a manufacturing operation to satisfy the demand, but they soon found that the production process was complicated and generated a large percentage of rejected parts. In semiconductor industry jargon, this was called a low-yield process, and it was not unusual for the yield of silicon transistors to drop below ten percent. Efficiency fluctuated wildly, occasionally generating better outcome but frequently resulting in near zero output. Such dry spells had a devastating effect on the military programs that relied on Raytheon's parts. In view of the shortages, the government began allocating the entire output of silicon transistors to crucial programs, causing delays in lower priority systems. We heard rumors of missiles being stranded on launching pads and serious time slippage in a number of projects.

Just a few months after I joined Raytheon, the company's silicon transistor production line ran into an unusually severe yield problem. The lunch talk in the Advanced Development Department, where that transistor had been designed and produced in small quantities, was that the difficulties were due not to inherent physical limitations, which had already been identified and overcome during the development stage, but to the incompetence of the manufacturing personnel. Another topic of conversation was that Raytheon was becoming too large and that its bureaucratic approach to manufacturing was responsible for many of its troubles. In our view, the production problems were caused by improper manufacturing procedures, which had to be changed in response to differences in new batches of silicon. Company rules, however, prohibited such modification without approval by several layers of management. By the time the manufacturing process could be altered, new difficulties often required further adjustments, which again would be implemented too late. "If only," our group said, "we could get those devices back here, we would straighten out the problems in no time."

It occurred to me that the situation presented an opportunity for a new company to produce devices superior to Raytheon's. There was no question that the demand existed and that little effort would be required to sell the product. "You could just go outside the factory," I told myself, grossly exaggerating the situation, "and shout 'silicon transistors for sale,' and you would be swamped with orders." It was clear that Raytheon's process was not working. I thought I could do better, move faster, and be more versatile in a small operation than my apparently unwieldy employer.

Despite this rosy optimism there were difficulties. All my previous semiconductor experience had been with germanium: I had never worked with silicon and knew little about its physical properties and the manufacturing processes required to produce silicon transistors. Also, I had no money to finance a solo venture.

The first problem was easy to solve. One of the more respected engineers in the laboratory was Jack Williams, who had been largely responsible for the development of the P-N-P silicon transistor. Somewhat of a loner, Jack did not take part in most work conversations or in social events outside the laboratory, but I got to know him well during my tenure at Raytheon. He was dissatisfied with living in Massachusetts. Hailing from Camden, Maine, he had inherited his parents' house and had a strong desire to return home. In later years I found that many Maine natives—or "Mainiacs," as they are sometimes affectionately called—feel a strong loyalty to their state. "Why don't you go back to Maine?" I asked him on one occasion. "Because there are no jobs there," he replied.

I believed that Jack would likely jump at the opportunity to join me in organizing a company to produce silicon transistors in Maine. By then I had thoroughly checked his credentials and learned that he was probably more knowledgeable about P-N-P silicon transistors than anyone in the industry. When I explored with him the possibility of a new venture, he seemed interested, although he told me many years later that the idea of starting a company had never occurred to him. He was confident in his ability to produce the devices and overcome the technical difficulties that Raytheon was facing. When I asked why he didn't solve those problems there, he replied, "Nobody will listen to me." We spent many hours discussing the equipment and space needed for our proposed venture and wrote a preliminary business plan. We estimated that an investment of one hundred thousand dollars would allow the new company to become profitable in less than a year.

How would we raise the funds? Venture capital was not readily available at that time—in fact, we were not even aware of its existence. It occurred to me that the State of Maine, in its desire to create jobs, might help us. I suggested to Jack that as a Maine native, he could apply for financial help from the state agency responsible for economic development. He did so, and even though his letter was not addressed to a particular individual, he received a reply within a week. A representative of the state wrote that he would like to explore this opportunity with us, and we arranged to meet for dinner at the newly opened 1200 Beacon Street Hotel in Brookline.

He expressed interest in our plans, which called for creating twenty-five jobs within a year, and told us about an intriguing situation in Limerick, Maine. Until a few months before our meeting, Limerick had been the site of a medium-sized semiconductor operation, owned by the General Electric Company (GE), which had employed five hundred people. The company had rented and renovated an old textile mill to house the manufacturing plant, but recently moved the operation to upstate New York to consolidate it with other GE facilities. The move left their former employees unemployed and offered an attractive opportunity to a potential new employer. The manager of the General Electric operation had decided to stay in Limerick, and his former company agreed to leave detailed records of their employees' work experience and qualifications. Hence, the town offered a facility fully adapted to the type of manufacturing we were proposing and a large, easily accessible pool of already-trained labor.

General Electric had a reputation for superior training programs and good management practices, so before the end of our dinner we decided to visit Limerick, inspect the facility, and meet its former manager. Our dinner companion told us that the state would not provide any financing, but that the family who owned the mill might either back our project or recommend another investor in the hope of renting the facility to us.

As soon as we entered the Limerick plant the following weekend, we realized the facility was much too large for our endeavor; the lobby alone had more space than we needed for our entire operation. The building had indeed been well adapted for producing semiconductors, and the previous tenant had left behind some of the manufacturing equipment. We explained to our hosts that we needed only two thousand square feet of floor space and that it would be difficult to carve out such a small area from that large facility. Despite our misgivings, the town officials arranged for an introduction to the landlord, a member of a prominent, wealthy Boston family.

We were fortunate to be organizing our venture at a most propitious time. My previous employer, Transitron, had just gone public, creating the first large fortune in semiconductors. The success of Transitron's founders was the talk of the town and drew the investment community's attention to opportunities in new high-technology enterprises. We worried that potential investors would consider us too young to manage our own company: I was twenty-eight, Jack a year older. At that time, companies were usually started by more seasoned entrepreneurs. The initial meeting with the owners of the Limerick building was encouraging. By their own admission, they understood little of our products and markets but they were intrigued enough to proceed to the next stage—an interview with a prominent Massachusetts Institute of Technology professor. After lengthy questioning, the professor endorsed our plan and we proceeded to negotiate terms of investment with the investors' financial team. Our age did not come up in any of our discussions.

The business and ownership structure we created, largely at the MIT professor's suggestion, made a lot of sense. It was clear that we should not locate our venture in the Limerick mill because that building was more suitable for a large manufacturing facility than for a small new operation. Affiliated with a metallurgical consulting company in the Kendall Square area of Cambridge, the professor proposed that the company rent us space and provide essential business services. He further suggested that one of the owners of the consulting company assume the post of president of our new venture to provide the leadership experience that we, as two engineers, apparently lacked.

The ownership of our company would be divided into three equal parts among the owners of the Limerick mill, the consulting company, and the remaining third split between Jack and me. We shook hands on the deal, which called for an investment of $100,000, and the next day, both Jack and I gave notice to our employer.

During the next meeting with our investors, the entire project nearly fell apart when a new member joined their negotiating team. While not denying the previous terms of the deal, he said that the financial structure had not been designed properly. Our understanding was quite clear in my mind, but our backers probably thought our discussions were not final, since we did not ask for a letter of intent, a common step in such situations. With no experience in negotiating a business deal, Jack and I had not insisted, or even suggested, that we commit our agreement to paper.

The changes introduced by the new negotiating team were substantial. They now insisted that the $100,000 would not to be invested but loaned to the company, and that the funds would be advanced in two increments of $50,000 at the financiers' discretion. I was greatly troubled by this development, but the change in financial terms concerned me less than the fact that our potential partners did not honor their original commitment. The loan offered tax benefits to the investors, and the two-stage infusion of funds was not illogical, since it gave our potential partners the opportunity to evaluate our performance before committing the entire sum. My main worry, however, was the integrity of our future stockholders. At that time I had no way of knowing they were people of excellent reputation, but even now I think they should have been more careful in making the original promises.

I insisted we should return to the original terms, but my arguments produced no change in the investors' position. At that point I told Jack I did not want to be in partnership with these people but that he was free to continue the project without me, and then I walked out of the room. I did not get far before Jack came running after me. He pleaded with me to take the new deal. It was easy for me to abandon our proposed venture: I had no family or other obligations, and I had saved enough money to live comfortably until I found another job—though none of those considerations entered my mind as I abandoned the negotiations. Jack, however, was married with three children, he had mortgage payments, and he evidently had insufficient financial reserves to support his family without a paycheck. After a brief discussion, I returned to the room, out of respect for Jack, and we summarized the new agreement. This time we committed it to writing and sent it to the investors' lawyers to prepare a formal document.

On more than one occasion, I have thought about Jack's move to rescue the deal. Had he been less persuasive or had I not returned to the table, I might have spent the rest of my working life in a big corporation. I'm sure I would not have gone far. I was a development engineer, and my technical knowledge would have quickly become obsolete in the fast-moving semiconductor field. Engineers could pursue careers in management, but I was not a corporate climber and probably would have remained in the lower ranks of my profession. While we might have found other investors or I might have become the president of another company, I owe thanks to Jack for acting quickly to reverse my decision.

As I look back on that early venture, I can only marvel at the brashness of youth. Neither Jack nor I had run any kind of commercial enterprise; in fact, I wonder if any high-technology ventures were started by teams with as little business experience or knowledge as ours. Not only did we not understand accounting, we did not even appreciate its role in a successful enterprise. Such basic terms as inventory control, marketing, and cost accounting were foreign to us. As development engineers, we had seldom left our laboratories to face customers or to dispense cash.

Paradoxically, it turned out our naiveté in business contributed to our strength. Not versed in sophisticated management practices, we reduced our financial philosophy to the most basic strategy, what accountants call controlling "cash flow." We believed, in essence, that to be successful we had to take in more cash than we spent. Our marketing philosophy was simple, too: We visited customers and listened to their needs. While such considerations seem obvious, our lack of experience forced us into a straightforward view of management without complicated theories. We produced daily reports showing cash, order backlog, shipments, and a few other vital numbers. The concise nature of that information gave us a clear picture that almost automatically suggested the course of future action.

The home of our new endeavor, which we named Crystalonics, was an old building at 249 Fifth Street in Cambridge, near MIT. The narrow three-story wooden structure belonged to the consulting company that was to become our mentor. That company occupied all three floors except for a 1,000-square-foot room on the top level, where we installed our equipment.

The procedure was a mirror image of my experience in Rugby. To conserve our limited funds, we built most of the manufacturing machinery ourselves. With help from our landlord, we constructed benches, a furnace, testers, and chemical processing baths. We ordered raw materials, jigs, small tools, and countless other items needed for a new operation. Some equipment had to be purchased, of course, but we kept those acquisitions to a minimum.

Within just a few weeks, all parts and fixtures had arrived and we were ready to start the development process. Just as quickly, we ran into our first major difficulty: We could not buy the raw material, silicon, to produce our transistors. Available from two commercial sources, it turned out to be completely unsuitable for our devices. Essentially, our manufacturing process required silicon with a narrow range of crystal imperfections. One supplier's material had too many of these imperfections, the other one too few. The commercially available material met all other specifications, but the property that gave us problems, the so-called number of dislocations per square centimeter, was a parameter we had overlooked before we started our company.

It was clear that by failing to determine in advance all the properties of commercially available silicon, we had committed a colossal oversight, albeit one that was easy to make in the early days of semiconductors. Raytheon had developed its own method of making silicon; the process for manufacturing transistors was coordinated with the company's internal materials capability to produce a satisfactory result. While we were at Raytheon, it would have been highly improper to test externally available commercial material for compatibility with the company's process, especially after we had decided to become our employer's direct competitor.

Making silicon transistors without silicon was like making wooden furniture without wood. We tried our best to find other suppliers and to convince the two sources to alter their processes to produce silicon we could use. We frantically worked to develop new manufacturing techniques to make them compatible with available raw material, but none of these efforts produced satisfactory results. It was obvious that we were heading for a grand failure. Through a stroke of sheer luck, we found another small start-up company in the nearby town of Lynn that was producing silicon for its own use. The president of that operation agreed to grow silicon to our specifications—just to help out fellow entrepreneurs. The name of the company, North American Electronics, was far more impressive than the company's physical plant, which was a garage. North American's silicon was more expensive because its fabricating facilities were primitive and inefficient, but it saved us from premature demise.

The new source of silicon did not eliminate all our problems. When we finally received the material and other component parts, we realized that Raytheon's manufacturing people were not nearly as incompetent as we had thought. We had been highly critical of their effort, but our results were inferior to theirs. Worse still, our ideas for improving production efficiency turned out to be totally misdirected. Raytheon's manufacturing yields had been low, but ours were zero.

Again, the situation looked desperate. Our first-stage financing of $50,000 was nearly depleted, and we still had no viable product. Despite valiant efforts, nothing seemed to work, and we simply could not fix the bugs plaguing our manufacturing process. The only solution was to develop new devices that could be produced within the limitations of our production methods. It usually takes months, or even years, to develop a new transistor. With money running out, the prospect of changing the entire product strategy of our venture did not look promising.

I remembered from my Transitron days that a customer had approached my former employer with a need for symmetrical transistors—specialized switching devices. Nothing ever came of that project because the devices were difficult to manufacture. But thinking it over, I realized that the limitations of our Crystalonics process would not present major impediments in producing symmetrical transistors. We ran a few experiments and our initial results were encouraging. We produced just two transistors, neither of which met our target specifications, but we thought that with further adjustments we would be able to obtain the desired results. This was the first glimmer of hope since our first attempt to produce practical devices, but with just a few thousand dollars left, we had to move quickly. But again disappointment was waiting for us: When we called the customer who had been interested in symmetrical transistors, he promptly informed us that the need no longer existed. They had solved the problem by other means.

Our knowledge of marketing was no greater than our business experience. We understood that we had to find other buyers, but we had only a vague idea of who those buyers might be. We knew our devices would appeal only to suppliers of military equipment, because their superior performance relative to germanium products made them too expensive for commercial applications. To identify potential customers, we did two logical things: One was to run an advertisement for our new symmetrical devices; the other was to visit the Pentagon. Our small advertisement in Electronic News cost one hundred fifty dollars, which represented a substantial portion of our remaining cash. That investment, however, produced much better results than the Pentagon visit, although the trip to the military headquarters proved to be most intriguing.

I had never been to Washington, D.C., and I approached my visit to the Pentagon with great trepidation. We still had not developed the process to produce transistors similar to those purchased by government contractors from Raytheon, but I hoped we would solve the problem in the near future. In any case, with money running out, we had to book orders immediately. My main worry regarding the Pentagon visit was not commercial. Until that time, my only contact with military installations had been either in Russia or, more recently, in Cuba. I had visions of heavily guarded buildings, countless security checks, and endless scrutiny of my credentials. With my foreign accent, European nationality, and six-year history in the Soviet Union, I doubted I would get past the front door of the mighty Pentagon.

All of these thoughts went through my mind when I asked the cab driver to take me from the airport to the Pentagon. "Which entrance?" he asked. When I suggested the main entrance, he mumbled something about there being no main entrance, and after a short ride he deposited me in front of a big door at one corner of the building. Far from being surrounded by guards, I found myself all alone in the street; the Pentagon seemed to be deserted. I opened the big door carefully and looked down a long, empty corridor. There was an eerie silence as I walked through the entrance, past closed doors on my right and large windows facing a courtyard on my left. Each door had a plate with a name and rank on it, but there was no reception desk and no one to direct me to the proper office. I felt like a trespasser, sure that at any moment I would be surrounded by armed guards who would accuse me of spying. But no one appeared, and after a few minutes, I knocked on a door and was rewarded by a loud invitation to come in. Beyond the door a uniformed military officer sat behind a desk. He seemed genuinely happy to see me, as if visitors were a rarity, and invited me to sit down and state my business. I went into a detailed explanation of our situation and told him that we needed a list of customers for our transistors. Most attentive, he asked a number of questions and seemed eager to help. He made several telephone calls and within minutes directed me to another officer for further information.

I thanked him profusely and left his office as though in a dream. Here I was, in the world headquarters of the United States Armed Services, arriving unannounced and being treated with utmost deference by a high-ranking military officer. The situation made me worry about the entire defensive security of the United States! It seemed far too easy to gain access to that building, and the gentleman I had just met did not correspond to my vision of the tough military commander. Nevertheless, I appreciated his immediate advice.

The officer at my next stop was equally helpful. He listened to my story, made a few telephone calls, and sent me to another office. There, at last, I faced an officer who was ready for me with a long list of contractors currently using transistors of the type we planned to produce.

He said he could not show me the list, but he read names of about three-dozen companies and gave me enough time to write them down. I was amazed at the quick success of my mission, although at that time I had no way of knowing we would sell only small quantities of those devices.

It was about eleven in the morning when I left the Pentagon with the list of contractors and called Jack with the good news. He told me we had just received a call from the Bureau of Standards in Washington in response to our advertisement. I immediately contacted the person who had made the inquiry, and since he was not available that afternoon, I arranged for an appointment the following morning. With the rest of the day on my hands, I traveled by cab to the vicinity of the Bureau of Standards, which was located on a wide avenue lined with impressive office buildings. There was no sign of any restaurants, but shortly after my arrival, the buildings disgorged masses of people. When I asked a young man to recommend a place for lunch, he invited me to join him and his friends in a cafeteria in one of the office buildings. My companions were intrigued by my story, especially the decision to visit the Pentagon. The man invited me to have dinner with him and offered me the guest bedroom in the house he shared with a couple of friends.

I thought about the engineer at the Bureau of Standards who had expressed interest in our symmetrical transistors. We had no data sheets describing those devices, but I had test information on the two units we had produced. I spent about two hours designing three different types of transistors, hoping that we would be able to produce them. I found a twenty-four hour typing and duplicating service and arranged for the needed literature to be typed and copied by the following morning. The typist was an attractive English girl who, incredibly, was from Kirby Muxloe, the village outside Leicester where I spent my first year in college. She produced professional looking data sheets and joined my lunch companion and me for a pleasant dinner, after which we took her home and retired to my new friend's house for the night. Those were the days when one could still trust strangers. Today I would not spend the night in a house belonging to someone I met in the street, and a woman would most likely turn down an invitation to dinner from two strangers, even though one of them had recently spent a year in her home village in England.

My presentation the next morning went well. The engineer wanted to use our transistors in a totally unexpected way, and after an hour's discussion and new specifications, I received the first order for our company. It was miniscule—four transistors for a total sum of forty dollars, but it was a beginning and included a promise of further procurement if the initial samples worked.

When I returned to Cambridge that afternoon, I found out about an even more promising development. The engineers at the Army Ballistic Missile Agency (ABMA), the predecessor to the National Aeronautic Space Administration (NASA), had seen our advertisement and wanted to talk to us. I scheduled an appointment to discuss their needs, then flew to Huntsville, Alabama, the following day to meet with the engineering team in charge of the Army satellite program. The Russians had already launched their "Sputnik," and the U.S. satellite project commanded a high national priority.

During the meeting I was informed that about a year earlier, the Army had given Philco, at that time a large producer of semiconductors, a contract to develop symmetrical silicon transistors similar to the devices we advertised. Just a few days before our advertisement had appeared, their contractor had told them that it would be impractical to develop the product they wanted. By coincidence they had paid Philco $50,000 to do the investigation, the same amount we had raised to establish our venture. We spent a few hours examining their circuits and designing a device to meet their requirements. Naturally, the parameters of the new transistor had to be compatible with our current manufacturing process. I received a promise of an order, which they confirmed in writing a few days later. I realized at the time that procurement for the project would be small, since only a few Army satellites would be launched, and before leaving the meeting I asked if there were other people I should see. They scratched their heads, but came up with a couple of names. After a telephone call, they confirmed that the other engineers would see me.

A half hour later I spoke with two engineers in another laboratory—a meeting which would have a profound effect on our fledgling company. The group I met worked on the Pershing Missile, a major Army project that was destined to be one of the main U.S. defense systems for many years. Over the next few hours, we discussed several of their circuits, and it appeared that the symmetrical silicon transistors would satisfy their needs. Again we designed two types of devices. The potential here appeared to be large by our standards, and I made sure to specify parameters that would be easy to achieve within the limitations of our manufacturing process. On the basis of having produced two moderately good devices and hundreds of rejects, I arrived at prices that seemed satisfactory to them. They promised a $2,000 order, which arrived within a week.

We were elated. In addition to participating in an Army satellite program, we had just procured a contract for one of the most demanding defense projects in the industry. It was not only an endorsement of our products but a confirmation that the small size of our company did not automatically disqualify us from working with major defense contractors. We had worried that customers would not wish to be dependent on a new, untried supplier producing devices not available from other sources. We were only a few months old, and with only two employees we could not have been much smaller.

On my return, we worked hard to optimize the process we needed to produce the promised devices. Jack had family responsibilities, but, as a bachelor, I had no problem working through many nights. The units we produced were satisfactory and we received more orders. The timing of those orders was most propitious. It allowed us to begin earning a profit just before our start-up money ran out.

It was a close call, and in reviewing our situation we realized that our grand scheme for starting a company had had a nearly fatal flaw. By the time we solved our manufacturing problems, Raytheon was in full production with excellent yields. Other companies developed similar capabilities. The resulting oversupply drove the prices to extremely low levels, and, in any case, the customers, tired of the difficulties in procuring our type of transistors, redesigned their systems and substituted components from more dependable manufacturers. We had hoped to raise $100,000; we received half that amount. We thought we were addressing a ready market with no competition, but by the time we organized our production, the demand had shrunk and a number of suppliers had entered the field. We assumed we could buy material to produce our devices, but we found no ready source that could satisfy our needs. Finally, we knew how to build our target products in a laboratory but underestimated the difficulty of applying that knowledge to mass production. It was lucky that with only $5,000 of our capital left, we were able to develop a new transistor we had not even contemplated at the start of our project. The symmetrical devices, for which we found an application at A.B.M.A. almost by accident, saved our company.

Our initial technical difficulties had done little to inspire the confidence of our investors, especially those belonging to the family we met through the good offices of the State of Maine. The changes in the initial financing terms had already generated tension in our relationship, and our backers developed further doubts about our abilities as we stumbled from one manufacturing problem to another. Not surprisingly, they refused to advance additional funds after the initial payment of $50,000. They viewed our success in obtaining the Army orders only as an opportunity to recover their investment. The consulting group, however, evidently retained some faith in our abilities and suggested two Boston real estate developers as possible successors to our original investors. After lengthy negotiations, the new partners bought one third of the company from our first backers, giving them a 25 percent return in six months. I was glad our initial stockholders were rewarded for their risk. Despite our differences, I felt respect and gratitude toward them. After all, it was their investment that made our venture possible.

As our company expanded, we began to hire more people to work on the production line. Our first new hires were two young women and, later, several other female assemblers. All my working life I had felt that the distinction made between professional employees and production workers is unfair to the lower-paid personnel. Usually the latter punch the clock and are not paid if they miss a day of work, whereas management and technical personnel do not have to account for the times of their arrival and departure, or for absence from the office. Being somewhat of an idealist, I reasoned that the undignified way of treating hourly employees had no place in my company, and that if people were treated fairly, they would respond in kind with honesty and loyalty. We had no time clocks; I simply expected our employees to come to work on time and guaranteed them full pay for any absence caused by illness, on condition that they notified us if they were ill. This was a most unusual arrangement at that time, at least in our industry, but I was sure the privileges would not be abused. Unfortunately, we soon encountered an exorbitant amount of illness among our employees. Hardly a week went by without most of our assembly workers calling in sick for at least a day. I could not quite bring myself to reverse our policy, but it was clear the company could not survive with such absenteeism.

After a few weeks of confusion, we hired an experienced foreman, who introduced conventional disciplinary practices, including a time-clock. The health of our hourly employees improved immediately. I was not happy about the need to control our young production crew, and I found it embarrassing that we had to signal to them so clearly our belief that they could not be trusted. But I was the only person with such misgivings. Not only was there a remarkable improvement in the health of our people, but our assemblers seemed much happier. The atmosphere became much more collegial and the rise in productivity became a source of inspiration for us all. In addition to achieving normal attendance for the hourly employees, our new executive, Alan, reorganized our manufacturing practices. He was good at scheduling work and knew a great deal about purchasing. We soon had a smoothly running production line delivering reliable products on a timely basis. We no longer had to rely on Jack's or my heroic efforts to remove manufacturing bottlenecks. Business was good and we gradually enlarged our workforce to meet the growing demand for our transistors.

With the production line under reasonable control, I was able to visit new customers and we could devote more time to developing new products. Toward the end of the first year, Jack devised a plan to produce a very fast switch that could be used in the computer industry. We concluded that this device would not only be several orders of magnitude faster than anything on the market, but that theoretically nothing could be faster, since the switch response could potentially be close to the speed of light. We knew that no one had ever proposed a similar approach. We had a vision of sweeping the market with our devices and making it possible for the computer industry to build machines with vastly expanded computing power. There was a great feeling of excitement when we decided to build a few devices to test the idea.

The experimental transistors did not meet our expectations. We assumed, as is often the case in such trials, that the concept was correct but that its practical implementation was flawed, so we built more devices to verify our theory. The second and third batches were no more successful than the first. Based on the tests and a more realistic appraisal of the original idea, we realized that there was a fundamental error in our logic and that our concept would not produce a fast switching element. During our investigation, however, we noticed a few unexpected phenomena, which, because their effects were slight and seemed irrelevant to our main purpose, we simply ignored. But now that we had found our original concept to be flawed, we examined those phenomena more closely and decided they might suggest a new approach that had been theoretically predicted by others but never practically accomplished: to build a very different type of transistor, a so-called field-effect transistor. One afternoon I built a small batch of experimental units designed to enhance the new effect. I worked through the night and by morning, I unambiguously confirmed we had stumbled on a device configuration that could produce field-effect transistors.

What is a field-effect transistor? To the uninitiated it looks like an ordinary transistor, but there are significant differences in their electrical characteristics. In those early days of the industry, transistors were replacing large, fragile, and unreliable vacuum tubes. But the first transistors used for this purpose lacked many desirable characteristics of the vacuum tubes they were intended to replace. Field-effect transistors combined the small size, low power consumption, and reliability of conventional transistors with the desirable electrical characteristics of tubes, and they also displayed other advantages not easily attainable from any previously available components. With minor exceptions, we designed our new units to utilize the same parts we had used to produce our earlier models. This was partly for convenience, but mainly because we did not have the money (perhaps $2,000) to pay for the tooling of special parts.

It took us two months to develop practical versions of our new devices, and all that time we worried that someone else might be engaged in a similar effort and announce the new transistors before we could. But luck was with us, and this didn't happen. When we were ready to unveil our products, we were determined to do it with as much publicity and vigor as our meager resources would allow. I invited the local reporter of *Electronic News,* the best-known weekly newspaper serving the industry, for an interview. The publication was sufficiently intrigued to give us a front-page article in their next edition—an impressive feat, I thought, for a company employing only a dozen people. Joel Cohen, our new applications engineer, and I scheduled extensive customer visits, dividing the country between us. Joel visited customers on the East Coast while I scheduled a five-week trip to the West. My itinerary included Denver, Albuquerque, Salt Lake City, San Diego, Los Angeles, San Francisco, and finally Seattle. I made between two and four customer visits each day, ranging from informal meetings with just a few engineers to lectures attended by two or three hundred people. It was an exhausting trip, but well worth the effort. Our transistors produced a lot of excitement in the industry and we arranged the tight schedule to show our new products to as many customers as we could. The most invigorating talk was at the Boeing Company, in Seattle, where I attracted the biggest audience.

We had a narrow window between January 1960, when we completed development of our devices, and March of that year, the date of the big electronics industry trade show in New York, where we feared someone else might announce competitive units. We need not have worried, because a full year passed before other companies began to introduce field-effect transistors. I shall never forget a front-page headline in a trade publication at the industry show in New York a year later proclaiming, "Texas Instruments to Compete with Crystalonics in Field-Effect Transistors." At that time Texas Instruments was the largest semiconductor company in the world, and we were probably the smallest.

In the meantime, we had the field all to ourselves and our marketing efforts were achieving good results. We received many orders but, curiously, most were for our original symmetrical transistors. I think our new offerings served primarily to make more people aware of our existence and to enhance our overall standing as a supplier of advanced semiconductors, with the results being a better reception for our conventional products. We learned that lesson well and subsequently devoted considerably more resources to developing new products than to advertising, reasoning that in addition to expanding our existing offerings, an exciting innovative device, even with limited market appeal, could create more publicity than an expensive promotional campaign.

We learned other business and marketing lessons, too. We realized that we were not in a position to compete directly against most of the other semiconductor companies. By our standards, they were giants with hundreds of millions of dollars at their disposal and a wealth of scientific power in their laboratories. The trick was to develop devices that were useful but that our competitors would not produce. Naturally doing that required knowing their plans. Such intelligence was easier to deduce than might be assumed, as long as one had an understanding of the structure of the industry. At that time, many—if not most—large semiconductor companies processed new developments through at least three work centers. Initial effort on a new device or technology might start at the company's research facilities, then, after the feasibility of the concept was established, it would proceed to their advanced development laboratory. After further work, the product would normally advance to a so-called preproduction group and eventually be released for production. It was not unusual for devices to remain within each of these centers for at least a year, resulting in a development cycle that seemed unnecessarily long.

Frequently, members of each group, especially the research and advanced development laboratories, published papers describing their work. We studied those papers, both to keep up with the latest advancements in technology and to try to predict the direction of our competitors' development strategy. Whenever we found ourselves on a collision course with one of these giants, we dropped our effort. We knew that our meager financial and human resources would be inadequate to confront large established companies in head-to-head competition. Instead, we had to find gaps in our competitors' product lines and confine our activities to areas neglected by the large suppliers. To offer products similar to those available from the giants of the industry would have been as suicidal as setting up shop next to a large department store and selling the same goods. The economies of scale and the variety of choice offered by the large store would make it impossible for the small shop to stay in business. Products such as expensive jewelry or specialized clothing, however, are frequently better handled by small retail shops or boutiques. And this was our plan: to become a small industrial boutique.

In general, our strategy worked well, although on one occasion we overestimated the external threat. Almost by accident we came across a novel way of making very fast switching diodes, known as Schotky diodes, and decided to explore the feasibility of manufacturing them. Within a few weeks of our decision, we noticed a lot of interest in those devices, not just in the technical press but also in the commercial electronic trade newspapers. Not until we had suspended our efforts did we learn that it took the larger companies well over a year to introduce the new product. We also learned that the diode described in the press had a number of disadvantages we may have been able to overcome with our approach.

Our success and profitability should have earned us the confidence of our investors, yet surprisingly we received only severe criticism rather than praise. We found ourselves at odds, not just with our financial backers but also with the consulting company that was supposed to be our mentor. They had decided that we were competent to run our little operation as long as it was in the development stage, but that the company now needed more seasoned management. Admittedly, we lacked many business and marketing skills in the beginning, but we had been learning fast. There had been little interest in helping us with direction when we were struggling, but once we reached profitability, they said we needed much more help.

This "help" came less in the form of advice and more in the form of restrictions on our freedom of action. Typical of the disagreements was the management of funds. Jack and I were not allowed to sign checks, however small, nor were we advanced funds for petty cash. It was most embarrassing not to have even a few dollars available to pay for deliveries or even postage stamps. Our many requests for limited check signing authority were denied. We argued that not allowing us to control occasional payments below one hundred dollars made little sense, since in many instances we prepared quotations or accepted orders that committed the company to transactions involving tens or even hundreds of thousands of dollars. Our explanations fell on deaf ears and were often dismissed with remarks such as, "We took you boys off the street, and now you think you are important."

In one sense it is easy to understand their position. We were one of the first so-called "high tech" start-up companies in the Boston area, and we had no business background. Also, at that time, engineers were stereotyped as people who lacked any ability to understand the business world. They had the reputation, which some of them did indeed justify, of being interested solely in developing the product until it was perfect. Taken literally, of course, this would mean developing something forever, without ever releasing it to production. While some engineers may be intelligent, the reasoning went, it was the accountants or lawyers who should be running companies, not engineers or scientists. Whatever the truth of the matter, a few concessions such as limited check signing authority and recognition that we were not "picked up off the street" would have gone a long way toward improving our relationship.

That improvement was not to come, and with friction visibly mounting, Jack and I found ourselves unable to work with them any longer. We found another group of investors who bought all the outstanding shares of our company except Jack's and mine, tripling our previous investors' capital in one year. This time, Jack and I insisted on acquiring fifty percent of the company and receiving full management rights. Our new backers did not interfere with our daily operations and we continued to grow and prosper. Unfortunately, the new partners ran into financial difficulties in other ventures and had to sell our company's shares a year later to raise money, but in that period they more than doubled their investment.

We tried to create interest in our products by visiting as many potential customers as we could, and most of them insisted on inspecting our facilities to make sure we had the manufacturing capacity and controls to deliver the ordered quantities of transistors. Although we worried about every inspection, since our manufacturing line was tiny in comparison with our clients' other vendors, I usually enjoyed those visits. They gave us opportunities to establish personal relationships with our customers, understand their needs and, perhaps equally important, learn about the final applications of our devices and the roles we were playing in a number of national efforts. It was rewarding to know that our transistors were used for important functions, including life support equipment on space missions, critical defense projects, and crucial communication satellites. Whenever we could, we asked for photographs and occasionally movies of the final equipment in action. These, especially the images of the first "space walk," invariably engendered a feeling of pride and achievement.

Much as I enjoyed hosting our customers, the three visitors who stand out in my mind were a banker and two people from academia. One day the receptionist (yes, by that time we had a receptionist who also acted as a secretary!) announced a visitor, Charles Cunningham, from the First National Bank of Boston. Charles was a tall, patrician-looking young man who settled in the chair facing my desk. His broad shoulders and powerful athletic build seemed to completely fill my tiny office. He introduced himself as an officer of the First National Bank of Boston and asked about our company. I tried my best to explain the intricacies of our business. He then asked if we had a bank, if we were borrowing money, and whether our current bankers ever called on us. I was bewildered by his questions and did not know how to respond. I told him we had an account with the nearby Harvard Trust Company and that I did not understand the purpose of his questions. I had no idea that banks loaned money; my previous Siberian and engineering experience had not prepared me for the business world, and I assumed that those financial institutions existed only for the benefit of customers who deposited their checks and maintained checking accounts. I'm not sure Charles had ever met anyone with so little financial sophistication. He patiently explained the role of banks in supporting companies such as ours and offered to arrange a line of credit. At the time of his visit, we did not need any additional funds; we were generating cash and had about $100,000 in the bank—not bad, in view of our starting capital of $50,000. Charles suggested that we buy certificates of deposit that would pay us interest instead of letting the funds languish in our account without generating any income. We followed his advice, and I remember being very proud of the fact that my first commercial transaction with a bank resulted in our company not borrowing but "lending" money.

The second interesting visitor came from the Harvard Business School. I had heard about this institution from several people, and it was my ambition to attend classes there some day to supplement the meager business knowledge I was acquiring on the job. One day our receptionist announced that an HBS student wanted to see me, and I eagerly asked her to usher him into my office. I do not remember his name, but he was a pleasant young man, modestly dressed in a jacket, flannel trousers, and a conservative tie. True to the academic fashion of the times, the elbows of his jacket were covered with leather patches. He explained that he was looking for material for his thesis on small companies, preferably small, high tech companies. He asked if he could interview me about the history and operation of Crystalonics. I was happy to comply and we spent a delightful afternoon together. His second visit was even more flattering, when he invited me to have lunch with his advisor, Professor Hosmer, who taught a course on small business.

After our lunch, Professor Hosmer invited me to make a presentation at one of his classes during the next semester. I was too flattered to turn him down, but when the time came for my talk, I was terrified. I had been hoping to be a student at the school, and now I was being asked to present a "case"—a method of teaching for which Harvard Business School had become famous. I was surprised when the presentation went well, and even more flattered when I was asked to return over the next several years to share my business experience. My talks happened when major and positive changes were being made there. Initially, all the students in my class were white males dressed in sports jackets and ties; as the years went by, the class became much more inclusive, as the student body began to include women and people of color—and the attire became much less formal.

The third visitor I recall with great pleasure was announced by the receptionist as Mr. Shannon. This visitor could not have been more different from Charles Cunningham, the self-assured banker. He was a short, gentle, middle-aged man dressed in a well-worn suit of nondescript color. He walked slowly and shyly into my office and remained standing until I asked him to sit down, when he carefully lowered his slight frame and sat on the edge of the chair. His voice was quiet and hesitant, almost a stutter.

He said that a friend at an electronics company in California had told him we were making field-effect transistors and that he had decided to walk over from MIT to learn more about those devices. Naturally I was overjoyed. Here, I assumed, was an MIT technician who wanted an explanation of our latest devices. I launched enthusiastically into an explanation of how our new transistors worked, taking care not to overtax the technical knowledge of my visitor. But a curious thing happened as I proceeded with my discourse. Based on the questions he asked and the comments he made—all still in a timid manner—I began to realize that this man knew much more about every aspect of field-effect transistors and, for that matter, other areas of electronics, than I did. At the same time, he was so genuinely curious and courteous that he did nothing to intimidate me; he was obviously there to learn, not to show off. But with every passing minute I came to the conclusion that I was in the presence of an unusual individual. Suddenly something clicked in my mind, and I could restrain my curiosity no longer. "You are not Dr. Claude Shannon, by any chance?" I asked. He almost stuttered as he answered quietly, "I . . . I suppose I am."

It would be difficult for me to imagine a more distinguished visitor. Claude Shannon was one of the nation's most eminent mathematicians, who today is known for creating the theoretical foundations of modern information theory, the workings of digital circuits, and the science of cryptography. He has been widely credited with making the computer revolution possible, and his intellect has been compared to that of Einstein. He was also a man of considerable breadth and humor. I had read a lot about his scholarly work, but he was equally well known for his sense of play. One story describes him juggling while riding a unicycle through the halls of Bell Labs. He also took delight in designing and building machines that were able to play chess, solve mazes, and read minds.

His presence had an additional dimension for me. While his public reputation was known among the scientific community, I had recently come across a more intimate source of information about him. A few weeks before his visit, I had met a young lady named Olga who was Professor Shannon's personal assistant at MIT and translator of his foreign correspondence and foreign articles.

After our first meeting, he came to see us at fairly regular intervals. By a strange coincidence, he was also a director of Teledyne, a company that eventually acquired Crystalonics in a completely unrelated transaction. I was greatly saddened when Professor Shannon died in 2001, at the age of 84.

OLGA

I DO NOT WANT TO GIVE THE IMPRESSION that I spent every minute of my time running Crystalonics. I was 29 years old and I did find time for a social life. One Saturday night in 1959 two friends and I passed the International Students Union, at Garden and Chauncy Streets in Cambridge. We were young men from abroad who had all worked for Transitron, so the Union's international flavor caught our attention. Loud music poured out from the building, and although we were due at a party nearby within a few minutes, we thought we had enough time to stop in.

There were as many people jammed against the club's walls talking as there were gyrating on the dance floor. The crowd was lively and, as I had come to expect from Cambridge students, friendly and intelligent. After a brief look, we decided to come back when we had more time.

Before we made our exit, I heard a woman's voice speaking a foreign language with a familiar intonation. The noise level was high, so it took me a while to realize that the woman was speaking Polish with a Russian accent. I turned around and saw an attractive young lady addressing a tall man.

"Ah, someone is speaking Polish with a Russian accent," I said, stating the obvious.

The woman turned toward me and smiled. She was in her early twenties, of medium height, with dark blonde hair and big blue eyes. Her round face and shapely figure suggested Slavic origin.

"Are you Polish?" she asked.

"Yes," I replied, "but I also speak Russian. Are you more comfortable speaking Polish or Russian?"

She pointed to her companion.

"Peter is leaving for Poland in a few days. I was testing his knowledge of Polish."

I learned that her name was Olga, and we exchanged a few innocuous remarks in English interspersed with occasional Russian words. She said she was born in Brazil of Russian parents and had come to Boston for a few months to improve her English. I was immediately drawn to her, but I thought it would be impertinent to ask for her phone number after such a brief meeting. Besides, she had an escort. Fortunately, one of my friends came to the rescue.

"Ask Olga to give you her phone number before we leave," he advised me in a loud voice.

To my surprise she complied readily. In later years I teased her about her readiness to see me. "Oh, yes," she assured me, "I fell in love with your voice immediately. I also realized you were a kindred soul. I would never have accepted anyone else so quickly."

It was not exactly love at first sight, but for the next few days I was preoccupied with thoughts of Olga. She struck me as a well-spoken, refined young lady, but I knew little about her interests or tastes. I had no doubt she wanted to see me again—after all, she had given me her phone number. Still, I worried about whether I would make a good impression on our first date. Movies seemed too mundane, dinner at a restaurant too risky. What if I chose the wrong cuisine? Would she feel uncomfortable if our first date was after dark? After much thought, I decided to invite Olga to a concert. Yehudi Menuhin was performing at Boston's Symphony Hall on a Sunday afternoon, and I felt his recital would provide an ideal backdrop for our first date. I bought two tickets and called Olga.

She recognized my voice immediately. Her response was encouraging.

"I would like to go out with you," she said, "but I have already accepted an invitation to that concert from an MIT student. But you can take me home."

Her voice was friendly, her Russian beautiful. Her directness and sincerity were disarming. Even on the phone I felt as though I had known her for a long time. After just a few remarks it seemed that we had a lot in common.

The arrangement Olga proposed seemed cruel to the MIT student. "Perhaps that would not be fair to your friend," I offered. "Could I see you later that evening?" All my doubts and nervousness were now eclipsed by my desire to see her.

"All right then," she said. "I'll be at home. Call me later."

I offered the extra ticket to my regular tennis partner, George Chizinski, and joined him for dinner after the performance. Half way through the meal I excused myself and called Olga to ask how she had enjoyed the recital. I expected a short reply but instead was treated to a long commentary. She liked certain passages, objected to the volume of the accompanist's piano in others, marveled at the missed notes, and described other details that had eluded me. There was no pretense in her voice, no desire to impress. It was simply the response of a deeply knowledgeable music lover. She asked me to come to her place at eight.

"George, I think I have a music critic on my hands," I jokingly complained when I returned to our table.

Olga's place was easy to find. She shared a basement apartment with another girl near Commonwealth Avenue. We spent a delightful evening together, conversing like old friends, with Olga describing her work for an insurance company and her recent recruitment as a technical translator for none other than Professor Shannon at MIT. Two hours passed quickly and we arranged to meet again. A week later I came down with a cold but saw her anyway. Magically, she cured me with a concoction made of tea, honey, and brandy.

We were married two years later, in September 1961. Over the next six years we were blessed with a son and two daughters.

I pause here to toast the "woman behind the man behind the gun," a cliché that is apt in our case. Olga became a devoted wife and a loving mother who inspired high ethical and educational standards in our children. Her role in my professional life was also fundamental. She was a tower of strength for me, providing solid emotional support, though she had no interest in technology or business. She valued our privacy and, other than seeing a few of my coworkers who had become friends, she had little contact with our employees. Executives often fall into the trap of thinking that the entire world revolves around their place of employment. Olga made sure our home provided a quiet escape from the tumult of my business life and in the process enabled me to put my professional activities in the proper perspective.

CRYSTALONICS
EXPANDS

BY THE FIRST HALF OF 1960, we had sixty employees, and even though we had already doubled our original workspace, we were rapidly running out of room both on the floor and on the benches. I remember picking up a small electric multimeter to check the voltage in a wall socket and being unable to put it back down because its resting place on the bench, perhaps four by six inches, was now occupied by something else. We had been assigned only two legal parking spaces next to our plant, and our employees regularly got parking tickets from the Cambridge Police Department.

It was time to move. We chose a nearby 10,000-square-foot building, which until recently had served as a Gerber baby food warehouse. We leased it with an option to buy, had the interior renovated to our specifications in just a few weeks, and moved our entire company over one weekend. The new quarters looked like a palace to us. Going from two thousand square feet to a building five times larger gave us the feeling we could expand indefinitely.

With an established customer base, greatly improved facilities, and a growing cash reserve, we were ready for new challenges. A number of our former colleagues had intriguing product and business ideas and wanted to start their own companies. It occurred to us that we could help them set up new ventures. With our market reputation as a thriving semiconductor company, we were in a position to give them a running start. Although it may sound insincere, the main motivation was not material gain, but rather a desire to provide our fellow engineers with some of the opportunities we had when we organized Crystalonics.

Two such situations occurred almost simultaneously. George Freedman, my former boss at Raytheon, who was by then working for another company, introduced me to two engineers who had developed a new technology for making special diodes. One of the two men, Joe Averback, worked for Raytheon, my former employer, and I knew him to be a competent, practical engineer. Joe's partner, Mark, had strong theoretical knowledge of semiconductors. I had a great deal of confidence in George Freedman's judgment and encouraged our latest backers, a major New York City-based financial institution, to fund the new venture. Remembering our own start-up problems, I was anxious to structure a deal that would give the entrepreneurs a feeling of independence from Crystalonics and confidence that no decisions at odds with their desires could be made by other stockholders. The outside investors contributed $50,000 for a 30 percent stake in the new company, which we called Varactron. The two entrepreneurs received a 50 percent stake with no investment on their part, and Crystalonics was awarded the remaining 20 percent for providing space, facilities, business services, and marketing representation for nine months. That structure would allow the inventors to concentrate on their work without worrying about their future role in the company. With our relatively modest allotment of stock, we could hardly be accused of taking advantage of the situation.

Using our purchasing channels, accounting personnel, and much of our equipment, the two founders made rapid progress and soon produced working samples of their products. Unfortunately, their work led to a dead end when they discovered that the technology they brought with them, while good in the laboratory, was not suitable for mass production. Also, the two inventors developed major disagreements on a number of issues. We tried to help in several ways. Jack, the cofounder of Crystalonics and now our technical director, quickly adapted our manufacturing techniques to their product line. The injection of our technical know-how made all the difference. Joe readily embraced our technology, and with Jack's help soon developed the product line the new company, Varactron, originally intended to market. We tried to mediate the dispute between the two principals, and when that failed, we bought the interest of Joe's partner. Joe was a hard worker and led Varactron to become a small but highly profitable company that eventually merged with Crystalonics.

The other joint venture we organized was not successful and perhaps confirmed the old dictum that if you want to have a friend, don't do anything for him, but let him do something for you. In late 1962 a venture capitalist introduced me to three engineers who had approached him with a plan to produce a novel semiconductor device. I met with the three men, Tom, Ryan, and Chris, and found their ideas intriguing. Ryan, the inventor of the concept, was well versed in semiconductor manufacturing technology. Tom was an application engineer whose job would be to help customers use the new device. Chris was to be the president of the new company and would lead the marketing effort. I advised the three founders to look for other backers and introduced them to several people in the financial community. When they failed to get support for their ideas, they returned with a proposal of a joint venture with Crystalonics. Over the next few weeks we worked out an arrangement modeled on the Varactron transaction.

The venture capital firm that introduced us agreed to back the project as long as the founders raised at least nominal seed capital from other sources. To fulfill this condition, the engineers found a seasoned manufacturing executive who became an "angel" investor in return for a share of the new venture and a promise of eventual employment as production manager and plant engineer. Crystalonics agreed to provide the space, equipment, and all business services for a period of eighteen months in return for a twenty percent share of the company. The founders, who now numbered four people, were allotted half of the company's shares, and the venture capital firm received the remaining thirty percent.

The new venture raised approximately $60,000, a modest sum for a semiconductor start-up, but more than our original capital, and at this point we were supplying the fledgling project with substantial resources. To conserve cash, it was agreed that Ryan would be the only employee until he developed the new device, while the other founders kept their existing jobs. The proposed product in no way competed with the activity of the founders' current employers, so the arrangement did not create ethical conflicts.

The first disagreement was not long in coming. In a few weeks, Ryan had made substantial progress in his development effort, but was still a long way from achieving a practical device. At this point, the other three founders decided to join the new company's payroll. I advised against that, arguing that, although Ryan had proved the feasibility of the new device, a lot of work remained to produce a working prototype, and salaries for four professional employees would rapidly drain the available resources. It made no sense to have a manufacturing manager on board when there was nothing to manufacture, a sales person when there was nothing to sell, and an application engineer when there was nothing to apply. My arguments fell on deaf ears, and the expenses of the new venture increased dramatically.

The added financial burden was not the only problem. I have noticed over the years that there are people who are endowed with a talent for offending others. Chris was one of those individuals. When he assumed the position of president, his behavior—the way he walked, the way he talked, and even his facial expressions—became those of a pompous, self-centered man with total contempt for those around him. Shortly after being installed in our facility, he started spreading rumors that the only thing Crystalonics had going for it was his new venture. According to him, we were going out of business and planned to rob his team's efforts to rescue our company. He did a good job convincing his people of his assertions, and even raised fears among our employees.

How he arrived at his conclusion I shall never know. At that point Crystalonics was a fast-growing, profitable company with a sound balance sheet showing substantial cash reserves and no debt. Perhaps it was paranoia or envy. Or perhaps he could not understand that there are people, in this case those of us at Crystalonics, who just try to help their fellow engineers. He looked for a hidden motive and suspected an elaborate conspiracy designed to steal the fruits of his labor to revive our own "failing" company. Why else would anyone go to the trouble of arranging financing for other people, spend a lot of managerial and technical time to help relative strangers run their venture, and expect only a modest return?

When the new device was finally announced, it created a lot of excitement in the marketplace. We received a number of orders, but only one or two initial customers were interested in additional devices. The reason soon became apparent: The devices did not meet the claimed specifications. Tom, whose job was to work with the customers, wanted to withdraw the product from the market until the technical problems were solved, but his three partners resolved the situation by firing him instead. It became clear that the venture was heading for a grand failure through the depletion of funds and the founders' attitudes.

We proposed several solutions. Jack thought he could help solve the technical problems. If that did not work, we had a number of ideas that Ryan could develop into saleable products to make the new company viable. I suggested we submit joint proposals to government agencies for development funds, so we could add Crystalonics' financial strength to the project and enhance its chances of obtaining a contract. I offered to maintain Ryan and a technician on our payroll to see if we could develop a product to rescue their company. One by one the proposals were shot down, with each denounced as a plot to appropriate their ideas. They came up with a much more innovative plan: Since the customers no longer wanted the product, the team accused us of deliberately sabotaging the sales of their devices and sued us for a million dollars. I was not totally surprised by their action. In the words of Ben Kessel, the president of Computer Control Company, who had turned down this group of would-be entrepreneurs when they approached him for financing, "They were a bunch of nuts."

What I found most disturbing was the way a respectable Boston law firm hired by our accusers worded the complaint. I accept the fact that everyone has the right to be represented in a court of law, but the complaint against us referring to our original agreement stated, "Although the plaintiff did everything required of it under said agreement, the defendant failed and refused to perform all of its obligations thereunder."

Even with the license to exaggerate that many lawyers take for granted, common sense should have suggested to our would-be partners that they could not possibly have done "everything required" without our performing at least some of our obligations, such as, at a minimum, obtaining financing and providing space for their new venture. But stating objective facts was not the practice of these people, who seemed to be devoid of conscience and deluded by their elaborate conspiracy theory.

The timing of the suit could not have been better from our adversaries' point of view. By the time they had squandered their resources, we were being wooed by several potential acquirers, and they were all aware that legal action could easily disrupt the sale. In such cases it is not unusual for the stockholders of an accused company, whether guilty or not, to pay off the accuser to protect the sale of their operation. This may have been the ploy of our accusers all along. Of course, I entertained no thoughts of caving in to blackmail. A year later, one of our potential acquirers, California-based Teledyne, Inc., quickly determined that the accusation had no merit and did not even ask for a part of its payment to be held in escrow as protection against a potentially unfavorable resolution of the litigation.

We did not pay our accusers $1 million, but eventually settled for $1,000 to end the lawsuit. The device around which the ill-fated venture had been formed was never developed by anyone else, because it was superseded by other approaches. There was a measure of poetic justice in the outcome: While fighting us, the founders squandered not only their company's money but also their personal resources. The backers lost their investment, but more than made up for it in the success of Varactron, which they had also financed. Crystalonics also benefited from Varactron's success, and we learned valuable lessons in human relations.

When I belatedly realized that I had overestimated my ability to persuade others to follow a logical course, I took steps to avoid similar traps in the future. I found that I could be much more persuasive with people who knew that I could order them to perform and, if need be, remove them from their positions. I had always managed by consensus, not by "ukaz" (dictate), and, hopefully I was as ready to accept advice as to offer it, but in this case our 20 percent ownership of the company was not large enough to convert my suggested remedies into positive action. When I founded other joint ventures in later years, I never again insisted on my partners' holding at least 50 percent of the company's stock.

In helping organize Varactron and Chris's company, I was guided by a tradition of mutual assistance immigrants brought to the United States. Many of them shared backgrounds of grave hardships in their countries, where they had often helped each other to overcome problems. After arriving here, they also frequently had to rely on their countrymen for emotional and even material support. In addition to my father's and my uncle's generosity I, too, had benefited from the help of many individuals. In Siberia our community rallied together. In England I was invited by Jim Foster and his family to their home for two weeks of quiet study before my final college exams. Before my departure from England, my colleagues in Lutterworth shared with me their latest scientific discoveries to equip me technically for my work in the United States.

Up to that point, support had been mainly a one-way street: Other than my contributions in Siberia, I had been the recipient, not the giver, of help. At last, having established a successful business, I was in a position to participate as a helper. I had arrived in America, the land of opportunity, with nothing, and in just two years, thanks to the favorable business climate developed by generations of Americans, I had been able to establish a successful company worthy of participating in sophisticated space programs and defense projects. I wished to repay the kindness of others by giving my former coworkers a head start in establishing their own ventures. I never imagined that people I tried to help would turn on me.

UNION ELECTION

OUR UNHAPPY eighteen-month involvement with Chris's company was not a major distraction or impediment to our progress at Crystalonics. During that time we developed new devices and improved techniques for our existing products. Our transistors were designed into a range of demanding defense and space systems, including manned space programs. Several were classified, but we generally knew what role our devices played in the final applications.

Our transistors were used for monitoring parameters such as position, speed, temperature, and fuel flow in launched military and NASA vehicles, and the results were relayed by onboard radio transmitters to ground controllers. Transistors involved in this process inherently introduced errors, which degraded the relayed information, but our symmetrical transistors, by virtue of their design, generated fewer errors than others available on the market and allowed more accurate control of the rockets. In addition to their superior electrical characteristics, our devices were smaller and lighter than similar competitive offerings, thereby saving critical space and weight in the launched vehicles.

We also provided devices for so-called "silent sentries" to guard Minuteman ballistic missile silos. Accurate sensors were needed to detect intruders and discriminate among people, animals, and inanimate objects. The sensors generated electrical signals in response to their findings, and those signals had to be amplified and transmitted to the supervisory personnel. Transistors used in these amplifiers invariably degraded the signals by generating internal electrical "noise." Our field-effect transistors were by far the lowest-noise devices and were widely used.

Not everything went smoothly, of course. Reliability problems were not uncommon in the early days of semiconductors, and field failures led to a few tense meetings with our customers. One meeting I remember well involved a short-range ballistic missile. When I was ushered into a large conference room filled with irate military and civilian personnel, a high-ranking official screamed at me, blaming our company for causing failures in their rockets. On hearing my foreign accent and unable to pronounce my name, he went so far as to accuse me of deliberate sabotage and threatened to have me investigated by the FBI. The atmosphere became tense, but after further discussion the meeting ended on a reasonably cordial note. It was not completely clear that we had been at fault, since the missile in question ended up at the bottom of an ocean and it was hard to perform a complete failure analysis. Based on transmitted data, however, there were strong reasons to suspect our devices, so we designed a cooperative program of reliability testing to minimize the potential for future failures. The customer continued to work with us partly because he was impressed with our cooperative attitude and partly because he judged our transistors to be the best available for his application. We took such complaints extremely seriously, and with advancing technology, we gradually tightened our manufacturing procedures and became a more dependable supplier, even earning the title "Vendor of the Year" from several of our most discerning customers.

Apart from a few such short-term problems, which we managed to resolve, the situation at Crystalonics became almost idyllic. I was still dividing my time between general management, sales, and working in the laboratory. Lab work was for me the most enjoyable activity, although gradually I had to curtail the amount of time I could devote to technical projects. We were growing, becoming more profitable, and

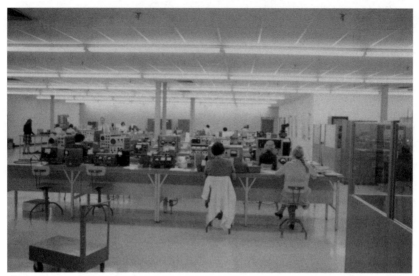

Crystalonics assembly line.

expanding our customer base both in the United States and abroad. For some time, the business as a whole sailed along smoothly, with no threatening clouds on the horizon. However, when those clouds did appear, they created not just a storm, but a hurricane that almost destroyed our company.

For some time Jack, my original partner, had been developing a new way to produce the silicon material that was particularly suitable for field-effect transistors. We had also hired a new engineer, Larry Bernstein, to improve the manufacturing efficiency of the P-N-P devices around which our company had been formed. As his experiments progressed, we realized that Jack's work, initially conceived for another purpose, was applicable to the devices we were manufacturing on the production line. By combining Larry's and Jack's efforts, we produced devices that were small, several orders of magnitude better, and more reliable than both our current product line and similar components available from our competitors. We could replace their products, but they could not compete with us, and we soon became the major player in our small specialty market. In the process of making competitive devices obsolete, we also radically altered our production methods, rendering irrelevant the techniques so well known to Alan, whom we had hired in 1959 as a production manager. Alan had done well over the years and was now a substantial stockholder of Crystalonics. Also, in addition to his production responsibilities, he was now the plant manager.

It is not unusual to run into conflicts between engineering and manufacturing personnel when a new product is moved into full-scale production. In our case we not only introduced a new product, but also replaced the entire manufacturing process. We changed every assembly step, yet retained all our people. It was as if the English language had suddenly become obsolete and the entire manufacturing staff had to learn to speak Chinese. Until this point, Alan had been doing an excellent job. He was a competent manufacturing manager, efficiently producing good product on a timely basis, and had a good understanding of the technology involved. He was also respected by his subordinates. By contrast the completely new approach developed by Larry put Alan, like everyone else, on unfamiliar ground. Larry, running a small pre-production line in the development department, was producing devices with consistently good characteristics, but Alan found it hard to achieve the same results on the larger scale of the main manufacturing line.

Frequent disputes arose, with the two men blaming each other for the high reject rate. Alan, who held the more senior position, accused Larry of developing the new devices with insufficient attention to their reproducibility. Larry insisted the manufacturing people had not followed the engineering instructions properly. There was some truth in both assertions, but on the whole I felt Larry's views were more valid. Alan had been with us almost from the start, and at that point owned ten percent of the company. Larry was a relatively new employee. To resolve the situation I suggested to Alan that we move Larry from the laboratory to manufacturing, where he would become a production engineer reporting to Alan. Larry, a mild-mannered and polite individual, readily agreed. Alan rejected my proposal because, in his opinion, "Larry could not be trusted."

My management skills and powers of persuasion proved inadequate to resolve the situation. Although we were making progress in improving our manufacturing efficiency, the tension between the two men increased and eventually Alan gave me an ultimatum: he would leave unless I fired Larry. I was sorry to see Alan go, but to submit to his demands would have been not only unfair, but harmful to the company. Alan left that day and I appointed Larry to be the operations manager, essentially giving him all of Alan's previous responsibilities.

In less than a week, Alan called asking to see me. We met the next day, and he told me that all our production employees were unhappy with Larry's management style. They also wanted to bring in a union, fearing there was little job security for anyone since Alan was let go. The only way to avoid a union election, according to Alan, would be for me to hire him back. He was willing to return even if Larry stayed with the company in another capacity. I knew it was not an idle threat. Alan's brother was our general foreman, and several people in key manufacturing positions were loyal to Alan. They were not happy about the recent management change and had already tried to undermine Larry's effectiveness. But it would have been unthinkable to me and to our management team to submit to Alan's new ultimatum. We examined several options, but in the end, we declined to reinstate him.

I was sorry to lose Alan. He had made valuable contributions and knew more about manufacturing than anyone in our company. But our new device designs had rendered his knowledge obsolete, and he found himself in the demeaning position of relying on Larry for solutions to even rudimentary technical problems. He surely felt that the change diminished his status and enhanced Larry's. The logical course for Alan, given his senior position in our organization, would have been to concentrate on the management aspects of his job and delegate technical matters to Larry. Such action would have allowed Alan to grow professionally while encouraging Larry in his technical endeavors. But this was not meant to be. Despite my strenuous efforts to coach him, Alan demonstrated an inability to rise beyond his current line position in our organization. Worse still, his actions proved that he could become an impediment to our growth. Lacking the grounds to credibly attack Larry's contribution, he fell back on the childish trick of smearing Larry's personality. I had every reason to believe that he would continue to undermine Larry's position in the future. If this was one reason for not reinstating him, the other, more important consideration was a simple matter of fairness: Having just promoted Larry to the position of operations manager, I could not strip him of his new responsibility just because Alan had changed his mind.

As to Alan's threats about the union election, I suspected that even reinstating him would not solve that problem. He had unleashed a process, and it did not seem likely that once it developed, anyone would be in a position to stop it. I decided we would just have to face what was coming.

The organizers from International Brotherhood of Electrical Workers (IBEW) appeared outside our plant almost immediately. At that time, I still held strong pro-union views, but I had never had firsthand experience with unions and knew little about them. As president and part-owner of a company, I should have leaned toward pure capitalism—a position I could have easily embraced after my exposure to the worst excesses of communism in Siberia. But I naively hoped that the world's social system would some day become a compromise between the extremes of capitalism and communism. Early trends in that direction were already appearing in the Soviet Union and Europe. Russia had begun tentative experiments with decentralization of responsibility in certain segments of industry, and European companies were taking steps toward sharing management oversight with employees by electing union representatives to their boards of directors. In the mid-1960s, it appeared that both systems could converge at a midpoint where employees would be in full partnership with management; everyone would be a part owner of the enterprise, and companies would compete in free markets. I felt that the unions in the United States had a major role to play in that conversion process.

The difference between my idealistic vision and the reality of union agitation became apparent immediately. The accusations and derision to which we were subjected by several hand-picked employees were ridiculous. Rumors about our alleged intentions to victimize our workers swept through the plant like wildfire and the working atmosphere deteriorated rapidly. I was approached again by several employees with an offer to call off the union if I brought Alan back. To this day I don't know how much the union knew about our internal situation. Each party to the conflict had a different agenda. Alan's brother and the employees who were his friends did not really want to have the union represent our workers, but were using the IBEW as leverage to force us to reinstate their champion. Others genuinely believed that a union would improve their working conditions. The union itself saw a company with a management crisis as a fertile opportunity to organize the employees.

The union's tactics of "fishing in muddy waters" were ugly. I objected to their alliance with Alan, and I was horrified at the pronouncements of their internal ringleaders and the disruptive plans they had in store for us after the election. According to them, Larry had had Alan fired in order to get rid of both him and all his friends. Supposedly, Larry would now begin making unreasonable demands on our employees and force them to work harder. The only way to restore the old atmosphere in the plant was to bring Alan back—which could be done only with the help of the union. With the union in place, the employees would have control over their fate and would not be subjected to unreasonable demands and conditions at work.

We retained a Boston law firm to help us fight the union invasion. The National Labor Relations Board promptly ordered an election. We waged a vigorous campaign, but it was an unequal fight. In union elections, companies rely primarily on loyal production supervisors to present the management view. In our case all the foremen were either Alan's relatives or friends, who strongly urged the employees to vote for the union. The predicament was largely my fault. I had had little experience in personnel management and had always tried to delegate as much responsibility as possible, and I had relied on Alan to hire the right production personnel. Because he had been a loyal employee and substantial stockholder, I felt that it would be an advantage to bring in people Alan knew and whose performance he could predict.

I tried to explain our position to our employees without much success. The process was complicated by the law's restriction of subjects that could be discussed and places where these talks could be held. For example it was illegal to call an hourly employee into my office for a chat. Presumably the law had been passed to prevent intimidation of workers by management, but the union organizers were quick to turn such restrictions to their advantage. One of the ringleaders burst into my office for a private chat just to provoke an unfair labor practice situation. The election results were worse than we expected. Fifty people voted for the union, twenty voted against.

Although the election campaign had been distracting for all of us, Larry wasted little time in improving the efficiency of the manufacturing line, and within just a few weeks our output almost doubled without any additional people and with the same consumption of material. I could not help feeling that Alan had anticipated this result and wanted to remove Larry before the comparison between the two men's capabilities became obvious.

The improvement left us with too many manufacturing and supervisory people. Normally we would have gone out of our way to avoid any cutback in staff, hoping that we could gradually increase our sales and that enough of our employees would either retire or leave voluntarily. But the election changed the atmosphere entirely. We no longer felt the same loyalty toward our employees, especially those who had attacked us during the campaign. Asking people to leave our employment has always been the most unpleasant and distasteful of my duties, and reduction of the workforce after the election was no exception. We selected fifteen employees of lowest seniority who, by coincidence, had been strong union supporters, and asked them to leave. We took this action on a Friday; the following Monday the union organizer came to warn me that if I did not reinstate those people immediately, we would have a strike. After I refused his demand, he left my office and within minutes fifty of our hourly employees left their benches and congregated outside the building. Twenty faithful, hourly employees stayed at their posts.

Crystalonics plant, Cambridge, Massachusetts, 1968.

STRIKE

IT WAS ALMOST A RELIEF to see the departure of the fifty striking employees. At least now it was clear who our opponents were; inside the plant we were among friends. We convened a meeting of our remaining assemblers, thanked them for their confidence in us, announced our intention to fight the strike, and asked for everyone's cooperation. We warned them of the harassment they could expect on the picket line and promised we would do everything in our power to minimize that annoyance by having a policeman on duty at all times. All the employees expressed their full support, greatly relieved to be rid of the agitators and in a position to speak their minds freely. We spent the rest of the day reorganizing the production line. Several engineers volunteered to work on the line to make up for labor shortage.

By the end of the day, a rowdy picket line had assembled outside the entrance to our yard. We watched with a great deal of apprehension as our employees crossed the line, but they suffered no insults or physical abuse. If we had to have a strike, we thought, it was good that the union staged the walkout while our employees were at work. That way, those who remained had to cross the picket line to go home. They found it an unpleasant but not impossible experience. Had the union called the strike after working hours, many employees, not knowing what to expect, might have been reluctant to cross the line coming into the plant. We anxiously awaited the next day, to see how many hourly employees would return to work, fearing that the loss of even one employee would encourage others to stay home. Fortunately all twenty reported for work.

With each passing day the picketers became more aggressive. There were incidents of pushing; the women began smearing passing cars with lipstick, producing streaks that were hard to remove. Surprisingly, the women were more aggressive than the men and also more likely to use foul language. The more obnoxious the picketers became, the more determined our employees grew to stand their ground. As often occurs in situations of shared adversity, the fight produced an almost festive atmosphere inside the plant; we were drawn together in a common cause. We tried to improve productivity and find new ways to increase efficiency. I made sure that I spent at least two hours a day performing various assembly tasks on the production line alongside our employees, and by the end of the week, we found our manufacturing output almost equal to what it had been before the walkout. But as the first week of the strike drew to a close, the strikers became more vicious and threatened the workers with retaliation over the weekend. We worried that our loyal employees would lose their resolve.

Several plans for fortifying our employees' steadfastness over the weekend were proposed, but eventually we settled on Larry's idea of a champagne party. We were heavily outnumbered, with fifty people on strike and only twenty assemblers on the production line, but that did not account for our total workforce. We also had forty professional employees performing various engineering, marketing, and administrative functions. That Friday we bought several cases of champagne, and about half an hour before the end of the workday, we assembled in our small cafeteria. It was so crowded that people could not move without bumping into one another. We started popping the corks and the champagne flowed freely both into and out of the glasses. Someone proposed a toast, and the voices grew louder as the celebratory mood filled the room. Just before the clock signaled the end of the shift, I climbed onto one of the tables, spread my arms wide, and to overcome the tumult almost shouted, "Don't beat up the people on the picket line!" We opened every building entrance and at once let loose all our people, who proceeded toward the gate in a joyous, half-intoxicated human wave, completely overwhelming the picket line. The stunned strikers recoiled in uncertainty, allowing the workers to pass without incident.

The afternoon of the party was the turning point. The union never regained its momentum, and one could sense a favorable outcome in the not-too-distant future. But in the remaining seven hard weeks of the strike, our endurance was tested almost to the breaking point. Like many of our people, I received numerous obscene phone calls at home as well as threats against my life and the lives of my wife and children. After a few days, I had our number changed to an unlisted one, but that only partially relieved my anxiety. I was suspicious of every shadow and noise inside and outside our house. I went as far as buying a gun. As a foreigner—I still held a British passport—I did not qualify for a pistol, so I purchased a small hunting rifle at Sears. I am not sure I would have had the confidence to fire it if anyone had broken into our house, but just taking that step helped relieve my anxiety.

Eight weeks of disruption is a major threat to the health of a small company, especially one that has to compete against corporate giants. Any decline in the quality of our devices, any disruption of deliveries, could easily have resulted in a loss of important and hard-won customers. Significant interruption of shipments would have quickly exhausted our meager financial resources. The strikers exploited such difficulties wherever they could. They did not resort to damaging our equipment, which would have subjected them to criminal prosecution, but they found a more deadly way to sabotage our efforts. Most of our customers were using our devices in their highly critical space and defense programs, and they expected us to meet extremely high standards of reliability. One of their requirements was so-called lot identification. It often took weeks or even months to process our devices through the manufacturing line and quality-testing procedures. During that time each batch had to be kept separate, which allowed us to eliminate an entire batch of devices should a problem be found. All the strikers had to do was mix up transistors among various lots to render the entire inventory useless, and they had done just that immediately before staging the walkout. Theirs was a sophisticated act of sabotage. Only a few people had full access to the segregated lots and not everyone understood the implications of mixing them into one indistinguishable group. We could only conclude that the strikers were coached by Alan's friends or, even worse, by Alan himself.

Life was difficult during those weeks, but as the strike dragged on, we found innovative ways to adapt to our new conditions. We were blessed with loyal employees, and the Monday after the champagne party everyone showed up for work. We tried to overcome each difficulty as it appeared. The smaller work force was the most obvious problem, and we compensated for that by applying technology to increase our output and by employing our professional staff on the assembly line. Delivery of raw materials and shipment of finished goods can be another problem during a strike, because truckers typically will not cross picket lines. In our case, however, we could fit a month's worth of supplies in the trunk of a car, and our finished products were small enough to be transported in automobiles. Third, we needed weekly deliveries of liquid nitrogen, which is normally transported in thermally insulated tanker trucks, but fortunately we were able to work out an arrangement with our vendor to deliver the gas at night. Finally, we ran up against the challenge of rubbish removal when our service company refused to make the weekly collections from our large trash container. There, too, we found a two-pronged solution. A number of our employees simply took bags of trash home in their cars. In addition, we found that several heavy men could jump on the rubbish inside the big container and compact the contents, greatly increasing our waste capacity.

At the beginning of the second week of the strike, we were asked by a government mediation agency to meet with the union representatives. The union had not yet been certified by the National Labor Relations Board (NLRB), and although we had no legal obligation to negotiate with them, we attended the first meeting. The lawyers advised us to have Larry represent the company. Since he was not the president, he could not be pressed into a binding commitment during the negotiations. That would leave us more time to examine the issues and plan our response.

We faced a peculiar problem during that second week: Our efforts to streamline the operation had been so successful that we found we could sustain our required production levels with just thirty people. That meant we would need to recall only ten employees. Our lawyer advised us that if the strike ended immediately, we might be forced by the NLRB to recall most of the strikers. If we could prolong the strike for another couple of weeks, he felt that we would not be legally required to bring our workforce back to its original strength. This was very sensitive information; if it leaked out, it might cause the union to abort the strike. We therefore made sure the union thought every day that we were on the verge of collapse. It was easy to convey this misinformation, because Alan's brother was still our foreman. We simply told him on a regular basis how desperate our situation was. I don't know whether he relayed our message to the union, but we achieved the desired result. The strike was not called off. The NLRB soon certified the union and we engaged in serious negotiations. Again it was Larry who attended the meetings.

Before long we came to an impasse. The union and our lawyers proposed two different contracts which appeared to be similar, but in reality differed considerably from each other. The union was not asking for more money; rather, their main demand was "super-seniority" for several employees who were its strongest supporters, to ensure they would be the last to be laid off in case of a cutback. I was not against normal seniority rules, but I strongly objected to arbitrary, preferential treatment for any employees. The union then suggested we could also choose several of our assemblers for super-seniority status. My response was that far from solving the problem of unfairness, the proposal made it worse by giving special status to even more workers. With the discussions producing no results, the union brought more senior people to the negotiating table. I attended one of the sessions and was impressed with the caliber of the new officials representing their side. They confided to me that they would become the laughing stock of their colleagues if they accepted the contract our lawyers had proposed, since it assigned all the problems to the union but gave them no power to act.

In the sixth week of the strike, we noticed strangers on the picket line. They were big burly men, whom I assumed the union had sent to intimidate us, and the action had the desired effect. We felt less secure, but we responded with increased vigilance. We made sure several management people were near the picket line to observe our employees when they reported for work and when they went home. The presence of our senior executives reassured them, and they all continued to come to work. Then one day in the eighth week, the union decided to end the strike and to negotiate the contract after the strikers had returned to work. They may have realized by then that there were no economic issues at stake, and that they had been generally misled by Alan and his allies. We readily agreed to their proposal, but offered to take back only thirteen people. That number may have seemed arbitrary, but we arrived at it after careful analysis.

As I have already mentioned, we needed a total of only thirty people, who had to be hired on the basis of seniority without discriminating against those employees who went out on strike. Had we followed strict seniority rules, we would have had to let go several people who supported us during the walkout. It was completely unacceptable to me to throw out people who had been loyal to us throughout this long ordeal. We solved the problem by splitting the manufacturing operation into several segments, with employment in each segment requiring different skills, and established several seniority pools. By trying a number of different combinations, we arrived at a situation where all our loyalists had seniority and thirteen vacancies remained. Despite strong initial objections, the union accepted our proposal and after eight weeks the strike ended. We continued our negotiations, but the union called the meetings at increasingly less frequent intervals, and by the end of the year it just faded away.

I understand that it is most unusual to expel a union after it is certified, and it was gratifying to prevail in what I believed was a just cause, but I found little reason to celebrate. The people who suffered most were the strikers. They left good, well-paying jobs to join the picket line. It was an exceptionally cold winter, and in order to survive their vigil they had to park their cars with the engines and heaters running as a refuge from the cold weather. They had been coerced into participating in the walkout by the ringleaders, and many did not even know why they were striking. On more than one occasion, when visitors to the plant asked them the purpose of their strike, the answer was, "I don't know." Their lack of social awareness and political sophistication was ably exploited by the organizers. This is probably best illustrated by the fact that, in their search for ultimate insults, and remembering my time in Russia, they often called me a communist. The sight of striking workers calling their company's president a communist was probably the most incongruous event in the whole unhappy episode, and even in our darkest hours, it never failed to bring a sad smile to my face. Most of them lost their jobs in the end; even those who returned were uncomfortable among their former adversaries and eventually found other employment.

Alan, who had triggered and perhaps even caused the drama, remained out of work, eventually opening a grocery store with his brother. He brought a suit against the company for overtime pay, as if a man in his position were entitled to additional compensation for overtime. He also tried to interfere with the eventual sale of the company. If his effort was designed to prevent Larry from developing his full technical and managerial potential, it was utterly unsuccessful.

I have heard that many people become fanatical during union fights. That was certainly true in my case. I could accept the possibility of my own company going out of business, but I could not accept the idea of handing over the reins to people with perfidious motives. Many on both sides of the strike paid a heavy emotional toll. Under continual threats on my family's life, I felt for several months that I had ceased to be part of civilized society and had been deprived of normal human rights. I felt somewhat like a criminal on the run—although such a person could at least run and hide. I had to be very much in view and pretend not to be affected by the events around me. In that I think I was successful, and the thought of giving up never entered my mind.

My colleagues and I learned many lessons from this unfortunate episode. In later years, I managed other operations that became targets of union organizing efforts. Fortunately those episodes were not caused by internal dissent but were merely routine union organizing drives. None was successful.

TELEDYNE

By 1965 IT BECAME increasingly common for companies around the country to buy other public or private enterprises. The resulting conglomerates, as they became known, grew rapidly by using their shares as currency to pay for their acquisitions, and the stock market rewarded that growth with high valuations. During that year a number of large companies approached us with offers of acquisition. By then, we had approximately two hundred employees and were enjoying profitable growth. Most of the potential buyers were not newly formed conglomerates but well-established operations, including Lockheed, General Instruments, and Radiation (a substantial customer located in Melbourne, Florida, that was subsequently acquired by another company). We were not under any pressure to sell, but the inquiries, which seemed to come on a weekly basis, encouraged us to think about the issue. The thought of trading the risky ownership of a fledgling enterprise in a competitive industry for hard cash looked increasingly attractive. Jack, the most security-conscious among us, was the strongest advocate of such a transaction.

After considering many options, we sold Crystalonics to Teledyne, at that time small, but growing fast. We chose Teledyne for two reasons: the personality of its founder and president, Henry Singleton, and the decentralized structure of the company, which allowed local management almost complete freedom in running its operations. I was thirty-five years old when we sold Crystalonics, and my proceeds, while not large enough for retirement, were sufficient to support our family for a few years.

Conglomerates have been widely criticized for killing the entrepreneurial spirit of acquired companies, stripping them of assets, and demoralizing the creative employees. Not knowing exactly what to expect after the sale, we assumed our new status with some trepidation, but our experience with Teledyne contradicted the gruesome stories we had heard about conglomerates. In fact, their treatment of us exceeded our most optimistic expectations. Crystalonics became a division of Teledyne, retaining its organization and operating under the same name; I was allowed to continue as manager of the new entity. Unexpectedly, the new arrangement afforded me more freedom than ever before. Our own board of directors had to be dissolved; we had had good directors at Crystalonics, and I would miss their advice. But in many ways, it was much simpler to make my own decisions without waiting for approval from a higher authority. I had also felt it was my duty to consult the employee stockholders, especially Jack, on almost every issue. After the sale, we still ran the operation as a team and consensus was important, but as long as we were profitable—and we always made handsome profits—Teledyne allowed me to make almost every decision. All in all, the management process was greatly simplified.

I did not see my boss, Henry Singleton, more than once a year. Teledyne required us to provide detailed monthly information including comparison of results with projections. We had most of the required data, although not always in the prescribed format, but it was a simple matter to reorganize our accounting system to conform to our new parent's wishes. Teledyne reports were superbly organized, and simply analyzing the information we entered into their corporate forms taught me a lot about our business—that is, when I began to understand the value of formal planning, market analysis, and accounting.

I had run Crystalonics largely by intuition, which was fine for a small organization where I knew everyone and could see everything at a glance, but I realized that to direct a larger company I would have to rely on more formal management tools. Teledyne provided those tools as well as informal lessons on how to use them. I absorbed many of those lessons, and my years with Teledyne made me a much better manager. They certainly did nothing to slow the growth of Crystalonics, which continued to thrive at an ever-accelerating pace.

When Teledyne asked me to run two of their other acquisitions in the Boston area, I began to see the reasoning behind the criticism of conglomerates. Both operations were in trouble, and both were losing their creative people. But those difficulties had begun before their acquisition by Teledyne, and most likely had precipitated their sale. In one case, the company ran out of product ideas; in the other, the founders developed serious disagreements. At the time of acquisition, the current financial results of the two operations did not fully reflect their deteriorating position, but management was already looking for a way out. Teledyne became a convenient scapegoat when problems surfaced after the acquisition. My experience may not be typical—I have seen instances of conglomerates putting short-term performance ahead of long-range goals—but such was not the case with the three operations under my care, where current profitability was well balanced with investment for long-term growth. Far from destroying their new associates, conglomerates often replace the failing existing management with more seasoned people and restore the acquisitions to sound financial health. Hopefully, this is what happened to the two additional enterprises entrusted to my care by Teledyne.

When we sold Crystalonics, I thought I would leave the new organization within a year or two, but I ended up staying for four years. The delay was prompted by my desire to ensure that the purchaser received a good return on its investment. I had been proud that each of our previous investors had made a handsome profit; those gains were easy to quantify by simply comparing each financier's proceeds from the sale of our stock with his initial investment. Since Teledyne had no intention of selling our company, I thought a better alternative would be to manage Crystalonics until my operation generated more cash for our new parent than was paid to our former stockholders. That happened within three years of the acquisition, after which I felt I had fulfilled my financial responsibility to my new employer. The second reason for staying was the pleasant working conditions. As I have already mentioned, I had more freedom than ever before, I was learning a lot and, under the Teledyne umbrella, I enjoyed the new association with interesting and creative people.

Four years after the sale of Crystalonics, however, I became restless. My work at Teledyne was becoming routine, and I thought it would be challenging to embark on another venture. When I contacted Peter Brooke, a venture capitalist with whom I had worked at Crystalonics, he was most receptive to providing the capital for a new enterprise, even though I did not yet have a clear idea for another start-up. After lengthy soul searching, I notified Teledyne of my desire to leave. I had no immediate plans for another activity and offered to stay for as long as necessary for a smooth transition, with the goal of leaving within two months. Teledyne's search produced a successor in four months, during which time I was asked not to announce my departure. It was a trying period, since I felt obligated to postpone important personnel additions until the new manager arrived, and current employees, unaware of my impending departure, could not understand my indecision. Eventually my successor came on board and I left Teledyne in January of 1970.

NEW VENTURES

MY DEPARTURE from Teledyne had been about a year in the making, but when it finally took place, the break seemed abrupt. The sadness of departure was softened by the warmth of my sendoff. The employees arranged farewell parties with speeches, reminiscences, and gifts. Perhaps most touching was a three-foot-long scroll signed by all my coworkers and a large bowl inscribed in Russian. It must have taken a lot of effort to find a Russian translator and to instruct the engraver in the art of Russian calligraphy. Joel Cohen prepared a thick scrapbook containing press releases, data sheets, significant letters, and articles that illustrated the historical development of my original venture. He also built a case to display the various products we had introduced at Crystalonics. I have treasured these items over the years, and they have provided a pleasant reminder of my first serious entrepreneurial effort.

These farewell activities occupied most of my time during the final week at work and contrasted starkly with the calm of the first Monday morning at home. It felt strange getting up in the morning without having to go to the office, but there was the exhilarating feeling of a new start. It is not often that we have an opportunity to shed all our troubles and start life anew. It was a pleasure not to think about the dozens of dull issues that arise daily in managing a business. I had started Crystalonics as a complete novice; I left Teledyne as a reasonably seasoned professional manager. In the early days, I had developed friendships with several of my subordinates, but those relationships were occasionally difficult to maintain with the growth of my first company. This was particularly true of the original Crystalonics employees with whom I shared many tasks at the start but whose duties remained essentially unchanged over the next few years, while I became progressively more immersed in the overall management. Still, I remained friends with most of them, and several of my former coworkers joined me in my later ventures.

Those were the positive developments. The other side of the coin was the feeling of isolation, of coming to a complete stop. I missed the activity, the many challenges facing my former companies, and the companionship of my team. There was a sense of the world moving forward without me. In addition, I had to support my family, which now included three small children. The proceeds from the sale of Crystalonics could sustain us for two or three years, but my new beginning would soon have to take a practical turn. Although I had several ideas that could form the basis of future commercial activities, I had not verified their feasibility before leaving my former employer. It would have been difficult to concentrate on future ventures while holding a full-time management position, and it would not have been fair to engage in such activities while I was working for another organization.

Overall, the sense of freedom more than outweighed the feelings of remoteness and uncertainty. My confidence was further enhanced by telephone calls from several business acquaintances just days after my departure from Teledyne. A few wanted my advice on business matters, one offered a job, and yet another proposed that I head a new high technology venture. Within two weeks I found myself being pulled in too many directions at once, and I decided to establish strict priorities about what kinds of opportunities I was prepared to investigate. In the end I did not participate in any of the situations suggested to me. Instead I embarked on a consulting activity that I thought would last for about a year and become a stepping stone toward building a series of high technology companies.

The year 1970 was not a good one for the economy. Unemployment was high in the Boston area and many companies were in trouble. While doing preparatory work for my next business venture, I thought I could be helpful as a consultant to one or two of these struggling enterprises. I approached Ray Miller, an officer at State Street Bank and a person with whom I had worked for several years at Crystalonics. He confirmed that, like many banks, his had several clients who were unable to repay their loans. One of those customers was a well-known local consumer electronics manufacturer who owed the bank two million dollars and could not meet its obligation.

I visited the company and spent several hours with the founder, who owned 80 percent of the operation. He was one of the first to design high-fidelity components. His company was an early producer of tuners, stereophonic amplifiers, receivers, and speakers which, when placed in two locations in a room, could produce more realistic sound than the previously available radios and self-contained consoles. The founder had not only started a company but had helped to establish a new industry with his completely new approach to high-fidelity sound reproduction. I had a strong interest in this field, and we had a lively technical discussion, but when I inquired about his company's financial difficulties, he denied the existence of any major problems and refused to acknowledge the need for corrective action. With the company on the brink of bankruptcy, he could not face the facts.

Such disbelief is, of course, common in all walks of life, not just in the high technology industry. At the end of their careers, people who have been prominent in their fields find it hard to accept the fact that their technologies and even their skills have become obsolete and their services no longer required. Frequently, in fast-moving markets, established products are displaced by newcomers using what Andrew Grove, former president of chip maker Intel, has called "disruptive technologies." These disruptions are especially difficult for old-guard managers to accept when the "upstarts" seem unworthy of the market respect they themselves had worked so hard to achieve. In the case of the American "hi-fi" market, the "disruption" had been caused by highly efficient Japanese companies. Foreign competition exposed longstanding shortcomings in companies such as my potential client's—deficiencies that had long been masked by the artificially high prices he could charge customers while enjoying a virtual monopoly in the marketplace.

We reviewed the financial condition of the struggling operation, however, and he asked me to visit him again. I saw him several times in the next few weeks, and while the visits were enjoyable—and hopefully useful to the owner—he still did not want to consider changing the way he was running his business. Meanwhile I was learning a great deal about the high-fidelity industry and the internal structure of his company. Even though I received no payment for these consultations, I had time to spare and what I was learning—not only about the hi-fi industry, but also about the consulting process—was a more than adequate reward for my efforts.

The company's condition continued to deteriorate, and I felt that if remedial action was not taken immediately, it would become increasingly difficult to reverse the slide. Sharing my sentiments, the bank decided to force the company to change its mode of operation. Unfortunately, it needed several weeks to establish its legal position for that course of action, finally doing so at a most inopportune time. We were about to embark on a family trip to visit Olga's relatives in Brazil. About half an hour before we were due to leave for the airport, I received an urgent call from the owner of the hi-fi company. In a voice that for the first time conveyed a sense of urgency, he informed me that the bank had pulled the loan and that unless something could be done quickly, the company would not survive. He urged me to take control of his operation immediately. We had previously had several false starts after agreeing on a course of action, only to see my client change his mind a few days later. I could not evaluate the urgency of the situation on the morning of his fateful call, and there was not enough time to verify the bank's position. I was reluctant to change our travel arrangements; with three young children, it had taken a great deal of preparation to organize this trip, and I did not want to postpone it at the last minute. To deal with the possibility that the company might collapse during the three weeks I would be out of the country, I called two retired executives, Ben Kessel and Ken Galucia, and asked them to step in and persuade the bank to postpone any drastic measures until my return. They readily agreed, and my client accepted their participation.

When I returned three weeks later, the company was still functioning, but its situation was precarious. Ben Kessel and Ken Galucia agreed to help me in a rescue operation. The company did not have sufficient funds to meet payroll for its several hundred employees later that week. With only two days until payday, my first step was to convince the bank to release the funds needed for payroll. The bank agreed to cooperate after we submitted detailed financial projections and a plan of action for the rest of the year. In the next twenty-four hours, our team of three consultants prepared the required documents and received the money to pay the employees. Now in control, we continued to work hard, and within four months, we had the company operating on a profitable basis.

During those four months we accomplished many things. It would be difficult and tedious to recall them all, but there were several highlights. Clearly the first requirement was to secure cash, the second was to return the company to profitability. We took two actions that generated immediate funds. Our client had a large inventory of self-contained consoles that did not sell very well—precisely because the company was now providing alternate ways to reproduce sound. Customers simply did not associate the company with the outdated products. We contacted a number of stores and offered them the consoles at a low price if they would pay cash on delivery. Over the next few days, one truck driver after another arrived at our warehouse, checks in hand, and removed our entire console inventory. As a result, we brought in about a million dollars. The second source of cash was a federal tax refund we were able to process quickly by convincing the Internal Revenue Service that the company had been badly hurt by foreign imports.

The new money quickly generated a burst of sales. The company had been in a painful position, owning an inventory of many almost-finished products that could not be shipped for want of a trivial final component, such as a knob. The vendors had refused to deliver these small items until their old bills were paid, and there had been no funds available to meet even those small demands. We disbursed the newly earned cash to our suppliers in ways that brought maximum benefits in new shipments, and the subsequent revenues increased rapidly.

The next task was to make the operation profitable. We accomplished that end by eliminating unprofitable product lines, streamlining major expenses of the operation, finding remedies for inefficient practices, and invigorating the sales force. We even found an organization that was prepared to buy the company for a price that would have seemed attractive to the owner before our involvement, but which he now refused to accept. He believed that the future now looked bright, and refused to sell.

With this happy ending, one might assume that our rescue team left on good terms with the owner and management. But that was not the case. Under a signed agreement, we were entitled to 12 percent of the company for our services, but the owner refused to honor that commitment, offering instead, a small cash settlement. Several members of the management team suggested that most, if not all, of the actions taken had been proposed and carried out by them, and that we were merely onlookers in that process. They were partially correct: The vast majority of remedies were, indeed, suggested and implemented by existing personnel. The reality was that they had not applied those remedies before our arrival. We involved the company's employees in every step of the turnaround process because they understood their business better than we did, but we supplied the drive, management expertise, and much-needed objective judgment. We were obviously dissatisfied with their settlement proposal, but instead of fighting it, we accepted the cash payment and left. The company ran into difficulties again less than a year after our departure, eventually found itself in bankruptcy, and was taken over by one of its foreign distributors.

I was disappointed that our efforts had had no lasting effect, but I did not regret my involvement, for I had gained valuable experience in turning around a troubled operation and learned a great deal about consulting. That year, I was also involved in two other consulting situations that were much less traumatic and more lucrative, so my overall income for the period did not suffer. However, my consulting activities confirmed my belief that I was not cut out to be an advisor; rather, what I did best was running my own enterprise. While the challenge of consulting was interesting, I did not enjoy the endless sessions I had to spend with clients' management teams, advocating ideas that were primarily their own but which I organized and presented in a form that made them easier to implement. In many cases, the clients' executives were reluctant to accept the resulting suggestions, perhaps because they came from an outsider. Occasionally, they even erected barriers simply to demonstrate their independence. This negative attitude may have been as much my fault as theirs, but it showed me that I functioned better as an implementer than as a consultant.

At the end of 1970 I was forty years old, still young enough to launch a new venture. I had developed several intriguing ideas and looked forward to the excitement of building another company.

POWER TRANSISTORS

BLH FORCE AND WEIGHT MEASUREMENT

Dynisco PRESSURE CONTROL SYSTEMS

DATA ACQUISITION CIRCUITS

BBF
GROUP, INC.

COMPONENTS AND SYSTEMS FOR MEASUREMENT AND CONTROL

Page from BBF Group, Inc., promotional literature, 1973.

BBF GROUP, INC.

BBF GROUP, INC. was incorporated on December 31, 1970. There was no particular reason why the event occurred on the last day of that year other than my lawyer's tardiness. Despite my constant urgings, which started in the fall, he simply did not get around to filing the necessary papers. It appears to me that lawyers, in general, share a common trait of procrastination and always manage to finish their tasks at the last possible moment. When I first asked my attorney to form BBF Group, Inc., and did not get a prompt response, I jokingly told him that I hoped he could complete the assignment before the end of the year. The joke was on me since, in fact, he filed the required papers on the last day of December.

The plans I developed for my new business were quite different from the strategy I had used at Crystalonics. I decided to begin by producing equipment for so-called "industrial process control," rather than becoming involved with other areas of electronics technology, such as computers and communications. Many giant companies were firmly entrenched in those fields, and it would have been difficult to compete with them. In my chosen application, there was less competition and the market appeared to be much more fragmented. In a field such as computers, one type of product can be produced most efficiently by large companies and sold to many customers to satisfy a wide range of requirements, whereas in a field such as process control, there is an almost limitless variety of specific applications, each of them needing its own solution. For example, producing gasoline requires different sensors and controls than producing pharmaceuticals, weaving textiles, molding tires, or pasteurizing milk. Such diverse applications, many representing a relatively limited financial opportunity, are usually better served by small companies rather than by the giants, who need larger market segments to sustain their growth.

In many instances, the technology used in industrial control processes still lagged behind the latest scientific advances routinely applied in the military and aerospace industries in 1970. During the Cold War, the armed services were eager to sponsor advanced technological research in order to stay ahead of the Soviets. The fruits of that research were not always easy to transfer to civilian industry because they were initially classified as secret, expensive to produce, and lacked apparent applications in the commercial sector. I felt, however, that extending advanced military technology to civilian applications would greatly increase the efficiency of many commercial enterprises. Although the advantages of such technology transfer were widely recognized, the process was not easy to implement. The main obstacle was that the military contractors who built the most advanced weapon systems knew little about commercial markets. While that may seem a trivial impediment, few large companies were able to overcome it. The internal culture of large military contractors was organized to satisfy complex, long-term requirements specified by a single huge customer, the U.S. Government. The culture developed among those suppliers—what became known as the "military-industrial complex"—was, and logically had to be, different from the versatile approach needed in the competitive, quickly changing, diverse civilian market.

Several major defense contractors tried to serve commercial customers by designing industrial products and establishing new sales organizations. At best, they met with mixed results, for it takes a long time to gain the confidence of new customers. My solution was to reverse the process: I planned to buy enterprises already well established in the commercial markets with a loyal customer base and transfer existing technology to them. That way my target customers would be buying advanced products from vendors they had dealt with and trusted for many years. The goal was to adapt innovations already in use in government programs to improve the efficiency of industrial processes.

It may be useful to review what is meant by industrial process control equipment. In its simplest form, it may be an instrument used to control the production of a consumer item, such as thin plastic film for wrapping sandwiches. Films of that type are extruded from molten plastic. To maintain uniformity and consistency, the temperature and pressure of the liquid fed into the die have to be accurately measured and controlled. The measuring devices, called transducers (not to be confused with transistors), serve to monitor and maintain the required manufacturing conditions. They function much like the thermostat of a home heating system, which is a simple kind of transducer that turns on the furnace when the house temperature falls below a desired level and turns it off after sufficient heat has been generated. In industrial practice, the transducers are much more accurate and complex. Oil refineries, power-generating stations, chemical plants, and food-processing facilities are extremely complicated environments that call for great sophistication in transducer design, requiring highly specialized devices that are difficult and expensive to produce. Because of the wide range of transducers needed by industry, each variety is generally manufactured in relatively small numbers, and their supplier firms are small as well.

When I was investigating the field in 1970, most of the transducer manufacturers were operations whose primary strengths lay in mechanical design and a thorough knowledge of customer applications. In the majority of cases, the customers needed not only transducers but also complex supporting electronic equipment. The transducer manufacturers were primarily experienced in mechanical engineering and so were not always at the forefront of electronic technology. They either supplied rudimentary electronic equipment to their customers or left them to buy those products from other vendors. Using parts from different suppliers often caused incompatibility problems and saddled the customers with the responsibility of constructing their own control systems. Consequently, many purchasers preferred to assign that responsibility to a single vendor.

This market condition presented an exciting opportunity for a new enterprise. If I could buy a well-established transducer manufacturer that lacked the latest electronic expertise and add advanced electronic technology, the operation could become an integrated supplier to a section of the process control industry. The value of electronic controls often exceeded the value of the transducer, so offering both products could double the sales volume of a transducer company to its existing customer base alone. I also hoped that the ability to supply a complete control system would attract new buyers and further increase the operation's growth.

I began a search for suitable acquisition candidates by examining the readily available catalogs and financial reports of relevant public companies. As often happens, I eventually found the right companies not through a laborious examination of data but through informal contacts. A fellow Lexington resident, Michael Hayward, whom I knew from my Crystalonics days, had started a small electronic consulting business called Dynamic Measurements Corporation (DMC), which he was interested in expanding into a manufacturing company. There were only two people in his operation, but Michael was a good engineer and had the specialized knowledge that could be applied to transducer applications. His company became BBF Group's first acquisition.

During my initial investigation, I received a call from Dick Carrara, who had worked for me at Teledyne and was now employed by Dynisco, a profitable operation producing pressure transducers used primarily in the plastics industry. Dynisco belonged to Microdot, a public company listed on the New York Stock Exchange. Microdot evaluated its long-term strategy and decided to sell Dynisco, which became our second acquisition. With that transaction, BBF Group, Inc., had two operations that could fulfill my original strategic purpose.

The two companies were small, however, with a combined total of one hundred employees, so I still pursued further acquisitions. Again, the next opportunity came unexpectedly. In analyzing the major costs of producing Dynisco transducers, I found that one expensive component was available from only two suppliers. I thought we could produce the item, a strain gauge, for far less than the price we were paying, but Dynisco management dissuaded me from launching the project, since making the components required specialized technology that would have taken us a long time to develop. "In that case," I said, "let's see if we can buy one of the two strain gauge manufacturers." The local supplier of those devices was BLH Electronics, a subsidiary of the Greyhound Company, of Greyhound Bus fame—a multibillion-dollar corporation engaged primarily in transportation, food, and financial services. It seemed impertinent to approach them with a proposition to buy one of their subsidiaries, inasmuch as BLH Electronics employed four hundred people, making it considerably larger than DMC and Dynisco combined. In addition to making strain gauges, it also produced industrial transducers for measuring force, weight, and pressure in applications that were not served by Dynisco. The new transducers, if we could add them to our capabilities, would fit beautifully into our product line and add an impressive group of customers who, as in the case of Dynisco, would become potential consumers of our proposed electronic instruments.

I asked one of the Dynisco managers, who knew a high-level BLH executive, to find out whether that company was for sale. We were astounded to receive a positive response on the first call. As it happened, our timing was perfect: The Greyhound Company had just decided to concentrate on its core endeavors and BLH, a relatively small manufacturing organization by their standards, did not fit into those plans. We acquired BLH Electronics in late 1972, and with our combined strengths, we became one of the largest transducer manufacturers in the industry.

Not long after buying BLH Electronics, we made one more acquisition to obtain a technical capability I considered essential to my business plan. It was becoming clear that semiconductor technology was making tremendous strides and would become increasingly important in the electronics industry. I thought that many of the techniques used in manufacturing semiconductors could be adapted to lower the cost of producing transducers. At the time, I was a board member of Silicon Transistor Corporation (STC), a semiconductor producer of power transistors used primarily in military applications. Because the operation was suffering heavy financial losses, the decision was made to sell the company. It was not an ideal fit with the rest of BBF Group operations, but STC's expertise could be developed to help our transducer effort, so we made the acquisition at the end of 1972.

Before buying STC, however, we drew up detailed plans designed to return the company to profitable operation. We closed their Long Island plant and consolidated all activities in their Chelmsford, Massachusetts, facility, eliminating unprofitable product lines and tightening manufacturing procedures. The acquisition process was relatively smooth because the principal STC investors had followed my past progress and had confidence in my abilities. They preferred to see STC as part of my company rather then operating independently under the direction of its own president, who was near retirement. It was most gratifying that the entire top management team, as well as other employees, agreed to move from Long Island to Chelmsford. I was somewhat less pleased that STC was a public company, and that by buying it we, too, would have our stock listed on a public exchange. Usually companies go public to raise capital and to be able to sell shares in a liquid market. I joked that, in our case, we assumed all the negative aspects of a public company, such as the increased scrutiny and expensive financial reporting required of listed corporations, without any advantages. We did not raise additional capital and the number of listed shares that became available was too small to arouse significant interest from Wall Street buyers. Nevertheless, I thought that the acquisition of STC's technology justified the transaction.

My primary guide in arranging financing for all these efforts was Peter Brooke. He liked my plans and, with two other investors, his venture capital operation, T.A. Associates, provided the initial capital for the acquisition of Dynamic Measurements Corporation. Peter was one of the most respected venture capitalists in the industry, and his contributions went well beyond financing. He was an invaluable advisor in corporate structuring, provided sound management counsel, and brought us many useful contacts in the financial community. At the same time, he was well aware of the limitations of his knowledge and did not interfere in day-to-day operations of the new company. Peter was the most influential director on my board, and I always consulted with him before making major decisions. But no matter how important the issue under discussion, few of my meetings with Peter lasted more than fifteen minutes. He had an incredibly fast and incisive mind, and could understand the gist of any problem immediately without wasting time on peripheral matters.

When Dynisco became available, I turned to Peter for additional funds. He was prepared to provide part of the capital required, but suggested that I approach a successful local high technology company to raise the balance. Having been associated with that company, he knew that its directors wanted to make investments in other industries. Although I knew its president well, I still approached our meeting with trepidation, perhaps fearing rejection in the same way any petitioner does, even though this seemed to be a straightforward business proposition.

The initial presentation went well. My potential investor and one of his top executives seemed genuinely interested in my plans, asked a lot of questions, and appeared to be satisfied with the answers. We agreed to meet the following day to continue our discussions. Often it is difficult to evaluate the results of a presentation, but judging from my audience's reaction, I felt there was an excellent chance that I would receive the required financing. I was correct in my evaluation of the interest I had generated, but when we reconvened, I discovered that this executive was not at all the person I assumed him to be. And in fact, my fears were more than justified, not by any weakness in my business plan, but by his hidden motives.

This person had an impeccable reputation for integrity, so when he asked me to join him in his office for further discussion the day after my presentation, his unexpected plan of action sent me into a state of shock.

"I really like your idea of a process control company," he began, "and I would like to participate in the venture."

"Wonderful," I replied. "It will be great to work together." He was known to be a very competent manager, and his company's growth proved that point. I had also served with him on another company's board, where I'd had the opportunity to see him in action. As with Peter, this executive's contribution could go well beyond his financial investment, and I was looking forward to getting his advice in the areas of corporate management and marketing strategy and to observing his well-known methods of dealing with employees.

"But there are some changes I would like to make in your proposal," he added.

"I expected that," I said. "I am sure we can work out an arrangement that will satisfy your requirements." But I was totally unprepared for his next statement.

"I don't want to be an investor in your company," he said. "I want my company to buy Dynisco and I would like you to work for me. You can realize your concept within my organization. Naturally, I'll give you a good salary and a generous incentive based on how well you perform."

"I'm not looking for a job," I said, "and I would really like to have you as an investor. Is there a chance that you will become a stockholder of my company?"

"Oh, no," he said. "I would like to work with you, but you should know that with you or without you, we are going to buy Dynisco."

I could hardly believe my ears. This man whom I had trusted with my plans and intimate details of my negotiations to purchase Dynisco was about to violate my confidence and the basic rules of ethics.

"That certainly is not going to be a very honest thing to do," I countered, "and it is not going to enhance your reputation for integrity."

"Well, you can be too honest," he said. "I have been too honest all my life."

I was astonished but not overly worried, because I had established a good working relationship with the two men who were running Dynisco. I felt sure they would not agree to this piracy, and without their consent, no prospective buyer would attempt to make the acquisition. I had a trump card in my hand and I decided to play it.

"One of the two men running Dynisco is a friend of mine and he wants to be part of my organization," I informed my competitor, "and the other one also expressed a desire to work for me. If you buy Dynisco, you run the danger of losing them both, and then what will you have?"

A triumphant and pitying smile appeared on his face. "I don't care if they stay or not. One of my top executives worked for Dynisco and he knows that business well. We'll do just fine without your friends. Of course, we would prefer to have them and you involved in this venture, but we are going ahead no matter what you do."

I felt disgusted, but not defeated. This turn of events was totally unexpected, and from the tone of my antagonist's voice, I had absolutely no doubt that he was serious about his plans. His company had cash available, and there was no reason why Microdot, the parent company of Dynisco, would not entertain an offer from another buyer. As far as I was concerned, losing this acquisition would represent a major setback. There were other transducer companies in the industry, but Dynisco seemed ideal for my plans. It was local, it was profitable, its growth could be enhanced by the injection of electronic technology, and it was for sale. I had spent many months surveying the industry and negotiating this transactions and losing it could jeopardize or, at best, substantially delay the implementation of my strategy. But I remained calm.

"It seems you have your mind made up," I said. "I would like a few days to consider your offer."

I had no intention of working for this man, nor did I want him as an investor now that I knew his response to my proposal, but I needed time to plot my strategy for dealing with this new situation.

"By all means, take your time. I'll look forward to hearing from you," he said, quite pleased with himself.

It was at times like this that my thoughts took me back to Siberia. I could not help but contrast the greed of this well-heeled individual, in the privileged position of running a successful company, with the generosity of my fellow exiles in the frozen North. Those poor people, going hungry themselves, would often share their meager rations with those burdened by greater need. The injustice of the current situation had a stimulating effect; I resolved not to be defeated by this individual who was determined to deprive me of the fruits of my thought and labor while my project was still struggling to grow its first tender roots, but I knew I had to act fast. Faced with what I considered to be a total lack of integrity, I decided that I, too, was free to use mild means of deception to gain time to raise money from other sources. I estimated that I had two weeks to negotiate the terms of my future employment before my interlocutor would lose patience and carry out his threat to make the acquisition. In those two weeks I would have to find the required capital.

My first stop was Peter Brooke's office. He, too, was surprised and disappointed at the turn of events. Peter, John Wright (a partner in Peter's firm), and I huddled to decide who would be willing to invest the required, not-insignificant sum at such short notice.

"There is only one person who will go for it," John said after just a few minutes, "and that is Charlie Lea."

"You are right," Peter and I said almost simultaneously. "If anybody goes for it in that period of time, it will be Charlie."

I remembered well the first time I met Charlie, ten years earlier when I was running Crystalonics, Peter suggested that we might decide to have our shares listed on a public stock exchange, and thought I should meet Charlie Lea, who worked for a Wall Street firm that could help us go public. Charlie called me, and a few days later we met in my office.

"Peter and I have been friends for a long time," he said, "and I understand you may want to go public at some point."

"That is correct," I replied, not really fully understanding all the implications of becoming a public company. We discussed the advantages and disadvantages of having publicly traded stock, and then I asked Charlie to tell me something about his company.

"Yes, I am with F. S. Smithers, and we are one of the oldest firms on Wall Street," he informed me.

"I assume you have taken companies public before," I guessed.

"Yes, we have," he assured me.

"And can you name some of them?"

Charlie sat up in his chair and with a straight face said, "One you may have heard of is IBM."

In the ten years since that conversation, Charlie had moved to another organization, and by the time we invoked his name as a possible BBF Group investor, he was working for New Court Securities, a New York investment banking firm owned by the Rothschilds. He headed what was then one of the country's largest venture capital pools. He had a great deal of confidence in Peter's judgment, and had also followed my progress from a distance.

We called Charlie and told him about our problem. Investors don't like to work under time constraints because they need time to evaluate the proposal, check out the people involved, talk to the proposed venture's customers, and do other so-called "due diligence" exercises to make sure the investment has a good chance of success. Such an investigation usually takes several weeks and is followed by the negotiation of investment terms, which are then formalized in a lengthy agreement. It is not unusual for this process to take several months, and the more we thought about it, the more unrealistic our two-week deadline appeared. Our challenge seemed even more daunting when Charlie informed us that the head of New Court Securities, whose endorsement was required for any major commitment of funds, was overseas and would not return in time to approve the investment. But Charlie was not one to give up easily. He asked us to come to New York and offered to try to bring the recently retired head of his firm to the meeting. Charlie felt that if he and the previous chairman, G. Peter Fleck, agreed on a course of action, the investment could be made.

Two days later Peter and I traveled to New York, and we were delighted to learn that the former chairman was able to attend our meeting. We were ushered into a large, dark-paneled conference room decorated with heavy antique furniture and conservative paintings of seascapes. A half-dozen people were already present, and shortly after our arrival, the chairman took a seat at the head of the table.

His appearance and manner did not bode well for our endeavor. A short, well-dressed man in his late sixties, his gait was deliberate, his gestures quick and precise. His face did not betray a sense of humor and his gaze implied a healthy dose of skepticism. Although his command of English was superb, I could tell from his accent that he was Dutch by birth. He greeted us cordially and, after a few preliminaries, asked us to state our business. His manner seemed to imply annoyance at the interruption of his retirement and impatience to return to his leisure activities.

I launched into my presentation, explaining my strategy of building a company by combining transducers with electronics. Only a few minutes into my talk, however, I realized I was in danger of boring my Dutch listener, so I wound down the technical aspects of the venture and tried another approach.

"In essence," I said, "I want to start a company in the field of electronics, and I have done extensive market research in the field. As in any business, I decided to manufacture a product that is in great demand. I have found such a product, and it is not only easily saleable, but the raw materials needed to make it are abundant and inexpensive. Also, the labor needed to convert the raw material into the finished product is practically free."

"In other words" I summarized, "we have an ideal situation: cheap, easily available materials that can be converted into the final product at low cost and then sold in a market that is eagerly awaiting its appearance."

I could see my audience's interest rising, and even Fleck's facial expression changing from skepticism to anticipation.

"What I propose to do," I said after a suitable pause, "is to manufacture successful companies. The raw materials are problem companies, which are plentiful and can be bought for a good price. In this era of acquisition, successful operations are eagerly sought and command high values. The labor of converting the former into the latter is my work, and I don't expect great rewards for my effort."

"Another way of putting it," I continued, "is that I want to be a pig farmer. Most companies operate like dairy farms. They sell the milk and keep the cows. I want to run my operation like a pig farmer who buys a little pig, grows it fast, sells it and then buys another small pig. That is what I want to do with my acquisitions."

I knew it was a high-risk strategy, and I did not want to present it in a manner that appeared frivolous. But to my great delight the description elicited the reaction I had hoped for. The chairman became more interested as I talked, eventually breaking into loud laughter. He had a sense of humor after all. He asked a couple of perfunctory questions, and then said that if everything checked out, he wanted to make the investment.

Charlie assigned one of his brightest subordinates, Roger Widmann, to carry out a fast investigation of my proposal. Roger, a thorough and energetic young man, devoted all his abundant energy to my project. He not only checked the prospects for BBF Group, but also spent considerable time examining my background. He must have been satisfied with the results, because we received the required capital before the expiration of my self-imposed two-week deadline.

My final—and most gratifying—act in this part of the fundraising effort was to contact the first potential investor, turn down his offer to employ me, and inform him that we had signed an agreement with Microdot to purchase Dynisco. I must confess to a feeling of satisfaction at winning this particular contest, although it was somewhat clouded by my disappointment in this man. He had been my collaborator for years, almost a friend, and an individual known for his integrity, his work with charitable causes, and prominence in Boston industrial and social circles.

The phrase "pig farming" that I used in my presentation to New Court Securities was actually more than a flip expression to attract attention. It was my attempt at describing a process that was to become known as a "turnaround" of troubled companies. Unfortunately, such turnarounds are often achieved by cutting expenses and eliminating employees who are essential for the future well-being of the company. In a typical financial turnaround, an acquirer cuts research and development funds, divests profitable divisions, reduces marketing expenses, sells buildings, and otherwise undermines the company's future. In too many cases such a strategy generates immediate cash that the purchaser can withdraw, leaving the operation a hollow shell badly prepared to face the future. In other situations, turnarounds are accomplished more honorably and productively. The acquirer brings with him sound management knowledge and new vigor that helps rejuvenate the operation.

I decided on a third approach, based on the belief that I was not a better manager than the people who were already running the companies I acquired. In fact, I rejected acquisition candidates that did not have a competent management team already in place. My contribution would be to make available the talent of those executives for performing productive duties, rather than allowing it to be wasted on efforts that did not directly contribute to their operation's progress. In this approach I consciously imitated practices I had learned at Teledyne.

Each company BBF Group acquired remained a separate entity. We also had a small corporate office, initially consisting of three people: a financial executive, a secretary, and me. The corporate office worked with banks, insurance companies, investors, and stockholders, essentially freeing the operating entities from the burden of those activities. Each one of our divisions and subsidiaries was completely self-contained, had a full management team, and operated under its own name. The remuneration of each operation's employees was dependent on the results of their own unit, not the performance of BBF Group. Unlike larger companies, we did not try to enforce uniform policies or reporting standards, but allowed each management team to institute the practices they considered suitable for their firms. In other words, we tried to combine the benefits of the small company (such as flexibility) with the benefits of large entities (notably, stability and resources), and on the whole that approach was successful. Invariably, after small adjustments and occasional changes in top management, the acquired companies performed better under the BBF Group umbrella than they had previously. The clearer definition of authority, greater freedom of action, an atmosphere devoid of political infighting, and liberal rewards tied to performance generated renewed enthusiasm among the acquired operations' management teams. That, in turn, resulted in better treatment of all employees, more productive efforts, improved growth, and increased profitability.

The other advantage was a general acceptance of new technologies by our companies. While the cooperation among them was never as close as I had hoped, the presence of diverse expertise and disciplines within the overall group opened access to the latest developments in several technologies. We soon added a fourth person, Joel Cohen, to our corporate staff to follow the latest developments in our various fields and act as an intercompany catalyst. I met Joel shortly after my arrival in the United States. He worked for me as an application engineer at Crystalonics, and then agreed to join us at BBF Group to promote technical cooperation among our companies. This job required a great capacity for diplomacy, to say the least, but Joel, one of the kindest people I have ever known, was perfectly qualified. I once told him that had he chosen an alternate path, he would have made an excellent rabbi or a fine and compassionate doctor.

It took a few months to become intimately familiar with the business details of our four companies and to agree on our course of action. By the middle of 1973, we began looking for other acquisitions. Since our business strategy seemed to be working, we investigated other transducer companies. We were far along in our negotiations to acquire a BLH competitor when our lawyers informed us that, under existing trade laws, we ran the danger of becoming a monopoly if we went through with the deal. Had we done so, we would have commanded approximately eighty percent of the market for force-measuring transducers, or load cells, as they were known. I was amazed and also pleased that a company the size of BBF Group, with fewer than a thousand employees, could be considered a monopoly in any business, but we followed our lawyers' advice and broke off negotiations.

With further thrust into transducers barred by antitrust considerations, I decided to explore other ways to promote the growth of our company. Electronic equipment consists basically of components such as transistors, resistors, and capacitors connected by wires and enclosed in cabinets. There are many ways to interconnect components, but the one that appealed to me was the use of printed circuits. This usually refers to rigid boards that support thin strips of copper, which serve as electrical connections. Several steps in the production of printed circuit boards are similar to those used in the manufacturing of semiconductors, and I thought our knowledge at Silicon Transistor Corporation could be used to develop a superior interconnection product.

Toward the end of 1973, Peter Brooke was approached by the owners of a company whose main product was a laminate material used by the printed circuit industry. It was not exactly what I had in mind for our new activity, but it merited investigation. I felt that we could infuse new technology into the operation and expand its product line to conform closer to my original plans, which in fact we did a few years after the acquisition. The company, Polyclad Laminates, was located conveniently in our part of the state, and we acquired it at the beginning of 1974.

Although by industrial standards we were still small, we began attracting the attention of brokers specializing in mergers and acquisitions. We regularly received letters offering companies for sale and inquiring whether we were interested in selling our operations. I usually ignored these letters, because most of them came from people of little substance. Their crude strategy was to find a company that could be acquired, then mail the name to hundreds of potential buyers, or, worse, advertise the availability of the operation in industry newsletters. One day, however, I received an unusually well-written letter from a Boston-based company claiming to represent a foreign client interested in BLH Electronics. I decided to contact the sender, not because I wanted to sell BLH Electronics, but to evaluate the agent in the hope that he might represent us in our search for new acquisitions.

The merger specialist was indeed impressive. The company, Weaver Associates, was located in a converted warehouse on Boston's waterfront, and their client was Bofors of Sweden. The inquiry was serious, and as the president of a public company, I had an obligation to investigate the opportunity. Our major stockholders expressed an interest in realizing a return on their investment but left the decision entirely in my hands.

BLH, the company of interest to the Swedes, was our biggest and most successful subsidiary. It also represented the key building block in our identity as a serious presence in the process control industry. Selling it would change the entire character of BBF Group. It seemed clear that we should either sell BBF Group in its entirety or not pursue the sale of BLH. Bofors, however, was not interested in all our entities. The Swedes offered to buy BLH and Dynisco and to lend me the money that, together with bank financing and my proceeds from the sale of BBF Group, would allow me to retain the three remaining divisions.

We discussed the terms of the proposed transaction, but before making the final decision I wanted to visit Sweden to determine whether we were dealing with reputable people who were in a position to help BLH Electronics and Dynisco grow and to ensure that the sale would neither jeopardize existing employees' jobs nor hurt the technology available to the industry in this country. I don't mean to suggest that the world could not exist without the operations we were negotiating to sell, but we were heavily involved in the space program, providing load cells that measured the thrust developed by rockets just before their launch from Cape Canaveral. We also supplied about ninety percent of certain pressure-measuring devices to the plastics industry and participated in a number of government defense projects. Disruption in the availability of our products could have created at least temporary problems for our customers.

Bofors being receptive to a visit, we flew to Stockholm and then to Karlskoga, close to the Norwegian border, where Bofors' headquarters was located. Karlskoga gave every appearance of a company town: It was clean, orderly, and almost entirely dependent on Bofors. My suite at the company-owned hotel contained photographs of people who had visited Bofors over the decades, presumably occupying the same quarters. The albums dated back to the latter part of the nineteenth century and included foreign ministers and important military figures who came to negotiate the purchase of arms that Bofors produced. The company was one of the most advanced manufacturers of guns, ammunition, and explosive materials. At one time Alfred Nobel, who later established the Nobel Prize, was one of its main stockholders.

We visited several Bofors manufacturing plants. One was a huge complex of dozens of shiny metal huts, each about six feet across, interconnected by pipes. The operation produced nitroglycerin, and the buildings were designed to separate the product into relatively small amounts to avoid concentrations that might cause a serious explosion. The walls of each hut were designed to collapse outward should a spark or flame cause an internal buildup of pressure. Because a blast can occur only in confined space, the precaution had prevented catastrophic accidents, reducing any potential flare-up to slow, harmless combustion. In its entire history of producing this dangerous material, Bofors had never had an uncontrolled explosion.

Sweden is famous for its underground hangars and subterranean factories. We were taken to a production plant built into the side of a hill, but as visitors we were not allowed beyond the main entrance. Judging by the amount of vehicular and rail traffic passing through the large gates, we decided that this mountain must contain a huge manufacturing facility. This observation was confirmed by the large size of Bofors' naval guns, which we were allowed to inspect.

At the farewell dinner, I sat next to the wife of the president of Bofors. She was a delightful Swedish woman who had attended the University of Kentucky and was a great admirer of America. After I finished a tasty meat dish, she asked if I knew what I had just eaten. I am not a finicky eater, so she need not have waited until the end of the meal to ask that question, but it turned out to be moose, of which they had an ample supply. The reason for the abundance was simple. Bofors tested their guns and shells on a wooded firing range that stretched for many kilometers outside Karlskoga. Not surprisingly, it was a place that people avoided. Animals, however, became accustomed to the noise and flying projectiles and, safe from human interference, thrived in that wilderness. Whenever the company needed fresh meat, a hunter was sent to shoot a moose at a time when no tests were being run.

The visit helped allay my fears about the prospective purchaser of our two operations. Bofors had been in business in one form or another for about two hundred years. A fine company run by solid people, they had plans for expansion to the United States. We spent two days negotiating the details of our proposed agreement, and I left feeling that if the transaction took place, the two BBF companies would be in good hands.

On my return, I still had to decide whether to recommend the sale to our board of directors. Initially it was not an easy decision. The employees supported the transaction; Bofors was a fine large company with considerably greater resources than BBF Group could provide. The investors, although not pressing the matter, were also in favor of the sale. I pondered my own preferences. Employing over one thousand people, we had prepared detailed plans for further expansion. The company was profitable, we had an excellent team in place, and we were pursuing numerous promising market opportunities. I had a choice of managing a public company with a large number of stockholders or fully owning a smaller private operation with four hundred employees. The prospect of continuing to build a large public enterprise was exciting, but a chance to grow a private operation from a smaller base was equally attractive. I was not an "empire builder," and the ultimate size of the company was less important to me than freedom of action. Reducing the number of stockholders to one would promote the privacy so important to me, simplify the decision-making process, and improve flexibility.

A consideration tipped the scales toward accepting Bofors' offer. As President of BBF Group, I was under obligation to our stockholders to commit myself almost exclusively to running the business. A friend who had built a Fortune 1000 biotechnology company had described his management philosophy in a message to his immediate subordinates: "Your first priority is business, your second priority is business, your third priority is business. Family and other things are your fourth priority. You have to be available to the company twenty-four hours a day, seven days a week. That is the commitment I have made. Tell me if you are not prepared to do the same. I'll not fire you, but you will never rise to the top ranks of this company." Those were admirable and, in certain situations, essential principles, and they resembled my own approach to work in the early days of Crystalonics when I was still a bachelor. But in 1976 I was not prepared to follow such a narrow path.

Russia revisited after the collapse of the Soviet Union, celebrating the signing of a joint development program between one of BBF's companies and a Russian scientific institute. I am right center; my son, Mischa, is in the foreground at far left.

BBF, INC.

A CORPORATION in the United States—or a limited liability company, as it is more colorfully known in Europe—occupies the very center of the capitalist system. Its reputation ranges from that of a soulless entity concerned only with the bottom line to that of a caring, loyal, and intimate kind of family. Since they arose as a significant economic and social force in the nineteenth century, corporations have been accused of imperialism, colonialism, heartless exploitation of foreign and domestic workers, destroying the environment, spreading pollution, preaching an ethic of greed, rewarding selfishness, and other deplorable behaviors. At the other end of the scale—and here, the praise of supporters is not nearly as loud as the reproach of detractors—companies have been complimented for providing good jobs and attractive working conditions, promoting their employees' professional advancement, developing new technologies that enhance living standards, sponsoring health programs, and enriching local communities.

The potential power of the corporation is directly related to the freedom of action it enjoys. If it conforms to normal standards of decency and integrity, it is free to operate in practically any part of the country. It can market an almost infinite choice of products and services domestically and internationally, and set the standards of behavior, compensation, and achievement for its employees. It is probably not an exaggeration to say that corporations operating in a free market environment won the Cold War by outproducing the centrally directed, rigid Communist industry. The well-managed corporation in a capitalist system can be a remarkably efficient producer of goods and services, easily surpassing the capabilities of most other types of organization. In short, corporations have a lot of power for good or evil.

The chief executive officer plays the paramount role in shaping the character of his company. In most cases, this is not an easy task, for he has to please several constituencies with conflicting interests. Stockholders of a public, or even a private, company frequently judge the president's performance on the basis of current profits, which puts pressure on management to boost immediate earnings at the expense of longer-term growth. Directors may dispute the strategic vision of the operation and disapprove of the president's plans. But even with total harmony among these various groups, the chief executive has an obligation to balance current performance with long-term success and to make sure the financial proceeds are divided fairly among management, employees, and stockholders.

At the end of our long negotiations with Bofors, I became the sole stockholder of BBF Group, or BBF Inc., as my remaining operations were now named, and I was in the enviable position of eliminating most of the above contradictions and constraints. I had no committees to watch over me and no other stockholders to satisfy. My only internal constituency was the employees, and I set myself the task of organizing BBF Inc. so as to expunge as many of the negative aspects of working for a commercial enterprise as I could. My goal in the new entity was to establish a pleasant working atmosphere and above-average professional and financial rewards for our people. As a private company, we could keep our employees' salaries confidential, no matter how large, which enabled us to design a system where financial rewards were directly proportional to the performance of each operation. Several salaries were, in fact, enormous in comparison with those at companies of similar size. Such generous compensation constituted a powerful incentive, which, in turn, made most of our companies the most profitable in their industries. On one occasion, we received a telephone call from a U.S. government agency charged with gathering statistical information on employee remuneration, inquiring about the reported salary levels for two of our top people. The payments seemed so high that the agency officials wanted to make sure there had been no mistake in our report.

To ensure that each group of our employees was judged solely on its own efforts, we eventually split BBF Inc. into four separate entities to allow a clearer definition of each operation's earnings and to prevent the shortcomings of one division from weakening the financial position of another. This reorganization also promoted a feeling of pride and a sense of ownership within each group. The corporate office, consisting of just three people including myself, continued its previous functions of monitoring and hopefully contributing to the progress of the four operating entities.

It would be an exaggeration, of course, to say that in organizing BBF I was guided solely by the interests of our employees, for my own interests also played a major part in the planning process. I had given a lot of thought to designing a corporate structure that would take into account my likes and dislikes, as well as my abilities and temperament. Having arrived at a particular situation, people often rationalize their path retrospectively, convincing themselves that it has been their desire all along to reach their present destination. I, too, have rationalized many of my past moves, even though originally I gave little thought to their ultimate outcome. But BBF Inc. was organized consciously along lines I had thought about and planned for a long time.

The structure of the organization and my role in it were also inspired by what I had learned at Teledyne and from venture capitalists. Teledyne had been successful at delegating authority to the heads of its operating entities, but it was a multibillion-dollar public company that needed tight control over its operations to satisfy their often-conflicting requirements and responsibilities. Despite the considerable degree of freedom afforded line management, Teledyne had to institute company-wide policies that were not always ideal for individual profit centers. Also, it could not afford wide disparity in compensation or benefit levels and often had to implement cash strategies to benefit the entire corporation rather than its individual division and had to enforce uniform accounting standards to control its diverse activities. I hoped to design a structure that would contain many positive aspects of the Teledyne organization and exclude most of its disadvantages.

Venture capitalists provided a different organizational model. Over many years of working with venture capital firms, I have developed a great deal of respect for them. They typically provide seed capital for start-up enterprises and large investments in young companies that have not yet reached profitability. Investors' advice can be invaluable to fledgling companies, and venture capitalists often serve on the board of directors, act as management advisers, and provide necessary moral support to the founders. Since venture firms do not aspire to run the company or even to be long-term stockholders, management can feel a sense of ownership without a need to conform to the policies of other companies, as long as their internal practices make business sense. The involvement of venture capitalists, however, also has some disadvantages. Their usual objective is to realize a gain on their investment in a relatively short period of time—typically within five years or less—certainly not more than seven to ten years. The young firm is expected to maximize its potential by the end of the period, at which point it is either sold to another corporation or becomes a publicly traded company. Such requirements do not normally conflict with the desires of the founders, but they can restrict freedom of action under certain circumstances. Also, venture capitalists, being accountable to their own investors, become impatient and make life uncomfortable for operating management if things don't go according to schedule. While pressure to perform is usually helpful, it is not always appropriate, especially when the venture capitalist is not experienced in a particular industry or has to follow a large number of investments and cannot devote the appropriate amount of time to evaluate each situation adequately.

In sum, the structure I envisioned had elements of both the Teledyne organization and companies sponsored by venture capitalists. I wanted to direct a minimum of three and a maximum of five separate enterprises, each based on technologies that I could easily understand. I preferred to have all companies within easy driving distance of each other, and I wanted to be their majority owner, with minority participation by key employees.

While the list of my requirements was not long, it created what I considered to be an ideal working situation for me. The reason for setting a minimum and maximum number of companies was simple: Each was to be autonomous, with its own president, bank account, manufacturing facilities, and distinctive name; I would be an advisor and mentor. I feared that if I had only one or two companies, I would have the time to become too involved and—unintentionally—lapse into micromanagement. In other words, I was aware of my tendency to participate in daily affairs in ways that might interfere with the companies' own management. What I wanted was for each operating entity to be truly independent and self-reliant, because those are the best conditions for building expertise and a feeling of ownership among the employees.

At the same time, acting as essentially a one-man board of directors and helping shape the overall strategy of each business, I would have to limit the number of operations to the point where I would have enough time to follow their progress. My somewhat arbitrary maximum of five companies proved to be a good estimate. With this number, I could effectively participate in the annual planning process, follow weekly bookings and shipments, advise on new product development, contribute to personnel policy, consult on the addition of key employees, and meet important customers.

My preference for technology-based companies stemmed from my educational background as an engineer and years of experience in operations using scientific disciplines to develop and manufacture innovative products. Equally important, I realized I was at least as interested in the process of new product development as in the business aspect of commercial enterprises. At one time, I even considered organizing a small private laboratory where I could engage in research and development, but I dismissed the idea because the effort and expense of furnishing a semiconductor laboratory would have been prohibitive. Also, it is hard enough to produce meaningful results when concentrating on just the technical aspects of a business, so part-time involvement in new product and process development would almost certainly lead to disappointment. A working relationship with three to five operations, all of them employing competent engineers and scientists in well-equipped laboratories, gave me excellent access to the process of innovation. I often participated in technical discussions, evaluated results, and occasionally I even designed experiments. I was always careful not to assume the leadership of any program or interfere with its orderly progress.

Our companies were all located within a two-hour drive of my office in Waltham, except for a subsidiary in California. Eventually, after the sale of the most remote operation, I could reach each of the remaining plants in forty-five minutes. This proximity made regular visits to our companies more convenient and urgent visits much more timely.

Although my main interests lay in new product development and our companies' growth, we did not neglect the more routine but equally important management controls of the business. Fully computerized, we could generate reams of useful information, but I never forgot the basic controls we had at Crystalonics. Like most managers, I hated surprises—especially unpleasant ones—and I realized that our timely, concise reports had been very effective at highlighting potential problems. At my first company, reports had been prepared daily; now, with our much larger enterprise, I felt we were stable enough to rely on weekly briefings. The reports, intended for both my managers and me, listed such vital signs as cash flow, orders received, purchases, employment, and shipments, both in absolute terms and as trends. To prevent information overload, I designed a one-page form that took only a few minutes to prepare and about the same amount of time to read, but that provided a clear and concise summary of the voluminous, detailed data generated by the finance and marketing departments at the end of each month.

My new corporate structure was also designed to fit my restless nature. I had seldom been content to stay with the same company for more than a few years. I found the challenge to survive and establish a solid profitable operation poised for future growth more exciting than the inevitable more repetitive management tasks. In the past, I had had to change jobs; now, I would be working with three to five companies at once. I could anticipate a degree of turnover, selling some firms and buying others, all the while pursuing new ventures whenever the time seemed appropriate.

I made a commitment to all our operating managers that each company could keep the profits generated, and that no cash, except for reasonable corporate fees, would be withdrawn from their operations. The corporate fees covered the expenses of my three-person office, and the company presidents—despite their occasional humorous derogatory comments—considered those fees to be reasonable. The retention of all profits at the source of their generation gave our employees yet another incentive to grow their operations. Naturally, complete retention of earnings was possible only if, apart from key employees, I was the sole stockholder. If other owners had been involved, they might have insisted on receiving dividends, to which they certainly would have been entitled.

If I did not receive dividends, how did I benefit from all these elaborate arrangements? After all, business is supposed to generate profits for its stockholders. The answer is that my motivations were not primarily financial. I drew a salary from the management fees we collected, but my pay was low. My main reward came from being involved in the work of our operations and in the act of building successful enterprises which, while small, participated in the country's major industries and sold their products worldwide. Building a successful company seemed to me as creative as carving a sculpture or producing a painting, with the added advantage that a corporation was a constantly changing and evolving entity. Like people, companies have character, personality, and moods that can range all the way from buoyant confidence to despair. Even more important, companies have a major impact on the lives of their employees. Creating an environment that nurtures the well-being of the staff was, to me, a fulfilling and worthwhile vocation.

I liked the idea of working with small private firms for many reasons. One was that in a private company I could indulge my desire to keep a low profile, away from the scrutiny and second-guessing to which public firms are subjected. Another was that it was thrilling to compete head-to-head with the well-established industrial giants and to try to produce more innovative products of better quality. Extremely important was the ability to set superior compensation for our key employees without the need to argue with other stockholders about what was "usually done." Finally, I felt that a small firm is simply more fun: flexible enough to stop on a dime, change direction, and go after a new market when the opportunity comes up. It's more exhilarating, like driving a sports car instead of a bus. Of course, the danger for the small businessman and the sports car driver is that you may be run over by the bus unless you know when to get out of the way.

This is not to say that the situation was totally devoid of potential financial reward. A successful company represents a certain market value that can be realized upon its sale. Occasionally, we were approached with an offer of purchase of one of our companies, and we did accept such offers several times. But in each case the transaction was either originated by the target company's management team or took place with their active encouragement. We never considered selling a company whose management did not enthusiastically support the sale. The proceeds of each divestiture were divided among the key employees and me. Since our employees knew that no sale would take place without their active support, they had confidence both in the security of their jobs and in their control over the continuity of their company's corporate identity.

Few of us have the luxury of working under ideal conditions, but I cannot think of a better professional situation than the arrangement I had designed for myself. Forty-six years old when BBF Inc. was incorporated, I still had many potentially productive years ahead of me. My previous experience included almost every aspect of running a small business: marketing, manufacturing, finance, engineering, and personnel. In my new capacity at BBF Inc. and its successor BBF Corp., I could engage in each operation as much or as little as I wanted. I could immerse myself in work almost to the exclusion of everything else, or

I could stand back and spend my time on other activities. Since I had no responsibilities to other investors, I could pursue certain projects at work almost as a hobby. Of course each company still had to grow and be profitable to stay in business and provide opportunities for its employees. Perhaps because of our corporate structure, in all but one case the financial performance of our companies exceeded the achievements of our competitors, bringing our staff and me a sense of pride and satisfaction. The underperforming operation was eventually sold to a competitor without any loss of jobs.

But there was one disadvantage to my new work life. For decades I had had the habit of walking around every manufacturing plant I directed—first as the hands-on manager, then as CEO—talking with the workers, listening to their stories, doing something or other with the instruments I knew so well. I especially liked to watch the loading dock when it was time to ship our finished products, for those shipments served as the most convincing proof that we were producing useful goods. With the new arrangements, I wanted to avoid curtailing the feeling of autonomy of my managers, so I rented space in an office building more than half an hour's drive from my closest manufacturing operation. There was, of course, no loading dock in the building to visit, and, at least initially, I felt that no one around me was doing anything useful. Indeed, for a while I felt like a parasite—and a lonely parasite at that. Unlike my previous places of employment, where dedicated people had worked long hours, my new building emptied at precisely five o'clock, intensifying my worry that I had entered an indolent, unproductive world. This environment took some getting used to, and to this day I miss the habit of experimenting, designing, assembling, testing, organizing, analyzing—all the minute-by-minute routines of engineering development and hands-on managing responsibilities.

It was satisfying to overcome the challenges of the marketplace. The competition was intense, and we fought some of the biggest and best-known corporations in the world. We usually did not cut prices, because our relatively meager resources would not allow us to outlast our competitors. Our strategy, rather, was to have the most advanced products, superior service, and the highest quality and reliability possible. We were able to achieve these goals because our small size and delegation of authority allowed us to work faster both in developing and in manufacturing new products. Also, our employees' sense of ownership and direct influence on results promoted a team spirit and desire to do everything possible to satisfy our customers.

My greatest satisfaction did not come from new technical breakthroughs or from our companies' growth, but rather from the professional development of our people. The process must have been similar to the joy experienced by a teacher who observes a child growing into a valuable, informed, and mature adult. The transformation was most obvious with professional people. Several of our company presidents had felt suppressed by previous employers because they did not conform to someone's stereotype of a management executive. We did not care how they ran their companies, as long as they achieved high standards of integrity, profitability, growth, employee welfare, and a sense of responsibility as neighbors in their communities. Each president set up his own style of management, and under those conditions several of them led their enterprises to worldwide leadership in their markets.

On the whole, the structure worked well. That is not to say that we achieved my ideal of having an oasis of sanity in this turbulent, confused world, but we came close. Competent people thrived because of the freedom they enjoyed. Though this same freedom made it more difficult to recognize the shortcomings of the less skillful managers, or outright dishonesty, the positive aspects of the system far outweighed the negative ones, and all the companies prospered. Occasionally we had to replace top people with individuals more adept at running small high technology companies—always a difficult and unpleasant task— but eventually we assembled remarkably dependable, honest, and capable teams of managers who ran their companies with consideration for their employees in an atmosphere largely devoid of internal politics.

It has truly been a privilege to have been—and to be still—at the helm of my companies, and I am forever grateful to the colleagues and employees who taught me so much about loyalty, honesty, the spirit of invention, and good humor. It is these remarkable people who have made my long journey through the world of free enterprise worthwhile, and I am proud that many of them have become lifelong friends.

Clockwise from upper left: In Lexington, Massachusetts with our three children, 1967; Olga and I at our daughter Nina's Medical School graduation, Washington, D.C., 1992; Michael (Mischa), Nina, Lisa, Olga, and I, 1995.

SOME FINAL THOUGHTS

AS I APPROACH MY MID-SEVENTIES, I live contentedly in my permanent home in the United States with my wife, Olga. We have been blessed with three children—two girls and a boy—and five grandchildren. Our daughters and son are well-educated, professional, decent people, and I think they inherited some of my father's characteristics of integrity, kindness, and respectful reserve.

I am still working, though not as much as earlier, and I am proud of how far I have come, both professionally and personally. When I started Crystalonics, we were a small operation with limited resources serving fields dominated by much larger, well-established competitors. Over the next four decades, our companies employed several thousand people. We maintained modest but effective research and development laboratories where our engineers and scientists made significant technological advances in their various fields. BBF Corp. eventually directed four companies, one of which, Dymec, is now the premier supplier of electronic devices that enable the power industry to monitor and regulate the complex equipment of the national power grid. Another of our companies, Lewcott, has become a world leader in the production of lightweight synthetic materials that are staples in many manufacturing, defense, and construction industries.

Despite the stresses inherent in nurturing small, new companies, I have been able to separate my working and personal lives, having always felt that one should not overwhelm the other. It is for me a point of pride that I have never owned a briefcase and have never taken work home. Except for the occasional business trip, I have always come home for dinner with my family. I never encouraged my fellow workers to call me at home, nor did I disturb their privacy during nonworking hours.

I attended most of my children's school functions, one of which stands out in my mind. During our son's college years, he led a singing group at Sanders Theater in Cambridge, Massachusetts. The twelve singers stood in a semicircle, and he was at one end, facing the center of the stage with his left side toward the audience. I looked at him and suddenly saw my father. The distance between us eerily erased nonconforming features and only similarities remained. I saw the same profile, the same stance, the same facial expressions.

This vision brought back many memories of our life in Poland and Siberia. I know my father would identify with his grandchildren and would be proud of them. I think he would see that his steady guidance of my early life and his self-sacrifice had not been in vain. It was because of his care that I emerged from Siberia without deep emotional scars and that the terrible deprivations I suffered during the war did not hinder my progress. Olga and I are intensely proud of our family. As for myself, I believe I have achieved a degree of professional success I would never have thought possible during those first sleepless nights in our lice-infested train bound for Siberia. But my father had a clear vision all along: He never gave up hope or his belief in my future. In the first letter I received from him in London in June 1947, he wrote:

My dear Bronek!

After receiving your telegram I immediately wired your uncle that you left Gdańsk on May 18th on the ship Eastern Prince. I hope that you were met in England at the port of the ship's destination.

Thank you very much for the booklet you sent me from Copoty, and above all for your attention towards me. The next day I received your two postcards. My dear Bronek! I agree with you that I wanted you to go and to be with your uncle in London because I see your future in this journey. You are still a child, you have not seen much of life. The war caught you at a very young age; your sufferings, hunger, and a whole range of misfortunes curtailed your aspirations to minimal levels, and in Poland you would never become the kind of person I so much want you to be. Under your uncle's guidance, you will have a wide-open field of opportunities. You have all it takes to become someone of substance. You are young and healthy. You have an introductory education and, if you only gather some inspiration and confidence in your future, I predict that with hard work you will not live your life as an average person.

If during the sickness of your mother (blessed be her memory) you were able to nurse her, work in mines on Sundays, keep us supplied with logs from the forest, cook, and at the same time be the best student in your class, I firmly believe that there are no difficulties that can keep you from energetically embarking on a course of final studies to achieve your ultimate goal. Dear Bronek, remember you are everything to me, I have no one else in life. I am putting all my hopes in you. Your future is also my future.

Our German housekeeper has stopped coming to work because she gave birth to a child. Again I have nobody at home. I sold your old suit from Krasnoarmieisk for six thousand. That is all for now. I am eagerly awaiting your letter.

Hugs and kisses, Your Father.

My poor, dear, long-suffering father. How could I not do my very best in life! How much I wish that he had lived long enough to follow my progress in America. I can only hope that he would think his sacrifices had not been in vain.

.